TOWARD EXCELLENCE

Create Enduring Business Success

ORLA KELLY
PUBLISHING

Pete Rogan and Stuart Rogan

Published in Ireland by Orla Kelly Publishing.

Orla Kelly Publishing,
27 Kilbrody,
Mount Oval,
Rochestown,
Cork.
Ireland

This book is dedicated,
with lifelong gratitude and heartfelt thanks,
to Barry Walters

ACKNOWLEDGEMENTS

I would like to thank (roughly in chronological order): Barry Walters, who gave me the chance to show what I could do, and helped me do it. Thank you for your faith, patience, direction, support, and not infrequent forgiveness! It made a life-changing difference. Andy Kelly, whose support and encouragement took me into the world of economic development and then self-employed consultancy. And Joan Cawdery, Susan MacLellan and Tracey Crozier for their encouragement, support, opportunities and wise advice at this time. Gary Brewer for his unstinting support, great ideas, countless opportunities and great diplomacy in helping me avoid some pitfalls, learn from mistakes and have the confidence to keep moving forward in the early days of the business. Jerome Finlayson and Professor Umit Bititci, whose generosity of spirit and endless patience helped me grasp lean, Business Excellence, Hoshin strategy and much more. Alison Matthew, Mike Breslin and Alison Clayton for the opportunities and encouragement over many years. Paul McFarlane, Steve Bald, Christina Noonan, Aydin Kurt-Elli, John Jess, Chris Peacock and Robert McGill for the ongoing encouragement, support and friendship. And Gary Roberts – what can I say, Gary? It's a book in itself, isn't it? Thanks a million

Pete Rogan

First, I would like to add my heartfelt gratitude to those who Pete has thanked, all of whom have also been seminal figures for me, many directly, others indirectly. I would, however, like to emphasise my thanks to Steve Bald, Sonia Bald, Paul McFarlane, Christina Noonan, John Jess, Chris Peacock and Robert McGill for their friendship and generosity. In addition, I'd like to thank Stephen Egan, Ray Jones, Martin Bald, Bob Patillo, Dr Agnessa Spanellis and Sheida Mohebpour for their paradigm-shifting inspiration and ideas. Special thanks also to Gary Roberts, Mike Millar, Ross Browning, Charlotte Reed, Mark Benger, Steven O'Day, Professor Umit Bititci and Aydin Kurt-Elli for their confidence and for opening up pivotal opportunities early in my career, with particular thanks to Gary for his personal example and resolute commitment to giving people the opportunity to learn, develop and be the best they can be.

Above all, I'd like to thank my co-author and Dad, Pete, for the opportunity to work together on the project of a lifetime and for his relentless dedication to making Toward Excellence a comprehensive, robust and powerful toolkit.

Stuart Rogan

FUTURE POSITIVE CONSULTING

We help businesses achieve and sustain success, using Business Excellence principles and practices to build organisations that are great to work for, buy from and invest in.

How We Do It

- We provide a coherent, time-tested system that has been built over three decades of research, practice, learning and refinement (and that continues to evolve), working in partnership with clients on live challenges and opportunities
- We use that to help each business figure out their own approach to Excellence
- Then we help implement, maintain and continuously improve that approach

Who We Work With

- Leaders and organisations committed to achieving sustainable success using the principles of Business Excellence.
- People who don't have years to spend researching, and who are looking for a time-tested model, trusted partners and proven, practical ideas and methodologies that work

ABOUT THE AUTHORS

Pete Rogan

Founding Director of Future Positive Consulting Ltd.

Pete Rogan brings decades of expertise in helping businesses achieve sustainable success. With a foundation in engineering, Pete transitioned into training and economic development, where he honed his ability to help organisations manage and develop their people effectively. Over his career, he has supported more than 200 organisations in achieving the prestigious Investors in People (IIP) standard.

In 1998, Pete founded Future Positive Consulting, which has since grown into a trusted partner for world-class organisations and fast-growing entrepreneurial businesses. Pete's work is driven by a passion for helping people get the best from their time, talents and efforts, professionally and in wider life, and for helping leaders build organisations that are excellent to buy from, work for and invest in.

Academically, Pete holds a first-class Honours degree in psychology and two Master's degrees: one in Organisational and Occupational Psychology from Birkbeck College, University of London, and another in Human Resource Development from Nottingham Trent University.

Away from work, Pete enjoys distance running and has completed more than 100 marathons and more than 500 half-marathons.

Stuart Rogan

Managing Director of Future Positive Consulting Ltd.

Joining Future Positive in 2016, Stuart gained a broad, practical education in business and management by immersing himself in client operations across a wide range of sectors. By 2019, he was consulting directly with leadership teams on strategy, operational management, process improvement, and leadership development.

As Managing Director, Stuart has led comprehensive business improvement programmes that have delivered significant operational and cost benefits for clients. His ability to develop and support the successful execution of strategy has made him a trusted advisor to leadership teams seeking to build well-managed, high performing organisations.

Stuart's enthusiasm and drive stems from a deep-seated passion for helping to build well-managed organisations, seeing their potential as a powerful vehicle for creating value and fostering societal benefit.

Beyond business, Stuart's interests are broad, spanning music, fitness, history, psychology, and philosophy— perspectives that enrich his approach to leadership and organisational development.

CONTENTS

PART FOUR: SOCIAL SYSTEM

APPENDICES

INTRODUCTION

'Every organisation is naturally in some state of transformation. The critical question is "To what?"' (Shigeo Shingo)

Founded in 1998, Future Positive consulting work in partnership with leaders who aspire to build organisations that are excellent places to work for, buy from and invest in. Businesses which, through their offering and their business practices, add genuine and enduring value to customers, colleagues and the communities they work in and with.

However, amid the noise, clutter and confusion of the different models, toolkits and methodologies, and the continuous stream of disparate improvement ideas, we discovered that it was hard to find a place to start and a way to proceed that we, and our more ambitious clients, could be confident would move us inexorably toward this aspiration.

We encountered many pitfalls for the unwary, including:

- Ending up simply **trying to patch up problems with last-generation management models** which (let's remind ourselves), are a product of the business conditions and thinking of the early 20th century and which have insurmountable systemic limitations in the face of mid-21st-century challenges, and need to be superseded

- **Being misdirected by fads and fashions**. There is a plethora of well-marketed panaceas for every ill, many of them trivial, focusing on one minor facet of deeper systems issues and failing to address root causes. It is hard to relate even the best of these to your aims, far less see how they fit together

- **Incoherence:** Ending up with a hotchpotch of approaches comprising 'a scrappy training in a great number of odds and ends' (as W. Edwards Deming described it). Principles, models, tools and methodologies that don't work as a coherent system

- **'Initiativitis':** Introducing one initiative after another which rarely deliver their full promise (and sometimes undermine each other) and do not build to a coherent business system

So we committed to do the research, make sense of all the information, sort the wheat from the chaff and design and field-test a system that might be of value to the leaders we aim to support.

On this journey:

1.   We found that the principles of Business Excellence provide the best foundation for building a significant business

> 'So many companies keep searching for some magic bullet but there isn't one, there is only good management.' (David Hutchins)

The broad field of Business Excellence captures the ways of thinking about business which superseded 20th-century 'command and control'. It continues to evolve in response to the fast-changing conditions of the 21st century, and is a bridge to ever more advanced and adaptive forms of organisation. While the principles and practices have been around long enough to have proved successful in globally competitive organisations in a wide range of industries, not every business has yet fully understood, adopted and benefitted from their value. This represents a significant - and potentially transformational - opportunity for many businesses.

2.   We built a coherent, practical, field-proven, time-tested framework, system and toolkit

Over the past 27 years we have comprehensively studied best practice in the field, identified the essential ingredients and system dynamics, and synthesised these into a coherent system. We then put our ideas into live practice, working with clients in a wide range of industries (and in various states of growth, change or trouble), tackling real opportunities and challenges. We continually applied, tested and refined our overall understanding, models, tools, materials, methods, skills and expertise through repeated ongoing cycles of continuous improvement. Through this, we learned a lot about what really works and what doesn't.

We then distilled this into a comprehensive, field-proven, time-tested, coherent:

- **Framework:** An overall conceptual meta-model outlining the essential building blocks of Business Excellence: the key variables and interactions. This allows our clients to see the whole picture of what is required to build a culture of excellence, and to assess their current status and identify actions that they are confident will move them forward
- **Toolkit and methodology** to successfully implement, sustain and scale this approach to get sustainable and increasing benefit

3. **We developed the expertise to help clients implement faster, better and more sustainably,** with less hassle and fewer missteps. To tailor the model to suit the unique needs of their business and to use it as the foundation for the development of their 'Way' (i.e. their own model, toolkit and approach)

This book contains the essence of what we've learned on this journey. It is a practical toolkit for leaders – like you – who have the ambition to transform their organisations. It will enable you to:

- See a clear path through noise, clutter and confusion to your vision of creating a culture of excellence
- Identify:
  - What success looks like for your business (the big vision, key principles and concepts)
  - Where you are (current status)
  - The highest-leverage possibilities for action
- Take action, confident that it will move you forward
- Review progress, learn quickly and plan what to do next, and keep going, cycling fast through improvement loops, innovating and building momentum
- Reach higher levels of capability and performance that you can sustain and enhance on an ongoing basis
- Customise this to develop your own 'Way', and keep it evolving, incrementally integrating useful enhancements

When applied with discipline and consistency, this high-leverage approach brings significant, enduring and compounding benefits. There are, first, the significant cumulative advantages that accrue over time. This creates a significant gap between what you achieve with it and what would have happened without it (and, likewise, a gap between you and competitors who aren't doing something similar).

Perhaps more importantly, it embeds a robust means of navigating the ever-changing landscape of opportunities and challenges, continually tracking and adapting to changes in the operating environment, investing the business with the ability to thrive in the good times and get through the tough times.

Work in progress – always

There remains much to learn about this continuously evolving field, of course. We continue to work to identify the most useful thinking, concepts, tools and techniques, and to present them in a way that is accessible and will allow you to create a consistent, coherent vision and take practical and effective action toward achieving it. (The subject of future revisions of this book and our forthcoming book Fit For the Future). So wherever you are on your excellence journey, I think you'll find something of real and enduring value for you here.

It took us a long time and a lot of painstaking (and occasionally painful) effort over three decades of working – often feeling overwhelmed, confused and uncertain, and meeting a surprising amount of indifference and resistance (both active and passive) – to develop and test the framework, toolkit and methodology, to integrate them into a coherent system, and to build the expertise. Our hope is that it saves you the time, trouble, risk and frustration of doing all of this and allows you instead to recognise and commit to the possibilities of what your business can be for the people whose lives it touches, helping you to get further, faster, more easily.

If it does, then it's been worthwhile.

Thank you for the privilege of letting us share what we've learned with you. The ambition is heartfelt and the progress hard-won. And I hope it may be all the more useful to you for that.

Pete

3.6 MILLION YEARS OF ORGANISATIONAL CULTURE

So, 3.6 million years back, we're living in caves. We hunt, we gather, we maybe relax of an evening, watching whatever's on the fire. Early continuous improvement experts note the waste and inefficiency, and from the Palaeolithic through the Mesolithic and into the Neolithic age we see the transition to the domestication of plants and animals, and to living in huts. Nice. And it only takes about 3.5 million years. But a bunch of people think this farming thing will never catch on.

Time rolls on. 3300 BC. Stone is out. Bronze is in. But not for long. Only about 1,500 years later (date varies according to your postcode), iron's where it's at. But then, around 500AD, the Iron Age begins to fizzle out. The Romans rock up. Trade becomes more widespread, communities get bigger. Ongoing innovation in infrastructure and farming continues. But a bunch of people think that metal will never catch on.

Manufacturing remains pretty small-scale, largely the preserve of specialised craftspeople until ... about 1760, when the Industrial Revolution gathers momentum. The 80 years to 1840 see machine production replace hand production, and early capitalist economies emerge. Factories appear and cities grow as the work in factories, most notably on textiles, draws in people from rural areas.

So popular is the first Industrial Revolution that they have a second one from 1840 to 1870. It's all kicking off now, with the increasing use of chemicals and steel, more mechanisation and more use of power from water and steam, and of course the coal required to produce it. Transport of goods and people leaps forward with the advent of railways and steam-powered ships. At the back end (circa 1860) the internal combustion engine is invented – heralding the next revolution. But a bunch of people think mechanisation will never catch on.

The 20th century

Enter the Machine Age. A seismic shift from craft production to mass production. Craft production of complex machines like cars was inefficient. A skilled craftsperson was needed to do almost every task. It was hard to make precision parts, and time had to be spent adjusting them to fit. And there was wasted motion as people moved around the workshop and built the product.

Fortunately, engineering improvements make it possible to manufacture, in volume, precision parts that are uniform, interchangeable and easily assembled. This enables Henry Ford, guided by F.W. Taylor's 'scientific management' principles, to simplify and standardise many tasks so that they can be performed by lower-skilled workers. The more complex and skilled work, including designing and improving processes, is handled by specialist professionals and managers. Highly significantly, this introduces a separation between those doing front-line tasks and those designing and improving them.

The moving assembly line is also introduced to cut down wasted movement of people. This all radically enhances productivity, improves quality and reduces costs. Reliable, high-quality, technically complex goods can now be mass-produced.

Ford (a fascinating and controversial character) also doubles wages and cuts the working day to eight hours. This is part of an expansive vision to use technology to provide reliable goods at prices everyone can afford, and to pay people enough to participate in, and benefit from, a growing economy. His ultimate ambition is to reduce poverty and release people from drudgery, freeing them to enjoy and expand their lives beyond the factory.

'We want to create for everybody the best life conditions possible, a high level of opportunity: a life that people will be glad to live.' (Henry Ford)

Identifying himself firmly as an industrialist, not a capitalist, Ford speaks of 'devoting business to the service of all of society instead of to the service of the few'.

A view comprehensively rejected by the next major innovator of organisational culture, Alfred Sloan of General Motors. His view is crystal clear: 'General Motors is not in the business of making cars, it is in the business of making money.'

Sloan ratchets up the rational thinking, breaking the business into divisions and departments, and relentlessly segmenting and de-skilling processes. His belief is that the whole enterprise can be optimised by isolating, controlling and optimising each individual component.

He drives centralised control. Top-level managers set short-term financial and productivity goals. They analyse and interpret data in reports they demand from managers. They make decisions designed to be cascaded down the hierarchy and followed. It is assumed that all the important information is in the numbers and that top managers do not need to know how the operation works to make effective decisions about it.

Good performance against short-term goals is rewarded by bonuses, increased budgets and promotion. Poor performance is punished by denying these rewards and by criticism, discipline and dismissal. Departments are played off against each other in the fight for resource, in the belief that internal competition will sharpen their performance.

White-collar experts design all processes and make any changes. Front-line people must follow this 'one best way' and have no autonomy to make changes or to show discretion or judgment in following procedures.

This approach conquers all before it and reigns supreme for decades. It provides the structural and cultural template – and, arguably, the moral standards – for large parts of the corporate world. So much so that it is still known as 'traditional management', as well as by its more descriptive names, 'command and control' or the 'financial results model'.

However... all is not well.

'Command and control brought great initial progress but created other significant problems and limitations which prevent it reaching an even better world.' (John Seddon)

Critique of the 'traditional' model

'Command and control has created organisations which are full of waste, offer poor service, depress the morale of people who work in them and are beset by management factories that not only do not contribute to improving performance, but actually make it worse.' (John Seddon)

There have been many excellent (and lengthy) commentaries on the limitations and problems of the 'traditional' model. Here's a brief summary. They are characterised by:

- Frenetic activity/constant firefighting (e.g. an end-of-month rush to achieve targets) that does not translate into sustainable, consistent and continuously improving performance
- Multiple, constantly recurring, preventable problems
- Departmental silos (vertical hierarchies) with constant friction between them, while nobody is responsible for managing the process that serves the customer (which runs horizontally across departments)
- Ever-increasing bureaucracy, rules and initiatives that increase cost, delay and distraction but add no value for the customer
- Fear and blame that stop problems being properly explored, understood and permanently resolved
- Managerialism – constant reporting and analysing of data and issuing of directives, but little real management/communication, far less leadership
- Out-of-touch senior teams (especially at corporate level): remote, aloof, disinterested in front-line colleagues and the problems that stop them doing a better job. Also often arrogant, complacent and change-averse
- Failure to thrive. Regular setbacks and crises stymie sustained, profitable long-term growth

After surviving crises in the 1980s and the 1990s, on 1 June 2009 at 8:00am, unable to supply an acceptable viability plan to the US Treasury, General Motors filed for Chapter 11 bankruptcy. It reported US$82 billion in assets and US$173 billion in debt.

Significantly and symbolically, they had been overtaken in 2007 as the world's biggest car manufacturer by Toyota, a company at the vanguard of the next evolution in management and organisational culture: Business Excellence.

Mid- to late 20th century – Business Excellence

The Business Excellence approach was framed by the Quality Movement in the middle of the 20th century (including W. Edwards Deming, Joseph Juran and Philip Crosby) and taken forward by organisations including Toyota. It achieved prominence with Womack, Roos and Jones's 1990 book *The Machine That Changed The World*. Business Excellence offered ways to improve not just profitability, but also the customer and employee experience. (See Steven Spear's *The High-Velocity Edge* for more examples from a range of organisations, including the service sector, public services and healthcare.)

The key principles are:

- Quality comes first – because if the quality is wrong, delivery performance, cost, customer satisfaction and productivity will all suffer
- Quality is defined as what the customer wants in terms of quality, cost, delivery and service
- Focus on the process – i.e. the means by which results are achieved. The process is relentlessly improved by identifying and removing anything that wastes time or money, or causes quality problems
- People are led. All colleagues are recognised and respected as the experts in their role. They are empowered to solve problems and drive the continuous improvement, and they have tools and training in practical problem-solving techniques to allow them to do this
- People are engaged and accountable. All colleagues are regularly given the facts and data to allow them to understand and improve processes and performance

This is the approach now followed by the truly world-class organisations (i.e. those leading all *genuinely competitive, global, consumer-led* markets for *quality* goods and services).

Given its straightforward common-sense principles and level of success, we might expect that every business is now following this more evolved approach. But we'd be wrong. A bunch of people think it will never catch on.

In reality, there are a range of responses to it. The majority don't recognise that these two distinct models exist, or fully appreciate the significance of the differences between them. Many have heard something about Business Excellence and dabble, trying out some techniques on a pick-and-mix basis, making little progress. Some implement the production tools and techniques without changing the underlying management system and organisational culture, and consequently fail to achieve significant sustained improvement. The few that fully grasp it commit to the painstaking, challenging, but ultimately rewarding process of developing a more effective management system and culture.

It is still possible, of course, to survive with the traditional approach in markets that are not as globally competitive (i.e. where there are few providers, all much of a muchness, so there is really nowhere else for an unhappy customer to go – for example, utilities, telecoms and banking), and in public services where, despite repeated failings and political and public pressure to change, there appears to be little real sign of that change happening.

So the traditional model, with all its attendant problems, trundles on. A key reason is that people don't fully recognise that better alternatives exist.

This is partly because the traditional model is simply what many of us grew up with and assumed to be 'normal': the way it always was and always will be. But that's my whole point. It's not, and recognising this matters. A lot.

> *'Most people imagine that the present style of management has always existed, and is a fixture. Actually, it is a modern invention.'* (W. Edwards Deming)
>
> *'By the 1950s it had become general practice at US corporations and at companies around the world. Today it is so pervasive that it is essentially invisible. It is simply how things are done.'* (John Seddon)

So… where are you and your business? Are you limiting yourself with a previous-generation management system and culture, or moving confidently into a future of sustainable success?

Spear and a loincloth, anyone?

PART ONE: INTRODUCTION

CHAPTER 1

CREATING SUSTAINED BUSINESS SUCCESS

Excellence and the alternatives

Every business culture, like every human personality, is unique, but it is possible to identify some broad categories and to gain some insight into how they are created and sustained, and into the results they produce. This can help us to understand the culture of our own business, create a vision of where we want to be, and take steps to get there.

Figure 1.1 shows four broad types of culture and the two key dimensions on which they differ: focus on performance and degree of engagement.

- The Business Excellence culture is our main focus here, as it offers the best prospects for sustainable high performance and benefits for all stakeholders in the context of 21st-century conditions, opportunities and threats
- Command and control cultures are based on the 'traditional' philosophy of the early 20th century. Obsolete in many industries, still prevalent in others
- Chaotic cultures lack focus and organisation and are minimally concerned with how people experience the business
- Cosy cultures tend to enjoy guaranteed business and lack focus, rigour and discipline in their approach to business management and improvement

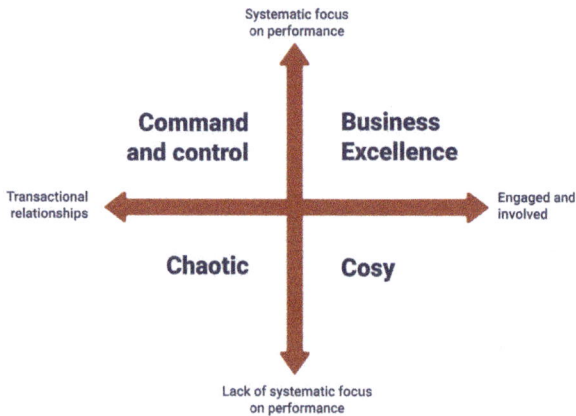

Figure 1.1: Culture alternatives

Let's explore this in more detail.

Business Excellence

In an Excellence culture, there is a relentless commitment to quality, continuous improvement and colleague engagement. This is communicated and supported from the top.

Figure 1.2 illustrates the dynamics.

Figure 1.2: Excellence culture overview

The ultimate aim is sustainable success, achieved by a focus on creating more of what customers value and eliminating the waste in processes. Performance is managed systematically at all levels with a strong focus on process effectiveness; constantly and actively looking for ways to enhance quality and productivity by identifying and removing the causes of errors, waste and inefficiency. Relevant measures and reliable data are used to inform discussions about performance, and to identify improvement opportunities. Appropriate time is made available for process improvement. Improvement projects are implemented effectively and seen through to completion.

Colleagues are actively and constructively engaged and involved. Managers understand that their role is to enable people to bring their full experience, knowledge and problem-solving abilities to the quest to deliver excellence and continually improving performance. This means ensuring that people are:

- Equipped with the right information, tools, skills and processes to allow them to succeed
- Actively and positively supported to perform:
  - Held accountable through regular, constructive discussion of performance and improvement
  - Coached effectively as part of everyday work
  - Listened to: concerns and problems that are preventing them from succeeding are understood and addressed
- Trained in process-improvement concepts, tools and techniques
- Actively involved in continuous improvement activities
- Able to communicate openly and honestly about performance and to analyse, discuss and solve problems, free from fear and blame

The simultaneous focus on performance and engagement creates an ongoing cycle of identifying ways to remove waste and add more value, using structured problem-solving to create effective and sustainable solutions. This all revolves around teamwork, both within teams and between different teams (vertically and horizontally) across the business to ensure that the whole system is improved end-to-end in a coherent way.

All of this creates the potential for an upward spiral of sustained and continuously improving high performance, and the agility to adapt to changing markets: a strong foundation for sustained competitive advantage.

This makes the business more attractive to buy from, work for and invest in because:

- The quality, reliability and competitive pricing that operational excellence brings helps to retain existing customers and attract new ones, and thus create a stable and loyal customer base
- With strong levels of colleague engagement, the organisation is better able to attract and retain top talent and get the best from them
- Having a solid and growing customer base, a stable and engaged team, and strong profitability, and being well positioned for growth, Excellent organisations offer better potential returns for investors

Alternatives to a culture of Excellence and their dangers

Cosy cultures exist where work is either guaranteed or has historically just rolled in consistently. The customers are either happy, undemanding, or have little power to change poor levels of service. People can pretty much work in their own way at their own pace. There is a belief that things will always be like this. That creates a measure of comfort, which can turn into overconfidence, complacency, and sometimes arrogance.

> 'Everything hinges upon luck and good feelings, upon the personalities of the people and the good will they share. Unfortunately, personalities, good feelings, good will and luck aren't the ingredients of successful organization, but the recipe instead for chaos and disaster.' (Michael Gerber)

This type of culture ticks along until some change in market dynamics, ambition or economic conditions brings pressure to deliver more, better, faster or cheaper. This can push the culture out of its comfort zone. Lacking the ability to adapt quickly, it is in danger of tipping toward chaos.

Cosy cultures can include smaller or younger entrepreneurial organisations with lots of positive energy that have not yet reached the point of needing to formalise and structure the business. Postponing that moment too long brings serious danger, as things can all too easily slip into Chaotic territory.

Long-established organisations can also reside in this category. Their challenge is more likely to be complacency, apathy and an 'it's always been fine, and my job is secure, so why change' mentality, and sometimes an attitude of indifference toward customers. They too are in danger of being driven into Chaotic territory if customer demands, financial or other pressures increase and their management system and culture are not sufficiently developed or mature to cope.

Even when ticking along nicely, though, the performance of a Cosy culture is usually mediocre (compared with its potential) because there is no sustained and disciplined focus on results and underperformance is not constructively challenged or addressed. This kind of culture can be okay to work for but lacks positive challenge, and is frustrating for colleagues when problems are raised but go unaddressed. It's an underwhelming experience for customers and not hugely attractive to invest in.

In a **Chaotic** culture there is inconsistency, disorganisation, a sense of chaos and regular conflict.

Here, there is no systematic focus on performance, though when things go wrong, people may discuss problems passionately – but leaning more on emotion and opinion than facts and data, and seeking to defend themselves and blame each other rather than trying to understand problems and identify and resolve root causes.

Communication and people-management are unsystematic and inconsistent. There is no structured or disciplined approach to continuous improvement. People react to circumstances, making snap decisions with little apparent logic or connection to an underlying strategy or plan, and often without consultation or real consideration of the longer-term and wider consequences. Managers see themselves as firefighters, there to resolve a constant stream of problems to 'get stuff out the door' and achieve short-term goals.

As a result, frequent mistakes are made, and most are made time and time again. Little is learned or improved. Quality is poor. People feel that they are not trusted, respected, informed, listened to, consulted, involved or properly thanked or rewarded. As a result, they are usually somewhat unhappy, stressed and disengaged, either through indifference or for self-protection.

Absenteeism is often high, and the business struggles to attract and retain talent. It is a constant battle to retain customers, maintain repeat business and upsell. Financial performance is often inconsistent and well below what the business is capable of. This makes it harder to attract long-term investment. All this creates a negative spiral of stagnation, frustration and underachievement.

Despite this, businesses in this space can survive and operate profitably if they:

- Have a highly specialist niche offering
- Operate in markets where customers and employees have nowhere else to go
- Operate in markets where customers will accept poor quality and service for a budget price
- Operate in markets where the competition is no better, or worse

In **command and control** cultures there is a strong emphasis on performance management, control and discipline, but little on engagement or empowerment. Where this is coupled with an overriding focus on short-term financial results, the measures and reward systems are geared more toward current financial performance than to building long-term capacity and customer loyalty or employee commitment. Relationships (with customers, employees and suppliers) tend to be transactional, sometimes exploitative and usually strained. Little loyalty or goodwill is either shown or expected in any relationship.

With this transactional mindset, engaging employees is not seen as important. People are viewed, essentially, as a cog in the machine. Strong cost control may mean that pay is kept as low as the market (or the law) will allow. People are hired and fired in line with short-term needs. Change is driven top-down – done *to* people rather than *with* them.

Colleague commitment and motivation is usually low; people tend to withhold the discretionary aspects of their potential contribution and are reluctant to take initiative, contribute ideas or go the 'extra mile'. Most just turn up and deliver the basics. Some give up, switch off and do the bare minimum. Others develop a negative attitude toward their work, the organisation and the management. In these cultures, people are, consequently, difficult to manage and motivate.

Absenteeism is high, and good people are hard to attract and retain. Management often responds to all of the above by taking a hard line. This just deepens the us-and-them attitudes all round, creating a spiral of mutual mistrust which makes it harder to communicate, motivate and solve problems, all of which filters through and impacts on quality, productivity, delivery performance and customer service.

The customer experience can range from good (for standard, low-complexity products and services), to disastrous, where products and services are mis-sold, over-priced, of poor quality or arrive late. Attempts to complain are met with impenetrable phone or online systems, bureaucracy, inefficiency, lack of genuine concern and sense of game-playing.

Some command and control organisations work hard at presenting an image of being customer friendly, environmentally responsible and good employers, but this is often window dressing in the name of brand image rather than indicating a genuine commitment.

Command and control cultures are typically found in industries whose business model is built around high-volume, low-margin products or services that can be provided by an unskilled or semi-skilled workforce, but they can also be found in high-skill environments like financial services. They are usually large companies in markets dominated by a small number of large players; for example, utilities, telecoms and banking.

If they are well run, their financial returns can be steady, making some command and control cultures attractive to invest in. Few, if any, however, are truly excellent in quality, customer experience or financial performance, being more expensive to run and less agile than the more customer-focused, lean and responsive Excellence cultures.

For more on this, see Appendix A – The limitations of command and control management.

The costs and consequences

Any kind of suboptimal culture, with low colleague engagement or lacking a systematic approach to performance management and continuous improvement, will create problems in seven interrelated areas. Each represents a recurring cost and impacts on results, reputation, profitability and growth, limiting the performance and potential of the business.

1. People problems

- **People withhold, or are unable to contribute, their discretionary potential** (i.e. things that they can choose to contribute or withhold, such as additional effort, goodwill, favours, flexibility, and ideas). As a consequence, much of the knowledge and expertise that the business is already paying for, and that could be put to use solving problems and improving things, goes untapped
- **Higher levels of grievances:** This includes formal grievances that need to be dealt with, taking up management time. It also includes grievances that are not formally pursued but that fester and feed resentment

- **Higher levels of absence, and the associated cost and disruption:** This includes overstaffing to compensate for historically high absence, the high cost of temps or overtime, and people working less productively or making mistakes while covering unfamiliar jobs
- **Higher employee turnover:** The most talented and committed people get disillusioned and leave because they are unable to fully use, develop and be rewarded fairly for their talent. The loss of knowledge and experience damages short-term results and hampers continuous-improvement efforts. There are recruitment and training costs, and other hidden costs associated with the disruption. Furthermore, when good people leave it can create a cascade effect, unsettling others who then start looking for the exit too
- **Poor labour-market reputation:** The business may come to be seen as an employer of last resort, rather than an employer of first choice. The top talent in the market is put off. This leaves the business to select from a pool of lower-performing, higher-maintenance people, who are less productive and harder to manage

2. Operational inefficiencies

- **Poorer quality:** More errors and delays, due to shortcomings in processes, communication, skills, motivation and levels of personal responsibility
- **Lower productivity** due to people problems, poor processes and the need for rework resulting from the poor quality
- **Increased costs** due to waste, rework, downtime, low productivity and absence
- **Poorer delivery performance:** Customer orders are late, incomplete or faulty

3. Unhappy customers

Unhappy customers due to problems with quality, delivery performance and poor client handling

4. Reduced revenue and profitability

- **Unhappy customers reduce their orders, look for price reductions, go elsewhere** and possibly spread the word about their discontent, which puts others off

- **Poor market reputation:** The business is not seen as an automatic/first choice due to quality, cost and delivery performance issues. This makes it harder to achieve sales, and to command the price necessary to maintain margins
- **Lack of competitive edge:** The competition builds a performance gap on quality, cost, delivery performance and customer service that is hard to close, and limits the price the business can charge

5. Managers are swamped with non-value-adding work, sucked into managing one level too low, and less effective

- Managers spend more time and incur increased hassle from dealing with the fallout from the problems outlined above:
  - Controlling and monitoring demotivated staff and dealing with absence, discipline and grievance issues
  - Dealing with avoidable operational problems
  - Dealing with complaints from customers that could have been avoided
  - Dealing with senior managers unhappy about quality, cost, delivery performance and customer problems resulting from the operational problems
- **Opportunity costs:** All managers get sucked into managing these avoidable problems, resulting in less management time being focused on their core responsibilities of facilitating sustainable, high performance and continuous improvement

6. Missed opportunities for improvement and growth

- Without a systematic approach to continuous improvement where people can get involved in solving problems and reducing waste, improving processes, efficiency, quality and delivery performance, and reducing cost, it will be hard for the business to achieve the levels of operational excellence that will provide the competitive advantage to create the strong platform necessary to win new business (and possibly retain existing business)
- Instead, the business is distracted by internal problems, and focuses less on what is going on externally. As a result, it may not be sufficiently alert to new market opportunities, technical developments or opportunities to improve how it does things

- Whatever opportunities are identified, the business may lack the responsiveness and drive to capitalise on them

- **Wasted potential:** The business fails to leverage the talent it has. Many small opportunities to involve people in using their talents to solve problems and drive continuous improvement are missed every day. These missed opportunities accumulate over time and come to represent a growing gap between the potential capability of the business and its actual performance

7. A doom loop that increases the risk of business problems or failure

When these aspects of underperformance become entrenched, the business becomes caught in a series of **negative double whammies** – situations where, simultaneously:

- Positive progress stalls

- Avoidable and costly problems are incurred

For example, where a business fails to equip people with adequate skills, it will not only fail to achieve the positive goals of high productivity and quality, but also, instead, incur costly errors and create dissatisfied customers. The time needed to solve the problems that are created robs management of the time and motivation they should have been focusing on tackling the underlying causes and making changes that will lead to sustainable long-term success.

This creates a doom loop of working hard, battling the same problems but never really getting out of it. Or worse, it can create a downward spiral cycle of underperformance and frustration that leads to sustained underperformance (and, in extreme cases, business failure) due to:

- **Stagnation:** The culture gets caught in a pattern of blaming and counter-blaming that keeps it locked in a cycle of self-perpetuating mediocrity

- With the burden of higher costs outlined above, and less discretionary contribution from people, the business becomes less efficient, flexible and customer-friendly, and more **crisis-prone and unstable**

- This increases the risk of **major failures**

- Carrying the unnecessary costs noted above, commanding poorer margins and having frailties around quality and delivery performance **increases vulnerability to market competition and economic or industry downturns**

- **Failing to create enough profit to reinvest** to maintain and enhance competitiveness

All of the above are examples of waste: wasted time, energy, money and other resources. All of which handicap and limit the business, and are, to a significant degree, self-inflicted and avoidable.

Questions:

- How much of this do you recognise in your business?
- What are the immediate costs of problems (inefficiency, lost business, quality problems, employee turnover, etc.)?
- What are the improvement and growth opportunities you can't get to because you are battling these problems?
- Is it worth doing something about?

Many organisations struggle to see the opportunities, create the vision, eliminate the challenges and develop a success culture.

Here's why

So why do businesses persist with approaches that predictably lead to the above problems? Why isn't every culture an Excellence culture? There are of course many reasons. including:

1. Lack of ambition and fear of change

Some businesses lack genuine ambition and a commitment to excellence and continuous improvement. Reasons include:

- Complacency: The business may be doing acceptably well as it is, and everyone assumes this will continue to be the case
- Lack of awareness of how to do any better, or an inability to implement changes

- Fear among managers that a proper performance-management system and meaningful performance measures will expose a catalogue of problems that they have failed to recognise, grasp or manage over a number of years
- Fear among managers whose limited vision, business understanding and abilities, and negative attitude and complacency, will be exposed by the challenge of change

2. Short-termism

Focusing on immediate results while neglecting (and perhaps actively damaging) the capacity of the business to generate better and more sustainable long-term returns. Short-termism is expensive and, ultimately, self-defeating. For example, saving money on basic training or postponing necessary maintenance exposes the business to operational problems and renders it unable to respond quickly to new opportunities and competitive threats, compromising long-term competitiveness.

3. Working harder, not smarter

Managers are paid to **deliver short-term results and simultaneously improve the business to ensure sustainable long-term success**. Many, however, seem to spend much of their time firefighting, battling against operational problems to serve customers. This leaves little time for identifying and eliminating the root causes of problems and improving processes, so they end up fighting the same avoidable problems time and again.

4. Trying to improve results without understanding the underlying systems that create them

The more a business sees short-term profitability as the overriding indicator of success, the more it is likely to rely predominantly on financial data to manage the company, particularly revenue and costs. This creates two potential dangers:

- **Pushing to increase revenue by any means:** This could lead, for example, to sales teams offering customers things that are difficult to produce cost-effectively, or offering credit that is unlikely to be paid back
- **Trying to reduce cost by any means:** Cutting specific line items simply because they are identifiable on management accounts, while failing to understand the full implication on end-to-end costs, usually creates the unintended negative

consequences of actually increasing overall costs and potentially damaging revenues by reducing customer satisfaction. For example, buying inferior tools or raw materials, or cutting back on training or maintenance, risks increasing operational costs through internal failures, customer complaints and returns, replacements and ongoing warranty costs.

The most sustainable way to increase revenue is to satisfy customers by providing the quality of offering they need at a competitive price. The way to do that cost-effectively is to understand what the customer wants and to gear the process to produce it efficiently by removing all waste from that process. This in turn relies on understanding the process and how it is performing.

5. Ineffective management processes

Management processes may go wrong in a number of ways. They may:

- Not be done regularly and systematically. They may be inconsistent or just be done in a reactionary way when a problem occurs
- They may focus on lag measures and have no means of measuring the real-time process performance that is driving financial and other metrics
- Be dominated by emotion and opinion, rather than facts and data
- Not follow the simple Plan-Do-Check-Act cycle (see Chapters 3 and 4) which ensures performance management is a systematic process, focused on performance analysis, learning and improvement
- Not include everyone, so that people who could make a significant contribution to improving things don't know what the issues are, and can't get involved
- Not be linked to the overall business strategy

6. Managers managing one level too low

The whole management chain often ends up managing (at least) one level too low, getting sucked into operational problems. This means either that the business is paying for an extra layer of management or that there is not enough focus on strategic improvement, or both.

7. Silo vs systems thinking

Rather than seeing the business as a system that works as a whole, the business is managed as a set of separate departments. These departments are set individual targets and rewarded or punished according to how well they are achieved, regardless of the impact that one team's approach to achieving their goals could have on the overall performance of the business. For example, Sales making deals for small quantities of highly specialised goods or services that Operations will struggle to deliver profitably. Problems are seen as localised and isolated rather than interconnected across the system. 'Us-and-them' attitudes develop between different functions, and between different layers in the hierarchy. There is firm adherence to functional and role boundaries, cultivating a widespread attitude of 'that's not my responsibility'.

8. No systematic approach to solving problems and continuous improvement

- A failure to differentiate between permanent problem resolution (i.e. identifying and removing root causes to prevent recurrence) and short-term fixes (which usually involve creating a problem somewhere else later) to 'get stuff out the door' or hit the numbers
- No toolkit for taking a structured approach to problem-solving, root cause analysis, developing and testing countermeasures, etc.
- No regular forums where people discuss performance using reliable facts and data, identify improvement opportunities, prioritise the opportunities and take action on them
- Lack of expertise: people haven't been trained to deal with routine issues, and no high-level expertise is available to deal with more complex issues

9. Fear and lack of trust

To make process management and continuous improvement work, people must be able to trust each other enough to speak openly and honestly about performance problems and the reasons for them, and work together to identify and test ideas to find workable solutions. However:

- People may simply be ignored
- Action may be promised, but never happen
- There is a fear of 'rocking the boat' and causing conflict
- Highlighting problems is perceived as negativity or blaming others, and:
  - People get defensive

- Things bec ome adversarial
- There is retribution (or a fear of it) from managers who feel criticised or made to look bad; for example, people may fear that they will be given difficult jobs, poor grades, etc.

10. Fragmented and incoherent approach to business improvement

Many leaders have never experienced an Excellence culture. As a result, they lack the vision, belief and know-how to create it in their organisation. They will no doubt have a clear intention to achieve success, but no coherent overarching philosophy, and, at best, it will done piecemeal, with slow progress and disappointing results. This includes:

- Ad-hoc gathering of concepts and tools, often driven by fads. The business does not develop a coherent philosophy and approach aimed at achieving an Excellence culture through increasing quality and removing waste by engaging people in continuous improvement activities, integrating and absorbing any useful new techniques that come along. Instead, the business lurches from one fad to another in reaction to problems and the failure of the last fad to make a lasting difference, causing dismay and confusion
- Not seeing initiatives through to completion before abandoning them, and jumping to the next thing

Many organisations claim to have good processes and management systems. They may indeed have systems, but there are often gaps and inconsistencies in how the systems fit together. They are disjointed and incomplete rather than forming a coherent suite of systems. There is often also a lack of discipline, drive and consistency in how managers use the systems.

Questions:

- How much of this is true for your business?
- How fully is it recognised and acknowledged?
- What headway is being made on addressing it?

Choose wisely – don't drift

'The only things that evolve by themselves in organisations are disorder, friction, and poor performance.' (Peter Drucker)

The Chaotic and Cosy cultures that develop without strategy or design can, as described earlier, easily becoming self-limiting, dysfunctional and change-resistant, and these can become deep-rooted and long-lasting.

Cultures built on 20th-century command and control thinking and practice will struggle in fast-changing competitive markets. And struggle to change.

Business Excellence offers a way of thinking, and a set of concepts, tools and techniques, better suited to the needs of businesses in competitive markets in the mid-21st century.

But experience suggests it is not for everyone. It takes uncommon vision, leadership, time, energy and enduring commitment to create. It involves risk and setbacks and will have its internal doubters and critics and meet with resistance, both passive and active. The benefits emerge only gradually, and in the early stages can be difficult to quantify. The only thing more risky, costly, frustrating and problematic is spending a career lifetime wrestling with the intractable problems of a sub-optimal and stuck culture.

What are your ambitions for your career and business? What results do you want to achieve, and how do you want to achieve them? What opportunities and challenges lie ahead for you and the business? Choose wisely. Don't leave it to chance.

CHAPTER 2

THE ANATOMY OF BUSINESS EXCELLENCE

Overview

Business Excellence is an approach to business management that aims to create an organisation that achieves sustainable success and has the agility to stay competitive amid the challenges of rapid and unpredictable change.

Business Excellence focuses on delivering what the customer wants, right first time, on time, every time, with zero wasted time or material. The management system is designed to make waste, quality problems and other performance problems visible, and to empower and enable front-line colleagues to address them.

Core principles

The core principles can be grouped into the 12 main areas outlined in Figure 2.1, which also shows how the principles relate and create a coherent whole, forming a fully integrated, dynamic socio-technical system.

Figure 2.1: Core principles of Business Excellence

Let's look at these factors in turn, starting with the three-way relationship at the top of the model between people, process and performance.

An organisation's success is tied to its ability to perform. That is, to provide valued, cost-effective service to a target market in a way that is commercially sustainable.

To achieve excellent operational and strategic performance and results requires engaged people working with an effective operational process. When led and managed well, this creates an upward spiral of engaged people who both follow and improve the processes, working collaboratively to tackle real issues: solving real problems and grasping real opportunities. This creates increasingly strong results, which further builds people's confidence, motivation and engagement and encourages them to improve further, finding ways to add greater value and remove waste.

The left-hand side of the model shows the 'technical system' – the chain of management processes, from strategic to operational to daily/process management. The purpose of these is to equip front-line colleagues with processes that are fit for purpose, lean, efficient, properly resourced, well managed and continuously improved.

On the right-hand side is the 'socio' part: the people factors and their interactions. These necessarily start with effective leadership attitudes and skills behaviours, running through to operational managers' effectiveness and that of the front-line managers who run the daily management process and directly enable and facilitate front-line colleagues' performance.

The model also, throughout, illustrates the interactivity and interdependence between the various factors. For example, if a leader has great skill, but not an effective strategy process, their effectiveness will be correspondingly diminished, and vice versa. An excellent strategy process in the hands of someone lacking the requisite understanding, skills and discipline to run it well will be similarly compromised. And so on up the chain of people, and the processes they rely on, to the organisation's front line.

The entire venture is founded on the thinking, principles and practices of excellence.

Finally, all aspects of the model are subject to continuous improvement, both in their own right and as a holistic, dynamic business system that adapts to its changing business environment.

Business philosophy

Business Excellence is based on a clear and coherent philosophy which represents a significant evolution from 'traditional' management thinking. Key tenets of this philosophy include:

- That sustainable and consistent success depends on **meeting the needs of all key stakeholders**; being first choice to buy from, work for and invest in

- **Operational excellence is the cornerstone of competitive advantage:** The ability to deliver right first time, on time, every time, is the key to creating valued, loyal customers

- **Process focus:** The quality of the process determines the quality of the result: well-designed and well-run, -maintained and -improved processes are the bedrock of sustainable success

- **Quality comes first:** The cost of poor quality is significant, and often avoidable. When product or service quality is not right first time, it drives up the cost of inspection, correcting internal failures and dealing with external failures. It also soaks up operational capacity, creates delays and impacts on delivery performance. Focusing on right-first-time quality minimises costs and maximises productivity, customer satisfaction and, in turn, sustainable, profitable sales

- **Respect for people:** Recognising people as proud, motivated experts in their roles who, if properly led, will take responsibility for managing and improving performance
- **Colleague engagement drives performance and improvement:** Recognising that everyone can make a difference, and needs to make a difference, engagement means connecting with people to develop and deploy discretionary and excellence potential; involving, enabling and empowering everyone in the business to be active partners in the management and improvement of performance
- **The purpose of performance measurement is to empower and inform:** Clear, understandable, visible performance measures should be available to all colleagues, in real time, and used to understand and improve performance (rather than target criticism)
- Recognising Deming's observation that **94% of performance problems are due to the system, not people**, when performance problems occur, asking 'How did the process let this happen?', not 'Who's to blame?'
- **Continuous improvement optimises short-term performance and underpins long-term success:** Sustainable success means building the capability to adapt quickly and smoothly to daily operational challenges, and to wider, longer-term strategic changes in markets, technology, etc.
- **Plan-Do-Check-Act (PDCA) thinking drives the management of daily performance and continuous improvement:** PDCA is a constant loop of: defining both a goal and the method of achieving it; executing the plan; reflecting on the outcomes; and applying what was learned to improve the approach and outcomes on the next cycle
- **Systems thinking:** Managing the business as a complete interconnected system, with the focus on optimising the performance of the entire end-to-end value stream, rather than individual elements in isolation
- **Pursuing perfection:** Perfection is defined as the complete elimination of waste so that the customer can be served exactly what they need, and only what they need, when they need it, with no delay and at minimum cost. It is recognised as not wholly achievable, but pursuing perfection will deliver the best of what is possible – excellence and continuous improvement
- **Constancy of purpose and long-term thinking:** The need for short-term results is balanced with the steady, disciplined building of the capability for sustainable long-term success

In Chapter 3, we expand this list and explore it in greater depth.

Leadership excellence

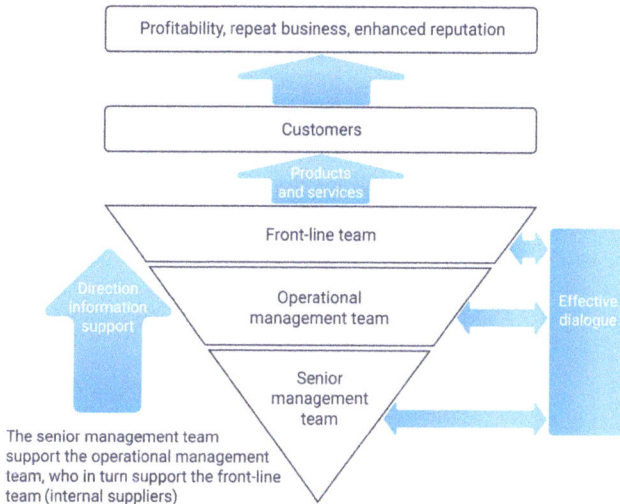

Figure 2.2: How leadership guides and supports operational excellence

Leadership in organisations that are committed to Business Excellence begins with leaders understanding, actively role-modelling, promoting and supporting the above principles.

A large part of this, as illustrated in Figure 2.2, involves providing direction and support to the people who do the work that serves the customers. Specifically:

- **Designing, overseeing and improving the strategic management system:** The processes that define, communicate and implement the strategy for the business

- **Overseeing and improving the operational management system:** Together with operational managers, designing, running and improving the systems that oversee the effective running of the operational processes

- **Being in touch with what is happening operationally:**

  - Through tiered meetings as part of the daily management process
  - Going to the front line as appropriate, to see and directly understand any significant challenges

- **Actively supporting continuous-improvement efforts, by:**

  - Directly executing the high-level improvement projects identified in the strategy
  - Monitoring the execution of strategic improvement plans at other levels
  - Removing barriers that have been escalated upward and are beyond the scope of operational teams to solve

Crucial to leadership excellence is setting the right tone and example for the culture; leaders living the values of the organisation, leading by example in their attitudes and behaviour, and working together effectively as a leadership team.

Underpinning this is the recognition that **quality begins in the boardroom.** As Deming emphasised:

> 'Workers are not to blame for poor quality or productivity. The workers don't determine the layout of the plant, the room temperature, the amount invested in research, development and training. They don't buy the equipment, tools and raw materials or determine the design of the product. In short, they don't determine 90 per cent of the things responsible for the quality of the product. [Furthermore] workers cannot change the system, only management can change the system. It is management's responsibility to change the system so that quality and productivity can improve and workers can experience pride of workmanship. Once that happens, worker input becomes a continual part of the improvement process.'

Engaging people

Recognising that everyone can make a difference, and everyone needs to make a difference, engagement means connecting with people to develop and deploy their discretionary and excellence potential: involving, enabling and empowering everyone in the business to be active partners in managing and improving performance.

Enabling and empowering means supporting people to:

- Perform, by providing the basic tools, training, raw materials, information and ongoing management support they need

- Solve problems and improve processes by providing information, time, and training in problem-solving techniques, and an environment free of fear where they can openly discuss and address improvement opportunities

The ultimate aim is to create a 'Thinking People System': a business system that unlocks people's wider capabilities and, as a result, becomes better at preventing and solving problems, and continuously improves. A system that is flexible, agile, responsive, resilient and stays aligned with the changing needs of customers.

The dynamic that fosters the simultaneous development of people, process and performance is illustrated in Figure 2.3: a virtuous cycle of enabling and empowering people to understand and improve processes, which develops people's process-understanding and problem-solving skills and also improves performance. This in turn provides motivation and encouragement to remain engaged in the quest to understand and improve the process further.

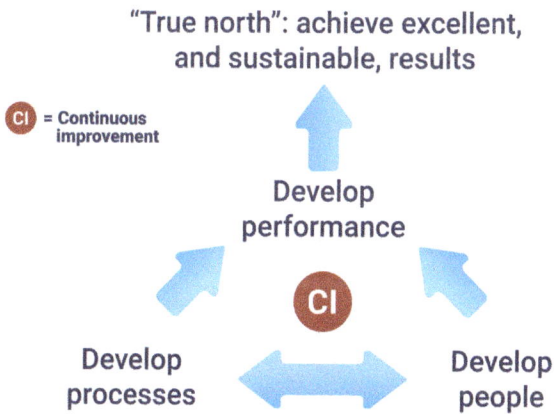

"True north": achieve excellent, and sustainable, results

CI = Continuous improvement

Develop performance

CI

Develop processes

Develop people

Figure 2.3: Simultaneous development of people, process and performance

The foundations for this are:

- Respect for people. Recognising that people are the experts on their own job, are motivated to perform to a high standard and continuously improve, and will do so if properly led, engaged, empowered and developed
- As well as empowering and enabling people, making it clear to them that their everyday responsibilities include both doing the job well, and improving how the job is done

- Agreeing challenging goals that stretch people and lead them toward a deeper understanding of, and sense of responsibility for, performance, processes and problem-solving

| *'Inspiring people is removing obstacles more than lighting fires.' (Peter Block)*

Key factors in enabling, supporting and promoting engagement are:

1. **Positive leadership:** Senior colleagues – starting at the top – leading by example, role-modelling the values, attitudes and behaviours that actively promote and support the principles and practices of Business Excellence

2. **Meeting hygiene factors:** Basic expectations which, if not met, will create a black hole of dissatisfaction and distrust that cannot be compensated for by any 'motivator'

3. **Clear expectations:** Of goals, standards and methods

4. **Tools, equipment and resources:** Of the right quality, available at the right time

5. **Capable processes:** Well designed, reliable processes, working within capacity

6. **Skills and knowledge:** Adequate quality and breadth of training

7. **Information on performance:** Timely, frequent and actionable facts and data

8. **Appropriate autonomy and responsibility:** The right degree of empowerment, authority, and responsibility to improve performance

9. **Accountability:** People must be answerable for decisions, actions, performance and results. Regular opportunities to discuss performance, problems and ideas are provided: scheduled, constructive forums, free from fear

10. **Effective coaching:** As part of everyday work to develop rounded, confident, responsible people with strong job skills, problem-solving skills and interpersonal and teamworking skills

11. **Structured problem-solving skills and tools:** The availability of a shared language and toolkit for structured problem-solving, with all colleagues trained to at least a basic level to enable them to contribute meaningfully to improvement activities

12. **Involvement in problem-solving activities:** To contribute insights and ideas to improve process and performance, and to simultaneously further develop their understanding of the process, and their problem-solving skills

Process excellence

Process excellence is the capability to deliver what the customer (internal or external) requires, right first time, on time, every time, at the right cost. The ultimate aim is to build a process that can produce predictable and repeatable results. Process excellence is the bedrock on which the success of the business is built.

Processes include all aspects of business performance, from research and development, marketing, sales, supply chain and operations, to logistics and after-sales service. (A process is anything with a clear, desired output, inputs, and a series of steps that are followed in roughly the same sequence each time.)

And, since business success is not the result of mystical events but of process effectiveness, it is necessary to explicitly focus on process design, management and improvement as a matter of strategic importance.

Process excellence is an expansive topic, and in some businesses it is highly technical and specialised. These eight factors are relevant to most. An optimised process:

1. **Is aligned with the Voice of the Customer (VoC):** It is understood who the customers are (internal or external), what they want, and (in the case of the paying customer) what they are prepared to pay for

2. **Flows:** Work and information flow efficiently through the process without defects, delay or unnecessary effort

3. **Is balanced:** Each stage of the process should run at the same speed ('takt time') as others, rather than some stages running faster or slower, causing work to build up in some places while others are underutilised

4. **Is even, and operates within capacity:** Process capacity should be closely matched to demand and the process should be neither significantly underutilised, nor overburdened

5. **Is standardised:** The best currently known approach to tasks should be captured, followed, and used as the baseline for further improvement

6. **Is properly resourced, organised and maintained:** The process should be resourced with sufficient:

   • People with the right skills, experience, attitudes and motivation

   • Equipment, tools and space

   • Raw materials and consumables

   • Time

The resources also need to be of the right quality, and available in the right place, at the right time, in working order, allowing people to work efficiently, with no avoidable down time across the working day

7. **Is error-proofed:** The key stages of the process (particularly those that are easy to get wrong, and with serious consequences) are error-proofed

8. **Is pulled, not pushed:** Activity is triggered only by a confirmed requirement, rather than in anticipation of demand that may not materialise

In Chapter 14, we'll offer an expanded version of this and cover each step in greater depth.

Daily management

Daily management (or process management) is the ongoing monitoring, course-correction and improvement of operational processes. Components of effective daily management include:

- **Measurement:** Process performance is measured, including quality, delivery performance and cost. Visual measures allow front-line colleagues to easily see if something is off track, enabling them to take immediate corrective action

- **Constant process monitoring:** Of key measures, workflow and other vital signs, to allow responsive:

  - Course-corrections, adjustments and fine tuning to keep performance on track

  - Running repairs: identifying and fixing problems before they escalate

  - Identification of deeper-seated process issues

- **Daily accountability meetings:** Daily management revolves around a series of tiered meetings, known as 'Three-Tier' meetings (though there may be more or less than three, depending on the size and complexity of the business):

  - Tier 1 meetings are the main forum for front-line managers and team members to review ongoing activities and results, identify and address immediate problems, and flag up wider problems. Immediate corrective action is taken where possible, and improvement opportunities that cannot be dealt with immediately are recorded for future actioning

  - The outcomes of the Tier 1 meetings are then fed into Tier 2 meetings at which the operational managers assess the performance of the entire value stream from end to end, handle any issues escalated to them, make necessary adjustments, and record any improvement opportunities that cannot be actioned immediately

- Similarly, the outcomes from Tier 2 (operational status, issues requiring discussion, decision or action) are fed up to the senior-level Tier 3 meeting

- **Individual check-ins:** To ensure that every colleague, every day, is engaged, accountable and has the opportunity to discuss any concerns or issues

- **Gemba walks:** Regular focused inspection of the workplace, and how work is being done, including layout, orderliness and cleanliness, condition of buildings and equipment, safety, and morale

- **Continuously improving operational processes:** Improvement opportunities identified through the above forums, and those percolated down from the strategic plan, are systematically captured, prioritised and addressed through using a structured problem-solving methodology that allows the root causes of problems to be identified and removed, to continually increase process capability, stability and resilience

- **Managing demand:** Demand is monitored and managed (its nature, timing and frequency) so it matches process capability and is not continually changing in a way that disrupts process flow and creates inefficiency

- **Resourcing, priming and maintaining the operational processes:** Providing the right people, tools, materials etc., all in the right place at the right time, to facilitate efficient working for the full day

Management effectiveness

The role of managers at all levels is to engage people in a consistent, constructive, adult dialogue to enable them to become high-performing, low-maintenance contributors who deliver sustained world-class performance and continuously improving results.

Managers are expected to thoroughly understand the work of the team they are leading. They are also expected to have strong problem-solving and coaching skills so that they can engage people positively to develop their understanding of performance and processes, and to help them become empowered and confident problem-solvers.

Success in management requires a broad range of attitudes, skills and other qualities, summarised in Figure 2.4.

Figure 2.4: Factors contributing to management excellence

We'll explore each one briefly in turn:

- **Attitude and approach:** Being positive, a problem-solver and taking responsibility for personal and team performance, and for making things happen

- **Self-management:** Emotionally balanced, calm, strong, resilient, persistent

- **Personal organisation:** Managing priorities, time and energy effectively

- **Interpersonal effectiveness:** Building strong working relationships with people with different personal styles. Able to handle challenging behaviours and difficult situations

- **Team player:** Collaborating effectively with others within their own departmental team, cross-functionally and at different levels

- **People management:** Able to organise, empower, coach and develop people, and to deal with underperformance and disciplinary issues

- **Leading the team:** Being able to get the mix of characters in the team to work effectively, solve problems, and improve processes as a unit

- **Managing stakeholders:** Ensuring that key stakeholders' expectations and perceptions remain informed and realistic so that processes do not become under-resourced or overburdened

- **Process excellence:** Ensuring that the processes are effectively designed, managed and improved, enabling people to consistently achieve excellent performance

- **Results:** Measures of effective management may include:

- Consistently strong, and continuously improving, performance against Key Performance Indicators
- Sustained progress toward strategic improvement goals
- Consistently high employee engagement scores
- Strong scores on leaders' 360-degree reviews

Beyond these expectations, which all managers share, there are specific responsibilities for front-line managers and operational managers.

Front-line managers

Front-line managers' responsibilities include:

- Daily management:

  - Daily accountability meetings (the Tier One meetings)
  - Constantly monitoring process performance and communicating with front-line colleagues to identify and address emerging problems early

- Coaching front-line colleagues effectively to develop the required skills, attitudes and behaviours

- Continuous improvement of the operational processes, and of the daily management process, in response to improvement opportunities identified:

  - Locally
  - In the strategic plan

Operational managers

Operational managers' responsibilities include to:

- Oversee and integrate the daily management of the core processes end-to-end across the business

- Ensure that front-line managers have what they need to provide front-line colleagues with the right tools, equipment, information and resources to succeed

- Coach front-line managers effectively to develop the required skills, attitudes and behaviours

- Oversee, integrate and monitor the continuous-improvement activities happening at the front line

- Actively engage in, and support, continuous-improvement efforts, helping remove barriers that front-line managers can't
- Continuously monitor and improve the performance of the daily management process and the operational management process
- Implement the continuous-improvement projects associated with the breakthrough goals in the strategic plan

Operational management system

Effective management, while requiring strong personal qualities, is not based on charisma or personality. Just as front-line colleagues need effective operational processes to deliver excellent performance, so managers requires effective management systems; processes that allow them to do their jobs effectively, systematically and consistently.

At operational level, this requires an operational management system: a coherent set of processes that oversees and integrates all the core operational processes end-to-end along the whole value stream and ensures that they operate, and continuously improve, as a coherent system.

The main functions of the operational management system are:

- **Monitoring and managing demand:** Monitoring of immediate demand (nature, frequency, volume) and longer-term projections to inform the planning, scheduling and resourcing of the operational processes. The overall stability, predictability and controllability of demand is also assessed, and ways are found to enhance the management of it to achieve greater process stability, predictability and control
- **Planning and scheduling activity:** To match process capacity and customer demand and ensure that processes are neither significantly under-utilised, nor pushed into overburden. All targets, activities and timings are communicated clearly, systematically and in good time
- **Aligning operations with strategic direction and goals:** Ensuring that:
  - The business is delivering on the operational business-as-usual goals on delivery performance, cost and customer satisfaction
  - The annual breakthrough goals set within the strategy process are cascaded to each operational area as appropriate, and executed

- **Resourcing the operational processes:** Ensuring that the processes are properly resourced with the right quality and quantity of raw materials, tools, equipment, consumables, space and working conditions, and the right numbers of people with the right skills, experience, attitudes and motivation. And that it is all in the right place and at the right time to maintain flow in the operational processes

- **Constantly monitoring the daily management processes:** Through overseeing the operation of the daily management process and gathering information fed in from the Tier One meetings, all key measures and other vital signs are constantly monitored to ensure the smooth flow of work through the operational processes and responsive:

  - Course-corrections, adjustments and fine tuning
  - Running repairs: identifying and fixing problems before they escalate
  - Identification and capture of deeper-seated process-improvement opportunities

- Managing and developing the front-line management team: Front-line managers are held accountable for fulfilling their responsibilities and are coached, developed and supported to perform well and continuously improve

- Continuous improvement of three different sets of processes, to continually increase their capability, stability, coherence, flexibility and resilience, and underpin long-term sustainable success:

  - Operational processes – end-to-end across the whole value stream, including all supporting processes
  - Daily management system
  - Operational management system

Strategic management system

The strategic management system is a coherent set of processes that ensure a consistent and structured focus on building the business's longer-term capability.

The strategic management system:

- Monitors the external environment for a range of factors including changing markets, customer needs, technology, and political and social conditions

- Monitors internal factors including people (morale, skills, retention, motivation, etc.), processes, technology and culture
- Analyses the information to establish the business's strengths, weaknesses, opportunities and threats
- From this, develops a robust long-term plan to mitigate threats and capitalise on opportunities. (What 'long-term' means varies between industries and businesses)
- Breaks this plan down into departmental and team plans, and cascades it through the business in a way that confirms the feasibility of the plan and secures understanding of it and commitment to it
- Supports and monitors the successful execution of the strategic plan (while ensuring that it does not cause problematic disruptions to business-as-usual operations)

Continuous improvement

For every business there is the ever-present threat of waste and inefficiency clogging up the value stream, compromising quality, cost and delivery performance. Even when products, services and processes are in good shape, in an ever-changing world with constantly increasing demands, there are always opportunities, and a need, to continuously improve.

To manage this effectively, the business needs a disciplined approach to continuous improvement in all parts of the business, and every aspect of performance. With continuous meaning continuous; a core activity, part of normal day-to-day operations – not triggered only by a crisis.

Creating a culture of continuous improvement requires:

- A **toolkit** to give people the means to map the value stream, identify improvement opportunities and take a structured approach to problem-solving; establishing root causes and permanently resolving problems
- **Empowering front-line people to drive continuous improvement:** To build ownership for performance and results, and simultaneously develop the process, people and performance, to build an organisation that learns and adapts quickly. This requires:

  - Training colleagues in continuous-improvement tools and techniques

- Support and encouragement for teams and individuals to take time to improve things
- Making expertise available to help guide and mentor teams, and bringing in more specialised problem-solving tools and techniques as required

- **Management systems that bring problems to the surface:** Focusing on improving how quickly and how well work flows through all processes (operational, management and strategic) allows barriers to be more easily identified and addressed.

Effective teamwork and collaboration

The interdependency between people and processes requires a team approach to managing and improving performance. The quality of teamwork depends on how well people across the business, and at different levels, understand, respect and trust each other, and communicate, share information, collaborate and work as a team to solve problems.

This takes time and effort to build and maintain, and can become fragile when things go wrong, but is essential to create the environment of collaboration and open and honest communication on which excellence depends.

Performance: excellent and sustainable results for all stakeholders

And finally, back to the ultimate aim: the creation of enduring value for customers, employees and business owners, so that everyone is motivated to continue their commitment to the business. This includes the business consistently achieving or surpassing targets for operational performance, customer satisfaction and profitability, and for colleague engagement, environmental performance and corporate social responsibility.

Summary

CI = Continuous improvement

Integrated technical system

Teamwork and collaboration

Operational and strategic excellence

CI

Operational process — Engaged people

CI

Process/Daily management — Front-line management

CI

Operational management system — Operational management

CI

Strategic management processes/system — Leadership

CI

Leadership thinking/Business philosophy

Figure 2.1(revisited): Core principles of Business Excellence

For the business to be excellent, the processes that produce the goods or services must be effective and efficient. For that to happen, the business must be able to systematically and continuously improve those processes.

This, in turn, depends on open, honest and constructive dialogue among people to recognise problems and work together to create solutions at, and between, all levels of the business. This requires the right tools and training in problem-solving and an operational management system and strategic management system that provide a relentless focus and discipline around high performance and continuous improvement.

The tone for all of this is set by how people are led, and in particular, the personal example in attitude, behaviour and competence that leaders set.

Questions:

- What are the strengths and improvement opportunities for your business?
- Is this journey for you?

CHAPTER 3

LEADERSHIP THINKING

Introduction

The nature and quality of leadership thinking is the foundation of excellence.
Figure 3.1 shows it in the context of the wider principles.

Figure 3.1: Leadership thinking in the wider context of the excellence principles

Business Excellence is based on what Deming called 'Profound Knowledge', a
philosophy comprising several core principles. Principles that differ significantly
from earlier, less evolved approaches. Achieving Business Excellence requires an
understanding of these leadership principles and commitment to them throughout
the organisation, starting at the top.

The principles are summarised below. This list is an expanded version of the principles introduced in the Chapter 2 overview. There are quite a few! Some are subtle. They are all important. They all relate to each other and overlap to some degree.

- Meet the needs of all stakeholders
- Operational excellence provides competitive advantage
- Performance comes from the process
- Sustained profitability comes from loyal customers
- Quality comes first
- Manage flow
- The purpose of performance measurement is to inform and empower
- Continuous improvement optimises short-term performance and underpins long-term success
- Pursue perfection
- Plan-Do-Check-Act (PDCA) thinking drives performance management and continuous improvement
- Remove fear and engage people
- Develop a Thinking People System – simultaneously developing people, process and performance
- Respect for people
- Empower front-line performance
- Foster accountability and responsibility
- Facts and data, not emotion and opinion
- Systems thinking
- Proactively invest in value-enabling time
- Teamwork
- Excellence begins (or ends) in the boardroom
- Recognise problems as improvement opportunities
- Take a structured approach to problem-solving
- Develop kata – make excellence a habit
- Constancy of purpose and long-term thinking

Let's explore them in more detail.

Meet the needs of all stakeholders

The assumption in Business Excellence is that sustainable success depends on satisfying the legitimate needs of all key stakeholders. That is, focusing on the quintuple bottom line – being first choice to buy from, work for and invest in while making a positive social and environmental impact– wins loyal customers, creates an engaged, high-performing team, attracts committed financial backers and secures a reputation as a socially and environmentally responsible business. All of which creates a strong platform for sustained success.

Operational excellence provides competitive advantage

'Sustained profitable growth is what the strategic planners of the world are always seeking, but find hard to achieve because their company's operations cannot deliver on their strategy.' (James Womack and Daniel Jones)

Operational excellence is:

- The ability to deliver what the customer wants right first time, on time, every time, to cost
- The resilience to do this consistently in the face of various challenges
- The ability to improve and adapt seamlessly to external change

In competitive environments where delivering on a promise is make or break, operational excellence is the key to both retaining and improving competitive advantage.

Performance comes from the process

Results are not mysterious happenings. Consistently excellent results can only come from excellent processes run by people who are well trained and engaged.

In Business Excellence, the primary focus is on continuously enhancing the 'means' (process and people) to improve the 'ends' (the results). Optimising process capability and performance by engaging and involving people in process design, management and continuous improvement.

The alternative is to focus on achieving an end goal without regard for the impact on the process. For example, pushing through more volume than it can handle, or constantly changing priorities to avert one crisis, only to create the next one, thus constantly sub-optimising both process and results.

Managers may also try to drive performance by 'tough' management – pushing people harder. This may provide an artificial short-term boost, but over time, no amount of pushing from managers, or positive attitude or effort from colleagues, can overcome the limitations of a process that is poorly designed, equipped and managed. It invariably results in demoralisation, adds to the sense of chaos and leadership incompetence, and may even lower productivity as people disengage and push back.

Sustained profitability comes from loyal customers

A fundamental assumption in Business Excellence is that strong and sustainable profitability is generated by loyal customers: customers who willingly return, are low-maintenance and who recommend the business to others. They are more valuable than a customer who is merely satisfied, will still shop around and may haggle over price. Loyal customers mean lower costs and higher sales because they:

- Require lower sales and marketing costs, as they require less persuasion and there is lower customer churn
- Tend not to rely on discounting
- Are more open to upselling and cross-selling
- Are more forgiving of the occasional hiccup, so there is less handling time, cost and distraction
- May add value by being unpaid advocates for the business, and also by working in partnership to help improve the offering

Quality comes first

There are two aspects to quality. The first is understanding what matters to the customer and designing a product or service that meets their needs. This need not necessarily be something technologically advanced or with all sorts of bells and whistles (indeed, pointless complexity can be a turn-off for some). It simply needs to do what the customer wants it to do, be available when they need it, and at a cost they feel offers value.

The second is developing an efficient process that delivers the product or service right first time, on time, every time. Getting things right first time means fewer defects. This minimises costs, maximises productivity, facilitates on-time delivery, and enhances customer satisfaction and profitability.

Phil Crosby debunked the myth that higher process quality means increased cost. He pointed out that getting quality right first time costs less than getting it wrong, since fixing any problems that we create absorbs time and money and incurs an irrecoverable loss of production capacity, lowering overall volumes and productivity.

His model (Figure 3.2) suggests that the activities required to prevent problems, i.e. to set up and run the process properly, take around 15% of operating costs. If, instead, problems are allowed to occur, the costs of inspection and fixing quality fails detected either externally or internally amount to around 40% of operating costs. On top of this there is what Deming called the 'unknown and unknowable' costs associated with creating unhappy customers who complain, want discounts, leave and discourage others from buying from us.

The upshot is that process quality must come first or we open the door to all manner of problems with productivity, reliability, customer satisfaction, cost and profitability. Investing time in getting the offering right and in getting the process right creates loyal customers and increases value-adding capacity. The very essence of working smarter, not harder.

Figure 3.2: The cost of quality

We'll discuss the importance of quality further in Chapter 5.

Manage flow

Flow is a crucial concept in Business Excellence: work must move through the value-adding process, without error or any unnecessary delay, movement, handling or processing. Anything else is waste – it costs time, money or other resources but adds no value.

Managing how work flows highlights the waste and allows it to be removed. This increases profitability and frees up capacity that could be used to grow the business, because:

a. Profit = selling price, minus the cost to make, minus the cost of the waste

b. Value-adding capacity = process capacity minus the capacity subverted by waste (defects and inefficiencies)

Flow should be managed end-to-end across the whole value stream, to ensure that the system is optimised as a whole.

The purpose of performance measurement is to inform and empower

Measurement, when used well, is a powerful tool for managing and improving performance. In Business Excellence, measurement has a clear purpose: to empower and enable people to manage and improve performance.

To facilitate this technically, performance information that is visible, understandable and actionable should be available to all colleagues in real time. Socially, this requires an environment where information is used to understand and improve performance; where colleagues can discuss problems, offer ideas and innovate in an environment free of blame and fear.

The combination of ongoing challenges, readily available performance information and fast problem-solving is what makes sport intrinsically motivating. With the intelligent use of performance measurement, any business can tap into this.

Continuous improvement optimises short-term performance and underpins long-term success

Sustainable success requires the capability for fast and effective problem-solving to respond successfully to daily challenges, to make ongoing improvements to process performance and to adapt to wider changes as markets, technology etc. evolve.

Culturally embedding a mindset of continuous improvement is vital because:

- A static system is a vulnerable system:

  - Entropy is always invisibly degrading processes. So the speed at which we counteract this must be faster than the rate of decay

  - The business has to respond to changing external conditions, so its rate of internal adaptation must be faster than the rate of external change

- Robust cost and quality competitiveness tends to result from the compounded accumulation of small improvements over time

- Without it, problems accumulate and are only addressed when crisis point is reached, and in a very reactive way. Improvement stops when the immediate crisis has passed and so the cycle repeats. In line with the principle of 'Pursue perfection'(see below), process improvement should be ongoing and not just stop when a set performance goal is reached.

Pursue perfection

Perfection is defined as the complete elimination of wasted time, effort and resource so that the customer can be served exactly what they need, only what they need, and exactly when they need it, with no delay and at minimum cost. It is understood that this is not completely achievable, but that the pursuit of perfection is necessary to deliver the best of what is possible – excellence and continuous improvement. Anything less opens the door to complacency, the acceptance of mediocrity and the risk of losing competitive advantage to hungrier and more ambitious rivals.

PDCA thinking drives performance management and continuous improvement

PDCA thinking (see Figure 3.3) is the disciplined and systematic approach that underpins the management of performance and continuous improvement at any level; strategic, operational-management or operational. It brings a structure to people's thinking and creates a constant iterative and incremental approach to management and improvement. It is the engine that drives Business Excellence.

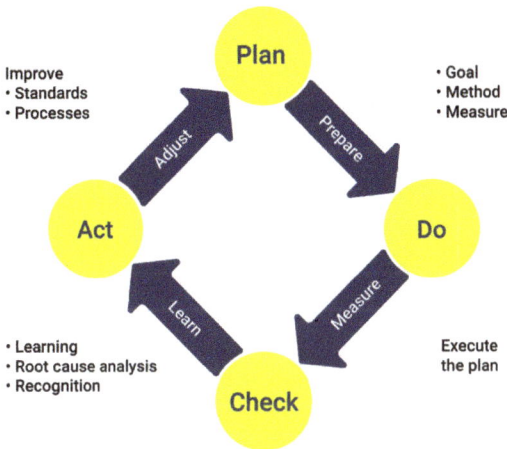

Improve
· Standards
· Processes

Plan

· Goal
· Method
· Measure

Adjust

Prepare

Act

Do

· Learning
· Root cause analysis
· Recognition

Learn

Measure

Execute
the plan

Check

Figure 3.3: The Plan-Do-Check-Act cycle

From a technical perspective, it is a constant loop of:

- **Planning:** Defining a goal, the method for achieving it and the measure by which success will be assessed
- **Doing:** Executing the plan
- **Checking** that the plan was followed and that the outcomes were as expected, and if not, ascertaining why not
- **Acting** on the lessons learned during Check, and adjusting the method, goal or measure to reflect what has been learned

From a social perspective, how 'Check' is run significantly influences the organisation's culture. If it is characterised by blame, the fear of it will likely cause people to shut down and disengage. Trust will diminish, and it may become contentious. Little progress will be made. A more productive approach is, first, to see problems as opportunities for process improvement and, second, to remove fear and engage people.

Remove fear and engage people

Deming memorably noted that in his experience, around 94% of problems and possibilities for improvement related to some aspect of the operational or management processes, with only 6% due to other factors, which may include bad weather and bad luck as well as individual errors. The best approach to understanding and addressing problems is therefore to view people as the solution, not the problem, and begin by asking 'How did the process let this happen?', rather than 'Whose fault was that?' This avoids fear and blame and engages people positively in the quest to solve the problem; it directs focus to the likeliest root cause and avoids the risk of alienating people, creating defensiveness and deflecting the focus from the source of the problem.

This is part of the wider aim to...

Develop a Thinking People System – simultaneously developing people, process and performance

The aim is to develop the culture to become a Thinking People System (or 'Learning Organisation'), where people are actively and positively engaged in managing performance, solving problems and improving processes.

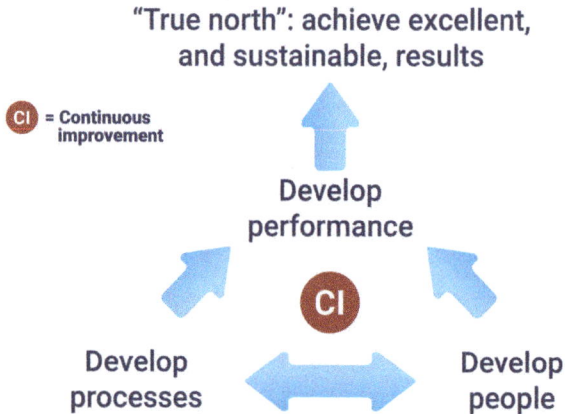

Figure 3.4: Colleague engagement/Thinking People System

The co-development of people, process and performance drives an upward spiral:

- As people are engaged, they take more responsibility for performance and results. This helps them understand what is happening in the process and how it can be improved

- This develops people's business understanding, process-knowledge, and problem-solving and teamworking skills
- As people learn and improve the processes, performance improves, creating an upward spiral.

This creates a culture that is able to learn, adapt and respond quickly and intelligently to challenges: a Thinking People System.

What follows from this is the principle that management and improvement is best done by front-line teams; the people who understand the processes best because they use them every day. They should have the capability to change the systems rather than be constrained by their limitations.

This is based on another of the key tenets of Business Excellence...

Respect for people

Respect for people includes treating them with dignity and courtesy, of course, but also involves:

- Recognising that the people who do the job are the experts in that job, and, if properly led, engaged, empowered and developed, will make a significant positive difference, through problem-solving and continuous improvement, to quality, customer service and process performance
- Treating people like capable and responsible human beings and providing a positive challenge to improve, learn, develop and pursue ambitious goals, and in the process stretch themselves, unlock more of their potential, and achieve more.

Empower front-line performance

Since it is the people at the front line who directly provide the product or service to the customer and manage the front-line processes, operational excellence depends on them being properly enabled and empowered to do this.

The role of managers at successive levels of the organisation, therefore, is as illustrated in Figure 3.5; to make sure that people have the right information, equipment, raw materials, training and support, when they need it.

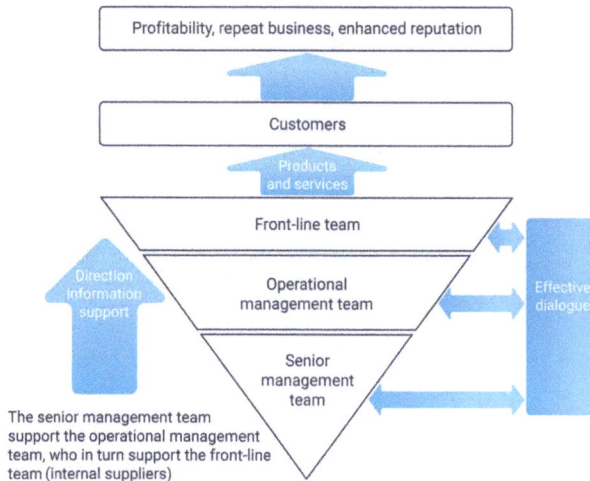

Figure 3.5: Enabling front-line colleagues

To make this work it is therefore necessary to...

Foster accountability and responsibility

Accountability means being answerable for decisions, actions and outcomes. Responsibility is having the ability, resources and autonomy to perform to the expected standard, make decisions and take action. People should be both accountable and responsible for the results they are paid to deliver. Starting at the top.

To facilitate this, the management system should be designed to do two things:

- Provide a tiered approach, to get the right accountabilities and responsibilities at the appropriate levels. Front-line teams should have accountability and responsibility for the operation and performance of front-line processes. Managers at successively higher levels should be accountable and responsible for progressively larger portions of the overall system performance

- Strike the right balance between accountability and responsibility at each level so that people are able to adequately influence the results they are accountable for

Facts and data, not emotion and opinion

The focus in managing and improving the process should be primarily on the facts and data gathered from the measurement of process performance, rather than on emotion and opinion. This is crucial in creating a culture where people engage in finding and removing the actual root causes and driving meaningful process improvement. When subjective opinion and emotion dominate, the quality of the dialogue suffers and can become a battle of egos and personalities, damaging teamwork and preventing people from developing a full and accurate understanding of the system.

Gut instinct, hunches, organisation folklore, pet theories and previous experience all, arguably, have their place in understanding and improving process – but there is a serious danger when they are used in the absence of sound facts and data about how a process is actually performing in reality, and whether our actions to improve the process are working in practice.

Systems thinking

Systems thinking means recognising that a business is a complete, interconnected socio-technical system and being able to discern its constituent parts, figure out the internal relations and dynamics and what the highest leverage variables are, so as to be able to intervene intelligently.

And it means doing this through positive engagement with others, since other actors not only affect the different aspects of the system, but are also a crucial aspect of the system.

Part of this is recognising that to improve any aspect of performance (quality, delivery performance or cost), every part of the organisation needs to be aware of, and accountable for, the impact it has on that metric, and be open to improvement.

There are two dimensions to this. The first is horizontal, optimising the performance of the entire value chain as it runs end-to-end through various front-line functions. The second is vertical, recognising that the operational processes will only be as effective as the management system they are embedded within. This highlights the importance of a properly designed and managed strategic management system, operational management system and process management. They need to be sound in themselves and integrated, aligned and coordinated vertically.

Proactively invest in value-enabling time

Broadly, there are three ways time can be spent in a business:

- **Value-adding:** Activities that directly contribute to creating the product or service that the customer wants and will pay for
- **Value-enabling:** The planning, organising, communicating, managing and developing, coaching, reviewing of performance, and process-improvement required to optimise the efficiency and impact of value-adding time
- **Waste:** Time spent on anything else; correcting defects or errors, waiting for information, raw material or equipment, doing things that the customer didn't ask for, doesn't want, and won't pay for, etc.

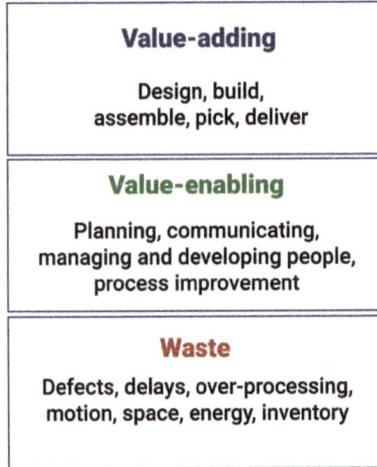

Value-adding

Design, build,
assemble, pick, deliver

Value-enabling

Planning, communicating,
managing and developing people,
process improvement

Waste

Defects, delays, over-processing,
motion, space, energy, inventory

Figure 3.6: Three ways that time is spent in business

There is an interactive relationship between the three. Enough value-enabling time needs to be invested regularly, and spent wisely and efficiently, to create an upward spiral. Otherwise, waste increases and value-adding time, efficiency and cost suffer, potentially creating a downward spiral.

As Figure 3.7 illustrates, it is easy to get trapped in a loop of firefighting and stagnation.

Errors and inefficiencies → Unhappy customers and staff

Poorly managed people and processes

Working long and hard on value-adding and unnecessary waste

Failure-driven demand

Over-busy: reactive, not proactive. 'No time' to plan, communicate, develop people and improve processes

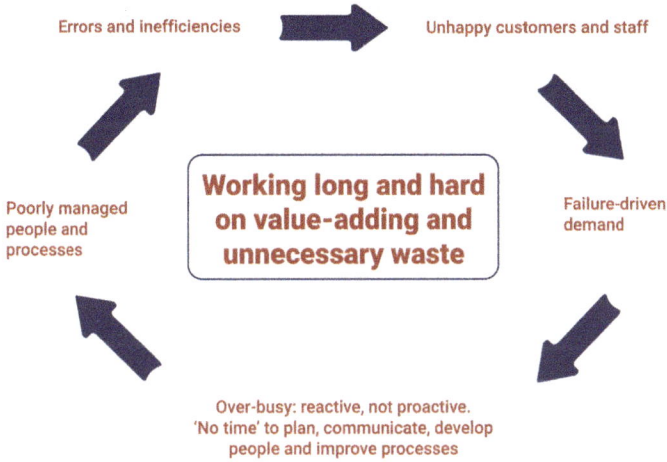

Figure 3.7: The mediocrity loop – working hard to stand still

But as Figure 3.8 shows, investing value-enabling time and learning to do it efficiently, well and with discipline can create an upward spiral of sustainable and continually improving performance.

Efficient, high-value service

Effective processes and engaged people

Working efficiently and effectively on value-adding and value-enabling

Happy customers and staff

Time made to manage and develop people and processes

Figure 3.8: The leadership loop – value-enabling time drives performance and improvement

Teamwork

Since every business is a system, its efficient working requires effective coordination which relies on cooperation and collaboration across different functions and between different hierarchical levels. Fostering teamwork has both a technical aspect and a social aspect.

The technical enablers of team performance are:

- Goals that:

  - Make overall performance pre-eminent. The optimisation of the overall end-to-end process should be made the primary focus for every team, with the optimisation of local processes that comprise this. This mitigates against the risk of destructive internal competition and the risk of a (supposed) improvement in one area (e.g. cost savings) having a significant unintended negative impact on the process overall (e.g. quality problems)

  - Align functional goals. The output goals of each process stage must be aligned with the needs of the adjacent stage to create smooth flow horizontally and vertically at hand-offs and along the entire process, coordinating the timing, volume and quality of the flow of material and information

- An effective operational management system to oversee and coordinate the whole system, monitoring performance and identifying and resolving problems. As part of this, appropriate forums should be designed to facilitate cross-functional communication, collaboration and problem-solving

Socially, achieving teamwork requires the right leadership, to develop collaboration as a cultural instinct and habit. As well as putting the aspiration for excellence and shared success front and centre, this will also include defining, living and embedding values that encourage collaboration and cooperation and discourage individualistic and destructive internal competition.

Excellence begins (or ends) in the boardroom

Leadership is the most important single determinant of success in Business Excellence. There is an attitudinal and behavioural aspect, and also the direct practical impact of how well leaders serve people by providing what they need to succeed. Let's look first at the attitudinal and behavioural aspect of leadership.

People look for positive and competent leadership: leaders who provide a clear positive vision to work toward, who lead by example, role-modelling the values, attitudes and behaviours of Business Excellence, and who have earned people's trust and respect.

At a practical level, leadership competence is measured by the degree to which people are enabled, involved and empowered. Key factors in enabling, supporting and promoting engagement are:

1. **Positive leadership:** Senior colleagues, starting at the top, leading by example, role-modelling the values, attitudes and behaviours that actively promote and support the principles and practices of Business Excellence

2. **Meeting hygiene factors:** Basic expectations which, if not met, will create a black hole of dissatisfaction and distrust that cannot be compensated for by any 'motivator'

3. **Clear expectations:** Of goals, standards and methods

4. **Tools, equipment and resources:** Of the right quality, available at the right time

5. **Capable processes:** Well-designed, reliable processes, working within capacity

6. **Skills and knowledge:** Adequate quality and breadth of training

7. **Information on performance:** Timely, frequent, actionable facts and data

8. **Appropriate autonomy and responsibility:** The right degree of empowerment, authority, and responsibility to improve performance

9. **Accountability:** People must be answerable for decisions, actions, performance and results. Regular opportunities to discuss performance, problems and ideas are provided: scheduled, constructive forums, free from fear

10. **Effective coaching:** As part of everyday work to develop rounded, confident, responsible people with strong job skills, problem-solving skills and interpersonal and teamworking skills

11. **Structured problem-solving skills and tools:** The availability of a shared language and toolkit for structured problem-solving, with all colleagues trained to at least a basic level to enable them to contribute meaningfully to improvement activities

12. **Involvement in problem-solving activities:** To contribute insights and ideas to improve process and performance, and to simultaneously further develop their understanding of the process, and their problem-solving skills

Since the bulk of the causes of low quality and low productivity belong to the management system and thus lie beyond the power of the workforce, leaders need to take responsibility for the design, management and improvement of the management systems that provide the above.

Recognise problems as improvement opportunities

In Business Excellence, problems are viewed as opportunities to learn more and more about how the process works and how to improve it, and to simultaneously develop people's problem-solving and teamworking skills.

The mentality is therefore to actively bring problems to the surface and solve them, rather than ignoring or covering them up and continuing to suffer the financial and operational consequences.

Take a structured approach to problem-solving

Taking a structured approach to problem-solving is vital. Without it, we can make all sorts of costly errors and not notice. We can fail to properly define the problem and go off at a tangent. We can miss the actual root cause and have the problem recur. We can take the wrong actions. And we can fail to follow through the PDCA loop and never really establish if the solutions we thought would work actually did.

One popular approach is A3 problem-solving (named after the size of the sheet of paper it was originally captured on). It walks our thinking through a series of logical steps that first identify the root cause, then develop potential solutions, test them and adopt those that are proven to work. These steps are:

- **Theme/background:** Define the broad area of focus, e.g. quality
- **Problem definition:** Tightly specify and measure the problem to accurately define it and the impact it has
- **Goal/target state:** Specify where we want to be at the end of this exercise
- **Root cause analysis:** Using various techniques, isolate the most probable root cause
- **Containment measures:** Implement any short-term actions required to prevent major problems while a permanent solution is found and applied

- **Proposed countermeasure(s):** What actions do we think will reduce or eradicate the problem?

- **Action plan:** Specify who will do what by when

- **Impact check:** A check-in to see if the action plan was followed and what the results were

- **Next actions:** If the countermeasures worked and the situation is where it needs to be, we close out the A3. If the countermeasures did not fully succeed, we go back to the beginning and double-check our thinking at each stage

Develop kata – make excellence a habit

An organisation can navigate challenging situations more effectively if it has deeply embedded habits and routines ('kata') for managing and improving processes. These disciplines should be the backbone of the management system. They also rely on leaders and managers, starting at the top, ensuring that they are run when they should be and to the right professional standard.

Constancy of purpose and long-term thinking

'Excellence is not a programme with a beginning and an end, but a philosophy that directs efforts at all levels of responsibility towards the more effective use of the resources available, to meet the needs of the customers.' (Jeffrey Liker and James Franz)

Business Excellence requires a long-term approach, balancing the need for short-term results with the steady, disciplined building of the capability for higher levels of sustainable success.

It is not a 'programme' that is ever done. It is a philosophy and a set of practices that need to be persisted with and constantly evolved over time.

Questions

Thinking about both

a. You as a leader

b. Your leadership team

Where are the:

- Existing strengths?
- Waterline issues? (as in 'sunk below the' and presenting danger)
- Breakthrough opportunities?

PART TWO: CORE PRINCIPLES

CHAPTER 4

THE PRINCIPLES OF PERFORMANCE MANAGEMENT

Performance management: Introduction

> *'Problems in organisations always come down to one of two things: a lack of clear goals or a lack of clear communication around them.' (Peter Drucker)*

Performance management is the process of defining clear aims and turning those aims into focused activities, tracking progress, identifying and closing performance gaps, and achieving sustainable and continuously improving performance.

It is the discipline at the heart of all great achievements in business, sport and other domains, applied wherever organisations, teams or individuals are serious about excellence in performance and focused on outcomes.

Central to effective management of resource, time and effort, performance management is at the very core of what leaders and managers are paid to do: achieve desired results in an organised, systematic, consistent and disciplined way.

Why it matters

Performance management is central to sustained high performance. It prevents problems and enables any that do occur to be quickly identified and addressed, allowing the business to consistently meet operational targets and continuously improve.

It allows the business to be flexible, responsive and resilient. To be better able to withstand, and adapt quickly to, challenges and changing operational and strategic circumstances.

It drives continuous learning and improvement, allowing the business to learn from successes and setbacks and progressively build better and better strategies and processes. It builds confidence and raises ambitions, driving an upward spiral of sustainable success and continuous improvement.

Further, this ability to learn, change and adapt quickly and well allows the business to capitalise faster and better on improvement opportunities and on market opportunities, thus potentially consolidating and stretching its long-term competitive advantage, and creating a gap between it and its rivals that will be hard to close.

Effective performance management is also the key to colleague engagement, motivation and team-building. Performance management provides the common purpose that people can unite behind, and the forums where people come together to communicate, collaborate, learn from each other, encourage each other, share ideas and create solutions. It provides the mechanism for measuring, recognising, celebrating and sharing the successes that help bind successful and resilient teams ever closer together. It drives involvement, empowerment, responsibility, productivity and continuous improvement and unlocks commitment, discretionary potential and excellence potential.

Despite all this, not all businesses manage performance conspicuously well. The costs of this are significant and enduring, and the bad habits self-sustaining. The risks associated with not managing performance well include:

- Lack of direction
- Loss of focus: struggling to identify and achieve priorities
- Unnecessary time, effort and resource spent on crisis management and firefighting, correcting problems – many of which could, with proper planning and communication, have been prevented
- Difficulty in getting people engaged, motivated, taking responsibility for performance, continuously improving and working as a team

- Failing to reflect on performance, learn from experience and identify areas for improvement, and instead repeatedly coming up against the same old problems and limitations

- Missing out on opportunities due to built-in limitations on productivity and quality and a lack of agility

- Not achieving the full potential of the business, teams or individuals

- Becoming increasingly vulnerable to competition, change, and economic downturns

The performance management process

Performance management is a conceptually simple discipline comprising a small number of straightforward principles and practices captured in the PDCA (Plan-Do-Check-Act) model outlined in Figure 4.1.

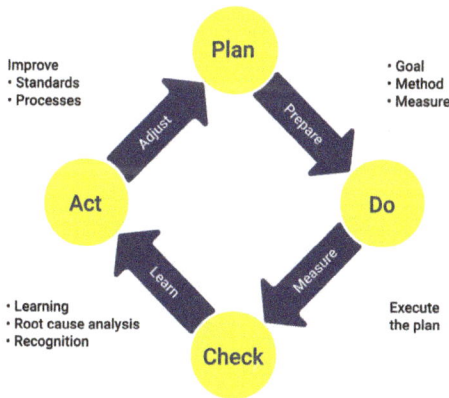

Figure 4.1: The Plan-Do-Check-Act cycle

Each of these stages is described below.

Plan

As the old saying goes, proper prior planning prevents poor performance. Planning allows problems to be spotted and solved in advance rather than encountered later in reality, when the damage is done and they are harder and costlier to fix. Research suggests that the leverage on planning time is significant: for every minute we spend planning, it is estimated that we save between 10 and 40 minutes in execution. We go further, faster with less hassle, for two reasons:

1. Most of us are overwhelmed with demands, challenges and opportunities. Selecting the highest-leverage ones to work on is the key to success. Not effort, not time. We'll simply never have the time and energy to do them all, so we have to be smart in choosing our priorities

2. Without planning we'll get sucked into the urgent, miss some of the important tasks, get poorer results than our time and talents deserve and become mired in failure-driven demand. (Demand placed on our time, energy and resources by a need to redo what we failed to get right first time)

Planning, however proven and effective it may be, is still either not done, not done consistently, or not done well by many managers who prefer to dive into action, unable to resist the emotional impulse to react to what arises rather than, as Steve Peters put it, staying mindful and 'responding with a plan'. The difference is significant: working smarter, not harder.

Do

Doing means, specifically, following the plan. This includes following the existing processes, procedures and standards. Sounds obvious. Not always done. When the plan is not followed, it creates two problems. First, diverging from the plan (which is, by definition, the best-thought-through approach) increases the chances of problems. Second, if the plan was followed, then it is clear what steps were taken and easier to identify where any problem occurred and take corrective action. If it is unclear what process was followed, it is harder to pinpoint and address the root cause of the problem.

Check

Reflection is the key to developing awareness and insight into what is driving performance and how it can be improved.

Making reflection a habit is one of the most powerful and high-leverage habits we can develop. Not taking time to reflect properly is a massive missed opportunity, and a massive risk.

Like planning, it is often short-circuited, particularly by those who are emotionally unable to resist the impulse to constantly react without sufficient appreciation of what is driving a situation, because it requires a little bit of space, time and thought (though typically less than 2% of our time).

To those who have not yet reached the level of emotional and cognitive maturity commensurate with effective professional management, it feels like a distraction from action and 'real business'. They often fail to recognise the trap that they are in – like the housefly trying to get through the window, exerting tremendous energy and anxiety, continuously repeating the same actions which get them no further forward. Not knowing what to do, they keep trying to do everything faster: they get locked into being busy and anxious, unable to slow down, think and learn.

As we master reflection and it becomes established as a habit, part of how we think and operate, it takes little or no additional time. Indeed, overall it saves time and adds value. When we're working as hard as we can, working smarter – thinking, planning, reflecting, learning – is the only way to reach the next level of performance capability.

Act

When lessons have been learned and the root causes of problems identified at the Check stage, action can be taken on the process – its goals, method or measures – in an attempt to improve results next time round. Then the cycle starts again.

The principles are universal and can be applied in any domain. As Christian Laing notes:

> 'The process is straightforward. It works for businesses and for Olympic athletes: simply measure, analyse and improve your performance. Then do it again and again and again. Just don't stop.'

Engaging people positively as active partners in managing and improving performance

Accountability and responsibility

Accountability and responsibility are central to performance management. Accountability is what people have to account, or answer, for. This includes performance targets, behaviours and attitudes. Responsibility is people's ability to respond. This requires that they have the time, resources, skills and experience to respond, and that they are also personally willing to do so.

Responsibility should feel empowering, accountability positive. Since most people's results most of the time will be positive, having responsibility and being accountable should be positive and confidence-building. When things go wrong, managers with the right style and approach will make sure that feedback and discussion are constructive and aimed at learning, guiding, supporting and encouraging improvement, rather than focusing on criticism and blame. (More on this shortly.)

If done properly, performance management will create an upward spiral. People will be happy to be accountable and responsible, as they get clear direction, praise and recognition, constructive feedback, opportunities to discuss problems, advice, reassurance, support and encouragement. This will equip them better to succeed, build confidence, and increase the odds that they'll want even greater responsibility and accountability. They are also likely to be more open and honest, more supportive and less blame-oriented toward others. In this way it breeds high-performing, low-maintenance people with drive, confidence and maturity, and a responsibility-focused (rather than accountability-avoidant or blame-oriented) culture.

Proactivity

Proactivity means doing all the above in a regular, systematic, disciplined way, rather than waiting for the problem or crisis to show up and get mired in firefighting and failure-driven demand: in short, being wise before the event, rather than during or after it.

Positivity

The spirit of how performance management is done is important. It should always be positive, forward-looking, solution-focused, developmental and supportive, even when things, as they inevitably will, go wrong.

There's an in-built element of a game about performance management (a definite goal, with problems requiring effort, skill and ingenuity to overcome and something meaningful at stake), and capturing some of that intrinsic sense of challenge, and the satisfaction in overcoming problems, can make it more engaging and energising.

Performance management meetings can themselves be engaging. The focus can (and indeed should) include recognition and celebration of individual and collective progress and achievements. Setbacks can, with some skill, be handled in such a way as to get people committed and motivated to address the underlying problems.

The magic of involvement

Including and involving people turbo-charges the performance management process and drives engagement. There's no mystery to how and why it works. Involving people in creating the vision and the goals means involving them in the process of thinking through for themselves, and discussing with colleagues, what success looks like, how it will be achieved, and how it will be measured. If people are able to decide for themselves what they want to achieve, and devise fair and appropriate measures, they are more likely to understand and to commit to the goals. Then, like a driver using a satnav, they're able to guide, monitor and manage their own progress toward their destination. If the targets and measures are imposed and not fully understood, or just plain arbitrary, people are less likely to identify with them or fully commit to them.

Seven invaluable things happen when people are actively involved in an adult way, all of which lead to greater business understanding, enhanced commercial awareness, improved teamwork, increased responsibility and a greater sense of belonging and engagement:

1. It develops individuals. As people engage in the debate they gain a fuller, more rounded and balanced understanding and appreciation of how the business works and how all the different aspects (customers, cost, quality etc.) are reflected in the goals. They understand how these goals interrelate, why there are potential clashes and contradictions (for example, in aiming to improve quality and customer satisfaction while controlling costs), and where balances need to be struck. These are things that can switch people off when communicated in a formal presentation, but when they are given the chance to discuss and ask questions, they internalise it more and it becomes more interesting, meaningful and motivating.

2. The goals are likely to be more relevant and pitched at the right level if they emerge from a discussion that everyone can contribute to. Goals are also likely to be more ambitious if people are consulted and the discussion is handled skilfully.

3. Most crucially, if people **agree** the goals (or at the very least **accept** them after discussion and explanation), they are more likely to not only understand them but to actively commit to them. There's a direct common-sense link between involvement and understanding, and commitment. This increased commitment brings a stronger motivation to succeed that could make all the difference when the going gets tough. People will think harder and persist more if the task is something they put their name to achieving rather than something that was imposed on them.

4. Discussing and agreeing goals rather than imposing them also shapes working relationships. It creates adult-to-adult rather than parent-to-child working relationships. Not only does this define the nature of individual relationships, but it also aggregates to define the nature of the culture. It moves the business in the direction of individual ownership of, and responsibility for, goals. To involve people is to treat them with respect as responsible professionals, and this is more likely to lead them to behave responsibly, professionally and with respect for others' perspectives, needs and goals.

5. It develops the team. A team, of course, is a group of people who need to collaborate effectively to achieve a common goal, so discussing and agreeing goals is one of the most relevant and beneficial team-building activities there is. This also creates a self-reinforcing positive loop: the tighter the team, the better the objectives, and the more appealing and motivating the objectives, the tighter the team becomes behind them.

6. Getting agreement on goals sets the business up for taking action. People know what action to take and why. This improves focus and motivation and increases the odds of successful execution.

7. Getting agreement on goals also sets the business up for the final phase of the performance management cycle; reviewing progress. Where performance measures have been agreed they are, once again, not only understood but perceived to be more relevant, legitimate and valid. Also, crucially, people understand the intent behind the performance measures and that the review process is there to help them learn and improve rather than to criticise and blame them, so they are more likely to engage in a mature and positive way.

What, where and how: content, communication forums and style

The three main components of successful performance management are content, communication and style.

Content

This includes a clear sense of purpose and an appealing and credible vision of future success, together with a set of clear goals and expectations that will allow success to be measured. This creates focus and motivation and provides the means to measure success and progress.

Communication forums

A systematic and disciplined approach to performance management is required. Regular, structured communication forums are needed to bring stability, consistency and drive to the process. Without these, the process will lose focus and momentum and will stutter to a halt. Forums will include team meetings and individual performance conversations.

Style

The style – the way in which performance management is done – is crucial. It significantly influences how people will feel about the process and react to it. If it is handled well, people are left focusing on the goals and feeling confident and motivated. If it is handled badly, people will be left confused and demotivated, focusing on how unproductive or unpleasant the process was. The style that is consistent with the principles of Business Excellence is to be encouraging, supportive, solution-focused and constructively challenging.

Dealing with successes

Our job as leaders is to be aware of performance and results, acknowledge, celebrate and reinforce success, and find out if anything has not gone well and why. Often though, too little is made of success. This is a wasted opportunity. Recognising success is the fuel that drives confidence and helps people feel good about themselves and their colleagues. When we feel good about one thing, it's also often easier to feel positive and optimistic about other things. This reduces our fear of problems and increases the odds of us initiating something and pushing through the difficulties to success.

Recognising and celebrating success needn't be elaborate. A simple acknowledgement such as 'thanks' or 'well done' during regular reviews can make all the difference. It doesn't take much time, creativity or expense to create opportunities and identify ways to acknowledge what people have done well. Missing any reasonable chance to acknowledge achievement, progress, growth or effort is a wasted opportunity to build confidence and ambition and to reinforce what you are looking for from people. It's also a missed opportunity to build goodwill and mutual respect and strengthen the relationship. It's free money we're leaving lying on the table at a time when it seems like business is so pressured, stretched and competitive that we could do with every bit of commitment, motivation, goodwill and help we can get.

Dealing with setbacks

Not every business (or, indeed, every manager or individual) has a healthy relationship with mistakes, either their own or others'. It's a sensitive area, a tightrope to be walked with skill and awareness. If the tightrope is walked successfully there is the prize of ownership, responsibility, learning and growth, but there is also the ever-present danger of dealing with it badly and generating resentment, damaging confidence, engagement and commitment.

The spirit of how we deal with errors, problems and setbacks is vital. The legendary Liverpool FC manager Bill Shankly had a great approach. He viewed mistakes as 'happenings'. They were simply things that had happened that he didn't want to happen again. So he sat with the team and discussed 'what had happened', 'why it had happened' and 'how it could be stopped from happening again'. At first pass it may sound a bit corny, but it makes sound psychological sense and works well.

There are three main ways to go when setbacks in performance occur. You can:

Ignore it

This avoids some possible short-term discomfort. You can hope that people's own awareness and motivation will lead them to spot the issue and solve it themselves.

However, usually nothing is learned, and people may believe that because you said nothing, you either didn't notice or don't care.

React negatively to it

Be critical, harsh or punishing in what you say and what you do. While this may make people aware of what is wrong and that you've noticed and that you care, if you offer little in the way of explanation, direction or encouragement, people will switch off and shut down. Criticism is like dynamite. It's very powerful but also has the potential to be destructive, and great care and skill is required in its use!

Being criticised harshly is upsetting and stressful for anyone. People who are stressed and upset and have had their self-esteem knocked don't tend to be good at listening, analysing and coming out of their comfort zone to try new ways of thinking and behaving. Some, fearing your reaction, will deny any error, make excuses or cover it up. Some will actively push back and become defensive and closed-minded, arguing and justifying their own position and blaming others (including you). The more they rehearse their own arguments, the more they persuade themselves that they are right and you are wrong.

Other people will just withdraw. Many will already have been feeling bad about the mistake. The criticism will just increase the sense of guilt and shame. Embarrassed, angry and afraid to speak out, their confidence and motivation damaged, they'll disengage from you and your opinions, ideas and suggestions and not learn or change. Either way, when we criticise with insufficient skill and judgment, the lesson goes unlearned and we're doomed to a repeat of the same mistakes. It's worse than useless – this approach is actively damaging.

React positively

Discuss the issue openly, honestly and in a calm, balanced, adult way, understanding the reasons, identifying the solutions and devising preventative measures to avoid recurrence. This is the most direct, most relevant and fastest way of solving problems and preventing recurrence. It acts as extremely well-targeted learning and development for individuals and the team. It brings improvements, with an immediate impact on results and relationships. Handled with maturity, skill and perspective, many problems can be turned into opportunities for growth, development, and individual and business improvement. As such, this is the very essence of working smarter, using intelligence to solve problems (indeed, using problems as the catalyst to improve awareness, thinking and increase collective intelligence).

Reacting negatively to mistakes creates a double whammy. Not only are the benefits of handling it well missed but, with relationships damaged and nothing learned, the risk of a recurrence (and more mistakes in other areas) has increased, not decreased. It's the high-risk, high-hassle, low-success approach. It makes no human sense or business sense.

THE DANGERS OF HARSH CRITICISM

Nothing can be learned without people opening themselves up to self-analysis and reflection, and people won't open up if there is any legitimate fear of harsh criticism and punishment, or if there is little chance of progress and little chance of being understood or getting to the bottom of the problem and finding a way forward. Destructive criticism motivates people to hide from responsibility for fear of being blamed, and to be unwilling to risk trying to improve anything in case it doesn't work out.

In extreme cases it creates a domino effect. People experience a setback; confidence, belief and morale collapse; motivation and persistence collapse; a numb acceptance of failure and helplessness descends. People accept defeat and await their fate with resignation. It becomes easier to give in and take the criticism passively than to try and fight the losing battle to solve the problems, or to fight back against the manager who is making things worse by turning the drama into a crisis. Things reach a point where it can't get much worse. The manager can't follow through on the worst of their threats and their escalation tactics run aground. Everyone is stuck in an unhappy, unproductive stalemate.

If we are purposely trying to create a command and control culture and stifle individual intuition, then this is an excellent way to break people's spirit. But if you've read this far, I suspect that's not what you're trying to achieve.

Cumulative effects –keeping it going

Like personal fitness, consistently strong business performance requires a persistent and disciplined approach. Failure to check progress and results sends the clear message that you're not serious, or to be taken seriously. This will affect not only short-term results but also the credibility of your process, and the credibility of your commitment to getting results. This will negatively affect long-term performance and improvement, and your credibility as a leader.

Effective performance management is like turning a flywheel; it takes some time and effort to build up the momentum and establish the process as habit and practice, building up confidence and trust in the process, in the measures and in each other. At first it feels like it is all hard work and no reward, but discipline and persistence pay off.

Summary

Consistent, strong, sustained performance is not down to luck, it's down to effective performance management. Performance management is a core organisational capability, and how seriously we take it directly reflects our professional commitment to success.

Performance management is the process of setting goals, measuring progress, learning, and making adjustments to ensure that the goals are achieved. It raises business awareness among colleagues, helping them to think more – and more clearly – about performance. It also helps to identify and correct anything that is preventing people from doing their best for the business. It hits the sweet spot of engagement, empowerment and motivation.

CHAPTER 5

WHAT QUALITY MEANS AND WHY IT MATTERS

Introduction

Eighty-plus years after the dawn of the quality movement, what quality means and the fundamental of importance of it in performance is still not fully understood, appreciated or acted on.

One of W. Edwards Deming's many invaluable contributions was the insight (iconoclastic at the time) that quality is the key to building a successful, sustainable business: quality, he argued, drives customer satisfaction and efficient production, which drives profitability, which drives sustainability.

In this chapter, we'll look at five key aspects of quality that are vital to understand and get right:

1. Defining quality

2. That quality creates loyal customers (the key to sustainable success)

3. That quality is free: it is the key to high productivity, low cost and sustainable, profitable growth

4. Why quality must be built in (it cannot be not inspected in)

5. The difference between quality improvement and quality assurance, and why it matters

Defining quality

An important distinction to draw in defining quality is between **external quality** (understanding what the customer wants and designing the product or service to suit) and **internal quality** (building processes that can reliably achieve external quality).

External (product or service) quality

External quality means achieving what matters to the customer. Specifically, ensuring that the product or service:

- Is designed to meet their needs
- Is delivered on time/is available when required
- Does what was promised
- Is delivered right first time, every time
- Evolves and improves as appropriate to meet customers' changing needs

Quality, however, does not usually mean achieving the highest technical specification. The customer may not require the product or service to be 'gold plated' to get what they need from it. They might instead value such qualities as ease of use, longevity, durability, reliability, low running costs, compact size, or value for money. Adding or over-engineering any feature that the customer didn't ask for, doesn't want and won't pay for would be a form of waste rather than value. Products and services that contain unnecessary features may be:

- Overly complex and, as a result, hard to use or unreliable, and more likely to frustrate than delight
- More complex to make, adding time, risk and cost, and therefore...
- More expensive to both make and buy
- Less reliable and/or more expensive to maintain

Internal (process) quality

Internal quality (or process quality) is ensuring that the processes in the business are capable of efficiently and effectively delivering what the customer wants, right first time, on time, every time. And that they are continually improving, and adapting to evolving customer needs.

External quality creates loyal customers

'The consumer is the most important part of the production line.' (W. Edwards Deming)

Deming argued that the starting point for creating sustainable business success was focusing on the customers, who, he pointed out, ultimately pay for everything.

The primary aim of any business must, he believed, be to create loyal customers. Customers who are more than just satisfied. Loyal customers, he suggested, have a disproportionate impact on driving the profitability and growth of the business because they automatically place repeat business, are not constantly haggling over price, and are open to conversations about buying new or additional products and services. They also help bring in additional (loyal) customers through referrals.

Deming's research showed that this category of customer generated between six and eight times as much profit as less loyal customers who came and went, haggled over price and were resistant to buying new or additional products or services.

Winning and maintaining this customer loyalty, Deming argued, requires strong, and continually improving, quality and delivery performance of goods and services. It also requires the ability to do this at an attractive cost, and profitably.

This, in turn, depends on the performance of the processes that design, build, distribute and support the products or services. Therefore, he argued, a business needs to develop a deep understanding of how its processes work, and continually improve them.

Quality is free

A historical misunderstanding about quality (still alive and well in places) is that quality is expensive. This is usually due to a misapprehension of what quality is. Phil Crosby offered the argument (at the time also heretical) that, far from being expensive, quality is free. That, indeed, it pays dividends to get quality right, since it is quite simply cheaper not to have to put things right that shouldn't have been allowed to go wrong in the first place.

Figure 5.1 illustrates his point:

- The activities required to prevent problems amount to up to 15% of operating costs. These include all the value-enabling activities of effective planning, organising, communication, developing people, process-priming, process management and process improvement (i.e. all of the things Morgenstern suggested need be done to work smarter, not harder)

- If we 'save' money by not doing them and instead allow avoidable problems to occur, the costs of inspection and fixing problems detected both internally, and externally by customers, amount to around 40% of operating costs. (Not including what Deming called the 'unknown and unknowable' costs associated with creating unhappy customers who may complain, require refunds or price reductions, walk away, and dissuade an unknown number of others over an unknown period of time)

Improving internal quality reduces costs because a job done right first time requires only the planned time and materials, not the additional labour and material costs associated with rework and getting disgruntled customers back onside (or, indeed, replacing those that don't come back).

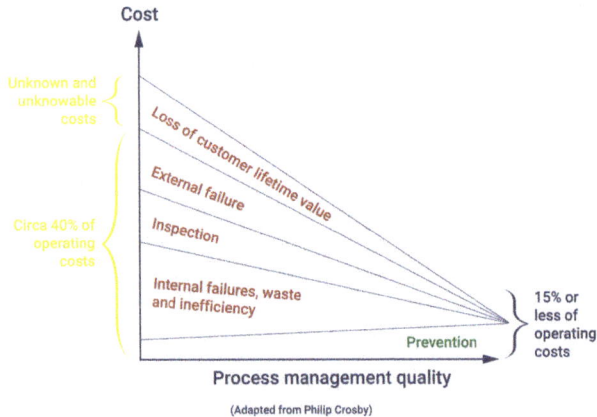

Figure 5.1: The cost of quality

Not only is quality free – it underpins sustainable growth

By extension, excellent internal and external quality means:

- More loyal customers
- Lower costs

- Better productivity
- Better delivery performance
- More available production capacity, since the process capacity (including labour, material, space and machine capacity) that was being consumed correcting quality problems is now freed up to increase the scope for growth

These are all conducive to growth and require no risk or capital investment.

Though it might sound like a statement of the blindingly obvious, not every business either gets this, or does this. Some, indeed, purposely pursue a strategy of reducing the time and money spent on value-enabling activities, only to incur the inevitable costs later. But because they have either no concept of, or no measure of, cost of poor quality (COPQ), it remains unmeasured and unmanaged. It nonetheless has a significant influence on financial and reputational damage.

Poor quality costs a fortune – and possibly the future

Businesses that focus narrowly on short-term profit keep a tight rein on production costs, ever vigilant for ways to reduce them. That's no bad thing. However, there are significant dangers if this is done through an inspection of financial data alone, rather than a fuller understanding of overall process performance.

First, when in this mindset, it is difficult to see the case for paying up front for prevention measures. Second, financial accounts show items needed to get the job done right first time; labour, tools, raw materials etc. But this data by itself does not fully or accurately identify where the waste, inefficiency or problems arise in a process. (A value-stream map with some in-process measures would also be required.) So, while the root causes of problems and inefficiencies go unaddressed, any financial restrictions and cuts will almost inevitably fall on the resources necessary to get the job right first time – creating internal and external quality problems and the need for costly rework.

This will almost certainly generate an overall end-to-end cost increase (particularly when service and warranty costs are included), reducing profitability and also affecting quality in a way that damages customer loyalty, making the customer harder to keep on board and sell more to. There is also a risk of knock-on reputational damage (recall Ford's finding that happy customers tell eight other people, but unhappy customers tell 20). This can reduce both market share and profitability and necessitate spending significant amounts trying to regain sales or replace them elsewhere.

But from within the restrictions of this particular way of thinking, all cost savings are cost savings, and without the will, tools or concepts to understand overall system performance and the COPQ, the wider impact on the business will be a reduction in both short-term profitability and longer-term growth prospects.

Quality must be built in

'Why spend all this time finding, fixing and fighting when you could have prevented the incident in the first place?' (Philip Crosby)

Quality cannot be inspected in. Inspection, as invaluable as it is in many circumstances, can only catch problems once they have occurred. Quality must be built in. Built in to the processes that create the product or service. The process must be designed, measured, managed and improved to achieve and maintain the capability to consistently deliver the level of internal and external quality required.

Quality improvement vs quality assurance

This final key point reflects the evolution in the last 70 years in our understanding and practice of quality management, and relates to the point that quality cannot be inspected in, but must be built in through effective process design, management and improvement.

The key distinction here is between:

- Quality assurance, with its emphasis on inspection and compliance, and
- Quality improvement, with its process-focused emphasis on improvement: using problems to learn about, better understand and improve the process

In reality, there's always a bit of both going on, but there are dangers in too much emphasis on inspection and compliance:

- Inspection procedures can quite easily become overly bureaucratic and obstructive, introducing unnecessary steps and activities, causing unnecessary delays and raising costs (increasing commercial risk unduly while reducing compliance risk)

- When focusing mainly on identifying problems and stopping quality failures rather than improving processes, the root causes of problems may not be identified and eliminated, and the capability of the processes that produced them may not be improved to build in quality and reduce the likelihood of future problems

Summary

1. Quality has two complementary aspects:

   - External – meeting customer needs for functionality, availability and cost. Achieving excellent external quality is the key to creating loyal customers who bring repeat business, are open to upselling, and who will recommend the business to others
   - Internal – being able to produce the goods and/or services right first time, every time

2. Quality is free: poor quality costs because it is usually much more expensive to do things over and have to handle customer complaints than to get things right first time. Focusing on getting quality right leads to lower costs, higher productivity and more loyal customers. This frees up capacity for growth, providing significant competitive advantage and a strong platform for sustainable success.

3. Any arbitrary cost-cutting that impacts on the ability to deliver quality, on time, will backfire, increasing costs, damaging profitability and hampering sustainable, profitable growth

4. Quality must be built in to processes through effective design, measurement, management and continuous improvement

5. The quality strategy must be focused predominantly on quality improvement, and not just on inspection and compliance

CHAPTER 6

VALUE-ENABLING TIME: THE KEY TO EXCELLENCE

Introduction

> *'If trying harder was going to reduce errors, it would have worked already.*
> *... Realize that your problem is caused by a systemic situation, not a lack of*
> *effort.' (Seth Godin)*

Achieving excellence needs more than time and hard work. The key, as Deming memorably noted, is mentality – a deep commitment to finding ways to work smarter: doing the work of figuring out how to continually optimise time, effort, equipment and resources, in the context of constant change.

The foundation for this is the systematic prioritisation of time to reflect, analyse, discuss, understand, innovate, experiment and improve things. And using that time in a disciplined and focused way.

Three ways to spend time: value-adding, value-enabling and waste

Time in business can be spent in three ways, on:

- **Value-adding** activities that transform the product or service in ways that add direct, chargeable value to the customer (i.e. that provide what they want, asked for and will pay for). For example, designing the product, cutting materials to size, assembling the product, picking the item, delivering the order, or serving the customer

- **Value-enabling** activities that underpin and optimise the value-adding activities. The important foundational work that makes the next day, week, month, year and the longer-term future better. These include:

  - Designing, planning, resourcing, managing and improving the underpinning processes

  - Leading, managing, coaching and developing people and fostering teamwork

  - Long-term strategic planning and implementation. Enabling the business to (a) survive, by identifying and dealing with emerging threats, (b) thrive, by spotting and capitalising on opportunities, and (c) developing the business as a system to be more adaptive to emerging opportunities, threats and other changes in its environment

- **Waste** activities that either add no value, or actively destroy value. Effort that is unnecessary, inefficient or creates the need for rework, or that damages processes, relationships, trust or reputation, or suppresses the development or expression of talent and reduces the scope for learning, improvement and growth

In any professional performance domain, the primary responsibility of a manager is to find the optimal balance between value-adding and value-enabling time, to minimise waste and to optimise both the amount and quality of value-adding time. This is the very essence of the craft of management.

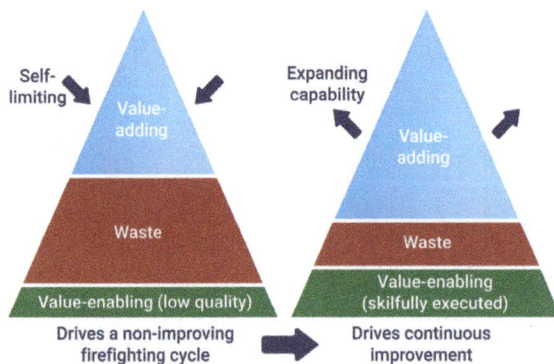

Figure 6.1: Three ways that time is spent and the resulting dynamics

The dynamic between value-enabling, value-adding and waste

The three categories of time use are dynamically interrelated, in both positive and negative ways.

The high-performance continuous-improvement cycle

Skilfully executed value-enabling work:

- Makes value-adding time more efficient, controlled, predictable and higher quality, which ...
- Minimises wasted time and resources, which ...
- Creates more time for value-enabling work (and for enhancing its quality) and thus opens up the possibility of creating a virtuous cycle of reciprocally expanding capability and possibility

All of which increases the value-adding capacity of the enterprise without risk or capital investment (see the right side of Figure 6.1).

The non-improving firefighting cycle

But this can also go in reverse (see the left side of Figure 6.1). When insufficient time is invested in properly designing, planning, setting up, resourcing, maintaining, monitoring, managing and improving operational processes, and in developing, coaching and managing people, the result is that inefficiencies, quality problems, delivery problems and poor productivity become embedded and systemic. This creates three main layers of deleterious effects.

First-order effects: loss of operational capability

The first-order effect is to impede flow, slow down processes, throw things out of sync and generally reduce the efficiency or effectiveness of value-adding time. This creates a nuclear fusion-type cascade; one problem knocks the process out of flow and creates another, logarithmically increasing failure-driven demand (unplanned and unpredictable additional demand on the system and its resources, created by a failure to get things right first time).

The net effect of this is to damage quality, cost, delivery performance and colleague engagement through:

- Wasting resource and process capacity through the need for rework (i.e. failing to achieve right-first-time quality)
- Overloading people, processes and managers, thus sowing the seeds of further problems
- Creating internal conflict and damaging teamwork and morale
- The time, cost and distraction involved in dealing with the increasing number of customer returns, refunds and discounts
- Reducing customer loyalty, sales, repeat business, up-sales and referrals, and the corresponding additional time and cost involved in replacing that lost revenue and margin

All of this makes performance difficult to predict and control (the core responsibility of a manager).

Second-order effects: loss of tactical capability

| *'Having lost sight of our objectives, we redoubled our efforts.' (Pogo)*

Operational exigencies can narrow managers' focus and time horizon down to firefighting in order to just 'get stuff out the door'. Value-enabling activities become (further) marginalised, are categorised as non-urgent and are (further) postponed, cancelled, or rushed and done badly.

This can compromise crucial tactical capabilities, including:

- The planning, setting up and resourcing of the process for the next shift, day, week or month
- The ability to improve operational processes through the identification and removal of the root causes of problems
- Managers' awareness of issues at the gemba (where the value-adding working is done) and lack of connection to, and support for, the people there
- Basic skills training and multi-skilling – potentially compromising operational flexibility and resilience
- Timely implementation of long-term strategic improvement projects, leaving the business vulnerable to changes in the business environment

Since total workload is the sum of value-adding work and failure-driven demand, managers can create for themselves an increasingly heavy and dynamically unpredictable burden and become less and less productive in a self-perpetuating cycle of entrenched, chronic, and often worsening operational problems: a 'non-improving firefighting cycle'(as Mike Rother called it). Managers in this situation, rather than managing the process and results, are managed by the process. At the mercy of the problems created by it.

Getting snared in such a stuck loop limits performance, improvement and the ability to thrive and grow. In extreme circumstances, it can threaten survival (see Figure 6.2).

Figure 6.2: The non-improving firefighting cycle

How bad can it be? Research suggests that, on average, 34% of time spent in UK companies is on preventable wasteful activity (with the highest level 70%).[1] That's serious – and, perhaps more worryingly, most organisations don't measure their cost of poor quality, so the severity of it can go unrecognised and unaddressed.

Third-order effects: loss of strategic capability

Positioning the business to survive and thrive long-term requires strategic capability: the time and expertise to step back, assess the threats and opportunities, evaluate existing capability, identify the gaps, create a plan, and execute that plan with discipline and persistence – all the while, dynamically learning and adjusting.

However, if every level of management gets sucked into playing one level too low and distracted by a morass of operational problems, the discipline of strategic management can become overlooked, and the capability to do it well, underdeveloped. As a result:

---

1   Source: Proudfoot Consulting: Global productivity report 2008: A world of unrealised opportunities

- There may be no clear, appealing vision of the better future we are working to create, and a corresponding loss of direction, sense of purpose, focus, motivation and commitment throughout the business
- Emerging opportunities and threats may be missed
- The capability to deal with these threats or opportunities may not be developed adequately or promptly
- The positive ideas and intentions that the business does have will not translate into long-term impact
- The business will be unable to get on the front foot and positively shape events, instead being at the mercy of them. Performance and rate of improvement will decline in relation to best-in class in the industry, creating a widening performance gap that will be increasingly hard to close

Worse still, leaders and managers may come to make the mass of avoidable problems that the business is snared in an excuse for not making time to adequately plan, manage or improve their people, processes or culture. Even worse than that, they may then accept this as the norm and assert that it is a fixed and unalterable reality, rather than a reflection of existing leadership attitudes and capability that they have the responsibility to change.

This mindset opens up the danger of getting into a stuck loop similar to Figure 6.2, but at a strategic level; i.e. across the whole organisation and over time, leading to institutionalised, self-perpetuating mediocrity at all levels – strategic, tactical and operational.

The real cost of this (the gap between what was possible and the current reality) is hard to measure – especially, of course, for businesses with underdeveloped strategic measurement systems. But not investing sufficient time and skilled effort in value-enabling activities is self-evidently the harder, riskier, more expensive, more time-consuming, more self-limiting and less efficient and successful road to choose. A false economy.

SMARTER WINS

Introduction

As far back as the 1930s, industrial engineer Allen F. Morgenstern encouraged us to 'Work smarter, not harder'. This was no glib cliché but, rather, very specific advice. An invitation to see beyond additional effort as the sole route to better results, and instead to apply our intelligence to devising ways to achieve more with less effort. To develop and optimise a system's capability rather than to simply maximise it within its current capabilities. This remains a central tenet of Business Excellence.

The limits of working harder

Getting the maximum from every business asset – equipment, space, people and resources – by demanding more (quality, cost, volume, variety etc.) or reducing resource, or both, makes sense. Such pressure can be a useful spur to learning, growth and creativity. It may eradicate complacency and lead to higher levels of productivity and efficiency. But there are two significant dangers.

First, when it takes any part of the system – equipment, people or relationships – past breaking point, danger lurks. Things struggle, strain and begin to burn out and break down:

- Equipment fails and reduces process capacity, reliability and manageability. Repair and replacement costs increase. Extra equipment may have to be purchased as back-up
- Quality suffers, deadlines are missed
- Customers complain, demand refunds or price reductions, or leave if problems continue
- Colleagues disengage. Relationships become strained. Grievances and absenteeism increase. People leave. Vital expertise is lost. Overtime costs increase. There is further disruption as new people join and have to be brought up to speed
- Underlying process inefficiencies and vulnerabilities go unaddressed as managers are maxed out and distracted by the need to tackle urgent issues
- Capability and resilience are degraded (either suddenly or over time)

Pushing everything to the max for a short period is occasionally unavoidable, or may represent a decent risk/reward ratio. And, as long as it doesn't go too far for too long, the damage can be undone and full capability restored in good time. But if it does go too far for too long, there's a real risk of getting stuck in a non-improving firefighting cycle, and of hobbling the performance and potential of the business in the long term.

Second, more effort alone will, at best, maximise results within the current limitations of the process. It does not address those constraints and bring any sustainable – let alone transformational – gain in capability and performance.

As Maslow's Law of the Instrument suggests, when we have a limited repertoire of tools or strategies, we may apply them in situations where they are inappropriate, and fail to develop alternative approaches that may be more suitable or effective. To paraphrase Maslow, 'to someone with a hammer, everything looks like a nail'. And then, to paraphrase Shakespeare, 'there are more things in Heaven and Earth than are dreamt of in this philosophy'. Enter stage left: working smarter.

Working smarter

Working smarter is taking sufficient value-enabling time and spending it well; planning, reviewing, learning and improving to optimise system capability, performance and rate of improvement.

In the technical processes, this will focus on improving workflow and right-first-time quality; systematically identifying and removing the causes of defects, inefficiencies and other barriers to help people to engage positively with the work and achieve excellent QCD performance.

In the social systems, this will focus on:

- Developing people's attitudes, skills and behaviours to help them perform and problem-solve better and more confidently
- Empowering people to improve their local processes and work with others to align those processes with adjacent ones
- Developing relationships and the mutual trust that allows for rapid and effective business-wide collaboration and problem-solving

The case for well-spent value-enabling time

Put simply, value-enabling means taking care of today and simultaneously building capability for the future. But, as Bonini, Kalloch and Ton pointed out:

'Companies often perceive a trade-off between short-term operational inefficiency and investment in the future. But it's a false trade-off. You're going to pay one way or the other. Either you invest in a well-paid, well-trained, well-motivated team and effective processes that will make your company better every day, or you incur endless high penalties for your mediocre workforce processes and culture, in the form of higher turnover, higher inventory costs, lower quality, worse customer service, and less responsiveness and adaptability.'

Investing in building capability may seem expensive, but the alternative – a poor-performing operation – is much costlier.

The highest-leverage way to use time

Value-enabling activities, then, are the highest-leverage way that managers can spend time because, when done well, they bring benefits in three key ways:

Tactically

Value-enabling activities boost effective planning, communication, performance management, people management and process improvement, which yields a greater degree of predictability and control over performance and results. This allows managers to:

- Be wise before the event – to plan effectively to avoid many foreseeable, and potentially costly and limiting, problems
- Spot issues early and make timely in-flight course corrections
- Spend sufficient time on implementing the strategic projects designed to prepare the business for the future and build the capability to deal with emerging opportunities and threats

Operationally

Value-enabling activities:

- Optimise operational value-adding capability

- Progressively reduce the waste and inefficiency embedded in processes by creating time, and building the skills, for (continuous improvement)

All of which improves quality, cost performance and delivery performance, and frees up process capacity for growth.

Strategically

Value-enabling activities enhance the business's capability to (a) see emerging threats and move to deal with them, and (b) see opportunities and act to successfully grasp them. For aspiring market leaders, effective strategic vision, planning and execution also builds the capability to:

- Shape the product or service (and possibly the industry)
- Develop the organisation's people and processes to perform better and more consistently long-term
- Make the business more adaptive as a system, to become increasingly adept at reading the environment and responding appropriately

Value-enabling activity is real management work requiring real management capability

Finally, since every manager is responsible for simultaneously delivering both short-term performance and longer-term improvement in value-adding capability, it is important to recognise that value-enabling activities are the real work of management. (The alternative being forever trying to maximise an underdeveloped process).

Perhaps in local, low-competition markets in low-complexity environments with fixed offerings, it is possible to survive with little or no value-enabling capability. But in competitive, complex and rapidly evolving environments where a business needs to operate as an adaptive, integrated system to thrive, it is a fundamental requirement.

Balance is key

The aim is to get the right balance of value-adding and value-enabling time, adjusting value-enabling time dynamically to suit circumstances and provide the right levels of productive capability, tactical adjustment capability and strategic-improvement capability to ensure that, ongoing:

- Existing processes are adequately designed, planned, resourced, maintained and managed
- Problems are spotted early, and solved faster than they are piling up
- Processes are continually improved

It's not a time problem

'How come we always have time to fix it, but not time to get it right the first time?' (Unknown)

The availability of time or resource is not the problem. If anywhere near 34% of an organisation's time (and associated resources) is routinely spent on activities that either add no value, or actively destroy value, then it is clear that time that could be invested in value-enabling activities is there, locked up in the waste created by inefficiencies and failure demand.

This is time and resource that could be invested in a focused and controlled, rather than reactive, fashion, in activities that enable, support and enhance the value-adding activity.

So if the problem is not a lack of time, what is it? It's usually one or more of the following:

- Mindset
- Lack of insight, skills and expertise
- Lack of discipline and emotional maturity
- Lack of accountability
- No overall management system

Let's have a look at each in turn.

Mindset

When managers who are embroiled in firefighting say they are 'too busy', they are right in the sense that they are overloaded. But in the whirl of activities, deadlines and adrenaline and emotional reaction, the whole ecology of where, how and why problems are arising, spreading and becoming ingrained is missed.

This is partly psychological. Constantly reacting to short-term pressure kicks in the fight-or-flight response, which:

- Narrows attention to the here and now
- Causes people to react rather than think
- Impedes the ability to think, both longer-term and systemically, to accurately perceive and analyse situations, and to prevent problems and find better ways of doing things

Being in firefighting mode is, strangely, a comfort zone for some who enjoy the heroics of reactionary problem-solving, but fear the challenge of managing smarter, i.e. taking responsibility for thinking strategically and for improving people and processes.

It is the responsibility of every manager to be self-aware enough to see this happening and pull out of it.

VERTICAL DEVELOPMENT

The ability to see the importance of making time for value-enabling work is a function of a manager's level of vertical development: that is, their level of consciousness of what is going on around them. Their ability to perceive, analyse, think and act at increasing levels of dynamic complexity and across longer timescales, recognising that working harder with ineffective systems is not the road to better outcomes. Progress requires that we work smarter. That we use our intelligence to see what is happening and evolve our thinking and systems accordingly.

Levels of vertical development

Here's a quick overview of the levels of vertical development. These levels represent different degrees of what John Vervaeke calls 'optimal grip' – our grasp of the realities of our situations, our understanding of the key variables in play and how they dynamically interact to create outcomes, and how we might intervene to improve those outcomes.

In line with Einstein's observation that one cannot solve problems with the same level of thinking that created them, each level represents a different stage of emotional and cognitive capability. The lower on the spectrum we go, the greater the emphasis on more energy, effort and force being the solution. The higher we go, the greater the focus on the quality of the intelligence that guides effort and action.

Let's explore the four levels, starting from the bottom:

- **Reactive/chaotic** level behaviours include firefighting, blaming and complaining. At this level we may (or may not) solve the problem of the day. But, having failed to address the underlying root causes, we will face the same problem again the next day, and the day after that

- At the **tactical** level we will anticipate some near-future operational issues and will plan accordingly to avoid or mitigate those we can. We'll also be tuned in enough to read how events are unfolding and make necessary in-flight adjustments. Generally, we'll do our best within the current constraints, but will not seek to understand and address the underlying process limitations

- At the **improvement-focused** level, we'll look at the process that is driving the current outcomes (including the problems). We'll (re)design, manage and improve the processes in our purview, address the underlying root causes and improve outcomes on an ongoing basis

- At the **strategic** level, we'll seek to understand how the whole business works as a coherent system, and where future problems and value-adding opportunities are likely to occur. We'll then move to address these proactively, building new, and higher-level, capabilities to create an increasingly more adaptive system over time. We will always be seeking to increase possibilities and improve outcomes for all stakeholders

What is seen or missed (and why)

Growth of consciousness (and thus management competence), then, can be understood by considering what is seen and not seen in terms of variables, dynamics, and the impact on outcomes in any given context.

The following are recognised and acted on at higher levels and are missed (or dismissed) at lower levels:

- 94% of problems come from system shortcomings and only 6% are due to a range of factors including bad weather, bad luck and human error. So the best route to better results is system improvement (process improvement or people development, rather than pushing failing systems harder or apportioning blame)

- There is a cost in planning, communicating, and managing and developing people, and a greater long-term cost in not doing so. But without thinking through the logical consequences of inaction, this cost only becomes apparent with hindsight, when the problem occurs or the opportunity is lost

- It's cheaper, easier and better to be wise before the event (rather than during, after or never). Ideally well before. Before the event, small shifts can create big differences to the outcome. During the event, even herculean efforts might not get us back on track. After the event, there may be no way back to where we started, far less to where we hoped to be. Therefore, avoiding problems with foresight, good planning, process design and people development is the most cost-effective, highly leveraged way to work

- We think, plan and act differently depending on the furthest look-ahead point in our systematic analysis and planning, i.e. if we are planning for the next day, year, phase of life, or even for the next generation. (And we'll probably get the future we failed to plan for)

Therefore, value-enabling activities (investing time and effort now for better outcomes later) do not get in the way of management work. **They are management work.**

Lack of insight, skills and expertise

Even with the right mindset, managers need to have the knowledge, skills and expertise to plan, manage and improve processes, and to coach and develop people. Not all managers fully understand what process excellence entails or how to achieve it (though a lack of insight leads some to be overconfident in this area).

Lack of discipline and emotional maturity

Even where managers have the right insight, skills and expertise, there can be a knowing-doing gap: a lack of discipline in running the routine meetings and the one-to-ones where performance is discussed, managed and improved at team and individual level. Discipline may also be lacking in the follow-through on improvement activities. Much of this is down to allowing a sense of urgency, rather than importance, to guide priorities.

Lack of accountability

The lack of management discipline is often the result of a lack of accountability. Managers are rarely measured or managed on how much time they spend on value-enabling activities, how well they perform them, and what the results are.

Simply hoping that managers will spend enough time, and spend it well, is never enough. It can't be left to chance. Value-enabling time must be time-blocked and non-negotiable, and managers must be held accountable for it and for how well it is invested.

No overall management system

The reason for inadequate accountability is usually some shortcoming in the operational management system: the integrated set of management processes that defines standards, sets goals, designs processes and holds people accountable, allowing the business to be managed and improved in a coherent, systematic, disciplined and consistent way.

While every manager at every level needs to have the right mindset etc., the best guarantee is having an effective management system that holds people accountable for the quality of the time invested in it.

Prioritising value-enabling time

The key to positive change is breaking the vicious circle and creating an excellence loop by understanding what value-enabling time is, why it is important, prioritising it, and becoming slick and disciplined at it (see Figure 6.3).

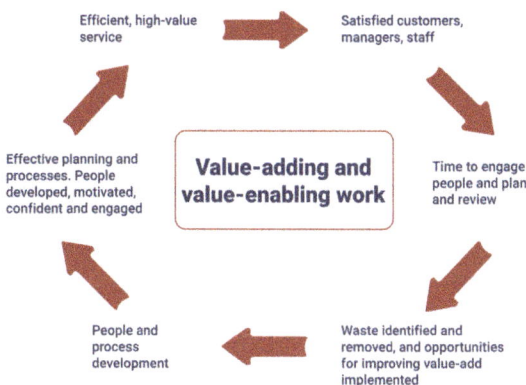

Figure 6.3: The excellence loop

Easy to say, difficult to do consistently well. First and foremost, it requires vision and leadership at all levels, starting at the top. Getting the five areas discussed earlier right can contribute to the solution:

- Mindset
- Insight, skills and expertise
- Discipline and emotional maturity
- Accountability
- Management system

Let's have a look at each in turn.

Mindset

The first step is recognising that investing enough time in value-enabling activities and getting them right is the key to maximising value-add, minimising waste and creating an upward spiral:

- Remembering that the core responsibility of leadership is to remove the causes of failure, improve the system and help people do a better job with less effort and greater satisfaction
- At an individual level, leaders making sure that their time management prioritises and assigns sufficient time for planning, reviewing, reflecting, learning and developing their personal attitudes and skills
- At team level, making it part of the operational management system
- At strategic level, building it into management systems and roles and responsibilities from the top, throughout the organisation

Insight, skills and expertise

Developing an understanding of process-management and process-improvement concepts, tools and techniques, to be able to make the best use of value-enabling time. Again, there are different responsibilities at different levels:

- At organisation level, recognising the strategic importance of developing the knowledge and skills of all colleagues
- Managers helping colleagues to hone these skills through their application to real challenges
- Every individual understanding the importance of developing and using these skills

Discipline and emotional maturity

Prioritising and protecting appropriate time to commit to value-enabling activities, understanding their importance and ensuring that they are not constantly pushed aside due to short-term pressures. It is also crucial to invest time and effort in learning how to perform value-enabling activities consistently well, and then doing so more effectively and efficiently on an ongoing basis. Once again, there are different sets of responsibilities for this at strategic, operational and personal levels, all of which need to be recognised and met.

Accountability

Ensuring that key value-enabling responsibilities are built into the standard work of leaders, managers and colleagues, and time-blocked, and that the accountability process routinely checks that they have been performed and are delivering results.

Management system

The best way of ensuring all of the above is recognising that investing sufficient time in value-enabling activities to achieve Business Excellence is ultimately a strategic issue, and that it needs to be reflected in the values of the business and built into leadership and management systems and roles and responsibilities, led from the top.

Summary

Well-executed value-enabling activities are the key to Business Excellence. They make the difference between working hard to move forward and working hard to stand still. Value-enabling activities ensure that processes are designed, primed, managed and improved to optimise performance, and to ensure that people are managed and developed effectively to both use and improve those processes. They reduce firefighting and dedicate time to building performance and value.

Value-enabling time must be prioritised. It must also be used effectively, which requires the right mindset, knowledge, skills and discipline. Every manager has a personal responsibility to do this, and for it to be done consistently well across the organisation, and over time.

PART THREE: TECHNICAL SYSTEMS

CHAPTER 7

MANAGEMENT SYSTEMS OVERVIEW

Introduction

Two fish swim past each other. One says, 'The water's lovely.' The other replies, 'What's water?'

Like water for fish, the management system, so fundamental, pervasive and all-encompassing, can be strangely inconspicuous in organisations. Even when its shortcomings lead to significant widespread problems, it can go unnoticed, unquestioned and unchallenged.

What is the management system?

The management system is the central nervous system of the business. It is the set of processes that measure and manage performance across the whole business, and at all levels: it plans, monitors and regulates performance, coordinates the various operational processes to promote coherent functioning day to day, and enables ongoing strategic adaptation.

The management system determines what gets measured, how the information is used and, crucially, what happens when problems are identified. It touches every person and every activity. It shapes the culture, influences people's attitudes and behaviours, and is a major determinant of business performance.

In an organisation committed to Business Excellence, the purpose of the management system is to:

- Ensure that every colleague has the right processes, information, tools, materials and training to do their job successfully
- Provide useable and timely performance information to allow people to for run, manage and improve their processes
- Engage people in an ongoing constructive dialogue that enables them to understand, manage and improve their processes to achieve sustainable success

An effective management system creates an aligned, informed and motivated culture that is equipped to achieve sustainable success. An ineffective management system risks widespread and entrenched dysfunctionality that will consistently constrain performance and progress.

This means that the design, management and ongoing improvement of the management system is a leader's most fundamental, and highest-priority, task, and the highest-leverage improvement that an organisation can make. As Bititci observed; 'Transforming measurement and management ... is not just a leadership issue, it is, given the impact on sustainable success, arguably the leadership issue.'

Components of the management system

The management system comprises two related systems: the strategic management system and the operational management system. These inform, guide and oversee the management of the core processes, as illustrated in Figure 7.1.

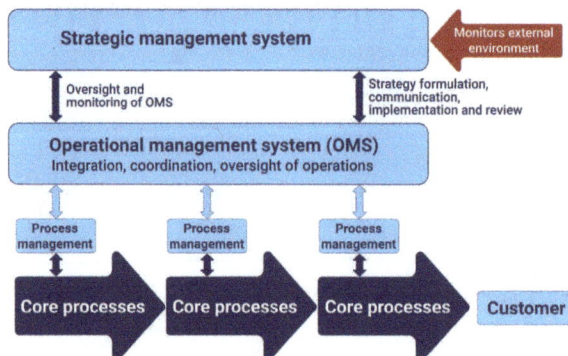

Figure 7.1: Management system overview

The strategic management system sets the purpose, direction, goals and strategy for the business. It:

- Defines the purpose, aims and values of the organisation
- Monitors the external environment to assess the status of markets, technology, legislation etc.
- Identifies the core capabilities the organisation requires to succeed in its chosen markets
- Assesses the current capability of the organisation
- Analyses and integrates internal and external perspectives and plans how best to achieve:

  - Operational control, to ensure that the operational processes perform optimally and improve continuously
  - Strategic breakthroughs in key areas, to achieve sustainably higher levels of performance

The operational management system is the set of processes that macro-manages ongoing business operations. Its functions include:

- Monitoring and managing demand
- Planning and scheduling activity
- Resourcing
- Integrating and coordinating the operational processes end-to-end along the value stream
- Aligning operational activity with strategic direction
- Overseeing and coordinating process management: the day-to-day measurement, management and improvement of front-line processes
- Managing and developing people

When designed and run well, these two sets of processes create a complete, coherent, aligned, integrated and coordinated system that choreographs action across the business, and through time, bringing the right degree of both resilience and agility.

Why it matters

The quality of the management system and the discipline and professionalism with which it is run have a significant influence on performance, culture and the organisation's ability to adapt and change.

When designed, managed and improved consistently well, it focuses energy and activity on productive endeavour, and creates genuine engagement and empowerment and a culture characterised by high standards, responsibility, teamwork and continuous improvement.

When it is inadequately designed, managed or maintained, the inevitable result is problems with performance, processes and culture, often creating entrenched dysfunctionality that constantly constrains and undermines performance and seems resistant to attempts at improvement.

Despite this, when looking to improve, many leaders focus on changing just about everything but the management system.

Let's explore in greater detail the impact that the management system has on:

- Business performance
- Management performance
- Culture
- Change

The impact on business performance

People rely on a well-functioning management system to provide them with the following, on time and to the right standard, as any problems here will immediately and directly impact performance:

1. **Capable processes:** Well-designed, reliable processes, working within capacity
2. **Clear expectations:** Of goals, standards and methods
3. **Skills and knowledge:** Adequate quality and breadth of training
4. **Information on performance:** Timely, frequent, actionable facts and data
5. **Accountability:** For decisions, actions, performance and results
6. **Opportunity to discuss performance, problems and ideas:** Scheduled, regular, constructive forums, free from fear

7. **Effective coaching:** As part of everyday work to develop rounded, confident, responsible people with strong job skills and problem-solving ability who work well with others and in teams

8. **Process improvement:** Time, skills and tools to identify and remove process problems

The impact on management performance

There is a danger that, without the focus and discipline provided by a well-designed and well-run management system, one of two things will happen:

- Short-term pressures will push managers into reactive mode. The immediate impact will be to compromise process stability and the predictability and repeatability of results. In the longer run, it will hamstring ongoing strategic improvement, keeping the organisation locked into limiting patterns of recurring problems and rendering it unable to achieve its full potential

- In less demanding environments, complacency and stagnation can easily set in, creating a culture of self-perpetuating mediocrity

The impact on culture

'Most companies are led, managed, and populated by thoughtful, hardworking people who want their organisation to succeed. The conclusion has become clear: it is not the people, but rather the prevailing management system within which they work that is the culprit.' (Mike Rother)

The management system also has a significant impact on culture; how people think, feel and act with regard to the business, colleagues and customers, and with regard to issues such as standards, quality, integrity and continuous improvement.

Most people turn up for work with a positive enough mindset. But their attitudes and behaviour can be bent out of shape by a range of issues whose root cause lies in the management system and the spirit in which it is run. For example:

- Unrealistic targets being imposed

- Frustration at things that stop them doing their job with pride and serving the customer, including, as outlined above, ineffective or inefficient processes;

wrong, late or inaccurate information; unavailable or faulty materials, tools or equipment

- Not having the authority, information, time, tools or forums to solve those problems themselves
- Being repeatedly ignored, criticised or blamed when raising the above issues
- Being told to improve their attitude when they get frustrated by all of this

There are two aspects to this. First, the question of how technically effective the system is, and the discipline and consistency with which it is run. Managers are unlikely to get from their people higher standards than they set themselves. So if the management system is poorly designed and run, people may justifiably conclude that leaders either don't value excellence or are incapable of leading it. And they may consequently believe that a focused and disciplined approach to performance and improvement is not required of them.

Second, there is the issue of how socially effective the system is, the 'spirit' of how the management system is run. The pivotal issue here is how performance discussions are handled. A management system designed and run with the intention of helping people understand and improve performance, and one that involves, includes and empowers people and fosters teamwork, respect and trust is likely to promote positive attitudes and behaviours, and to generate greater accountability, responsibility, and joint problem-solving.

If, however, performance discussions focus on highlighting failure and apportioning blame, people are more likely to become fearful, defensive and blame oriented. Even more so if they are not given the tools, information, problem-solving training, empowerment and time to address them. To make matters worse, if people's reticent behaviours are ascribed to 'attitude problems', despite the root cause being the management system (the leader's responsibility), levels of cynicism and distrust will deepen further.

Over time, this creates a culture where people won't take responsibility or initiative for fear of what might happen if they make a mistake. As a result, quality, financial performance and customer satisfaction are likely to be underwhelming, inconsistent, and resistant to improvement. This also creates a context where people may be tempted to game the numbers in an attempt to avoid negative attention.

It is tempting to think that, because people in excellent organisations demonstrate positive attitudes and behaviours, working on attitudes and behaviour is the way to change a culture. But, as with many aspects of excellence, there is a danger in trying to reproduce the observable aspects without looking deeper to understand the underlying principles and the underpinning systems.

Just as water won't run up hills and you can't push with a rope, working on attitudes and behaviours alone won't change a culture. Culture is, rather, a reflection of how the management system shapes people's attitudes and behaviours around performance, quality, errors, customer service etc., so no amount of behavioural training will improve the culture or levels of engagement if the management system keeps undermining trust and disempowering people.

The impact on change

The ultimate aim of most change is to help people improve performance by serving customers better and more profitably. The levers typically used to achieve this are technology, processes and structure.

But the pivotal influence of the management system on performance and culture is often, mysteriously, overlooked. This is a significant omission, and potentially fatal to the success of any change initiative, because problems are commonly misattributed to other causes, which consequently drives a constant stream of fads and superficial fixes that leave the core problems unaddressed. Worse, sometimes the problems are even compounded when the failing management system is ratcheted up with more targets, more inspections, more criticism, blame, fear and threats. (A great example of working harder, not smarter.) All of this further compromises the trust, teamwork and process-improvement capability the organisation needs if it is to evolve.

Indeed, some high-profile, big-budget and high-risk structural, technological or training interventions are unnecessary and even counterproductive. Greater improvement could have been achieved more easily, more quickly, and with less cost and risk by changing the management system to better engage, enable and empower people to run, manage and improve their processes and performance.

Simply, and self-evidently, without an adequate management system, nothing will work well for long.

Developing an effective management system

The management system, Dean Spitzer observed, must be both technically and socially effective:

- **Technically:** To define the measures that provide the information that allows the business to be managed and improved. The system should provide:

  - **Focus:** It should measure and manage the factors most relevant to success
  - **Integration:** Create a coherence, (a) horizontally, making sure that the measures are aligned all the way along the value stream so that work flows smoothly from end to end, rather than stuttering through poorly coordinated silos, and (b) vertically, to align with strategy

- **Socially:** To engage and involve people in managing and improving the business. The system should provide the right:

  - **Context:** A constructive, professional environment that enables and empowers people to improve process performance
  - **Interactivity:** To engage people as active partners in process management and improvement by providing:

    - Appropriate forums to review and discuss performance information and develop an ever-improving understanding of the processes
    - Continuous improvement tools and training, and adequate time and scope to use them

We'll take a look at these four sub-categories in more detail, starting with context, then exploring focus and integration, and concluding with interactivity.

Context: management system purpose

Empowerment, if it is to be more than wishful thinking, needs a supportive context.

For organisations committed to Business Excellence, the purpose of the management system is to actively engage people in an ongoing constructive dialogue that enables them to understand, manage and improve their processes to achieve sustainable success.

The context therefore requires the right environment; one where people are (a) responsible and accountable, (b) free from fear or blame, (c) focused on value creation, and (d) able to develop a deep understanding of how their processes work.

Let's look at these in turn.

Accountability and responsibility

Accountability is being answerable for one's decisions, actions and outcomes. Responsibility is having the ability, resources and autonomy to perform to the expected standard, make decisions and take action. To get the best from people, everyone must be both accountable and responsible for the results they are paid to deliver. An effective management system will therefore strike the right balance between accountability and responsibility and be appropriately tiered, to get the right accountabilities and responsibilities at the right level:

- Front-line teams should have accountability and responsibility for the method, performance and results of front-line processes. Colleagues are responsible for ensuring that standards are followed, and that when delays, defects or equipment problems are discovered, they are immediately corrected, or escalated for appropriate support

- Managers at successively higher levels should be accountable and responsible for progressively larger elements of the overall system performance and escalations from the process areas in their purview

This allows performance to be monitored more closely, in real time, and for problems to be identified and resolved faster, by front-line people, with more serious problems being escalated upwards, to be dealt with at the most appropriate level.

Finally, in a culture of excellence, accountability and responsibility are likely to be experienced positively as improvement-focused dialogue, coaching and support.

Freedom to lead... and freedom from fear and blame

The management system will only be as strong as the social aspect, and the effectiveness of the social system depends largely on trust; the trust people have in the aims of the system, the effectiveness of the technical and management systems, the relevance and accuracy of the measures, and how far they can trust their managers to respond intelligently and constructively to problems and improvement ideas.

Leadership effectiveness means:

- Removing blame, which leads people to shut down and be defensive or to game the system, rather than being open, honest, cooperative and solution-focused. Dealing with problems by asking 'How did the process let this happen?' rather than 'Whose fault was that?' is more likely to set the right context for enabling and encouraging people to take responsibility for processes, performance and results

- Removing the fear of failing to meet unrealistic goals with inadequate processes, resources or support, and instead encouraging and coaching people to set and pursue their own ambitious goals

Focus on value creation

While improving process efficiency and removing waste is important, the primary aim of any process is the creation of value. That is, understanding what the customer wants, will use and will pay for, and developing the optimal way of consistently delivering and continuously improving it. As John Seddon put it, 'Doing the right thing, rather than the wrong thing righter.'

Without a clear focus on value creation, it is all too easy for people to lose sight of their purpose and how best to achieve it.

Develop a deep understanding of processes

'If we are to manage the performance of our business processes, we need to better understand their anatomy and behaviour.' (Umit Bititci)

In order to improve a system, it is necessary to understand how it works. That means identifying the main steps, and the key variables and interactions, and then experimenting by attempting to improve the process by making changes, guided by structured problem-solving tools and thinking. This will require sustained effort, constancy of purpose and an environment where continual improvement is encouraged.

This is an ongoing upward spiral of model-building, testing and revision to get everything to fit, creating a coherent picture that develops an ever-deepening understanding which in turn informs more effective action and ever-better results.

This model-building is also vital, because as Deming pointed out, 'Without theory, there is no way to make sense of the information that comes to us in an instant.' Performance information, by itself, no matter how fast, detailed or frequent, tells us little and does not allow us to be confident that the action we take on the system will work.

We need, therefore, to develop the capability to move quickly and accurately from:

- **Data:** Raw and unprocessed, to derive useable...
- **Information:** By extracting the important signals, themes and patterns hidden in the data, to give it meaning and relevance to derive...
- **Knowledge:** An understanding of what factors drive performance, which allows us to develop...
- **Wisdom:** Deep, rich insight that allows people to take consistently good and timely action

Creating a context where the focus is on value creation, developing and acting on a robust understanding of how the process works, and getting the right balance between empowerment, support and accountability, ensures effective control and improvement of processes, enabling organisations to learn, innovate and change rapidly, and creating the agility necessary to thrive in increasingly unpredictable and fast-changing environments.

The focus of measurement: what gets measured gets managed

Process control measures

At the operational level, control measures are required to help understand, manage and improve how the process is operating in real time. These include:

- **Results measures:** These measure the outcomes required from the value-creating processes (the 'ends'). The core of these are invariably the QCD (quality, cost and delivery performance) measures. They should align with the voice of the customer and reflect the levels of performance that are required for the business to be competitive
- **In-process-measures:** These are measures of the key variables in the value-creating process that have the biggest impact on results (the 'means'). They allow the flow of work through the process to be tracked, in-flight adjustments to be made, emerging problems to be spotted and solved in real time, and opportunities for ongoing process improvement to be identified

Both sets of measures need to be honed through time and experience from the 'trivial many', which can create confusion and obscure the true picture of what is happening, to focus on the 'critical few'.

Strategic measures

For strategic improvement, measures must look beyond the routine 'vital signs'. Transformational measures should be sought. Factors that could create a transformational breakthrough in strategy, approach and results. For example, Southwest Airlines' focus on aircraft utilisation and, as the main driver of that, turnaround time, was the key to revolutionising their business (and, arguably, their industry).

(The topic of measurement is covered in fuller detail in Chapter 9.)

Integration: ensuring alignment and coordination of the value stream end-to-end

The management system – both the measures and the forums – should form an integrated whole that recognises the interconnectedness and interdependence of the various processes, and connects the business as a coherent entity cross-functionally and vertically: focusing on the performance of the whole, rather than the individual parts in isolation.

Cross-functional integration

Since the value stream runs horizontally across the business, through various departments, cross-functional integration is required to ensure:

- The smooth and balanced flow of work end-to-end
- The coordinated improvement of the whole value stream; identifying the biggest constraints, and also ensuring that changes in one part of the value stream do not have unintended negative consequences on others

Vertical integration

Vertical integration coordinates the different levels at which performance is managed, and aligns the vision and strategy with daily operations.

Vertical and horizontal are of course related, as each successive vertical level is responsible for the integration of the corresponding lower-level processes.

Interactivity: the degree to which people are involved

Interactivity is the engine that engages, empowers and unlocks individual and collective potential by involving people in understanding and improving processes. Achieving this requires the right climate, access to useable information, and appropriate forums to review and discuss performance information and develop an ever deeper understanding of the processes. Relevant and timely forums, and the ability to contribute to them, are crucial if engagement, empowerment, accountability, responsibility, innovation etc. are to be meaningful, and for people to properly develop the necessary attitudes and skills, which can only be fully developed by working on real business problems.

People also require continuous-improvement tools and training to enable them to be active partners in problem-solving.

Fostering interactivity is, in and of itself, a powerful force for positive change. Sometimes purely social interventions alone – letting people decide what to change – can deliver significant performance improvements.

There are four components of this that we will explore in turn:

- Creating a positive, productive climate
- Providing access to relevant and useable information
- Creating appropriate discussion forums
- Provision of problem-solving tools, training and opportunities

Creating a positive, productive climate

As discussed earlier, the key to excellence is developing an increasingly full and accurate understanding of the value stream and empowering people to manage and improve it. This technical understanding can only be developed through a social process that fosters:

- Open, honest, constructive dialogue that is based on, and also builds, trust and respect
- The inclusion of multiple viewpoints and, for the greater good, a willingness to listen, cooperate and be flexible in pursuit of excellence
- Solution-building: progressively building knowledge, wisdom and solutions through constructive dialogue

- Willingness to experiment and accept missteps that result from well-intended attempts at improvement, as part of a learning process
- The professional discipline to follow through on agreed actions

Providing access to relevant and useable information

To facilitate this, people need information that is up to date, relevant and presented in a way that they can understand and act on. The information should be displayed in clearly in operational areas ('comms zone'), accessible to everyone, where teams can meet to review and discuss performance and solve problems.

The information should provide real-time insight into process-performance and a clear line of sight to strategic priorities. It should include:

- A strategy overview
- Process measures that reflect how work is flowing through the value stream
- Output measures of process performance
- Tracking of improvement projects and their impact

For consistency, and to support integration, this broad structure should be replicated across the organisation and at different levels.

Creating appropriate discussion forums

People also need regular forums to discuss the above information and manage, maintain and improve process performance. Consistent with the need for effective vertical and cross-functional integration, the forums should align daily management with strategic priorities.

The forums should collectively form a tiered structure, anchored by 'daily management' meetings across the business where every front-line colleague is involved in a review of the previous day and a look ahead to the current day. Issues should be dealt with locally and immediately where possible, and larger issues escalated as appropriate to the tier(s) above. They must also support effective cross-functional collaboration to ensure that the end-to-end process runs smoothly and stays focused on meeting customer needs.

These forums should also:

- Be regular and frequent: run at the speed of business (i.e. not so often that they add nothing, and not so infrequent that vital issues don't get caught in time)

- Maintain ongoing, focused and positive discussion of performance (without which some form of complacency or negativity will creep in)
- Foster trust, strong working relationships, collaboration and the joint problem-solving that underpins excellence.

Provision of problem-solving tools, training and opportunities

People also need the tools and training to identify problems, find their root causes, and permanently resolve them. And they will need adequate time to do this, and genuine empowerment to experiment and make changes.

How to begin

The start point for enhancing a management system depends on a number of readiness factors including level of ambition, existing culture, leadership style, level of continuous improvement expertise, current degree of process-management capability, and levels of trust.

The best place to start is often with the social system; educating people on process-improvement tools and techniques, providing time to experiment and empowerment to improve processes. This can build dialogue, trust and understanding, can make people enthusiastic for more involvement and responsibility, and progressively draw more and more people in.

Another powerful early step is to map out both the strategic management system and the operational management system and, for each, identify, analyse and prioritise improvement opportunities.

Then do the same for front-line teams with their respective operational processes. As Deming pointed out, people need to see the process, and how it connects and flows, before they can figure out how to measure and improve it.

Setting up the comms zones where people can access performance information, and establishing regular forums for reviewing and discussing performance, is also a significant step forward.

The above steps will build a platform of trained and empowered people with access to information and discussion forums, establish traction, and progressively build momentum as people begin to identify and successfully complete process improvements.

Understanding the territory

Building, managing and improving an effective management system is not for every leader, only for those serious about, and committed to, Business Excellence. And so, before embarking on improving the management system, it is important to fully understand the territory and what you're getting into. In particular, note that:

- **Every organisation must find its own solution:** There is no standard approach. Every organisation must develop and continually evolve its own approach

- **It takes time and much trial-and-error learning:** Transforming both the social and technical aspects of the management system will take time, and you may have to start small (and localised). No one gets it right first time. Indeed, Cowley and Domb suggest being 'prepared for chaos in the first year of the new system'

- **It should be evolutionary, not revolutionary:** It is a constant process of model-building, testing, revising and refining until everything hangs together in a coherent framework of concepts. A process of discovery, iterative and highly interactive

- **Don't expect perfection:** There are no perfect measures or perfect management systems

- **The big change is social and cultural:** 'Performance measurement will always be used to monitor and control, but when people see that it is used more for the purpose of improvement, then everyone will know that a change is truly taking place' (Dean Spitzer)

- **Expect the 'wall of resistance':** As Bititchi highlights, existing approaches, despite often being both ineffective and unpopular, are often entrenched philosophically and operationally, creating 'resilient self-reinforcing systems that are resistant to change, and encourage practices and behaviours that jeopardise sustainable performance'

- **It's a tough gig, but ultimately worth the effort:** Developing and maintaining an effective management system is hard to achieve, but given the competitive advantage, agility and sustained benefits that can ensue, worthwhile. In highly competitive industries, it is simply essential

- **It's never done:** In designing effective management systems, as with every other process, learning and improvement never stops

The good news is that there will be many improvement opportunities so that you can progressively uncover increasing scope for evolutionary improvement for years to come.

Summary

It is important to recognise the all-pervading influence that the management system has (for better or worse) on all aspects of organisational performance and culture.

Only management system that uses information to help people understand and improve performance, and that properly equips and engages front-line people to manage and improve performance, will create a culture of excellence and deliver the much-lauded (but rarely fully realised) aims of empowerment, engagement, responsibility, accountability, initiative, creativity and continuous improvement.

The design, operation and improvement of the management system is the leader's responsibility – their most important responsibility, and the most powerful lever for managing and improving business performance.

The keys to designing an effective management system include:

- **Context:** To provide a positive, professional environment for discussions about performance and improvement
- **Interactivity:** To actively engage people in a constructive and empowering dialogue about managing and improving performance
- **Focus:** Identifying the 'critical few' operational and strategic measures
- **Integration:** Ensuring coherence, both vertically and cross-functionally

An effective management system designed on these lines creates a powerful engine for enduring excellence. While achievable, and ultimately worthwhile, it is neither easy nor quick. It is arguably the leadership priority for many organisations and should be the first, and most important, part of any organisational change or improvement effort.

CHAPTER 8

WHY MANAGEMENT SYSTEMS GO WRONG

Introduction

A poor management system can seriously impair an organisation's ability to perform and improve, and it can also create a deeply dysfunctional culture.

To understand why, let's explore what can go wrong in the four key areas Dean Spitzer identified:

- Focus
- Integration
- Context
- Interactivity

Focus

Effective management relies on effective measurement, which means measuring:

1. The outcomes that matter most, and
2. The underlying factors that drive those outcomes

Figuring this out can be hard, painstaking work. Even when we've worked out what to measure, there's another set of challenges around figuring out how to measure it.

The only way is to work it out gradually by trial and error (i.e. over several PDCA cycles). Few at the top of organisations are able or willing to invest the time or effort to take that particular journey, and so the measures many businesses end up with tend to be simplistic, based on outdated ideological assumptions about what *should* work rather than knowledge of what actually *does* work.

Here are just a few of the more prominent examples of how we can get the focus wrong:

- Measuring the wrong things (the biggest category)
- Unclear information
- Constantly shifting goalposts

Measuring the wrong things

Measuring the wrong things focuses attention on, and therefore prompts action on, the wrong thing. This arises when we fail to focus on the purpose of the business – to meet the needs of the customer profitably. It sounds unwise, but it happens. A lot. Here are just a few examples.

Activity measures

These highlight activity while telling us nothing about the value of that activity. Not all activity adds value: the wrong activities can destroy value.

For example, measuring how quickly calls are answered and how many calls are taken each hour can yield superficially impressive data, but tells us absolutely nothing about the achievement of the actual purpose of the system, which is first-time call resolution. Indeed, it may be serving to undermine the purpose, damage customer satisfaction and increase costs, because if the customer's query is not resolved first time, the customer is passed around or has to call back (sound familiar?). This creates what Seddon called 'failure demand' – an unnecessary demand created on time and resources due to a failure to get things right first time.

In short, activity measures can drive behaviours that destroy value rather than create it. Other examples of activity measures that tell us nothing about the achievement of purpose include home visits completed, inspections conducted, and sales calls made. Nothing about achievement of purpose there anywhere.

Productivity measures

These are a close cousin of activity measures. Productivity is often measured as some kind of ratio between what comes out and the resource that went in. Again, however, it is not measuring whether the process is achieving value, or meeting customer needs right first time. For example, we could be (very productively) working on things that are not a priority for the customer, or making (highly efficiently) items that go into stock and might never be sold.

Examples of distortions introduced by productivity measures include:

- Producing something that is not immediately needed (and may never be needed) just to make the utilisation of people and resource look good

- Not putting enough labour hours on the job, so that the outputs-per-person looks good, but quality is poor and/or people are overworked

- Knowingly providing inadequate product, information, answers etc. to count a transaction as complete

- People working on the easy and quick tasks while the urgent but difficult work piles up (sometimes poetically described as 'parking and creaming')

'Look good' measures

These create an illusion of action and progress – but tell us nothing about things that really matter to the customer or business profitability (quality, cost and delivery). Indeed, they are sometimes chosen to divert attention away from difficult, underlying problems that really need to be highlighted, understood and solved if the business is to move forward and thrive long-term.

Examples include:

- Investment in technology – many investments in technology are not successful

- Staff qualifications – I have come across businesses that have trained large numbers of people in process-improvement skills and never give them a chance to use them

- Reorganisation – many reorganisations are counter-productive, as they cause disruption but often fail to address the real reasons for performance problems or poor teamwork, which are invariably process or management systems issues

Comparison measures

A comparison measure is where a data point is compared to a reference point; for example, a customer specification, an average or a management target. The conclusion is either 'It's okay' or 'Do something'. As Wheeler notes, this approach inevitably results in 'periods of benign neglect alternating with periods of intense panic ... [an approach] completely antithetical to continual improvement.' That's bad enough. But comparison measures don't allow us to understand how natural variation in the process affects the outcomes, and so we risk:

- Misinterpreting and overreacting to certain results
- Failing to properly grasp the full picture of process performance, and missing real opportunities for sustainably improving it

Here's why:

- All processes (and therefore the results they produce) demonstrate some degree of variation
- A process is 'stable' (statistically speaking) if it consistently and repeatedly generates a set of results within certain limits (the upper control limit and lower control limit)
- The process may be stable, but not producing the desired results (for example, the control limits may fall outside the customer specifications), i.e. it is not 'capable'

If a process is stable but not capable, the process needs to be studied, understood and improved. This is because, in a stable process, the variation is created by 'common causes', i.e. factors inherent in the process. An example might be how temperature affects the behaviour of raw materials.

If a process is not stable (i.e. not consistently and predictably operating with certain limits), this suggests the presence of 'special' or 'assignable' causes which are destabilising the process – for example, machine breakdowns. A process has to be made stable, by identifying and removing these assignable causes, before it can be properly examined, understood, managed and improved, to enhance its capability.

If, however, the process is stable, to treat every divergence from the some notional ideal as a special cause is not only futile, but is actually likely to destabilise the process.

So, the problem with comparison data is that it completely misses the impact that process variation has on results, and creates the significant danger of demanding action on a result that is just due to the natural variation in a stable (if imperfect) process. Explanations may be demanded, but since no assignable cause actually exists, any resulting explanation is, as Wheeler observes, likely to be a 'work of fiction whose only purpose is to pretend that something is being done about a perceived problem'.

If the goal is beyond the capability of the system, the system will have to be changed by understanding and addressing the common causes. And to do this, we need to understand the Voice of the Process (VoP). Primitive and simplistic comparison data won't do.

(Control Charts and other measures provide more meaningful and accurate insight into the behaviour of the process and enable continuous improvement – but this is a complex topic in its own right and beyond the scope of the present book.)

Wrong time frame

As Bititci points out, short-term measures can act against the creation of sustainable long-term performance: 'In managing the performance of our business, it is quite easy to increase its value in the short-term by simply stripping away capability.' Goals need to balance short-term performance with the building of sustainable long-term capability.

Unclear information

Approaches to information gathering, analysis and presentation that may look impressive, but simply intimidate, bewilder and confuse, and provide little useful, actionable insight. This may include:

- **Volume of data:** Generating and gathering lots of data with no real pattern to it, or clear link to how it helps us understand or improve the system

- **Complex analytics** that provide little or no insight

- **Impressive scorecards,** dashboards and 'war rooms' that provide neither the information nor the environment for people to discuss and improve performance

- **Information unavailable to the people whose role it is to operate and improve the process.** As Michael Hammer pointed out: 'Measurement systems typically deliver a blizzard of nearly meaningless data that quantifies practically everything in sight, no matter how unimportant; that is devoid of any particular rhyme or reason; that is so voluminous as to be unusable; that is delivered so late as to be virtually useless; and then languishes in printouts and briefing books, without being put to any significant purpose ... in short, measurement is a mess.'

Constantly shifting goalposts

Asking for different data (or different configurations of the data) or 'special reports' depending on what the current crisis is, rather than having a stable, useful set of measures. Hugely distracting, time-consuming and confusing.

Integration

Focus is about picking the right core measures. Integration is about ensuring that measures are complete, connected and coherent enough to allow us to understand, manage and improve the whole system – as a system – rather than managing the business as a collection of dislocated parts and hoping that they will all, by some miracle, work together in a seamless, choreographed way.

Unfortunately, the outdated rationalist notion persists that if each component of a system is optimised, then the whole system will be optimised. This simplistic view overlooks the obvious: that the interdependencies between the components need to be recognised and managed if the whole system is to be optimised. What happens at the interfaces between sub-systems matters. Alignment between the different parts of the system matters. Without it, things don't flow, and costs, delays and quality problems increase.

The core problem that arises from a lack of integration is a lack of a clear understanding of how the business works as a complete system, serves its customers and adapts to changes in its markets and environment. As John Seddon highlighted, 'Most managers fail to develop even the most rudimentary theory that allows them to jointly, interactively predict cause and effect, and then test, learn and improve.'

The ensuing problems can all be summarised by one word: 'sub-optimisation'. The various manifestations of this include:

- Different functions working at cross-purposes to optimise their own numbers, rather than optimising the whole. For example, most businesses experience some tensions between sales teams whose bonuses depend on the revenue value of business won, and operations teams for whom the complexity, mix and timing of the work influences their ability to do it, and from a financial perspective the actual profitability of that work
- Focusing on cost reduction without considering its impact on short- and long-term quality, productivity and delivery. While cost always needs to be

understood and managed, there are dangers in the simplistic assumption that a cost reduction automatically improves either short- or long-term profitability. First, from a financial perspective, it is often better to focus effort on increasing profitable sales by providing quality products and service, rather than risk compromising the offering and losing customers. Second, there is the ever-present danger of false economies, where pursuing cost reduction without understanding the consequences in the value stream actually increases the cost of poor quality in the long term due to the expense of fixing the problems it creates, and the loss of reputation and repeat business incurred

- Loss of synergy and the creation of unnecessary operational conflicts as different functions protect their own finances, efficiencies and schedules when overall process-performance and customer satisfaction is better served by 'taking one for the team' and, for example, sharing resource or reprioritising

- Loss of synergy and the creation of unnecessary conflict around business improvement: people working passionately and hard on the wrong improvement priorities and in the wrong way. Ideas that sound good in principle, but whose impact on different parts of the value stream, and the end result, have not been fully thought through. The result is often 'push down-pop up' problem-solving; for example, sales secure work that cannot be delivered to the promised quality and timescales, causing operational problems, late delivery, customer dissatisfaction and poor colleague morale

Context

Context is about who measures, who decides what to measure, for what purpose, and what happens if performance problems are identified.

The context can range from control to empowerment. At the 'control' end of the spectrum, organisations set measures at the top, defining the purpose of measurement as upward reporting to allow senior managers to monitor and control performance. The response to performance problems is typically with criticism, directives and warnings of consequences if performance does not improve.

At the 'empowerment' end of the spectrum, the purpose is to enable colleagues to understand and improve process performance. Front-line managers and colleagues help to shape measures that allow them to do this. When problems occur, front-line people use the information to identify and remove root causes and improve the process. When done consistently well, this means that processes are both under control and continuously improving.

In the middle of the spectrum, where many organisations sit, there is a lack of clear purpose, focus discipline, and consistency around measurement, so they miss the potential benefits.

The context is less conducive to effective management and continuous improvement when:

- Measurement is used to monitor and control rather than engage and empower
- It is adversarial
- Goals are arbitrary and unrealistic

Let's explore this.

Using measurement to monitor and control rather than engage and empower

Monitoring and control is an important part of measurement. And there are different ways in which it can be achieved.

The Business Excellence approach focuses on control of the processes that generate the results, by using measures that enable front-line colleagues to understand and improve their processes.

The main alternative is to attempt to control people. This could include: ensuring compliance with set policies, processes and standards; ensuring that people follow directives (whether they make sense or not); or exhorting people to achieve goals by any means. Or all three! Control may be exercised through rewards (giving or withholding them) or through criticism, blame and formal discipline. The risk here is of fostering fear, defensiveness, resentment, and a reluctance to take responsibility.

Monitoring and control require upward reporting, and there are potential dangers here also.

Clearly, top-level managers need to understand what is happening in the business and take appropriate action in good time. However, when information is gathered, aggregated and sent upward for analysis and action (rather than using it immediately on the front line to make decisions and improve processes), there are risks, particularly in an adversarial context. These include:

- Filtered and skewed information which amplifies good news and suppresses bad

- Information that is too abstract to allow any kind of meaningful analysis, or to enable root causes to be identified; e.g. data aggregated across time periods or across several departments

- Information arriving too late to allow timely action, e.g. end-of-month reports

Gathering, analysing and presenting information carries a cost and distracts managers from their core responsibilities of engaging with people to manage and improve process performance. Many reporting processes are wasteful and inconsistent, and destroy rather than add value.

Adversarial approach

'When the relationship is adversarial, people will be motivated to outwit the control system.' (Leonard Greenhalgh)

Aside, of course, from lack of respect and emotional intelligence, choosing an adversarial approach to managing performance stems from the belief that goals are accomplished by effort alone (and that failure is due to individuals' motivation). There are two (often subconscious) aspects to this thinking.

The first is **management by results**. The assumption here is that all that is required to get results is to set a goal and rigorously monitor action and progress so that people work hard enough to achieve it. The strength of this approach is that it focuses attention, mobilises effort and mitigates against complacency. Where certain conditions are met, the effects can indeed be positive and powerful.

These conditions include the goal being achievable, and that people have effective processes, problem-solving tools and training, empowerment, time and useable information, and work in an atmosphere that supports innovation and improvement. These factors also make **management by means** possible, i.e. they enable people to figure out how the value-creating process works, continually enhance its capability, achieve breakthrough goals, and move toward Business Excellence.

When these conditions are not met, management by results descends into browbeating people into committing more time and effort; working harder, not smarter. In the long term, this is a recipe for conflict, inefficiency, mediocrity and stagnation.

The second concept in play here is what McGregor famously called Theory X - the assumption that most people are lazy, untrustworthy and self-interested and have to be given a target, and then monitored, controlled, pressured, criticised and possibly intimidated into performing.

As Deming suggested, however, the reality is closer to McGregor's Theory Y – that most people do a good job if they have the right tools and resources, and that 94% of performance problems stem from process, not individual, failings. In other words, where people underperform, a responsible manager should look first at the process, information and resources people had, and at how they selected, inducted, trained, managed and coached their people.

And even if performance problems do come down to a person's attitudes or behaviour, this neither necessitates nor justifies an adversarial approach. It requires mature professional management.

Arbitrary and unrealistic goals

Goals set by senior managers are typically communicated with a sense of certainty and confidence intended to convey not only the necessity of achieving them, but also that they are also founded on solid information, rigorous rational analysis and watertight planning.

But such an impression is often misleading. Deming suggested from his experience that many targets were estimates which had no firmer basis than 'stargazing'. John Seddon went further, suggesting that no reliable method exists for setting a target and consequently, what we see is mostly guesswork, with many goals being spurious, and some 'outright deceptions'.

Problems typically arise when:

- A target is set without full consideration of system capability (and might thus overstretch it or underutilise it)
- There is a lack of flexibility in response to changing conditions (also potentially leading to overstretch or missed opportunities)
- The people who are tasked with achieving the target, and who are most familiar with the process and its capabilities, are not involved

Pursuing any poorly derived goal has negative consequences:

- **Operationally:** If there is a significant mismatch between capability and demand, this either overstretches and potentially destabilises the value stream (compromising quality, cost, delivery performance and long-term sustainability), or fails to use its full capability

- **Socially:** Working toward a target they can't meet, and constantly failing and being criticised, demoralises and disengages people. This also fosters disdain for their leaders' lack of insight, ability and integrity and creates the moral context that some feel legitimises 'gaming' – i.e. distorting processes or data to get the 'right number'. (This is discussed later)

Problems occur when the target number on some measure is arbitrary, and not set on the basis of an analysis of market strength and business capability. Reasons can include:

- An unrealistically high target set by a powerful stakeholder with a vested interest
- Lack of analysis. For example, the ubiquitous 'last year plus 10%' (why 10?)
- Departmental managers trying to set goals as low as possible, to reduce the risk of failure and increase the odds of exceeding target, looking good and being rewarded

Some targets go beyond just being poorly focused. They actually shift the focus away from achieving the system purpose (i.e. to serve the customer efficiently and well), to meeting the metrics, regardless of the actual impact on customers, profitability or long-term capability.

When we looked at focus, we saw how activity measures, productivity measures and look-good measures have the capacity to do this. In the contact centre example, the actual purpose is first-time call resolution, but where people are measured and managed on the volume of calls handled, and average call time, there is a greater incentive to get the customer off the phone fast rather than to take time to understand and solve the problem right first time. This results in the creation of failure demand. In this example, the demand on system resources (time, people, equipment, etc.) increases because the customer either bounces around other departments, or has to phone back, or both, each time using more time and resource as they re-explain the story, getting increasingly irate and dissatisfied. Performance looks good when assessed by the narrow and misleading call-volume metric and when factors such as customer satisfaction and cost of poor quality, which would provide a fuller and more balanced picture, are not measured.

It is also possible for the system purpose to be deliberately subverted; for example, where the emphasis is shifted from serving customers profitably to maximising profitability by any means.

Interactivity

The interactivity of measurement is the degree to which people are empowered to use the information from the measurement system to make changes to:

- Their work processes
- The measurement system itself

Unless they are able to use performance information to make changes to the things that are causing problems, if they are criticised and challenged on performance, people are likely to be frustrated, defensive or simply disengage. (Which, ironically, may invite further criticism of 'bad attitudes'.)

Where people are not able to influence the design of the measures and goals, they may conclude that measurement is just being used as an instrument of control rather than empowerment, and may view it with disdain.

Gaming

Brian Joiner observed that when people are pressured to meet a target, they can do three things:

- Work to improve the system
- Distort the system
- Distort the data

Where the context doesn't support the first of these, we are inviting problems. The ingenuity that should have been directed into problem-solving and innovation around processes gets directed into the dubious art of gaming, i.e. finding ways to present favourable numbers.

Rules get bent or broken. Short-cuts can be taken with (among other things) customer service, quality, and health and safety. From the predictable (e.g. cutting training budgets to reduce short-term costs) to the illegal (e.g. LIBOR fixing), to self-destructive institutionalised accounting fraud (e.g. Enron), examples are legion, with, as Spitzer observed, its more mundane manifestations played out daily in organisations around the globe. These manifestations include:

- Hiding unfinished work so that the backlog is not visible
- Falsifying outputs; for example, counting quality failures as completed work
- Fudging numbers:

- Premature revenue recognition
- Deferring expenses
- Use of special charges
- Capitalising operating costs

These can create the illusion of strong current performance, but run the significant risk of longer-term sub-optimisation and damage to results, trust, engagement and culture.

While most colleagues recognise these problems because they live with them every day, many senior managers are either unaware of, or unconcerned by, what is going on.

The challenges of changing the management system

Getting the management system right can be a messy, complex business: like trying to do a complex, three-dimensional, moving jigsaw, with too many pieces and no picture on the box. Worse, those trying to do this are often venturing into this area with people who don't understand the concepts, get the point, want to get involved, or even trust each other. Including, and often especially, at senior level, often with people who think they learned everything they needed to know about this 25 years ago.

Because of these challenges, and because, sadly, few senior managers fully appreciate the nature and significance of these challenges, fixing the management system is often put in the 'too difficult' tray and ducked completely. Instead, CEOs change structures, processes or roles, or adopt new technology, and generally rearrange the furniture. While creating (in some minds at least) the impression of decisive strategic action, this invariably just creates further disruption, mayhem and demoralisation.

> 'As a result of ignorance about performance measurement, many executives try to fix everything else in their organisations except measurement, and find that the problems are never solved – because the source of so many organisational problems is a defective measurement system.' (Dean Spitzer)

Transformation

Many challenges around colleague engagement and sustainable improvement are due to an almost subconscious reliance on limiting, traditional measures that keep us trapped at a level where we fail to properly illuminate, understand and solve problems, and just keep recreating them. No amount of tinkering will help. Fundamental assumptions need to be addressed.

The good news is that we can now recognise measurement dysfunction and understand the reasons for it. The further good news is that better alternatives are available. Transformation of measurement, and consequently of culture and performance, is possible.

The four categories Spitzer defined that helped us understand the problems also provide a structure to help us move forward:

- Create a positive **context** – one where measurement is used to drive improvement
- **Focus** – develop measures that:

  - Relate to the purpose of the system (the voice of the customer)
  - Help colleagues to discuss, understand and improve performance
  - Foster the building of long-term capability to underpin sustainable competitive advantage

- The **integration** of all measures into a coherent framework, that links measures:

  - Cross-functionally, to help integrate functions and enhance collaboration
  - To strategy and the development of long-term capability

- **Interactivity:** Developing, with people, measures that they trust and can use to improve

CHAPTER 9

EFFECTIVE MEASUREMENT

Introduction

The purpose of an effective measurement system is to provide relevant and timely information to allow the people responsible for a process to:

- Set the process up for success and prevent problems
- Facilitate in-flight tracking and quick and effective course-correction
- Identify ways to continuously improve the process to make it more efficient, robust and resilient
- Provide a basis for meaningful, positive responsibility and accountability in all of the above

Measurement has both a technical and a social aspect:

- **Technical:** First, to identify measures that offer the most useful insight and the greatest leverage to manage and develop the process; second, to promote coherent functioning across the organisation, and through time, by ensuring that these measures are integrated horizontally (end-to-end along the value stream) and vertically (aligned with strategy)
- **Social:** To create a context where measures are used to help the people responsible for the process to understand how they influence performance, and to engage and involve them in its management and improvement

Why this matters

> 'What gets measured gets managed, and what gets managed gets done.' (Peter Drucker)

From a technical perspective, measurement is crucial to the effectiveness of the PDCA cycles that power performance and improvement throughout the business. Measures are defined at the Plan stage. At the Check stage, we can assess to what extent the action taken has produced the expected results, learn about the nature and size of any gaps, and work out next steps.

From a social perspective, a good measurement system also strongly and positively influences people's behaviour, aligning their thinking and actions with organisational purpose and strategy, fostering engagement with it and creativity in the pursuit of it.

Done well, this constitutes a core organisational capability that affects every process, person and result in the organisation.

Measurement is also central to leadership and management; the capability to foresee, plan and manage, anticipate events, avoid problems by attending to the right measures at the right time, and create opportunities.

For many organisations, taking a more comprehensive, coherent, rigorous, systematic and disciplined approach to measurement can represent a significant evolutionary advance in strategic and operational capability.

While there are costs associated with measurement, the cost of not measuring is significantly greater, due to the operational inefficiencies and missed strategic opportunities that result from the inability to stay fully focused on purpose, prevent problems, and make rapid and effective course-corrections and improvements at all levels of the organisation.

Top tips

In designing measurement systems, it is useful to:

- Use both results (lag) measures and in-process (lead) measures
- Define both the desired outputs and the desired outcomes
- Go beyond the simple vital-signs measures and develop potentially game-changing, transformational measures

- Boil metrics down to the critical few from the trivial many
- Measure what needs to be measured, not just what is easy to measure
- Integrate measures horizontally and vertically
- Translate raw data into actionable wisdom

Let's explore these in turn.

Use both results measures and in-process measures

Results or output measures track process outputs: the 'ends'. They are, typically, the QCD measures (quality, cost and delivery performance). They are of course vital, but by themselves are insufficient to achieve process control, as they have two significant limitations:

- They are **lag measures**. By the time the information is available, it's too late to alter the course of events in that cycle. As the old saying goes, if you can see it, it's too late. Wise we may be, but only after the event, and we have to wait for the start of the next cycle to make changes. It's like a football coach trying to manage by looking at the results in the Sunday paper. It's hit-and-miss, slow, expensive, and lacks the agility necessary to deal adequately with fast-changing situations
- A results measure – for example, profitability – may be an aggregate measure, determined by a range of variables in the preceding process(es), and so **cannot be *directly* managed**
- The key to effective management is to understand and skilfully influence the means: the factors that drive the results

So, in-process or lead measures add a number of invaluable things to management capability. They:

- Identify where, when and how to intervene (what levers to pull)
- Allow problems to be prevented (think of aircraft pre-flight checks)
- Allow problems to be spotted and solved early (often in real time through visual management)
- Ensure that the process is balanced (i.e. each stage is running at the same speed and on time) and flows smoothly so that there are no bottlenecks or delays
- Include input measures that track the quality and availability of the resources the process depends on

Define both the desired outputs and the desired outcomes

It is also important to distinguish between outputs and outcomes. Outputs tend to be narrowly defined and short-term. Outcomes are the wider and longer-term impacts on all stakeholders. For example, one could posit that the output of the oil industry is oil and money, while the outcomes include heat and power for homes, industry and transport, but also negative externalities such as pollution and climate change.

For ethical reasons, organisations committed to Business Excellence generally take both outcomes and outputs into consideration.

Develop transformational measures

In business processes, as with human health, measures of 'vital signs' are fundamentally important, but don't have the scope or detail to help you build toward excellent performance. We must also, therefore, discover what metrics have the greatest potential to transform our thinking, approach and results.

Here are some simple examples of transformational measures at different levels:

- At results level, measuring cash-out to cash-in time can radically change the way that people look at cycle time and inventory
- At a process level, measuring cost of poor quality (COPQ) – the cost of defects, rework, refunds, replacements etc. – can have a transformational effect on a team's approach to quality and continuous improvement
- At a strategic level, transformational measures are typically intangible factors such as talent, leadership, employee relations, culture, agility, resilience, ethics and sustainability. Transformational measures can also come from rethinking traditional measures. For example, measuring and managing customer relationships (how they feel) instead of customer service (your technical response levels)

The critical few

> 'Businesses that do not scrupulously uncover the fundamental drivers of their units' performance face several potential problems. They often end up measuring too many things, trying to fill every perceived gap in the measurement system. The result is a wild profusion of peripheral, trivial or irrelevant measures. Amid this excess, companies can't tell which measures

> *provide information about progress toward the organisation's ultimate objectives and which are noise. If companies can't prove basic causality, they certainly can't determine the relative importance of the measures they select. And not being able to weigh these measures makes it hard to allocate resources ... for example, does a dollar invested in product development yield a higher return than a dollar spent on customer retention. ... [and] particularly when bonuses are at stake they place greater weight on measures whose targets they know they can hit.' (Christopher D. Ittner and David. F. Larcker)*

There lurks in measurement the potential for the classic error of not knowing exactly what to measure, and so measuring everything and ending up with a confusing muddle of data that we're not entirely sure how to respond to. It is therefore important to whittle measures down to the 'critical few' from the 'trivial many'. This means for:

- **Strategic measures:** Finding those that are pivotal in building organisational capability and competitive advantage

- **Results measures:** Identifying those that are crucial to the operation of the business. These are typically designed around the SQCDE measure (safety, quality, cost, delivery performance and colleague engagement)

- **In-process measures:** Finding the factors that are crucial to control any particular process (which are unique to each process and must be determined by those working with it)

Measure what needs to be measured

Two bits of useful advice here are, first, don't just measure what is easy to measure. Easy but meaningless metrics will only create distraction and unnecessary work. As Seth Godin advised; 'If you're not going to use the data to make a decision, don't waste time on it.' Second, if you need to get it right, you need to find a way to measure, review, manage and improve it. So don't exclude something just because it is difficult to measure. Sometimes there is no quick, simple or objective way to measure something important but, as Deming argued; 'Everything that should be measured can be measured in a way that is superior to not measuring them at all.'

There are two related factors to consider: accuracy and objectivity. Regarding accuracy, Deming helpfully pointed out that 'measures only need to be accurate enough to serve the purposes for which they were intended,' that 'an inexact answer is almost always good enough' and that we should aim for 'appropriate accuracy'. Regarding objectivity, getting a credible numerical measure of, for example, colleague engagement sounds like it could be expensive and almost impossible to track in real time. But a simple check-in with people at the daily meeting provides information with enough accuracy and validity on which to base some immediate constructive intervention.

Integrate vertically and horizontally

Measures should form an integrated and coherent system that reflects the interconnectedness and holistic nature of the business as an entity, and which focuses on the performance of the whole, rather than the individual parts in isolation. Measures therefore should be integrated both horizontally and vertically.

Horizontal integration ensures focus on the end-to-end performance, coordination and improvement of the whole value stream which runs through the business cross-functionally, through various departments, reflecting the interconnectedness and interdependence of multiple elements across the organisation. This helps to identify and address cross-functional performance and coordination issues, and fosters understanding of how the system works, and how it can be managed and improved as a whole. It also actively promotes cross-functional dialogue and collaboration, and reduces the dangers of misalignment such as loss of synergy, conflict and process sub-optimisation.

Vertical integration ensures alignment of vision and strategy with daily operations. The measures of process performance should be aligned with the corresponding departmental measures, which in turn should be aligned with the top-level success measures set out in the strategic plan.

Translate raw data into actionable wisdom

As Deming pointed out; 'Without theory, there is no way to make sense of the information that comes to us in an instant.' In other words, performance information, by itself, no matter how fast, detailed or frequent, tells us little and does not allow us to be confident that the action we take on the system will work. We need therefore to develop the capability to move quickly and accurately from:

- **Data:** Raw and unprocessed, to derive useable...
- **Information:** By extracting the important signals, themes and patterns hidden in the data, to give it meaning and relevance, to derive...

- **Knowledge:** An understanding of what factors drive performance, which then allows us to develop...

- **Wisdom:** Deep, rich insight that allows people to consistently take informed and timely action

The key is to understand how the process that we are trying to measure works. This involves first identifying the main process steps, key variables and interactions. The next step is to experiment by attempting to improve the process through making changes guided by structured problem-solving tools and thinking. Thus a coherent picture is gradually built that allows, as Dean Spitzer put its, an 'increasingly deeper understanding that leads to progressively better actions that drive desired results'.

Getting the psychology right

The success of measurement depends, ultimately, on the degree to which people constructively engage with it, which in turn depends on the psychological relationship with measurement that is created. This includes:

- The issue of control (who controls what and how)

- The purpose: is the measure designed to produce actionable information, or is it a target?

- What happens when a performance issue is identified

Performance control, not people control

In Business Excellence, the aim is to get the process under control – i.e. operating in a way that is stable, predictable and repeatable – and for this control to be achieved through informed and intelligent effort by the people responsible for it. This differs markedly from the historical command and control approach which aims at the control of people by passing down orders, standards, targets, processes, rules and specifications, and checking up to ensure compliance. In the latter, it is assumed that:

- The processes designed by managers and experts are perfect and will not need any significant in-flight adjustment or ongoing improvement, regardless of what conditions they might have to operate under

- Even if they did, the people who work in the process cannot be trusted to do this

These assumptions are generally viewed as incompatible with the realities of mid-21st-century business, where there is a need for a fast and effective response to handle the ongoing rapid and unpredictable change.

In Business Excellence, using measurement to provide insight rather than oversight, to enable and empower people to control the processes that they are responsible for, is not regarded as a nice-to-have but rather as an essential; not only for motivation, but also to foster the engagement necessary to navigate the array of challenges and opportunities, and to optimise the process in the short and longer term in the face of them.

Measure vs target

A measure is of course just an aspect of system performance that we choose to track. And there are two main ways to use any measure:

1. To provide information about the performance of the process so that the people responsible for the process are able to manage effectively through various challenges, and to continuously improve it over time. The big upside of this is a more controlled process and sustainable improvement. A potential downside is that, without the right level of professional discipline, it will drift into complacency and mediocrity. Hence the need for genuine leadership rather than just supervision

2. As a target. This can open up a number of potential dangers:

   a. If a stretch target is set (i.e. one beyond the current capability of the system) and people have the right continuous improvement tools, training and time to incrementally improve process capability to achieve this (working smarter), all may be well. In the absence of a structured and disciplined approach to improvement, however, or where the stretch target is to be hit immediately, it can only be achieved by throwing more time, effort or resource at it (working harder). This of course may be an occasionally necessary last-resort measure, and powerfully effective. But it is also unsustainable, potentially risky and not the right approach for delivering sustained, stable, and continuously improving, world-class performance. Pushing people and the system into overdrive may get increased output, but if the trick is pulled repeatedly, the result is likely to be system degradation (of tools, equipment, resources etc.) and damage to motivation as people get disillusioned, switch off or leave

b. With a target that people perceive to be unrealistic, unfair or exploitative here may be gaming, including passing on faulty work, or sales people promising unmeetable timescales or offering unauthorised discounts

c. Target fixation: with a singular focus on, for example, productivity, people may, deliberately or otherwise, take their eye off performance on other metrics, such as quality, safety or colleague engagement, and consequently tip the process/system out of balance

d. Another risk is that, when they reach the target, people stop, despite many opportunities for improvement remaining – for example, in further reducing error rates or cycle time. It is called continuous improvement for a reason!

Using measures as information allows us to optimise the whole system as a coherent piece and improve it sustainably in the longer term and ongoing. Using measures as targets can narrow the focus down to maximising a restricted range of measures in the short term and inadvertently hobbling the capability for ongoing system-wide improvement.

Measures and values

What gets measured also generally reflects what matters to the business, and there are choices here that have implications for colleagues' engagement and motivation (and for business reputation more widely).

Top-line measures that are narrowly focused on shareholders' short-term interests (for example, profitably) tend not to be especially motivating to colleagues, particularly if it is felt that their own and their customers' interests will be secondary, and will possibly be deliberately undermined in the pursuit of them.

In contrast, where organisations include, in addition to profitability, a wider and more balanced set of aims, then generally, people are more likely to engage. These aims might include to provide a meaningful, valued service to clients and a positive work experience for colleagues, as well as concern for the wider social and environmental impact of the business.

Criteria for an effective measurement system

To summarise the above, an effective measurement system should comprise a suite of measures that work together to give comprehensive insight and provide timely, actionable information without being overwhelming. Individually and collectively, measures should be:

- **Aligned** with the purpose of the process and the Voice of the Customer (VoC)
- **Relevant:** Measuring the factors with the highest leverage and that mean something to the people involved
- **Useable:** Help the people responsible for the process to take informed action
- **Up to date and timely:** Measured and made available at the right time (as close as possible to real time) to allow in-flight adjustments to be made to keep performance on track
- **Visible:** Directly accessible
- **Accurate and reliable**
- **Sufficient:** Measuring all the key factors in the process
- **Vertically aligned:** Part of a cascade from strategic to operational
- **Horizontally aligned**, end-to-end, cross-functionally, along the value stream

In addition, at a strategic level, measures should:

- Track the development of competitive capabilities – the intangible assets that do not appear on your balance sheet, such as agility and ability to innovate
- Reflect changing customer expectations of quality, cost, delivery, experience etc.

How to achieve this

A good place to begin is to define the purpose of the process and the results we want from it – the 'results measures' which collectively comprise the Voice of the Process (VoP). These need to reflect and be aligned with the results the customer wants, the VoC.

Then there's the painstaking task of methodically uncovering the most useful process-measures – the critical few factors that allow us to have the biggest influence on the value-creating process. Following these steps may be useful:

- Look at the process and identify, as well as you can from existing practice, data, experience and intuition, which variables appear to have the greatest impact on the desired results

- Develop a plan for gathering data on these variables (it may be best to use a manual data collection process first, then automate) and figure out how best to make the information available so that it can easily be understood and acted on
- Use this data to facilitate visual management and inform the daily meetings where issues can be identified and plans for addressing them made
- Establish a fuller understanding of causality and the points of greatest leverage by running safe-to-fail experiments aimed at improving the processes
- Once you have identified the key variables, decide on the best way to gather, analyse and present the information to allow clear and effective monitoring and to keep meetings short, relevant and action-focused. One approach is to use the traffic light system and exception reporting. Green denotes 'acceptable performance', amber 'outside acceptable levels, but remedial action in progress', and red 'cause for concern'. This means that there is no need to discuss every measure at every meeting, only the red items, allowing the time to be used more productively on addressing high-leverage issues

This same broad approach can be used at all levels, from strategy to front-line operational processes.

In all of this, remember:

- There is time and cost to measurement systems, so they need to deliver and be lean (deliver right-first-time quality, and deliver exactly and only what is required)
- The benefits of interactivity. The degree to which people understand and buy in is likely to mirror the degree to which they are involved
- The development of measures is emergent: we usually begin with measures that are provisional and based on educated guesses. Greater validity and accuracy comes in time through learning about their use in practice
- Perfection in this is neither possible nor necessary; causality will never be fully understood
- Transforming both the social and technical aspects of the management system is something of an art form. It will take time and much trial-and-error learning to get right. And it is never done. As with everything else, further honing and improvement will be ongoing
- Start small (and localised). Establish good practice and then build out from there. Trying to change multiple parts of a management system at the same time is mind-bogglingly complex and risky.

CHAPTER 10

THE STRATEGIC MANAGEMENT SYSTEM

Introduction

The strategic management system is a set of processes that macro-manages, engages and empowers the whole organisation. It:

- Monitors externally for developments in markets, technology, legislation etc.
- Analyses the internal and external perspectives and develops an appropriate strategy for taking the business forward which addresses both:
  - The maintenance and ongoing improvement of the business fundamentals
  - Breakthrough activities aimed at achieving significant improvements in business-critical areas
- Oversees, monitors, manages and improves the operational management system – which in turn manages the core processes

Figure 10.1 illustrates where the strategic management system fits into the wider picture.

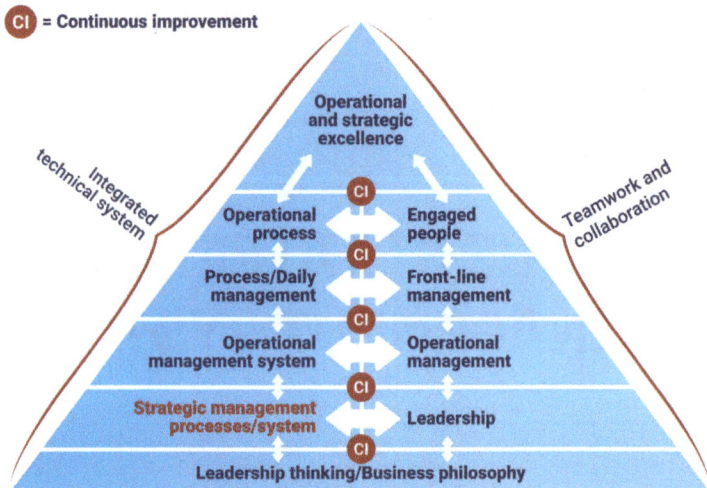

Figure 10.1: The strategic management system in context

Hoshin Kanri: overview

The best model on which to base the design of the strategic management system is Hoshin Kanri. It is based on the principles of Business Excellence (including colleague involvement and continuous improvement at all levels) and promotes, supports and embeds those principles throughout the business.

The premise of Hoshin Kanri is that optimising organisational performance is best achieved by ensuring that everybody in the organisation is working toward the same end, fully understanding the long-range direction and goals of the organisation, working to a coherent, measurable plan and actively involved in defining, implementing and reviewing that plan.

Hoshin Kanri is a cyclical process which begins by assessing external factors, internal capabilities and current performance, deriving from the analysis of these a vision and a strategy setting out high-level objectives for breakthroughs and business fundamentals for the next three to five years. These objectives are then cascaded down through the organisation and translated into achievable actions.

The cascade process involves discussion between different levels and functions in the organisation to ensure that the plans are feasible and widely understood, and to secure ownership of them and genuine commitment to them. The plans at each level are measurable, allowing for ongoing monitoring, learning and adjustment, and for the development of ever-deeper understanding.

Structured problem-solving methods are used at all levels to involve and engage people and help them to implement the breakthrough plans and consistently manage and improve daily operations.

Finally, there is an ongoing review process which, like the cascade process, actively and constructively engages colleagues at all levels in identifying, understanding and resolving issues. The performance of the strategic management system is itself subject to review as part of this process, to assure that it too is continuously improved.

The purpose is not only to set and implement strategic goals, but also to empower people to take responsibility for measuring, analysing and understanding situations and creating, implementing and managing plans for improvement, and to develop a level of comfort, familiarity and a natural sense of professional discipline with measurement, feedback, accountability, responsibility and continuous improvement.

Why it matters

The primary advantage of an effective strategic management system is the alignment of goals, both within each level of the business and between the levels, as illustrated in Figure 10.2.

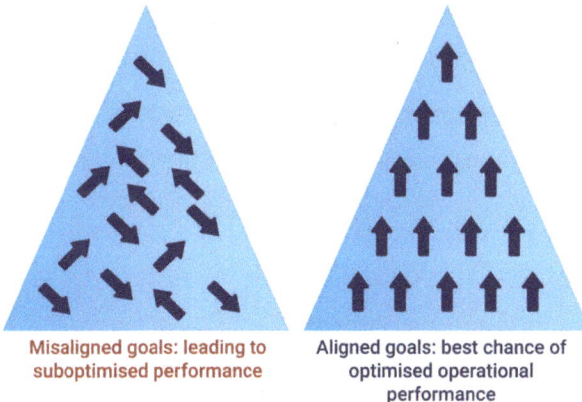

Misaligned goals: leading to suboptimised performance

Aligned goals: best chance of optimised operational performance

Figure 10.2: Alignment of goals

A properly designed and run strategic management system ensures that an organisation remains focused, aligned, and able to consistently and reliably deliver excellent operational performance and achieve its long-term strategic goals. It sharpens and maintains focus on critical issues and gets everyone on the same page, clear about the 'big picture' and their part in achieving it. Ensuring that operational and strategic management are both effective and integrated with each other helps to maintain consistent performance and continuous improvement, and prevents the avoidable crises that stem from complacency or drifting out of touch with changing market conditions.

It also helps to avoid problems frequently encountered with strategy processes, including:

- Poor structure, leadership and implementation
- Unclear vision
- Measures that are narrowly focused on financial outcomes and inadequately focused on performance drivers
- The involvement only of senior managers with little, or no, meaningful wider engagement
- The selection of strategic goals based more on emotion and opinion (feelings, hunches, gut instinct) than on facts and data
- Arbitrary and unrealistic targets
- Strategic planning not being integrated with operational planning (so adequate time and resource to deliver strategic goals is not planned)
- Action-planning lacking focus, visibility, measurability, coherence and alignment
- No systematic review of action plans to drive and manage implementation

The strategic ratchet

A well-designed and well-run strategic management system allows the business to systematically and consistently ratchet up sustainable improvements in capability and performance. As shown in Figure 10.3, each year the previous baseline is consolidated through effective operational management and then built on by:

- Operationally-led continuous improvement activities
- Breakthrough activities (which require a tight and focused process for choosing strategically important priorities and implementing them effectively)

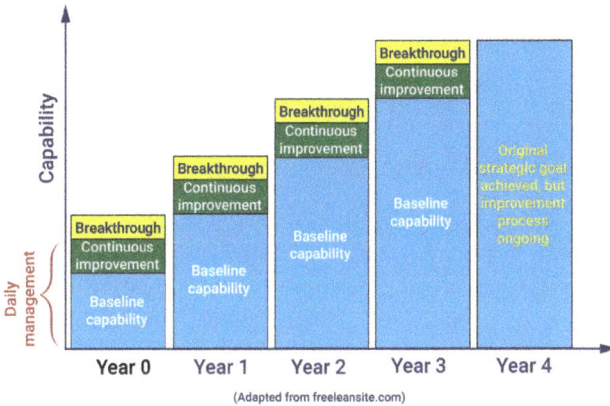

Figure 10.3: The strategic ratchet

Getting the right responsibilities, actions and behaviours at the right levels

As Figure 10.4 illustrates, an effective strategic management system helps to achieve the right balance in how time is spent in the business between:

- **Operational management:** Setting up and resourcing processes properly, and monitoring process performance to pick up and address problems early so as to stay on track to achieve target

- **Continuous process improvements** from opportunities identified through ongoing process performance reviews and colleagues' ideas

- **Significant strategic breakthrough improvements** in capability aligned to the emerging threats and opportunities

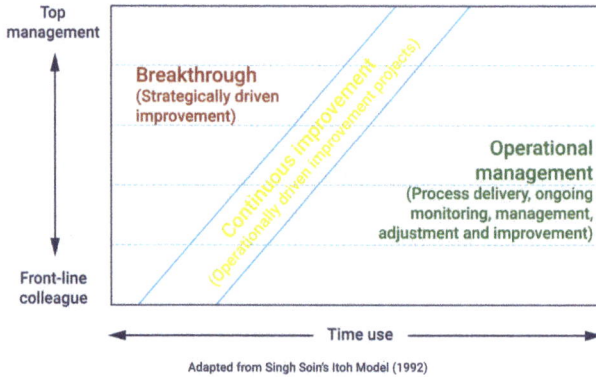

Figure 10.4: Structuring time at different levels

It also highlights, structures (and makes measurable) responsibilities at different levels:

- **Colleague-standard work:** Delivering operational performance and contributing to the monitoring, management and improvement of the process
- **Manager-standard work:** Leading daily management and kaizen in their area (monitoring and improving local processes), and also contributing to breakthrough projects
- **Leadership-standard work:** Overview of the operational management system: planning, implementation, review and support of breakthrough projects; and the integration of both across the organisation

As operational management is improved to control and improve the efficiency of operational processes, the time saved can be invested in improvement activities, which will make a significant impact on success in the long run. Thus, a well-designed and -run strategic management system helps the business to progressively increase its capability for change and improvement.

A strategic management system built on Hoshin Kanri principles is simply indispensable for any business committed to Business Excellence. It is what integrates and coheres all the other management and operational processes into an optimised system. As David Hutchins points out, without it we may get no further than 'a rudderless set of tools and techniques that will only produce results on a hit-and-miss basis, with many of the improvements of dubious value'.

Strategic management system: structure, content and process

We'll explore the model in two steps: first, its underpinning structure, and then the process that brings it to life and sustains it.

Structure and content

The structure comprises (as illustrated in Figure 10.5) three main blocks with various elements:

1. **The overall mission, purpose, values, success drivers and success measures:** This captures the essence of why the business exists, what success looks like and how that success will be achieved

2. **Long-term/strategic plan** (typically looking three to five years ahead). This comprises:

   - **Business-as-usual objectives:** These relate to the performance and improvement of any core processes that have not been singled out for significant 'breakthrough' improvement. These processes are to be managed and subject to ongoing, local, continuous improvement to maintain the required standards of performance

   - **Waterline objectives:** Goals that relate to upgrading any capability that is currently below the 'waterline' of minimally acceptable capability, or those that are likely to fall below that line in the time period

   - **•Breakthrough objectives:** Improvement goals in a small number of areas that will build new levels of useful capability critical to achieving the vision, but that are not yet at that standard. These will become the focus of breakthrough projects

3. **Annual operational (deployment) plans:** These plans specify how the waterline, breakthrough and the business-as-usual objectives will be delivered operationally. They are typically annual plans, capturing what needs to be achieved in the next year to stay on track to achieve the three- to five-year strategy and, ultimately the long-term vision. There may be several layers to this cascade, depending on the size and structure of the business. The plans become more concrete and specific as they cascade down through each department and any layers until the specific actions that will be taken at the front line on any given week/day are identified. These plans will include

measures so that progress and performance can be meaningfully monitored and managed.

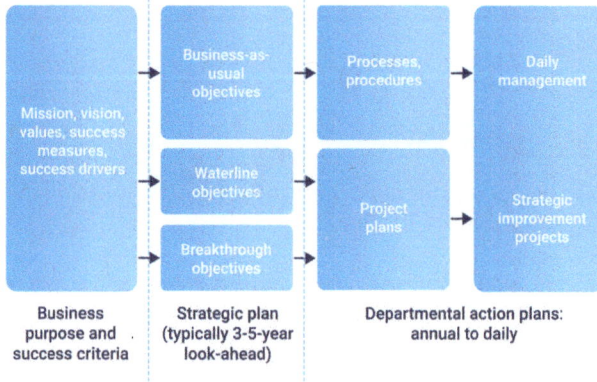

Adapted from Juhani Anttila

Figure 10.5: Strategic goals flowdown

Strategic management process

Now let's look at the process for developing the content, integrating the different elements, engaging people and locking the whole thing into a loop for continuous organisation-wide learning and improvement. The process is illustrated in Figure 10.6.

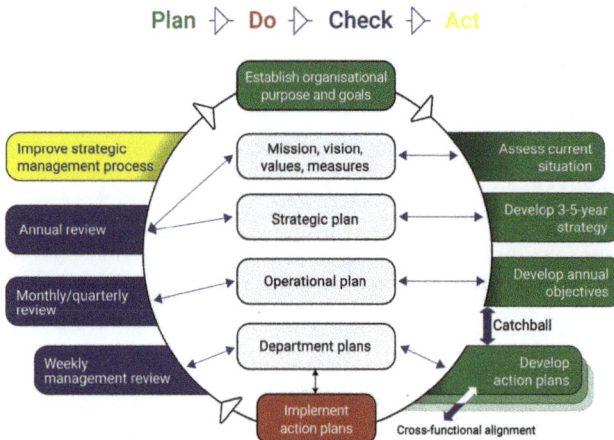

Figure 10.6: Strategic management process overview

Establish organisational purpose and goals

First, the overall mission, purpose, values, success measures and success drivers are established. These provide context for assessing the current situation and setting the strategic plan.

Assess current situation

The next step is to assess the current situation, both internal (existing performance levels and business capabilities) and external (market dynamics, competitor awareness, and social, technical, economic and political factors).

Develop the three- to five-year strategic plan

In this phase, the gap between the vision and the present position is established. If necessary, work is done to establish the root causes of any gaps. The waterline areas for improving capability over the next three to five years are then established and breakthrough objectives are developed. Objectives are also set for the performance and ongoing management improvement of the core processes that need to run consistently well and be subject to locally-driven continuous improvement.

Develop annual objectives

Next, the objectives are developed to deliver the progress that needs to be made in the next 12 months to achieve the three- to five-year breakthrough objectives. Goals also need to be set for the processes that will run as business as usual (though typically, these will be 'on rails' and will need little or no adjustment from the previous year).

This begins the 'deployment' part of the process. Implementation plans are developed which are focused, clear and measurable.

Develop annual departmental action plans

In this phase, goals for each area are identified and agreed. These are developed using 'catchball', a collaborative, iterative process where the objectives, timescales and resource requirements are discussed and agreed between the people involved at different levels (and also cross-functionally) to ensure the feasibility of the approach, understanding of it, and commitment to it.

The process repeats until all the objectives are translated into defined tasks and assigned to individuals.

Implementation

The plans are put into action.

Daily/weekly review

This local, ongoing monitoring and review is predominantly of the core processes and allows tactical adjustments to be made to deliver operational performance. Progress on breakthrough and waterline objectives will be included. Here, continuous improvement tools such as value-stream mapping and structured problem-solving are used to understand problems, and to identify and remove root causes.

Monthly review

The next tier of the review process involves structured monthly (or more frequent, if appropriate) reviews of action, progress, learnings and next steps. This maintains focus, discipline and appropriate urgency and allows any major problems to be highlighted, understood and addressed. These reviews happen at each level for which objectives have been set. The reviews are concise and focused, using the previously agreed action plans and measures to monitor progress. The focus is usually on exception reporting (where things are off target). At this level, as at every level, structured problem-solving tools are used to understand problems and to identify and remove root causes.

These reviews are likely to be part of the regular monthly operational review, but can be carried out as a separate strategic review if required/desired.

These reviews are 'rolled up' through the organisation (to mirror the earlier downward cascade processes) to maintain coherence and alignment.

Annual strategy implementation review

The annual review looks at action, progress, results, current position and learning points on both the:

- Strategic plan, and
- The strategy planning, deployment and implementation process

Lessons from both can be taken forward into the following year's process.

As with the monthly reviews, annual reviews are focused and concise, using the previously agreed action plans and measures, incorporating all the review information rolled up from reviews earlier in the cycle.

Improvement of the strategic management system

Any lessons, either on strategic content or the strategy process, are learned and adjustments made prior to the start of the next cycle to ensure that this process, like every other process in the business, continually improves and evolves.

Then the whole process repeats...

Two final, crucial points to underline about this process:

1. The importance of the catchball process in shaping, communicating and gaining commitment to the goals, and in involving everyone at appropriate points in the review process. This is where the engagement and empowerment of people happens. It is this that enables people to contribute fully to the delivery of operational goals and the improvement (both strategic and ongoing) of processes. This type of adult and focused dialoguing is what develops the culture that supports Business Excellence

2. It standardises the strategic management process, and is a crucial aspect of leader-standard work. This gives senior managers a defined process to work with, which can help to improve the consistency and quality of their contribution

Getting started

'If you want dramatically better results, you have to do something dramatically different.' (Michael Cowley and Ellen Domb)

Building a strategic management system on the principles of Hoshin Kanri is a necessary journey for leaders and organisations that are committed to optimising their business and achieving Excellence.

This is a long-term exercise. It involves an iterative process of continuous, patient development over many years. It takes a lot of work and commitment. It is a genuine test of leadership vision and skills.

So it's not for everyone. But if you've read this far, it may well be for you.

So, where to start? This will be different for every organisation. Much will depend on the organisation's state of maturity and readiness, including:

- Existing leadership style
- Understanding of Business Excellence principles, tools and techniques (at all levels)
- Existing culture and levels of colleague engagement, and trust between different functions and different levels
- Sophistication of existing operational management processes, process mapping and structured problem-solving

The journey typically begins with a period of assessing readiness and laying foundations (what Cowley and Domb called the 'zero'th year'). This would typically include:

- Engaging the senior team and establishing/building understanding and commitment
- Conducting an initial strategic assessment of internal capability and external factors
- Strengthening the daily management processes to ensure sufficient operational stability, and to create time for breakthrough activities
- Picking one important breakthrough issue to use as a pilot
- Involving people in rolling out the pilot
- Reviewing and establishing the plan for the following year

The first year is likely to be chaotic, disjointed and frustrating. The second year may see the first full-scale pilot, but again, may be run as much for learning as for immediate and direct progress (though there will be both).

There is no shortcut past this 'storming' phase as new ways of thinking and interacting, and new tools and approaches, are trialled, improved and bedded in. However, getting past this in itself builds a key organisational competence; the ability to progressively build a coherent system, and above all, to display the steady professional discipline to both maintain, and continually build and improve. This sheer stick-to-itness differentiates the business and its leadership from the many who 'tried everything and nothing seemed to work'.

For anyone not in the position to drive this organisation-wide, it's possible to start on a limited scale in your area, prove the concept and see what you can influence from there.

Finally, bear in mind that embarking on this journey is, for most businesses, a 'good-to-great' endeavour. There is no immediate crisis. The time is there to build and improve steadily. As Hutchins points outs, 'The business has survived okay – what we are trying to do is increase the rate of performance improvement and ... on a steeper curve than the competitors.'

CHAPTER 11

CREATING A STRATEGY MAP

Introduction

The strategy map is an essential leadership tool as it provides a clear, complete and coherent picture of how the business operates as an interconnected system, and of what drives success. It promotes intelligent and successful decision-making, fosters colleague engagement and supports sustainably strong and continuously improving performance.

The benefits of developing a strategy map

A clear strategy map helps to:

1. Manage performance effectively, because it:

    *   Identifies the factors that drive performance and how they interact and affect each other

    *   Helps differentiate between the genuinely important 'vital few' activities and the distracting noise of the 'trivial many'

    *   Maintains a balance between short-term operational performance and long-term capability building

2. Improve cross-functional teamwork, coordination, cooperation and joint problem-solving by helping people understand how the business works as a system and how each part affects the others

3. Enable people to understand how their actions affect success. This in turn helps to engage and empower people, getting them more actively involved and taking greater responsibility for managing and improving performance

4. Ensure consistent, sustainable performance. The strategy map reduces the risk of focusing too much on one thing, knocking the system out of balance and undermining overall performance: For example, the drive for increased profitability can compromise quality or customer satisfaction, introducing failure-driven demand and associated inefficiencies, creating tensions and frustrations, and undermining sustainable financial performance. (Similar distortions can occur in the other direction by focusing too much on quality, customer satisfaction or employee satisfaction.) While it is tempting to push a system hard in one direction for short-term results, there's always a price to pay. No system works well for long when it's out of balance

Without the clear, comprehensive picture a strategy map provides, strategy and goal-setting is likely to be too loose, subjective and 'gut feel', driven by too narrow and rigid a set of measures, and characterised by focus jumping from one thing to another, rather than a consistent, balanced focus on all relevant factors being maintained.

Creating your strategy map

A generalised example is shown in Figure 11.1.

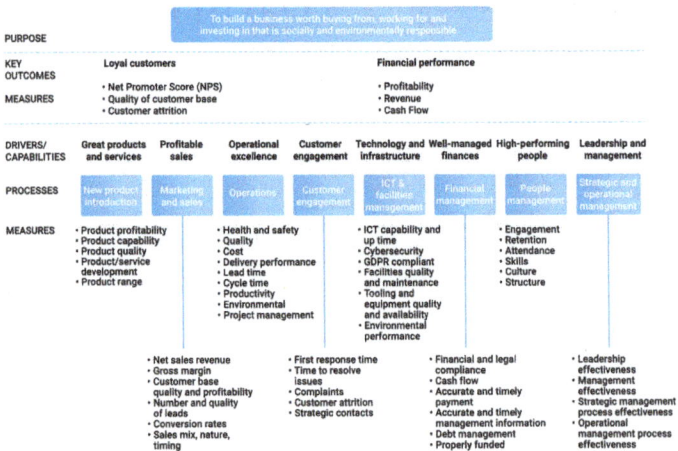

Figure 11.1: Top-level strategy map

There are four steps in creating a strategy map:

1. Identify your overall purpose
2. Identify your key outcome measures
3. Identify the core capabilities that underpin success
4. Derive from this the key measures that will allow performance to be managed and improved consistently and sustainably

Let's look at each of these in turn.

Step one: Identify your purpose

This is typically a short sentence or paragraph capturing the top-level criteria for success. For example:

> *'Toyota will lead the future mobility society, enriching lives around the world with the safest and most responsible ways of moving people. Through our commitment to quality, ceaseless innovation, and respect for the planet, we strive to exceed expectations and be rewarded with a smile. We will meet challenging goals by engaging the talent and passion of people who believe there is always a better way.' (Toyota Purpose Statement)*

Step two: Identify your outcome measures

The next step is to identify what the most important outcomes are for your business. Commercial organisations, for example, will need to have loyal customers and strong financial performance to survive and thrive. Increasingly, organisations also include social and environmental outcomes as being central to their purpose.

Step three: Identify the core capabilities

Next, identify the core capabilities and the underlying processes that the business requires if it is to deliver the desired outcomes. These capability areas will typically include:

- Great products and services
- Profitable sales
- Operational excellence

- Customer engagement
- Technology and infrastructure
- Financial management
- High-performing people
- Leadership and management

Step four: Derive the key measures

The final step is to decide how success in each area will be measured. The measures will be used to drive the agenda of management meetings – making them more productive, and cutting down time spent, by focusing everyone on the highest-leverage topics.

Now that you have a good first working draft of your strategy map, it is ready for the 'catchball' process which will hone the plan, develop the next-level plans and develop the concrete action plans, and in the process, inform, involve and engage colleagues at all levels across the organisation.

Summary

The strategy map helps to identify what success means, the factors that underpin performance and how these can be reliably measured. This allows meaningful goals to be set for strong operational performance, continuous improvement and strategic breakthroughs.

CHAPTER 12

THE OPERATIONAL MANAGEMENT SYSTEM

Introduction

The operational management system is the central nervous system of the business. Figure 12.1 locates it in the context of the wider business systems.

Figure 12.1: The operational management system in context

In Business Excellence, the purpose of the operational management system is to provide holistic and coherent management of all aspects of business operations. To:

- Ensure that every colleague has the right information, tools, materials and training to do their job successfully

- Measure process performance so as to provide useable and timely information to manage and improve the processes

It plans, schedules, measures and manages performance throughout the business, across all functions and levels. It aligns and coordinates the operational processes to create a coherent, coordinated, balanced, thriving operational system.

The operational management system is, as the name suggests, a system: a collection of processes with a clearly defined purpose, customers, inputs, outputs and process steps, and regular and consistent timing.

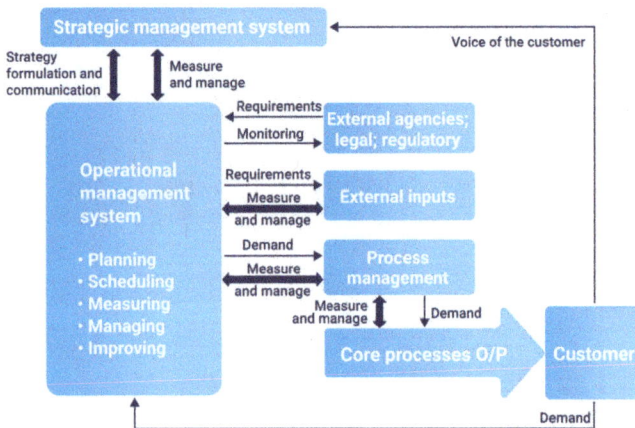

Figure 12.2: Interactions within the technical system (in detail)

As shown in Figure 12.2, the operational management system does two interrelated things. It:

1. Operationalises the strategy, translating the goals into practical action
2. Oversees the routine functions and activities of the organisation to ensure that the strategic goals are successfully achieved

Its core activities are planning and scheduling operational activity, measuring and managing operational performance and overseeing the ongoing improvement of the underlying process.

The operational management system interfaces with the strategic management system, with the strategic plan providing overall direction, specific goals and, through the values it sets out, setting the tone for how its activities will be pursued.

The operational management system feeds into the strategic management system information regarding both operational performance and underlying capability, to highlight any need for tactical course corrections and to ensure that an accurate picture of internal status is available as part of the strategic review process.

The operational management system also interfaces with the process-management processes across the business. These oversee the design, management and improvement of the front-line operational processes. From the operational management system will come information regarding the nature, timing and volume of demand for each process, and also information pertinent to the parts of the strategic plan which that part of the operation is responsible for.

Measures of the performance of each operational process will also be fed back to the operational management system, discussed by the managers responsible and, where appropriate, relevant course corrections will be made (both operationally and strategically). Short-term performance information and data aggregated over weeks, months and the full financial year will be fed back to the strategic management system to inform discussions between the relevant managers on any required course corrections, and to also inform the next round of the strategy process.

The operational management system also interfaces with the providers of various external inputs (which could be anything from stationery suppliers to agency workers to long-range weather data). Requirements are communicated to external suppliers, and performance is measured to inform ongoing dialogue and coordinate effective action.

Finally, to ensure that the company's operations are compliant with all legal standards, and with any standard the business subscribes to voluntarily (for example, Investors in People), there is communication with the relevant agencies to understand requirements, monitoring of the business by those agencies and dialogue to guide and support successful compliance.

Key factors

There are three key factors in getting the operational management system right: its design, management and improvement.

Design

- Identifying the operational management system owner
- Designing the operational processes as a coherent system end-to-end along the value stream
- Designing a set of measures that are integrated and aligned end-to-end
- Vertical alignment of management processes and measures
- Designing the management forums (including meeting structures and agendas)

Ongoing management

- Overall organisational load (capacity and demand matching)
- Overall organisational planning and scheduling
- Overall organisational resourcing
- Ongoing monitoring and management of end-to-end performance
- Engaging managers and ensuring cross-functional teamwork
- Compliance: ensuring the operational processes comply with regulatory requirements

Continuous improvement

- Oversight, coordination and monitoring of operational process improvement
- Implementation, oversight, coordination and monitoring of strategic improvement projects
- Continuous improvement of management processes
- Improvement of the improvement tools, training and processes

Let's look at these in more depth.

Design

Operational management system process owner identified

The owner of the operational management system must first be identified – the person responsible for the overall design, management, improvement and performance of the system as a whole. This would normally be the CEO (or equivalent). While this step may sound obvious, not every organisation (or CEO) recognises that ownership of the operational management system is a central part of the CEO role.

Operational processes designed as a coherent system end-to-end

The network of interdependent operational processes should be mapped and configured as a coherent operational system that is aligned, coordinated, and integrated horizontally to create optimal flow of work end-to-end along the entire value stream.

Designing an integrated and aligned set of end-to-end measures

As discussed in Chapter 9, each operational process should have its own in-process and output measures, which are designed as part of the local process management. A key purpose of the operational management system is to oversee and cohere these and ensure that these local measures:

- Are fit for purpose- that they accurately measure the performance of each process and the value stream overall
- Support flow and balance along the value stream
- Align the operational processes as a whole with the VoC

Vertical alignment of management processes and measures

The operational management system should also be designed to create vertical integration and align operational goals with the strategic direction and goals of the business. Within the strategy process, both business-as-usual and breakthrough goals should be set as part of the annual plan, derived from the longer-term plan (typically covering five years). Both should be cascaded to operational management level and then to process level as appropriate.

The activities necessary to achieve the breakthrough goals should be incorporated into the operational planning and woven in with the business-as-usual activities to ensure that they are scheduled, appropriately supported and resourced, and cascaded down to process management level. Reports and other relevant signals and information should also be fed back up through the different levels of the operational management system and to the strategic management system so that both ongoing performance, and progress toward the breakthrough goals, can be monitored and reviewed.

Management forums mapped (including meeting agendas)

The forums that comprise the operational management system should be mapped out to ensure that they:

- Coordinate and align the operational process end-to-end
- Coordinate and align the goal-setting, planning and reporting processes vertically
- Have a clear purpose, and agendas that are focused on the relevant process measures

We'll show you an example map shortly, but first let's look at the management control and reporting system (MCRS) - the network of plans, reports, measurement tools and discussion forums that manages operational performance. This is the core of the operational management system.

While the description below is, necessarily, a simplification, it outlines the key considerations and MCRS design principles.

Management control and reporting system

The MCRS is a performance management loop of forecasting, planning, execution, control, reporting and review, as shown in Figure 12.3.

Figure 12.3: Performance and control loop

Forecasting, planning, controlling and reporting will of course run across a range of timeframes: monthly (or a longer interval), weekly and daily (or a shorter interval), and every business will have to create its own unique approach, tailored to its own needs.

Figure 12.4 shows a generic, simplified example of MCRS design.

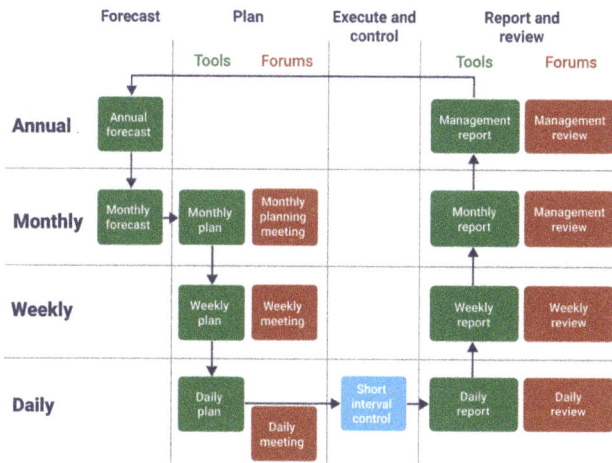

Figure 12.4: The management control and reporting system

MCRS design begins by considering the Forecast column. A business will usually have an annual forecast for activity, revenue, costs and profitability, which will flow down to a monthly forecast, adjusted to reflect changing circumstances.

The monthly forecast informs the monthly plan and schedule, which are discussed and agreed at a monthly capacity planning meeting. The monthly plan can then be distilled down into a weekly plan, which can be discussed and agreed at the weekly planning meeting. Similarly, the weekly plan can then be distilled down into a daily plan, which can be discussed and agreed at the daily planning meeting, completing the Plan column.

Drift is best managed with regular checks and corrective action. Figure 12.5, which looks at how the frequency of review and control points influences the degree of performance drift, illustrates this.

This is short interval control (SIC). Checks will be carried out at least daily and, depending on the nature, requirements and speed of the process, as often as hourly.

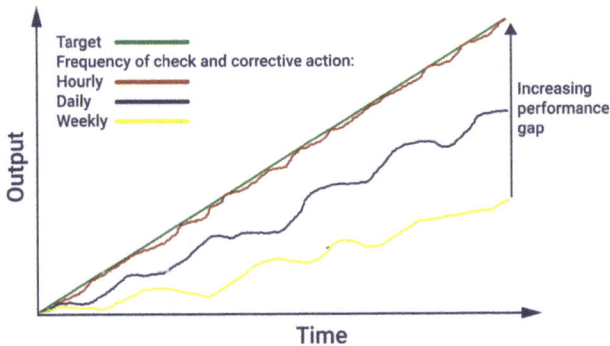

Figure 12.5: Control frequency and performance drift

Report and Review begins with a daily report compiled from the SIC information which is discussed at the daily reviews. A typical agenda for this would be:

- **Planned:** What output was planned for this interval?
- **Actual:** What was the actual output?
- **Variance:** What was the nature and size of any difference? What is the cumulative difference for the day?
- **Reason:** Why did the difference occur?
- **Action:** What will be done to get back on track and prevent recurrence?

General status from the daily front-line meetings is communicated upward. Current or emerging problems that may affect the local process, other adjacent processes or the system overall are flagged up and, where appropriate, escalated for appropriate decision, action or support.

The information from the daily reports is compiled into the weekly report. The results are discussed at weekly meetings to identify any relevant corrective or process-improvement actions.

The process repeats, chunking up to monthly management reports and the annual summary report. These are discussed at the respective meetings, where progress against financial goals is also tracked.

The design of the MCRS must incorporate all the functional requirements to support operations, including planning, procurement, material handling and dispatch.

Completing the management and communication system map

To these core MCRS forums must be added the other forums essential for engaging people and running the business, including health and safety meetings and continuous improvement meetings. The full management system map may look something like Figure 12.6.

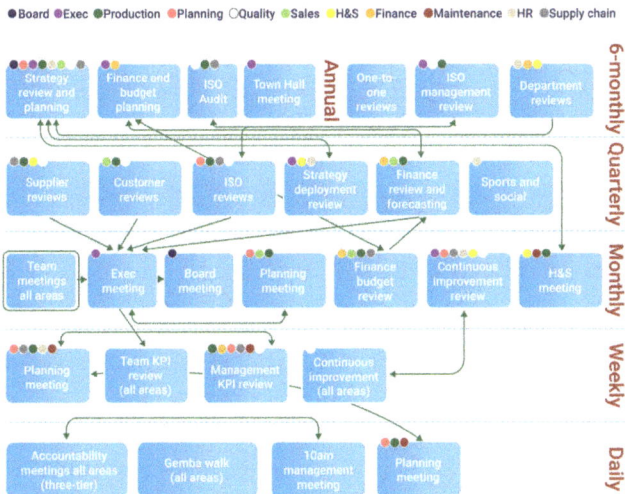

Figure 12.6: Full management and communication system map

Finally, each forum should have a clear purpose and agenda, focused on the relevant process measures.

Ongoing management

Overall organisational load managed (capacity and demand balanced)

A key purpose of the operational management system is to create smooth end-to-end flow and to keep the process consistently operating within capacity, avoiding both a) the inefficiency of running with overcapacity, and b) overloading the process, creating stresses and strains that in the short term lead to quality problems, and in the long term to the degradation of both the process and colleague engagement.

This means that, first, demand must be understood: its volume, nature and frequency over the short and longer term. And second, the capacity of the process end-to-end, especially any potential bottlenecks or points of failure, must be understood, again over the short and longer term.

The two must then be compared and the resultant information used to either manage demand or adjust process capability. Or, more likely, both.

This is of course, in practice, highly dynamic – part art as well as science. It's always better to err slightly on the side of short-term inefficiency rather than risk long-term process degradation with frequent incursions into overload.

Overall organisational planning and scheduling

Following on from the above, overall operational activity should be planned and scheduled to match customer demand and process capacity, to deliver on-time-in-full without inefficiency or overloading the process.

And of course, the planned targets, activities and timings must also be communicated clearly, systematically and in good time to each of the local processes, to facilitate proper execution and coordination across the organisation.

Overall organisational resourcing

The core processes must be properly resourced with the right quality and quantity of raw materials, tools, equipment and consumables, and the right number of people with the right skills. All of which need to be in the right place at the right time.

A key purpose of the operational management system is to oversee and coordinate the network of internal processes that feed each other, and the processes for bringing in external resource and making it available at the right time. This must be planned not just on a daily or weekly basis, but across the full business cycle, looking ahead to anticipate changing seasonal requirements or other circumstances likely to affect the nature or volume of demand.

Ongoing monitoring and management of operational performance

When the appropriate measures and forums have been designed, these should then be used in a systematic and disciplined way. The various meetings should be run on time, to an agenda, in a constructive fashion. As we will discuss in Chapter 13, in the short term, the flow of work and all key measures and other vital signs should be consistently monitored at the front line to allow for responsive course-corrections. A key part of this is the daily standup – the short start-of-day meeting. This forms tier one of the three-tier system (as discussed in Chapter 2).

Engaging managers and ensuring teamwork

The management process should empower, engage and support people to deliver excellent and continuously improving performance. At a technical level, this includes providing:

- Effective operational processes, tools and resources
- Performance data that can be used to understand and improve how the processes are performing
- Forums that give people the opportunity to discuss performance, problems and ideas in an environment focused on constructively resolving problems and free from fear and blame

Equally important is effective people management to ensure that each individual has:

- Clear expectations
- Appropriate skills and knowledge
- Ongoing coaching
- Accountability for personal attitudes, behaviour, performance and results
- Empowerment to solve problems, including continuous-improvement training, and appropriate time, authority and support

There should also be accountability at all levels of management, from top managers to those on the front line, to ensure that all of the above is being done in a systematic and disciplined way, and where it is not, that it is picked up, corrected and the underlying reasons identified and dealt with.

Finally, the design and operation of the system should actively foster, promote and support teamwork across the organisation and between the different levels.

Compliance: ensuring the operational processes comply with regulatory requirements

The operational management system should ensure that all operational processes are compliant with regulatory requirements, including health and safety, financial and any industry-specific requirements. The measurement system should be designed to track key regulatory requirements and to ensure that these are built into the agendas at the appropriate forums, to highlight them to the colleagues responsible. Similarly, the measurement system should track the setting and completion of actions to address any shortfalls in this area.

Continuous improvement

Oversight, coordination and monitoring of end-to-end process improvement

While the continuous improvement of the local front-line processes is the responsibility of the front-line managers and teams, it is necessary to monitor and manage these at operational management level to avoid the dangers of:

- Working on the wrong priorities, e.g. speeding up a process that is not a bottleneck
- Changes in one process (e.g. making cost reductions) having unintended negative consequences in others (e.g. taking quality below an acceptable standard)

There will also be cross-functional improvement projects that require cooperation and coordination between different functions, and that need to be monitored and managed at operational management system level.

Ongoing improvement projects should also be monitored in a structured, disciplined way, at operational management system level, to ensure that they get completed on schedule, and that the benefits are incorporated via appropriate process changes and become standard practice.

Implementation, oversight, coordination and monitoring of strategic improvement projects

Within the strategy process, breakthrough goals should be set as part of the annual plan, derived from the longer-term plan. These should be cascaded to each area as appropriate.

The activities necessary to achieve the breakthrough goals should be incorporated into the plan and woven in with the business-as-usual activities to ensure that they are scheduled and appropriately supported and resourced. Central to this is making sure that the people involved in each breakthrough project are given adequate time and are all available at the same time as each other, to allow the project to progress on schedule.

As with the locally generated continuous improvement projects, the progress of the breakthrough projects should be monitored as part of the regular review process.

Continuous improvement of management processes

As with every process, the operational management system must itself be reviewed and systematically improved. Ways should always be sought to improve the quality, speed, accuracy and efficiency of information-gathering, analysis, presentation and decision-making, and the communication of those decisions.

The quality and efficiency of the various discussion forums should also be periodically reviewed and improved.

Though primarily the responsibility of the local process owners, the improvement of both the front-line processes and process management in each area should also be monitored and tracked at operational management system level.

Improvement of the improvement tools, training and processes

The continuous improvement process, tools and training must themselves be analysed and improved, for two reasons:

- To allow improvement opportunities to be identified and exploited faster and better
- To be able to successfully tackle increasingly more complex and subtle problems

Summary

The shape that the operational management system needs to take will be influenced by the unique mix of factors specific to a business, including the product or service, the tasks involved, the people, and technology. And, like any set of processes, it too will be subject to both short-term adaptation and longer-term improvement.

CHAPTER 13

PROCESS MANAGEMENT

Introduction

Process management is the monitoring, management and improvement of the front-line operational processes, to ensure that they deliver what the customer needs, right first time, every time with maximum efficiency and minimum waste. Figure 13.1 locates it in the context of the wider business systems.

Figure 13.1: Process management in context

Process management is itself, of course, a process. It has:

- **A clear purpose** (described above)

- **Customers:** The operational process and the people who work with it

- **Inputs:** Information from the operational management system and performance data from the operational process
- **Outputs:** Information and communication to manage demand, to trigger the input processes and to coordinate with the wider operational management system
- **Process steps:** For the gathering, analysis, presentation and discussion of information, and for making and communicating decisions
- **Takt time:** Regular and consistent timing

Figure 13.2 illustrates in greater detail how process management operates.

The performance and capability of the process (the VoP) is monitored, as is the VoC (data on customer service and satisfaction), along with information regarding process demand (what is required of the process and when) which is fed in from the operational management system. The resulting analysis is then shared and discussed with:

- Front-line colleagues, to inform any in-flight adjustments or process improvements
- The operational management team, to Inform any required alterations in demand, resource adjustments or other course corrections

Process management also coordinates activities with the various input processes which supply the required material, information, tools, people and sundries to the front-line process.

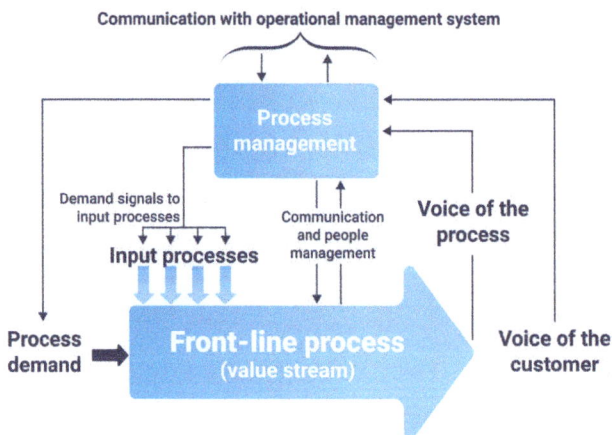

Communication with operational management system

Process management

Demand signals to input processes

Input processes

Communication and people management

Voice of the process

Process demand

Front-line process (value stream)

Voice of the customer

Figure 13.2: Process management and the front-line processes

Key factors

There are three facets of process management: design, ongoing management and continuous improvement.

Design

Before an operational process can be successfully managed and improved, its fundamental structure must be sound. This means:

- Identifying the process owner
- Mapping the value stream and designing (or redesigning) it to flow smoothly
- Designing the process measures and aligning them with the overall business strategy and with other processes
- Designing the management forums (e.g. daily, weekly and monthly meetings)

Ongoing management

This includes:

- Load management (matching capacity and demand)
- The planning and scheduling of process activity
- Resourcing
- Priming and maintaining
- Ongoing performance monitoring and management
- Engaging, managing and developing people
- Ensuring compliance with regulatory requirements

Continuous improvement

This includes:

- Ongoing kaizen improvements
- Identifying, capturing and prioritising improvement opportunities
- Tracking and managing ongoing improvement projects in a disciplined way
- Training colleagues in the fundamentals of structured problem-solving

- Making process-improvement specialists available to help with more complex problems
- Improving the process management process itself

Let's look at these in more depth.

Design

Process owner identified

The owner of the process must first be identified - the person who will be responsible for the overall design, management, improvement and performance of that process.

This is particularly important where the process is used across different shifts and where there is a risk either of no one taking responsibility for the overall integrity and improvement of the process, or of different people changing the processes in different ways, creating inconsistencies and misunderstandings.

Value stream designed for smooth flow

The next step is to make sure that the fundamental structure of the process is sound. This creates a capable, fit-for-purpose process and establishes a standard that can subsequently be improved upon.

The best way to do this (initially at least) is to map the process using a length of brown paper and coloured sticky notes. Here's a quick overview of the suggested method, known as value-stream mapping . (We'll talk about this more in later chapters, and a fuller explanation is provided in Appendix B.)

First, record who the process owner is (shown in orange) - the person responsible for its design, management and improvement. The 'SIPOC' tool then provides a useful structure for the main body of the map.

Along the top, (shown in red) map out the:

- **Suppliers:** List the main suppliers who are feeding information, tools or material into the process
- **Inputs:** List the information, tools, equipment, raw materials or sundries that the process requires

- **Process steps:** Set out the process steps, from left to right, in sequence from beginning to end (shown in yellow)

- **Outputs:** List the value-added products, information, services or experiences that the process is intended to create

- **Customer(s):** List the customer(s). Bear in mind that the customer(s) may be internal (the adjacent process steps), or a retailer, rather than the end user

- With the core structure mapped out in this way, you can capture further useful detail on the success criteria for the process (shown in blue), including:

- The **Voice of the Customer (VoC)** – what the customer has actually asked for. This is usually defined by some kind of measure of quality, on-time delivery and service (and cost if it's the end customer)

- What you understand the **purpose** of the process to be. Ensure that it aligns with the VoC. (They don't always, which makes this a crucial check)

- The **measurement** criteria that are used to monitor process performance, again ensuring that these are aligned with the VoC and process purpose

Next, capture information relating to the management of the process (shown in green), including:

- The operating plan for whatever look-ahead period is available, and how this both manages and balances the **demand** on the process (its timing, frequency and volume) and the **capacity** of the process (the factors that influence capacity and their current status)

- How and when the process is being monitored and managed

Finally, 'pain points' (not illustrated) can be noted, where there is significant waste or where there are other improvement opportunities.

Mapping the process in this way makes the key parameters visual, allows the process to be designed to flow smoothly, and enables significant problems to be identified and addressed.

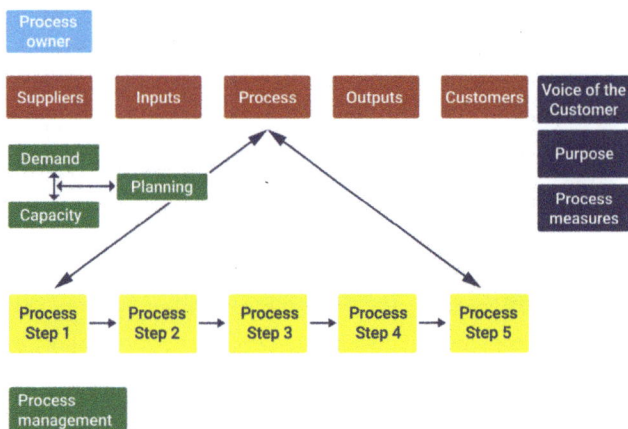

Figure 13.3: Process map template

Designing process measures and aligning them with strategic direction and other processes

'Make your workplace into a showcase that can be understood by everyone at a glance. In terms of quality, it means to make the defects immediately apparent. It means that progress ... measured against the plan, is made immediately apparent. When this is done, problems can be discovered immediately, and everyone can initiate improvement plans.' (Taiichi Ohno)

Properly designed measurement is necessary to enable people to manage and improve the process both operationally (in real time), and strategically (over the longer term).

Output measures and in-process measures are both required. Output measures show overall process performance. They are likely to include the QCD measures of quality, cost and delivery performance. They are lag measures, showing the results of actions already taken.

In-process measures are real-time measures that allow problems to be spotted and corrected in real time. These lead measures also provide an early-warning system for potential problems. They ensure better control of the process and more accurate prediction of process performance.

Measures should be:

- Aligned with the requirements of the internal or external processes or customers they supply
- Aligned with the strategic direction, measures and goals
- Relevant and sufficient (conveying useful information, and measuring all key factors in the process)
- Useable, providing information that can be easily understood and acted on immediately by those working in the process
- Accurate and up to date
- Visible – immediately accessible

The latter point is particularly important as it facilitates 'visual management': making available information that shows the process status and allows people to intervene. There are two levels:

- Live data – for example, warning lights or floor markings that indicate where material, equipment or people should (or should not) be. This level of visual management allows problems to be identified clearly and early by the person doing the job, enabling them to see directly and immediately when something is off course and to make informed, autonomous decisions and take timely and effective action
- Charts and graphs displayed in comms zone areas that show medium- to long-term patterns and trends, and that can be discussed and acted upon at the regular scheduled meetings where longer-term improvements are made

Management forums designed and scheduled

The forums where performance will be discussed need to be designed and scheduled. This would typically include:

- The daily stand-up meeting: A short and focused five- to ten-minute meeting at the start of each day, the purpose of which is to review the previous day, to draw any lessons, and to plan the day ahead and anticipate and prevent potential problems. (These are also referred to as 'Tier 1' meetings: the first tier of the daily performance update process.) The agenda would typically be:
  - **Planned:** What output was planned for this interval?
  - **Actual:** What was the actual outcome?

- **Variance:** What was the nature and size of any difference? What is the cumulative difference for the day?
- **Reason:** What led to the difference?
- **Action:** What will be done to get back on track and prevent recurrence?

- A gemba walk: The manager walking the work area (or otherwise checking with people) to ensure standards are being maintained, spot any potential problems, and be visible and available
- Weekly and monthly meetings: To look at trend data, to identify themes and patterns in process performance, and to look ahead to the next period
- One-to-one reviews and ongoing coaching

Each forum should have a clear, defined purpose and agenda so that it can be run in a disciplined way to a consistent standard, so that best use is made of the time.

Ongoing management

Load management (matching capacity and demand)

Process demand should be monitored (i.e. its nature and timing/frequency), both in the short and longer term. Process capacity must also be assessed and understood and the two compared to inform the planning, scheduling and resourcing of the processes, so as to either manage demand or adjust process capacity. Or both.

This sets up the process to flow smoothly and ensures that it consistently operates within capacity, neither lapsing too far into inefficiency due to over-resourcing, nor being driven into overload. (Alternatively, when not done well, it sets up the process to run unevenly and inefficiently.)

Within the strategy process, both business-as-usual and breakthrough goals should be set as part of the annual plan, derived from the longer-term plan and cascaded through to each process as appropriate. The activities necessary to achieve the breakthrough goals should be incorporated into the planning and woven in with the daily activities to ensure that they are scheduled and appropriately supported and resourced. The impact this has on process capacity must also, therefore, be factored in.

Planning and scheduling process activity

Following on from the above, operational activity, with the strategic implantation activities woven, in should be planned and scheduled to match demand and process capacity, so as to deliver on-time-in-full without inefficiency or hitting overload.

The activities necessary to achieve the strategic breakthrough goals should also be incorporated into the planning and woven in with the daily activities to ensure that they are scheduled and appropriately supported and resourced.

Targets, responsibilities and timings should be communicated clearly, systematically and in good time to the people who run the process, to facilitate effective coordination.

Resourcing

The process must be properly resourced with the right quality and quantity of raw materials, tools, equipment and consumables, and the right numbers of people with the right skills, attitudes and motivation. All of which need to be in the right place at the right time.

Priming and maintaining

It is also important that the process is properly set up at the start of each day/ shift so that work can begin without unnecessary distraction or delay, and that it is maintained to a standard that allows efficient working with no avoidable downtime for the full day/shift.

This includes taking a systematic and disciplined approach to:

- 5S (Sort, Set in order, Shine, Standardise, Sustain) – having everything that is necessary to accomplish the task in working order, and in the right place
- TPM (total productive maintenance) – maximising equipment availability/ uptime and overall equipment efficiency and effectiveness

See Chapter 14 for more on 5S and TPM.

Ongoing performance monitoring and management

Once the measures and the management forums have been designed to an operable standard, they must then be run in a systematic and disciplined way to monitor and manage the process.

The flow of work, key measures and other vital signs should be consistently monitored in real time, to allow for:

- Course corrections, adjustments, running repairs and fine-tuning
- Problems to be spotted and fixed before they escalate
- Deeper-seated process limitations to be identified

The Tier 1 daily stand-up meetings should run every day, on time and to agenda, and the wider and longer-term patterns and themes should be picked up and addressed at weekly and monthly meetings, which should also be run in a disciplined fashion, on time and to agenda.

Engaging, managing and developing people

The management process should empower, engage and support people to deliver excellent, and continuously improving, performance. At a technical level, this includes providing:

- Effective operational processes, tools and resources
- Performance data that can be used to understand and improve how the processes perform
- Forums that give people the opportunity to discuss performance, problems and ideas in an environment free from fear and blame and focused on constructively resolving problems

Equally important is effective people management to ensure that each individual has:

- Clear expectations
- Appropriate skills and knowledge
- Ongoing coaching
- Accountability for personal attitudes, behaviour, performance and results
- Empowerment to solve problems, including continuous-improvement training, and appropriate time, authority and support

Ensuring compliance with regulatory requirements

The process manager should ensure that the process is compliant with regulatory requirements, including health and safety, financial and any industry-specific requirements, by remaining aware of these and building them into the process goals, standards and reviews.

Continuous improvement

The aim of process improvement is to increase the capability, stability, coherence, flexibility and resilience of the process, to underpin long-term success and sustainability.

There are two broad directions from which improvement opportunities might come: those that are identified locally in the course of operating and managing the process, and those cascaded down from 'breakthrough goals' set as part of the strategy process.

Within the locally identified opportunities, there are some for which there is a fairly clear and obvious solution that can be acted upon immediately – the kaizen improvements. There are others for which there is no immediately obvious solution or root cause. These require fuller investigation using structured problem-solving.

The key criteria for well-managed process improvement therefore includes the following.

Fast implementation of kaizen improvements

Ongoing kaizen improvements (obvious quick fixes) should be flagged up to the process owner and implemented immediately.

Improvement opportunities identified, captured and prioritised

The performance-improvement opportunities that are identified through the various management forums should be captured on an opportunities list, systematically prioritised and worked through using a structured problem-solving methodology that allows the root causes of problems to be identified and removed.

Management of the improvement projects

The activities and resources necessary to complete the locally identified improvement projects and to achieve the breakthrough goals should be incorporated into the planning and woven in with the business-as-usual activities to ensure that they are scheduled and appropriately supported and resourced.

Central to this is making sure that the people involved are given adequate time, and are all available at the same time as each other, to allow the project to progress on schedule.

All improvement projects should be monitored in a structured, disciplined way to ensure that they are successfully completed on schedule, and that the gains are sustained by embedding the improvements into standard practice.

Colleagues trained in structured problem-solving

All front-line colleagues should be trained in structured problem-solving techniques so that they can be empowered to systematically and successfully work through the major improvement opportunities in their area.

Expert support available when required

Expert support from process-improvement specialists should be available to coach and assist teams when they face more complex issues, to help resolve the issues and simultaneously enhance the team's expertise.

Improvement of process management

The approach to process management should itself be reviewed and improved; in particular, how the measures and the discussion forums work in practice. Ways should always be actively sought to make them more effective and, where possible, simpler and leaner.

Summary

Process management is the design, monitoring, management and improvement of the front-line operational processes, to deliver what the customer needs, right first time, every time with maximum efficiency and minimum waste.

This requires three things:

- Getting the fundamental design of the process right
- Taking a systematic and disciplined approach to measuring and managing the process in real time, as well as identifying and addressing longer-term trends and patterns across weeks and months
- Capturing and prioritising the improvement opportunities identified and systematically addressing them using structured problem-solving

CHAPTER 14

PROCESS EXCELLENCE

Introduction

A business's success depends primarily on its ability to achieve the quality, cost and delivery performance that will create loyal customers; customers who return enthusiastically, bring more business and recommend it to others. And this requires consistent excellence in both the processes that deliver customer value, and the processes that feed and support them.

Figure 14.1: Operational process in context

Processes are the building blocks of sustainable success

Delivering what the customer wants – be it a product, a service, software, valued knowledge, information, or a particular experience – requires a process; a series of steps that have been proven to consistently deliver the promised outcome.

Processes are the building blocks of the system required to deliver sustainable high performance, and those processes need to be effective, individually and collectively.

What process excellence means

Process excellence is the design, management and improvement of processes so that they:

- Create loyal customers
- Produce the right thing, in the right amount, with the right quality, at the right cost, at the right time
- Do this without waste (unnecessary steps, delays, resource or expense)
- Be stable and in control, producing results that are predictable and repeatable
- Have the resilience and flexibility to handle fluctuations in demand and other short-term challenges
- Have the agility to adjust to longer-term strategic change and to remain relevant and competitive

Why process excellence matters

The quality of the process is the biggest single influence on results. People's contribution is determined by the quality of the processes they work in. It is impossible for colleagues to consistently outperform a poor process.

> *'If your business requires heroism from your employees to keep customers happy, then you have bad service by design. Employee self-sacrifice is rarely a sustainable resource.' (John Seddon)*

Effective processes allow front-line colleagues and managers to do their jobs efficiently and well, and to produce controlled, predictable and sustainable results. Without effective processes, even the best people will struggle, there will be problems with the basics, and people will become frustrated and disengaged. Managers, instead of managing the people and the process, will then be at the mercy of process problems (and the people problems created by the process issues), and will be less able to achieve consistent performance and results.

Process excellence is the bedrock of Business Excellence and is therefore of strategic importance. So understanding it, and being able to lead and engage colleagues in designing, managing and improving processes, is a fundamental management responsibility.

Achieving process excellence

Throughout the business, starting at the top, achieving process excellence requires the right:

- Mindset – understanding of, and commitment to, the overarching principles, key concepts and standards
- Understanding of the practical tools and techniques that allow for successful implementation
- Discipline and accountability, built into the management system, for the design, management and improvement of the process

A key part of the mindset in process excellence is aiming for perfection. While perfection is unlikely to be achieved, the constant striving for improvement will achieve excellence and provide an advantage over competitors that are not similarly committed. The danger in failing to set the business's sights on perfection is that this can breed a 'good enough' mentality that opens the door to complacency and its attendant dangers.

Key aspects of process excellence

Process excellence is an expansive topic, and in some businesses it can be highly technical and specialised. Here, however, are 14 core, interrelated factors that are relevant to just about every process in every organisation:

1. Understand value (VoC)
2. Build in quality and minimise the cost of poor quality (COPQ)
3. Flow
4. Evenness
5. Operate within capability
6. Dynamic resilience
7. Balance
8. Standardise
9. Prime and maintain
10. Resource effectively
11. Error-proof
12. Pull
13. Measure
14. Manage and improve

Let's explore these in turn.

1. Understand value (VoC)

'Value' is the utility or benefit the customer wants from the product or service and is willing to pay for (i.e. what they want it to help them to do, achieve or experience). Value is defined by the customer, but many businesses *assume* they know what the customer wants, rather than developing a continually evolving, clear and accurate understanding. There are significant dangers in this.

So the first step in process excellence is to understand the VoC in sufficient depth and clarity.

From this, the purpose of the process should be defined. Purpose is also often assumed rather than properly thought through. For example, the purpose of a contact centre could be defined either as 'to achieve KPIs for high productivity and minimum call duration', or as 'first-time call resolution'. These are very different definitions of purpose and have significantly different implications for how the process would be designed, measured and managed – and, ultimately, its performance.

When the purpose has been defined, measures should be designed and aligned with the VoC. Misalignment between the VoC and the process measures can have serious consequences. At the extreme, we could have a process that is efficiently producing a technically excellent offering with perfect quality, on time, that insufficient numbers of customers actually want.

Finally, it is important to remember that it is not just the needs of the end-user that must be understood. Our direct customer may be an intermediary, such as a reseller. And most internal processes serve internal customers – the people who perform the next step in the value stream.

2. Build in quality – minimise the cost of poor quality (COPQ)

Defining quality

External quality means providing what matters to the customer and delivering it or making it available when required. But quality does not necessarily mean the highest technical specification. The customer may not require something 'gold-plated', but may instead value ease of use, longevity, durability, reliability, low running costs, compact size, or value for money. Adding features, or over-engineering any feature that the customer didn't ask for, doesn't want and won't pay for, constitutes waste rather than value.

As Seth Godin observed, 'When enough features are added, the system breaks down and fails.' More options and functionality may add little or no value, can make it harder to navigate and to access the small number of key things the customer wants, and create more opportunities for failure.

Internal quality (or process quality) is ensuring that the internal processes are capable of efficiently and effectively delivering what the customer wants, right first time, every time. And continually improving, and adapting to evolving customer needs.

Quality is free

Philip Crosby argued that, far from being expensive, quality is free. That, indeed, it pays to get process quality right, because, self-evidently, it is cheaper not to have to put things right that shouldn't have gone wrong in the first place.

Figure 14.2 illustrates his point:

- The activities required to prevent problems add up to less than 15% of operating costs. These include all the value-enabling activities of effective planning, organising, communication, developing people, process-priming, process management and process improvement. (All the activities that are the essence of working smarter, not harder)

- If we 'save' time and money by not doing these activities, and instead allow avoidable problems to occur, the costs of inspection and fixing problems that are detected internally, or found by customers, amount to around 40% of operating costs. (Not including what Deming called the 'unknown and unknowable' costs associated with getting disgruntled customers back onside or replacing those that don't come back)

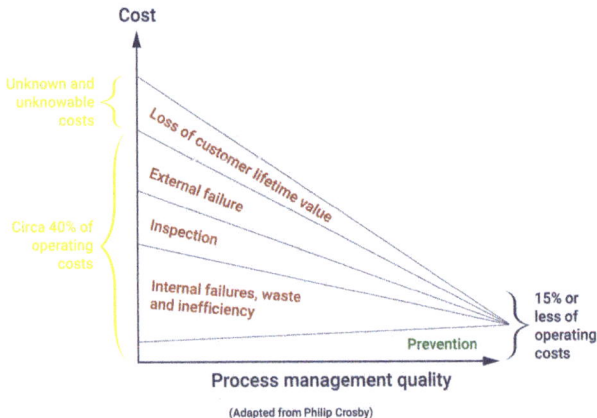

Figure 14.2: Cost of quality

So improving internal quality reduces costs because a job done right first time requires only the planned time, activity and materials (customer-driven demand), not the additional labour and material costs associated with rework and recovery (failure-driven demand).

But if a manager has either no concept, or no measure, of COPQ, it is likely to remain unnecessarily high, unmanaged and problematic, limiting the success of the business.

Build in quality

There is a crucial distinction between:

- **Quality assurance,** with its emphasis on 'after the event' inspection and compliance, and

- **Quality improvement,** with its emphasis on 'before the event' process quality and improvement

The key point is that quality cannot be 'inspected in'. Inspection, as invaluable as it is in many circumstances, can only catch problems once they have occurred. Quality must be built in. That is, the process must be designed, measured, managed and improved to achieve and maintain the capability to consistently deliver the level of internal and external quality required.

3. Flow

What flow is and why it matters

Flow is the movement of work (material and information) through the value stream, with the output from one part of the system matching the input requirements (timing, volume and form) of the next.

Flow is a crucial concept in process excellence. The aspiration is perfect flow – for the work to move through the entire value-adding process end-to-end, within, and between, all process steps without error, delay or unnecessary processing: to get the in-process time to be the same as the processing time.

In other words, the process should do exactly, and only, what is required. And only when it is required to meet customer need. Any activity or resource use that does not add value is what Ohno called waste (or 'muda'); inefficiencies that create unnecessary cost, hassle or delay.

Waste damages processes and limits their potential because it reduces:

- Productive capacity, restricting business growth (because Productive Capacity = System Capacity minus Waste)

- Profitability (because Profitability = Price minus Cost to Make minus Cost of Waste)

- The time that managers spend on strategy, growth and improvement (because they are being sucked into dealing with avoidable operational problems and, consequently, managing one level too low)

The other side of the same coin is that the removal of waste is often the easiest and lowest-risk way to increase profitability, enhance productive capacity and free up management time for higher-leverage strategic activity.

Improving flow by removing waste

There are various ways to identify process problems and limitations. The best way of finding those with the biggest impact is to look for barriers to flow. Removing these offers the most direct and certain route to increased process efficiency and reliability.

Ohno identified eight categories of process problems that create 'waste' (or 'muda'):

1. **Defects/rework:** Work that does not meet customer requirements and has to be redone (failure-driven demand).

2. **Transportation:** Unnecessary movement of material or information, which takes additional time and effort and could increase the chance of something getting damaged, misplaced or forgotten about

3. **Inventory:** Excessive stock or work in progress

4. **Motion:** Unnecessary physical, mental or emotional effort (including stress) in accomplishing a task

5. **Waiting:** Idle time while people await information, materials or decisions. Or when the process stops, slows down or is otherwise disrupted for any reason

6. **Over-processing:** Unnecessary work, detail, features, paperwork, forms, checks, reports, bureaucracy etc. Value-add is activity that changes 'form, fit or function' in ways valued by the customer. But any activity that does something that the customer neither asked for, wants or will pay for is waste

7. **Overproduction:** Producing more volume (of anything) than there is known customer demand for

8. **Underutilised human potential:** People lacking core skills, not being sufficiently enabled or empowered to make decisions or contribute improvement ideas, or otherwise unable to develop or perform to potential

To Ohno's list we can usefully add the following:

1. **Space:** Excessive floor space, shelf space, desk space, or any form of inefficiently used physical capacity

2. **Energy:** Wasted heat, light, fuel, electricity, gas, battery power etc.

3. **Transaction costs:** The time and effort it takes to foster cooperation, collaboration and innovation. Low trust increases transaction costs, while mutual trust can lower them dramatically

Making value flow by removing the above wastes optimises process:

- Velocity
- Quality
- Cost
- Lead time
- On time in full (OTIF) performance
- Profitability
- Value-adding capacity
- Agility

Waste can be present for so long and be so resistant to repeated attempts at solution over many years that it becomes deeply embedded, systematic, invisible and normalised. Once this happens, it is ignored until there is a crisis – either an instantaneous failure or, more usually, a slow-motion disaster. So reviewing the above list regularly, and taking appropriate corrective action, is important if we are serious about excellence.

4. Evenness

Evenness is the dynamic matching of capability and demand, to maintain flow and consistently deliver to promise in the face of fluctuations in various internal and external factors.

Unevenness (or 'mura') can potentially result from anything that introduces variation. This includes:

- Anything that disrupts flow (i.e. the 11 wastes listed above)
- Fluctuations in demand, including:

  - The **nature** of that demand. For example, new work vs familiar work: complex work vs straightforward work: lots of small, bitty jobs requiring frequent changeovers vs a long uninterrupted run of doing one thing
  - The **timing** of the demand. Is there confirmation well in advance, or is it last-minute? Are there constant tweaks and modifications to order volumes or specifications?

- The **frequency** of demand. Do orders arrive at regular intervals (or to a predictable pattern), or irregularly and unpredictably, creating gaps, lulls and surges?
  - The **volume** of demand. Are volumes reasonably steady or are some orders significantly bigger than others, or some times of year significantly busier than others?
- The support processes failing to provide the right resources at the right time, every time (raw materials, tools, consumables, supplies or information required to do the job)
- Equipment unavailability or breakdowns; IT problems
- Inconsistencies in approach through a lack of agreed standards, existing standards not being followed, or people being asked to do tasks they haven't been trained to do
- Any process steps that could create a single point of failure (SPOF). For example, a specialist process that only one person is trained to do, which becomes vulnerable if that person leaves or is absent. Or if there is only one specialist machine, which is oversubscribed and has become a bottleneck
- The front end of the process not being managed well and, as a result, the later steps being rushed to make up for lost time and to 'get stuff out the door'
- Expediting – unplanned reactive changes by managers to schedules or activities

Unevenness, in turn, can create various problems:

- It can, in and of itself, disrupt flow
- Gaps or lulls will mean the process is over-resourced relative to demand, and thus inefficient and incurring irretrievably lost cost and productive capacity
- Surges in demand that take the process beyond its capability will drive the process into overburden (this is discussed further in the next section)

Evenness can be enhanced by:

- Matching process load to capability, by managing demand and skilful scheduling
- Ensuring staff are flexible – sufficiently skilled and confident to step into other roles successfully
- Ensuring that the process is properly designed, maintained and error-proofed (see the sections below on 5S, TPM and error-proofing)
- Increasing process flexibility to allow capacity to be adjusted to meet fluctuations in demand

Unless it is infinitely resourced, there are, inevitably, limits to process capability. The capacity, flexibility, responsiveness, reliability and resilience desired are all strategic choices that should be informed by the VoC. There are always trade-offs to be made and these must be recognised, understood and managed. If they aren't, we can end up in the fantasy world of offering the customer things that we can't deliver reliably and profitably, which will in turn create further dangers to long-term profitability, reputation and growth.

5. Operate within capability

Process capability is defined by a number of factors, such as the available time, space, tools, equipment, materials, and people's abilities (including their ability to work effectively under pressure or in adverse circumstances).

Overburden occurs when the demand on the process exceeds capability. It can result from unevenness tipping the process beyond the point where it can run efficiently and effectively. Or it can be a result of deliberate policy to push the process beyond its limits ('maximisation' – see sidebar). Organisations are particularly prone to this when:

- They take on work opportunistically without full consideration of its impact on process performance and profitability
- A strong focus on cost and productivity metrics creates a risk of under-resourcing processes and making them vulnerable to unexpected problems (e.g. absence) or increases in demand

When any process is pushed beyond capability and into overload (or 'muri'), it degrades and risks:

- Quality and delivery performance being adversely affected, increasing failure-driven demand (rework and complaint-handling costs)
- The impact on flow reducing process capability, creating a vicious circle of overburden that gets increasingly harder to escape
- Customer loyalty being adversely affected, making it harder to retain customers and maintain reputation
- Squeezing out value-enabling time, which means that planning, review and process improvement gets less time and attention. This increases the odds of further avoidable problems occurring, and leads to waste and inefficiency becoming embedded

- Needing to spend more time and resource than should have been necessary on process recovery to get things back on an even keel. Or, worse, if overburden is acute and does not allow enough time to reset the process to properly start the next cycle (day, week etc.), people will be repeatedly set up to fail

- Capability degradation:

  - Equipment being damaged because maintenance is missed, or because it is pushed beyond operating limits

  - People becoming fatigued and disillusioned by their managers' unwillingness or inability to manage effectively, leading to disengagement and an increased risk of conflict, grievances, disciplinary proceedings and the best people leaving, diminishing the pool of skill and experience available to the business

All of this can compound over time and lead to permanent degradation of systems, equipment and infrastructure, culture, trust, the skills pool, and goodwill. In the longer term, this can lead to the business:

- Gaining a reputation as being not sufficiently trustworthy to give repeat business to (far less new opportunities)

- Being progressively drawn into carrying excessive stock, equipment and other resources. Thus waste becomes embedded and institutionalised

- Being at significant risk to long-term competitive advantage if improvement capability does not exceed the rate of change in the business environment

All of this makes over-driving processes (either as policy, or through mismanagement) expensive, risky and self-defeating.

A high-performance system needs to run with a sufficient safety margin to protect it from overburden: a time and resource buffer that gives it enough capability to make in-flight adjustments and fix itself as it goes so that it can function optimally in the face of a range of challenges. This buffer is also crucial for long-term success, because it provides the time and space for people to work to increase the capability of the process and adapt it to ongoing changes and opportunities in the business environment.

The rule of thumb is that a well-designed manufacturing process should not be run at more than 95% of capacity (because of the risk that the inherent variation in any process could easily tip it over into overburden). Excellent service processes (with higher inherent variation in the nature and timing of demand) would typically not be run at more than around 80% of capacity.

It is possible to game the process for a while, by pushing it routinely into overburden and pretending that this is strong, ambitious management. But, for the reasons outlined, that approach will invariably be inefficient in the short term and hobble profitability and growth in the long run.

Learning to design, manage and improve processes for excellent, optimised performance is the only route to excellence.

OPTIMISATION VS MAXIMISATION

Optimisation

Systems have an optimum level of performance; the highest level that they can run at sustainably without tipping into overburden, and do that cycle after cycle.

Excellence is reaching and maintaining this level and, where possible and desirable, enhancing capability to increase it.

This requires not just building core performance capability, but also building in resilience; the ability to:

- Be disruption-resistant; to function in the face of a degree of difficulty
- Recover when disruption does occur

Resilience requires:

- An 'anticipate and prevent' mentality/practice to find and remove vulnerabilities before they are exposed
- A 'stop and fix' mentality/practice to spot and correct problems that do arise before they become disruptive
- Time and resource to provide the capability to:

  - Absorb/buffer enough of the inherent variation and foreseeable problems to stop them tipping the process into overburden
  - Detect and diagnose problems early and carry out running repairs
  - Improve the process to remove vulnerabilities

This does not mean adding expensive, redundant 'just in case' capability (which would just be waste). It is about assessing the nature and level of risk to the process, gauging the right amount of time and resource required to buffer it, and deploying this resource strategically and intelligently.

(Think of an aircraft engine. It needs to be, by design, as lean as possible; light, safe, efficient and reliable. So resilience is built in through design and build quality, problem detection capability and a maintenance schedule that replaces critical parts well before the end of their projected life cycle.)

Maximisation

Maximisation, theoretically, means pushing a process hard to extract every last drop of productivity. The reality, of course, is that not knowing or respecting the limits of the process may (or may not) squeeze out some measurable short-term performance gain, but will definitely increase the risk of process elements degrading, and risk tipping the process into a downward spiral of compounding lower quality, reduced output and, possibly, eventual system failure.

Maximisation is based on a 'break and fix' mentality. But waiting until a process breaks to intervene incurs:

- Immediate, irrecoverable loss of production (in ways that are potentially unpredictable and uncontrollable)
- Higher repair costs if what fails creates secondary consequences that would not have otherwise occurred (e.g. a vehicle engine is destroyed because the timing belt was not replaced as per the maintenance schedule)
- Collateral damage – to colleague morale, customer confidence and wider reputation

(There's also 'break and walk': allowing systems to degrade by failing to invest in resilience, using the 'saved' cash to inflate short-term financial performance figures and continuing to push systems until they are seriously compromised, in perpetual crisis or collapse. And then walking away and leaving the mess to someone else.)

The difference between strategies (as with all 'work smarter, not harder' issues) depends on the vertical development level of managers; their level of understanding of complex, dynamic systems, and their ability to foresee (and care about) the long-term consequences of their decisions.

6. Dynamic resilience

Following on from the above, the process should be resilient in the face of the challenges that the customer might reasonably assume they are paying us to deal with.

Dynamic resilience (maintaining resilience in a changing operational and strategic context) requires building:

- **Productive capacity:** As discussed above, the ability to routinely and consistently meet the customer's needs (including the projected variance in them) without hitting overburden

- **Recovery capacity:** The ability to restore homeostatic balance, i.e. to:

  - Routinely get the system reset, primed and ready for each cycle

  - Restore capability and get back on track after disruptive setbacks

- **Absorptive capacity:** The ability to identify, assimilate and deploy relevant new information, knowledge, concepts and ideas. (This determines how fast and well the business can learn)

- **Adaptive capacity:** The ability to maintain allostatic balance – to evolve thinking and practice to successfully respond to emerging threats and opportunities (and, indeed, to create new opportunities or lead the development of industry best practice)

7. Balance

A balanced process is one where each stage runs at the same speed, so that no steps are either a bottleneck or are waiting too long for material or information from preceding steps.

Poor balance can mean inefficiency in one part of the process and, simultaneously, overburden (and all the problems associated with that) in other stages of the same process, thus potentially affecting end-to-end flow and overall process quality, efficiency and cost.

8. Standardise

Why standardise

A standard is simply the best (or least worst!) way that the business has currently found to do something: the hymn sheet we're all meant to be singing off.

Capturing and consistently following standards is the foundation of the business's ability to reliably produce the best results it is capable of. Standardisation prevents the avoidable and unnecessary variation in the system that might result from things being done in different ways by different people. (Such variation, of course, contributes to inconsistent quality, inefficiency, unnecessary cost, unevenness and overburden.) Standardisation also makes it easier and quicker to share information, collaborate and coordinate.

Standardise what?

It is often useful to standardise:

- Tools and equipment (to reduce changeovers and to simplify training, maintenance and procurement)
- Methods (to reduce variation and facilitate better teamwork and multi-skilling)
- Training (rather than have people trained or assessed in different ways by different people)

Setting and evolving standards

It is important that the standards are relevant and accepted. To increase the chances of this, the people who use them should be involved in their design, implementation, monitoring and continuous improvement.

Finally, standards provide the baseline from which the value of any suggested improvements can be properly tested and proved. Any proposed improvement must make a measurable, meaningful and sustainable difference to one or more of the key process measures, such as quality, cost, delivery or safety, and must not have any significant unintended negative impact on the others.

9. Prime and maintain

To allow people to begin work immediately at the start of the day/shift and work effectively to the end of it, without unnecessary interruption, processes must be properly primed and maintained. This means ensuring the availability of tools and equipment that are in working order and able to last the full working day without downtime or loss of efficiency.

Two key disciplines that support this are 5S and total productive maintenance (TPM).

5S

5S ensures that everything necessary to do the job right first time without delay or interruption is available and accessible. It involves colleagues in maintaining an organised, efficient, safe and clean workplace. The five S's are:

- **Sort:** Dispose of the unnecessary. Bin what you don't need. Red-tag if not sure. Store other things that are not immediately needed
- **Set in order:** Ensure that there is a place for everything and that everything is in its place. Arrange things according to frequency of use
- **Shine:** Clean and check – ensure that everything is ready for use immediately
- **Standardise:** Having established the best way to sort, set in order and shine, make that a standard in itself. Communicate and manage it
- **Sustain:** Establish all of the above as habit and review and improve regularly

TPM

Total productive maintenance maximises equipment availability/uptime and overall equipment efficiency and effectiveness. This includes ensuring that tools and equipment are:

- Properly maintained
- Calibrated
- Charged/fuelled up
- Available where and when required

TPM and 5S are the basic disciplines upon which efficient performance is founded (what can people do if they don't have working tools and equipment?) While it is clearly common sense, it is equally clearly not common practice. Many businesses struggle every day with such avoidable issues, and often have a poor (and sometimes unprofessional) attitude toward being reminded to keep things clean, tidy and in order. Make sure that you and your team completely understand the importance of 5S and TPM and that following them is an ingrained habit.

10. Resource effectively

Processes also need to be effectively resourced at the start of, and throughout, each day to allow people to work without unnecessary interruption due to the unavailability of materials, consumables or information, and to ensure that the process is adequately staffed with the right numbers of people with the right levels of skills and experience.

This requires attention to the input processes that feed into the core value-adding process, including:

- The supply chain feeding in the right quality and quantity of raw materials (and other relevant supplies) at the right time
- Management processes feeding in the right information regarding demand, schedules etc. to the right people at the right time
- HR (and managers) ensuring that there are enough trained people available

Many resource issues, such as out-of-date technology and under-skilling, may not give rise to problems immediately, but they are likely to hobble the long-term strategic development of the process toward excellence, so it's important to keep one eye on how things will need to develop strategically to anticipate future resource needs.

11. Error-proof

Process steps that could be especially vulnerable to mistakes should be error-proofed so that they:

- Are easy to get right
- Are difficult to get wrong
- Highlight clearly when errors are made

This helps prevent safety or quality problems, particularly in situations where a momentary loss of concentration might cause a significant issue. Error-proofing can take many – sometimes creative – forms, depending on the nature of the task. For example:

- Clear labelling
- Floor markings to indicate walkways, storage areas etc.
- Colour-coding to quickly identify that the wrong tool, wrong component, or something else is in the wrong place, e.g.:

- Only red-painted tools go on the red board, blue on blue, etc.
- The adjustment nut on the machine is painted green and only the spanner with green tape on it is the proper size for it

- Physical shape, size or orientation to stop the wrong thing going in the wrong place, e.g.:

  - An HDMI connector that can only be plugged into the right socket, and the right way up
  - An unleaded fuel nozzle that won't fit into the pipe on a diesel vehicle

- Shadow markings to depict what goes where on floors, benches, shelves, in cupboards or on toolboards, and what way round they should be for ease of use
- Confirmation prompts, e.g. 'Are you sure you want to delete this file?'
- Warning lights or buzzers, error notifications
- Warnings on packaging, e.g. 'Open other side!', 'This way up!'
- Automatic cut-outs that trigger when safety is breached, e.g. the dishwasher stopping if the door is opened during operation

12. Pull

A key aim in process excellence is to achieve just-in-time (JIT) performance: providing exactly, and only, what the customer wants, exactly, and only, when they want it. This requires:

- Perfect flow
- Getting demand information (i.e. what we need to do, when) to the right parts of the process, accurately and in good time

The pull concept is based on the 'supermarket model', (or 'kanban' system) where the customer picks exactly what they need when they need it, triggering a chain of events that replenishes what was used in good time; i.e. demand is pulled through the process, with downstream activity (starting with the customer) providing a full, accurate and immediate trigger for the next upstream stage (and then rippling further back upstream).

The alternative is a push system where scheduling is determined by a centralised process, and possibly based on forecasts and estimates. The dangers with this include:

- Overproduction – creating excessive inventory that might not get used, will lie around taking up expensive storage space, and may go out of date
- Underproduction – missing opportunities because the system cannot respond fast enough
- Delay and error in the information-management process may compromise process responsiveness, quality and cost performance

Consequently, for process excellence, activity should be pulled by external customers and internal processes wherever possible, and pushed only where absolutely necessary.

13. Measure

Effective measurement is fundamental to understanding, managing and improving processes both tactically (in real time), and strategically (over the longer term).

Effective measurement will include both output measures and in-process measures. Output measures show overall process performance and are likely to include the QCD measures. They are lag measures, showing the results of actions already taken. (The lag, of course, could vary from minutes to months, depending on the frequency of measurement.)

In-process measures are real-time measures that provide an early warning system, allowing problems to be spotted and course corrections made immediately ('in-flight'). These lead measures ensure better control of the process and more accurate prediction of process performance.

Effective process measures also help the team to develop a deep understanding of how the process works: what the process variables are and how they interact to shape the results. This, in turn, allows for better, faster and more accurate identification of process problems and their root causes. Effective process measures also allow the impact of improvement actions to be objectively assessed.

Measures, particularly in-process measures, are not necessarily numerical, nor presented at a central location. They can include visual or auditory signals that allow any aspect of the process to be understood, managed and improved by the person doing the job, enabling them to make informed, autonomous decisions and take timely, effective action. For example, indicator lights, dials, gauges, or floor markings that indicate where material, equipment or people should (or should not) be.

Measures should also be:

- Aligned with the purpose of the process and the VoC
- Relevant and sufficient (conveying useful information, and measuring all key factors in the process)
- Useable, providing actionable information that is easy to understand and act on immediately
- Accurate and up to date
- Visible – immediately accessible

14. Manage and improve

There are three main pillars to effective process management and improvement:

- Daily meeting
- Gemba walk
- Improvement time

The daily meeting

The daily meeting is the engine of process management. The excellence mindset is that every day matters: that every day is a day when we need to simultaneously deliver, improve, pick up and sort the small issues that could quickly grow into disruptive problems.

The daily meeting will typically follow the core agenda of:

1. Review and learning:

    - **Planned:** What was planned for yesterday?
    - **Actual:** How did it turn out?
    - **Variance:** What was the difference between planned and actual (on any factor in any direction)?
    - **Reason:** How do we explain the difference, and what can be learned from it?
    - **Action:** Is any corrective action to be taken today as a result?

2. Planning for a successful day, including corrective actions and other value-enabling activities

Beyond sticking to basic meeting discipline it should be fairly informal, and always positive: focused on performance and improvement.

This is probably the single most important forum for colleague engagement, and running the daily meeting, and running it consistently and well, is a statement about, and demonstration of, a manager's commitment to process excellence and colleague engagement. As is a failure to run it consistently and well.

Gemba walk

The gemba walk is where a team leader physically walks the process to ensure that all looks and feels well, and checks in with the people involved, picking up and discussing any emerging issues. (The gemba is 'the place where the productive activity happens'.) Where a physical walk is not possible, this can be achieved by regular short check-ins with people. The frequency of these should be determined by the speed at which problems can go from small to serious. (So, weekly or more frequently.)

Improvement time

Time should also be purposely created to work on improving the process. (It won't happen otherwise.) This is likely to involve some combination of smaller kaizen projects or longer/larger/more strategic improvement projects. A typical standard for excellent organisations is about 5% of working time, or ca. two hours per person per week. That might sound a lot, but is usually comfortably less than the time lost to failure-driven demand and other wastes and inefficiencies.

Summary

Process excellence underpins operational excellence, the basis of the business's competitive advantage. The ability to engage people in the design, management and improvement of processes is a vital management responsibility and competence.

Though each business is different, applying the following key concepts will provide a strong foundation for process excellence that can be continually built on and refined:

1. Understand value (VoC)
2. Build in quality and minimise the COPQ

3. Flow

4. Evenness

5. Operate within capability

6. Dynamic resilience

7. Balance

8. Standardise

9. Prime and maintain

10. Resource effectively

11. Error-proof

12. Pull

13. Measure

14. Manage and improve

While process maximisation is counterproductive, as it runs the constant risk of overburden, process performance can be optimised to run more effectively and efficiently and to continually improve, with greater resilience and with less downside risk. This can only happen when everyone understands the above thinking and the process excellence criteria.

To close, a powerful quote from Seth Godin that neatly captures the essence of process excellence:

> 'If your customer service strategy consists of reacting to problems and mollifying angry customers, you'll always be behind. Life becomes a fire drill and work becomes an endless chore.
>
> 'The alternative is to invest in cycles that lead to better systems. Because better systems put out the fire when it's really small. And to invest in design, because better design leads to clearer promises, which are easier to keep. And to invest in quality as the focus of production, because keeping your promises creates delight and lowers costs so much, it pays for itself.'

CHAPTER 15

THE POTENTIAL PERILS AND PITFALLS OF PERFORMANCE IMPROVEMENT

Introduction

As we begin our exploration of performance improvement, first, a word of caution regarding the potential perils and pitfalls for the well-intentioned but unwary pilgrim. This may help to avoid:

- Inadvertently damaging the very processes and outcomes they seek to enhance
- The frustration and confusion which have led many to lose faith and give up

Setting the scene

Business competitiveness derives from the ability to deliver consistently excellent quality, cost and delivery performance profitably, often in the face of constant challenge and change.

Building the capability for continuous improvement optimises short-term performance and underpins long-term success by enabling the business to adapt quickly, smoothly and well to both daily operational challenges and wider, longer-term strategic change in markets, technology etc.

This makes continuous improvement a core organisational capability, and increasing the rate of improvement a strategically important task. (The corollary is that the inability to improve the right things quickly, well and sustainably may be the single biggest barrier to performance improvement, growth and progress.)

Defining continuous improvement

Effective continuous improvement focuses on doing two things: adding monetisable value and removing waste – in that order, since it is adding value that pays the bills. Let's explore these further.

Adding value: creating loyal customers by discovering, and consistently delivering, what they want and will pay for

As Deming reminds us, the central aim of a business, and golden opportunity number one, is to create loyal customers so as to secure the consistently profitable revenue streams that are the lifeblood of the enterprise. The difference, he notes, is that satisfied customers may still shop around and look for discounts, but loyal customers willingly return and lead to lower costs and higher sales because they:

- Require lower sales and marketing costs (and reduce customer churn)
- Tend not to rely on discounting
- Are more open to upselling and cross-selling
- Are more forgiving of the occasional hiccup, so there is less customer handling time, cost and distraction
- May add value by being advocates for the business

The keys to creating loyal customers are to a) discover, and b) consistently deliver what they want and will pay for. That is:

- Understanding with sufficient clarity, depth and accuracy the Voice of the Customer (VoC) – what existing and potential customers want and will pay for, including their unmet needs. And to continually and actively track this to keep it fresh and relevant
- Delivering consistently well by ensuring that the value-adding processes are:
  - Aligned with customer needs
  - Consistently delivering to promise
  - Evolving to meet emerging needs

All of this serves to consolidate the pool of existing customers and attract new customers through reputation, and in turn to optimise revenue growth and pricing. It also positions the business to gain first-mover advantage in the face of evolving opportunities and threats.

Removing waste: delivering effectively and with optimal efficiency

Waste, as discussed in Chapter 14, is anything that consumes time and resource but does not add monetisable customer value. Waste is public enemy number one. It actively destroys value, damages profitability and hobbles growth potential in two main ways:

- The financial cost of waste comes right off the bottom line, and
- Waste misappropriates already-paid-for capacity that should be producing chargeable value

The good news is that the reverse is also true. Every cost saving goes right onto the bottom line. And every defect avoided and every bit of waste removed improves workflow, delivery performance and productivity and frees up more revenue-generating capacity (including people's time, energy and enthusiasm) to do more productive and profitable things.

Potential pitfalls: overview

There are seven potential pitfalls to be mindful of if we are to ensure that our improvement work is optimally effective rather than a missed opportunity or, indeed, actively counterproductive. These are:

1. Looking for the wrong thing in the wrong place: missing the fundamental importance of process quality
2. Failing to prioritise the strategic and systematic bolstering of value creation and profit improvement
3. Not being obsessive about the systematic reduction of waste as part of everyday management
4. Not knowing what poor process quality is costing
5. Applying counterproductive approaches to performance management
6. Adopting counterproductive approaches to continuous improvement

7. Not optimising the leadership and management systems and behaviours first

Let's explore these in more detail.

1. Looking for the wrong thing in the wrong place – insufficient emphasis on process quality

Our aim – and the key to creating loyal customers – is to build, maintain and continuously improve the capability of the overall business system to deliver, profitably, what the customer requires: that is, right-first-time QCD performance – and to do so consistently and reliably.

The highest leverage on results is, therefore, the quality of the system from which they derive. This means ensuring that every process in the value stream, from research and development, marketing, sales, supply chain and operations to logistics and after-sales service, and every aspect of the operational and strategic management processes, individually and as a whole, is thoroughly understood, properly designed and managed, and continually improved.

Leaders and managers who are serious about excellence thus tend (and indeed need) to be obsessional about achieving this level of process and systems quality.

There is therefore (potential pitfall #1) a danger that where the fundamental importance of the principle of process quality is missed and there is, consequently, insufficient emphasis placed on it in the management of business performance, the business risks looking in the wrong place for the wrong thing and potentially reducing the impact, and increasing the risks, of its improvement efforts.

2. Failing to prioritise the strategic and systematic bolstering of value creation and profit improvement

The primary business of business is of course to find and serve a customer profitably. Correspondingly, a part of every manager's role is entrepreneurial; to be enterprising and innovative, to have a portfolio of ideas for winning new business and increasing revenue and profitability, and to be actively pursuing these and tackling and solving the barriers that lie in the way of their achievement.

But sometimes, managers can get so focused on managing the money that they forget how the money gets made.

From this observation arises our second caution: to prioritise, in the management and improvement of business performance, the cost-effective bolstering of value-add. Consistently checking that we are providing what the customer wants and will pay sufficiently well for, and that we are in tune with their unmet and emerging needs. That the VoC is clearly understood and that the process remains aligned with it. Otherwise, as John Seddon pointed out, our attempts to improve our process may just lead us to doing the wrong thing righter.

3. Not systematically and routinely minimising and eliminating waste as part of everyday management

Waste is present in various forms in all business systems. It is in the operational processes, operational management processes, strategic management processes and the social processes of communication, people development, teamwork and collaboration. Waste is, quite simply, anything that consumes time or resource and impedes the smooth flow of productive activity but either adds no value, impedes value creation or actively destroys value.

Waste is, by definition, a process quality issue. It manifests in two main ways: defects and process inefficiencies.

A defect is any piece of work that does not meet requirements and has to be scrapped or redone. Defects create what Seddon called failure-driven demand; a demand created on the process by the failure to get something right first time. Defects can occur in any system. Operational management system defects might include failure to provide correct or timely information or resources; the cancellation, or poor conduct, of performance conversations; or failing to hold people accountable. Strategic management system defects might include missing key threats or opportunities or, more generally, focusing business resources on vanity projects or boondoggle (unnecessary or pointless work).

Process inefficiencies include:

- Transportation: unnecessary movement of material or information
- Inventory: excessive stock or work in progress
- Motion: unnecessary physical, mental or emotional effort
- Waiting: idle time when the process is disrupted for any reason
- Over-processing: unnecessary detail, features, paperwork, reports, bureaucracy etc.
- Overproduction: producing more (of anything) than there is a confirmed need for

- Underutilised human potential: people unable to develop or perform to potential
- Space: any form of inefficiently used physical capacity
- Energy: wasted heat, light, fuel, electricity, gas, battery power etc.
- Transaction costs: social friction that impedes cooperation, collaboration or innovation

Many of these concepts were derived from an industrial context, but the keen mind will easily relate them to any service or management process. For example:

- Waiting, in a management process, might be people hanging on for decisions or information (one of us worked in a business where the annual budget for the year beginning in April rarely appeared before June)
- Over-processing might mean unnecessary information being either required or given
- Overproduction may manifest as too many short-notice meetings which add little value, and not enough well-run meetings to deal with the essential planning and review of performance

Since such waste is ubiquitous, managers need to systematically and routinely minimise and eliminate waste as part of everyday management. But it's rare that sufficient focus placed on this.

4. Not measuring the cost of poor quality (or not knowing what poor quality is costing)

A related problem is that neither the cost of the missed opportunities for adding monitisable value, nor the cost of the waste, is easily visible. This is likely to be at least partly because they are relying on standard financial and operational measures which, on their own, do not provide the required depth, speed or granularity of insight.

Though every defect and inefficiency does of course reliably turn up somewhere in the numbers, the extent, location and nature of these, the system dynamics that created them and the root causes, are untraceable with standard financial and operational measures alone. More problematically, they provide no insight into what action can be taken to sustainably reduce defects and inefficiencies. This renders many of them, literally, unmanageable. Consequently, this embedded 'hidden' waste is a significant determinant of the upper limits of business performance and progress. It is managing the business: managers are not managing it.

Such is the seriousness of this that Joseph Juran coined the term 'hidden factory'; this highlights both the hidden nature of this waste and the magnitude of it – and, more importantly, that it is systematically and consistently produced as a by-product of any suboptimally designed or managed process.

But the waste is, of course, not hidden at all. It is just difficult to see using standard measures and management practices. Change where we look and how, and the waste and what drives it become highly visible. This is where the thinking, tools and disciplines of continuous improvement are vital. They are a necessary adjunct to standard financial and operational performance management, as they make visible and addressable the raft of hitherto unseen, ill understood and unaddressed, dynamically interconnected issues that limit both short-term performance and profitability, and long-term growth and prosperity.

So a vital opportunity for improvement is often to the measurement and management systems, to render the waste more visible and thus addressable. A key aspect of this is providing the people working in the process with timely, actionable information. This empowers them to make in-flight course corrections to keep daily performance on track, and to make longer-term improvements to fine-tune the process, keeping it aligned with the ever-changing VoC and fit for purpose strategically.

IDENTIFYING THE COST OF WASTE

Philip Crosby's cost of quality (COQ) model powerfully illustrates three things:

- The cost of waste
- The underlying causes and dynamics
- How much of it can be avoided in the first place by improving process management

First, Crosby outlines the major categories of cost associated with process quality; that is, how much it costs to get the quality of the product or service right. These are:

- Problem **prevention**
- **Internal failure** – this includes defects detected and corrected in-process, plus all the forms of process waste and inefficiency we discussed earlier

- The cost and time associated with **inspection** to stop any undetected defects reaching the customer

- **External failure** – defects reported by customers which create the need for expensive recall, rework, refunds, replacements, investigations and additional customer-handling time

To Crosby's list can usefully be added Deming's notion of the unknown and unknowable costs of lost client lifetime value; the cost of lost sales attributable to customers who walked away, bought less, negotiated discounts, or dissuaded others from buying.

Crosby called the total cost of waste in the business (internal failure, inspection and external failure) the cost of poor quality (COPQ).

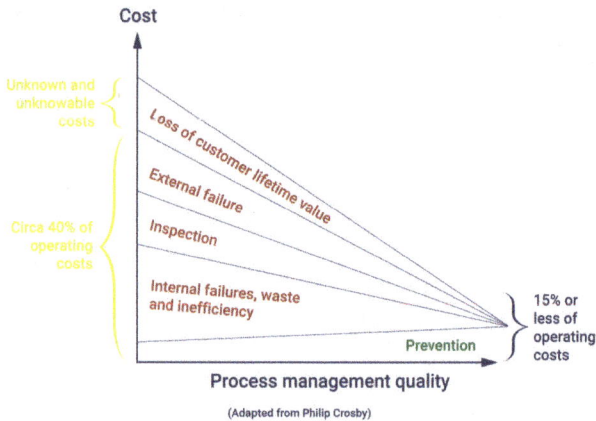

(Adapted from Philip Crosby)

Figure 15.1: Cost of quality

Deming, Crosby and others estimate that the total COQ (how much it costs to get the quality of the product or service right) can be between around 15% and 40% of operating costs (not including the 'unknown and unknowable'). This is illustrated in Figure 15.1.

Figure 15.1 further demonstrates Crosby's central point that prevention is the key variable (and the highest-leverage point for profit improvement) as it reduces the COPQ (waste) significantly. He famously stated (in his book title) that 'quality is free' – it more than pays for itself. (Not exactly a wild claim since, self-evidently, waste is money down the drain, and as Deming pointed out, someone gets paid for both making and fixing defects.)

> What Crosby calls prevention might be better described simply as effective process management; the design, management and improvement of the process to make it capable of consistently delivering to promise with minimal waste.
>
> In short, the QCD results depend on process quality, which in turn depends on process management, operational management and strategic management quality. This takes us back to Deming's point that 'quality begins in the boardroom' and reminds us that the role, the fundamental responsibility, and the very essence of the craft of leadership and management at all levels, is to optimise the performance of the systems in their purview which form the performance management chain that delivers key business outcomes.

5. Applying counterproductive approaches to performance management

There are four main performance management tactics that can be actively counterproductive. They all derive from assumptions and thinking from the 1930s command and control philosophy – a hangover from the days before systems thinking which still unconsciously permeates leadership and management attitudes. These are:

- The cost-cutting trap
- Working harder as the main improvement strategy
- Problem management
- Variation management

Let's explore these in turn.

The cost-cutting trap

Reducing non-value-adding cost is, clearly, a central part of waste reduction. But waste prevention and reduction is significantly more strategic, ambitious, skilled and surgical work. It goes further and deeper than cost-cutting, in four ways. It:

- Explicitly serves the primary financial goal of the management and improvement of profitability
- Aims to find and remove all waste, including, but not limited to, unnecessary cost. It looks, with greater insight, into more places, more skilfully, thoroughly, systematically, rigorously and tenaciously

- Is explicitly aimed not only at maintaining the integrity of the entire sociotechnical system as waste is removed, but also at enhancing the system so that it can consistently deliver low-cost, high-quality work and has the resilience to withstand a range of potentially destabilising challenges
- Is part of day-to-day management, not a problem response

This stands in sharp contrast to imposing acontextual cost reductions on a process. Cost reduction that does not take account of system dynamics is highly unlikely to lead to improved efficiency, because there are, more often than not, unforeseen negative consequences.

Here's why. Costs include:

- Those which directly support the **value-adding** activities that deliver the product, service or experience that the customer pays for. This includes labour, tools, raw materials etc.
- **Value-enabling 'prevention'** activities such as maintenance, training and continuous improvement which ensure that the value-adding activities run optimally
- **Waste:** Any activity that consumes time or resource and disrupts workflow but adds no value

Value-adding and value-enabling costs are usually highly visible in standard management accounts. But, as discussed, waste that has become structurally embedded in a system is not visible through standard financial or operational measures or management processes.

When the iceberg of waste is not visible because a business is not looking in the right place in the right way, and is lacking the insights, tools, strategies and skills to surgically and skilfully remove it, and when there is pressure on costs, it is by definition mainly the (more visible) value-adding and value-enabling activities that get targeted, rather than the actual problem (the waste) being systematically and rigorously identified and removed.

Therefore, poorly targeted cost reductions imposed on a process carry a high risk of turning out to be false economies. This is playing process Jenga and runs a significant risk of undermining and destabilising the process, driving up the COPQ, i.e. creating more defects, delays, customer dissatisfaction and need for rework etc. All of which, self-evidently, costs time and money to fix, while also potentially resulting in a loss of business, customer confidence and reputation. (All the while doing nothing to increase value-adding capacity.)

As Deming pointed out many decades ago: 'Organisations that focus on improving [right first time] quality automatically reduce costs, while those that focus on reducing cost automatically reduce quality and actually increase costs as a result.'

That's not effective or responsible financial management.

Any strategy of 'cut, cope and hope', no matter how it is dressed up, is a significant and unnecessary business risk because of the very real unforeseeability (and immeasurability) of the full consequences of the damage done to the process and outcomes, both immediate and long-term.

Low cost-to-produce should be baked in as a strategic goal and consistently pursued through a rigorous process of continuous improvement. See the sidebar below.

LOW COST OF PRODUCTION AS A KEY ELEMENT OF STRATEGY

Aspiring to be the lowest-cost producer makes strategic sense. Achieving this does not of course mean that the business is second-rate to buy from, work for or invest in, as Thomas Hout's 2025 research suggests.* Quite the reverse.

The strategy of being the lowest-cost producer, and how it is pursued, stands in stark contrast to a cost-reduction strategy that hollows out the business by reducing product or service quality, technical capability, people development, management capability and improvement capability.

Being the lowest-cost competitor, Hout discovered, is a deeply embedded cultural capability, built over time by continually finding more cost-effective ways to keep customers happy. This is mainly about people and creativity, and thus relies on strong colleague trust and engagement.

This is achieved by:

- Studying how every customer group is served and looking at those interactions from every angle
- An obsession with operational excellence, process excellence, workflow, logistics efficiency, and keeping overheads low
- Developing, over time, a rich understanding of the processes, obsessive attention to detail, reliable real-time operating data for decision-making, the development of in-house standards and process specifications, and rigorous hiring and training practices

> • Distributing intelligence and improvement capability throughout the organisation, to enable the people doing the work, at every level, to solve the problems they confront
>
> As Hout argues, the difference between a business that can turn out twice as much as another is often the intelligence and discipline applied to each of hundreds of tasks in the long chain of work over time.
>
> *Thomas Hout, The Secrets of Extraordinary Low-Cost Operators, Harvard Business Review, April 2025

Working harder as the main improvement strategy

> *When we look at organizations, brands or individuals with a reputation for quality, it's not at all clear that they accomplish this with more effort. Because that's simply not sustainable. The people who work at a Lexus plant aren't more tired at the end of the day than those that make the Cadillac Escalade. It's not about effort. In fact, focusing on effort is almost guaranteed to ensure that your quality problem will persist. Quality is a systemic issue, and if you're not working on your system, you're not going to improve it. "How do we do this work?" is a much better question than "Who isn't trying hard enough?"' (Seth Godin)*

Managers may try to drive performance by applying pressure and communicating a sense of urgency. Pushing people harder. Some well-judged and skilled manifestations of this may keep people focused and eradicate complacency. In some circumstances, such pressure can be a useful spur to learning, growth and creativity.

But no amount of effort will enable even the most skilled and committed colleague to consistently outperform a process that is poorly designed, resourced and managed. As Deming observed, 'A bad system will beat a good person every time.' In such circumstances, pushing, commanding and pacesetting may even lower productivity, as people disengage and push back.

Higher-productivity colleagues are generally those who work in better systems. Systems that enable them to work with speed, precision, efficiency and agility. The train driver who can now complete in four hours a journey that took 22 hours in 1849 isn't working five times harder. They work in a better system.

Transformational change is characterised by advances in the intelligence of the design, management and improvement of what is done and how it is done. That's the defining feature of the journey from the caves to here, and our best bet to get to better from here.

When working harder hits diminishing returns and begins to degrade capability, there's only one way to improve: to work smarter. That is:

- Skilled, disciplined and systematic strategic management to select and work on the right strategic priorities
- Skilled, disciplined and systematic operational and daily management to optimise the process for right-first-time quality and to continually build capability by:
  - Properly designing, setting up and resourcing processes to avoid foreseeable problems, and enabling people to work productively by giving them the right tools, resources and information, and effective processes
  - Making the defects and waste highly visible with effective in-process measures and value-stream mapping tools (see Chapter 16 for more on this)
  - Taking a rigorous, systematic and disciplined approach to the reduction of waste and defects
  - Making sure that people have been professionally recruited, selected, inducted, trained and managed
  - Holding people accountable to a professional standard, and coaching and supporting them on an ongoing basis, to achieve the expected standards of performance and contribution

Problem management

Problem management is finding ways to cope, and struggle on, without addressing the root cause of an issue. There are six broad manifestations:

- **Ignore it:** Don't acknowledge it, far less raise it, for fear that it may reflect poorly on us, give us more work, or that it is beyond our capability to fix and may just open up another can of worms that will cause further trouble
- Hide the problem by **manipulating the results or gaming the system**
- **Blame-shifting:** Blame someone else. Get the attention off us, or at least deflect or obfuscate sufficiently that less (or none) of the responsibility for addressing the issue falls on us
- **Benign neglect** – taking the view that because certain problems have been around for a while, have resisted numerous attempts at solution, and are

experienced by other businesses, nothing can or needs to be done. This, to some minds, legitimises the normalisation of some problems. The result is that it bakes in the resulting COPQ as a fixed cost

- **More horsepower** (a close cousin of working harder) – throwing additional time, people, kit or other resource at a situation. This is often successful in driving straight through barriers to 'get stuff done/out the door'. But raw power is expensive, clumsy, indiscriminate, somewhat addictive, and often leaves behind a trail of destruction, including burnt-out people and wildly inefficient, patched-up, unbalanced processes. Additional horsepower also masks the underlying problems and fundamental process limitations, meaning that the barriers to performance are not understood and removed and will continue to require the application of this expensive approach in perpetuity – also baking in the expense of the additional horsepower as a fixed cost

- **Expediting:** Managers jumping in to change the priorities or workflow or to divert resources. This can get the urgent and visible problems solved, but there is invariably a price to pay that is not immediately obvious, such as increased resource costs and workflow disruption. This stores up problems for tomorrow that might subsequently need expediting, creating a stuck loop

There are understandable reasons to adopt problem management. (For one thing, it is a decent self-protection strategy.) Acknowledging that there are problems on your watch is not comfortable. There is often trepidation about taking responsibility for them, as it opens us up to potential criticism. Then there are the risks, difficulties and vulnerabilities in trying to actually solve the problems.

Problem-solving is a messy, non-linear process full of blind alleys, setbacks, failed experiments and misunderstandings. It may look like we don't know what we're doing. (And, of course, we don't, or it wouldn't be a problem.) The amateur sees fumbling incompetence. The professional sees a problem-solver in action, working their way to a solution and reaching breakthroughs that a) no one else will and b) would not otherwise have happened, while at the same time setting an excellent example of leadership. (Business is, after all, about getting paid to profitably solve some kind of problem.)

In short, problem management just means that the problems will recur ad infinitum. It is expensive. And it keeps us stuck. It can not only lead to the original inefficiencies becoming embedded, but can also introduce and embed an additional layer of waste in the form of resources that need to be spent to compensate for the original problem. For example, having extra people, kit, space and inventory permanently on hand to ride out the recurring exigencies, further driving up the fixed costs associated with the COPQ and diverting further time and energy away from the actual leadership priority – solving the endemic system problems and moving the business forward.

Invariably, the time, effort and resources that are routinely and systematically wasted dwarf the time, effort and resources required to solve the problem. In choosing to leave the problems unaddressed, we make a commitment to this ongoing resource drain. Hence our encouragement here to recognise the limitations and dangers of problem management.

Progress requires a firm commitment to problem-solving rather than problem management; to actively lead and encourage people to bring problems to the surface and address them. To recognise that problems are actually treasures of hidden waste and variability that you want your people to find and eliminate through continuous process improvement. The attitude with which organisations approach this issue is an important test of the mindset and capability maturity of leaders and how they think about and act on problems and improvement opportunities. It requires that leaders have developed the systems-thinking capability to understand these dynamics, and the emotional intelligence to be able to resist the temptation to constantly react, firefight and bulldoze through at a purely tactical level, and to think and act strategically and recognise that their overriding responsibility is to ensure that the processes are fit for purpose and continually improving over the long term.

Variation management (misunderstanding process variation and how to manage it)

First, let's define some key technical terms that are vital to an understanding of process performance and improvement:

- **Variation:** All processes (and therefore the results they produce) demonstrate some degree of variation. Perfection is unavailable

- **Stability:** A process is **stable** if it consistently, repeatedly and predictably generates results within certain limits, no matter how good or bad those results are. (These limits are technically known as the **upper control limit** and **lower control limit**)

- **Capability:** A process is **capable** if it is producing results that meet customer specifications (the VoC)

The aim is, of course, to build and maintain a process that is both capable and stable.

The value of these concepts is that they allow us to identify two important possibilities. That:

- A process may be stable but not capable (i.e. it may be underperforming consistently in predictable ways – a bit like our local football team)
- It may be intrinsically capable, working well on a good day, but is not stable

Recognising the difference is absolutely vital if we are to intervene effectively.

Improving a process

Should a process not be delivering what we require, the first issue to check is stability. When a process is not stable, this suggests the presence of 'special causes' which are destabilising it; for example, frequent machine breakdowns or internet outages. The first step toward improving a process is therefore to make it stable by identifying and removing these (often external) special causes.

Then, if the process is stable but not capable, the remaining variation is created by 'common causes', that is, factors inherent in the fundamental design, structure and management of the process such as poor resourcing, lack of balance, poor communication, insufficiently well-trained people etc.

Therefore, the process itself needs to be studied, understood in depth, and systematically and progressively developed to improve right-first-time quality, shorten cycle times, reduce variation and generally get it into better fundamental shape (i.e. prevention).

Dangerous misunderstandings from failing to understand the difference between special and common causes and how to respond appropriately

When there is a failure to differentiate between special causes and common causes, experience suggests, managers with good intentions tend to try to constantly address them all – often in a reactive way. But this runs the risk of seriously undermining both stability and capability. Here's why.

If the process is stable (operating within predictable limits that are due to inherent process limitations, i.e. common causes), to treat every variation as a special cause is not only futile (because it is not the root cause), but will also destabilise the process further because this is, by definition, adding another source of variation. And then maybe another one to respond to the problems caused by that... and so on. This is a phenomenon called 'tampering'. (Check out Demings' classic Funnel Experiment, which illustrates this tragicomic principle.)

So, where managers routinely tamper, demanding explanations and action on a result that is due to the natural variation in a stable (if imperfect) process, they court significant dangers because, since no 'assignable' cause actually exists, any resulting explanation extracted from a beleaguered manager is (as Wheeler observed) likely to be a 'work of fiction whose only purpose is to pretend that something is being done about a perceived problem'. And if acted upon, it will create further instability.

If the stability and capability goals are fundamentally beyond the capability of the system, the system will, as discussed, have to be enhanced systematically by understanding and addressing the common causes.

To further emphasise a recurring theme in this chapter (and to anticipate potential pitfall #7): such a reactive and – quite literally – misguided response would never be a legitimate outcome from a well-designed and well-led management process.

Viewed through this lens, we can see that demands for such action under these circumstances suggest an improvement opportunity somewhere in the management system (and by implication, in leadership). Otherwise there is the risk of creating the tragicomic scenario that those demanding the urgent action – which is likely to drive the business into a non-improving mediocrity cycle and cause constant frustration all round – are the very people responsible for failing to prevent the issue in the first place.

6. Adopting counterproductive approaches to continuous improvement

It is worryingly easy to fall into the practice of false continuous improvement and fool ourselves that we are making useful progress, when in fact we are instead simply wasting further time, effort and resource. Below are six common counterproductive approaches to continuous improvement:

- Not addressing process constraints
- Failing to take a systems approach
- Disrupting overall systems balance and coherence
- Putting in additional checks, steps or processes
- Failing to take a systematic approach to problem-solving
- Leaving it to 'experts' and failing to involve colleagues and develop improvement capability

Not addressing process constraints

Two common, related problems where a systematic approach to continuous improvement is not taken are a) failing to address the 'rocks in the river' (genuine barriers to workflow), and b) addressing issues that are not. (See Figure 15.2.)

As Eli Goldratt points out, if what we choose to work on is not a constraint or bottleneck, then such 'point improvements' do not flow through to impact on the QCD of the end-to-end process, or improve process stability, reliability and resilience. This means that such 'improvement' activity is, in the saddest of ironies, itself waste!

Addressing issues that are not constraints includes automating processes before sorting out the fundamental design and alignment with the VoC. It also includes just asking people for 'good ideas' and other miscellaneous boondogglery.

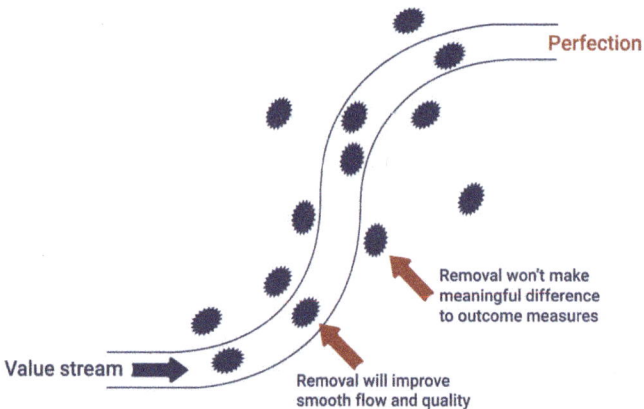

Figure 15.2: Focus on removing problems in the value stream

Failing to take a systems approach

Failing to take a systems approach runs not only the risk of missing the 'rocks' and wasting time and effort on 'non-rocks', but also the additional risk of counterproductive push-down-pop-up problem-solving; solving a problem or saving time, money, effort or resource in one operation, only to create a bigger problem elsewhere as a result of unintended negative consequences. For example, procurement saves money on components, but warranty costs increase by a larger amount as a result of the components being less reliable over time.

Disrupting overall systems balance and coherence

Any change, no matter how well planned, runs a risk of disrupting overall systems balance and coherence, both in how we change parts of the process along the value stream (as discussed above) and in how we address aspects of process performance such as quality, cost, delivery performance or colleague engagement. As mentioned, there is a danger that a poorly managed pursuit of cost reduction can drive up cost through compromising quality, introducing failure-driven demand, reducing customer satisfaction, and generally undermining sustainable financial performance.

But similar perils can, of course, occur by focusing too much on any single facet of performance without consideration of the systems impact, including any well-intentioned acontextual focus on quality, customer satisfaction or employee satisfaction. While it is tempting to push a system hard in one direction for short-term results (or in response to some 'initiative'), there's always a price to pay. No system works well for long when it is out of balance and its coherence is compromised.

Putting in additional checks, steps or processes

Also to be avoided is the practice of responding to problems – in the name of quality improvement – by putting in additional checks, steps or processes. This bureaucratic approach guarantees more waste, as it increases complexity and gives people more things to do with no additional time, since it is not something the customer will consent to pay more for. This typically just squeezes value-enabling time, leaving less time for planning, reflection, problem-solving, people development etc. As a result, the quality of these processes suffers and we risk falling into a mediocrity trap.

Failing to take a systematic approach to problem-solving

Even where improvement ideas meet the above criteria, there is a danger of failing to follow through on them effectively through a lack of discipline and coherence. The discipline of structured problem-solving is required; that is, working systematically and in sequence through the stages of problem definition, root cause analysis, solution development, action planning, implementation, review and learning, and embedding of gains. Without this discipline, attempts at problem-solving are likely to lack coherence and fail.

Leaving it to 'experts' and failing to involve colleagues and develop improvement capability

A final misstep is to get 'experts' to undertake improvements (taking the rather destructive view that processes are 'designed by experts to be run by idiots'). Where this happens, people tend to feel criticised and alienated, and consequently resist it. There is also no transfer of skills or knowledge to allow them to maintain or build on the change, or to develop and mature their own problem-solving capability. So the gains often deteriorate quickly and can't be reproduced.

7. Failing to start with the leadership and management systems, attitudes and behaviours

'Workers are not to blame for poor quality or productivity. The workers don't determine the layout of the plant, the room temperature, the amount invested in research, development and training. They don't buy the equipment, tools and raw materials or determine the design of the product. In short, they don't determine 90 per cent of the things responsible for the quality of the product. [Furthermore] workers cannot change the system, only management can change the system. It is management's responsibility to change the system so that quality and productivity can improve and workers can experience pride of workmanship. Once that happens, worker input becomes a continual part of the improvement process.' (W. Edwards Deming)

Responsibility for avoiding the aforementioned pitfalls by actively promoting excellence in performance management and continuous improvement sits with the leadership and management team. And the further up that chain we go, the greater the level of responsibility and the potential leverage.

The most immediately actionable and highest-leverage opportunities for improvement are thus in the management systems, and the attitudes and behaviours, that flow from the top through the business to front-line colleagues and enable (or constrain) their ability to deliver consistently excellent and continuously improving performance.

The spine of this is:

- Accountability for process and results, starting at the top, cascading to the front line, with each level holding the next level accountable for holding the next level accountable

- Timeboxed value-enabling time, and its specified use for planning, performance conversations, performance review and continuous improvement, being built into standard work for leaders and managers at all levels. A non-negotiable, core, mission-critical obligation

But this is far from common practice.

Hence our final, and arguably most important potential pitfall is not fully recognising or acknowledging the significance of management systems and leadership attitudes and behaviours, and not recognising them as the principle opportunity, and the necessary point of departure, for performance improvement.

This is, of course, not in any way intended as criticism of the vast majority of well-intentioned, hard-working, highly committed and savvy leaders and managers. Quite the reverse. It is an invitation to examine the leadership and management paradigm that informs and underpins their thinking, behaviour, decision-making and, ultimately, their outcomes, and to consider if adding to and evolving that paradigm further might serve their own, their colleagues', their company's and the wider social interests even better in the long term.

> 'Efforts and methods for the improvement of quality and productivity are in most companies fragmented, with no overall competent guidance, no integrated system for continual improvement.' (W. Edwards Deming)

WHY IS CONTINUOUS PROCESS IMPROVEMENT NOT COMMON PRACTICE?

- Let's explore the wider reasons why systematically well-executed and culturally embedded continuous improvement capability remains far from common practice.

Lack of strategic leadership

Senior managers don't always value, lead or support continuous improvement. They may:

Not fully understand it or appreciate its value and strategic importance

- Not fully grasp its holistic nature or the relentless and obsessive focus required every day. This leads many to erroneously assert that 'We already do this' or 'There is no waste in my process'

- Fail to prioritise it
- Lack sufficient faith in front-line people, believing that they couldn't, shouldn't or wouldn't get involved in processes improvement

Lack of management direction, discipline and support

Following the lead they get from above, middle managers may also underappreciate the importance of continuous improvement (and value-enabling activity generally). They may also, being under pressure from above to achieve short-term goals, get sucked into firefighting – forever heroically battling through all the problems caused by faulty processes, rather than fixing those processes.

Part of this is that many suffer from the 'no-time fallacy': the passionately held belief that they 'don't have time for improvement activities because they have a real job to do'. This overlooks three things:

- Improvement is part of the day job
- Their time is being spent dealing with all the avoidable problems created by the process issues they won't make time to fix. They have created the catch-22 situation that now traps them, perpetually limiting their process capability, and therefore their own performance and that of their team
- Over the medium- to long-term, improving processes rather than continually working around problems saves time and money

People can't get involved (lack of opportunity and empowerment)

Because of the above, people may not be given the time, or regular forums, to discuss performance and to identify and pursue improvement opportunities in any systematic way. They are not held accountable to a rigorous professional standard. Neither is there is usually any meaningful real-time performance data that would allow people to identify issues early and nip them in the bud.

People don't have the tools or training to take a structured and systematic approach

Neither managers nor front-line colleagues are trained in continuous improvement tools and techniques. Tools are either:

- Non existent, or
- Too complex and specialised: people are put off and don't know where to start

Without the right tools and training, attempts at continuous improvement can actually make things worse. Discussions can become dominated by emotion, opinion and blamestorming, with people reacting to symptoms, jumping to conclusions and failing to get to the root causes. Superficial solutions emerge which are then not fully implemented. So the problems recur and everyone becomes frustrated with the 'improvement' process and less committed to it.

Culture of avoidance, fear and blame

In addition, the following also mitigate against people showing initiative and taking responsibility for continuous improvement and problem-solving:

- A sense that there is nothing in it for them except work and risk: that it is focused exclusively on improving financial returns for shareholders
- A climate of either fear or indifference that discourages people from highlighting problems
- A habit of blamestorming rather than problem-solving if problems are discussed
- Nothing getting done when valid issues are raised
- People being punished and criticised for wrong turns and mistakes while, in good faith, trying to make improvements

Summary

Business Excellence focuses on delivering what the customer wants, right first time, on time, every time, with zero wasted time or material. The engine of this is the management system and culture, which sets the ambition, expectations and standards, and which consistently and professionally holds people accountable for both performance and improvement at all levels.

We have identified seven potential pitfalls in the achievement of performance improvement. Being alert to them may prevent us getting stuck and frustrated, and wasting much time and effort.

The opposites of these seven potential perils and pitfalls can usefully point us firmly in the direction of good practice. Let's conclude by looking at those.

Seven ways to avoid the common perils and pitfalls of performance improvement

1. Look for the right thing in the right place. Recognise the fundamental importance of process quality. Hard-wire the design, management and improvement of business processes and the collective system into the management system and culture

2. Prioritise the improvement of sustainable profitability through taking an entrepreneurial attitude toward understanding and meeting current and emerging customer needs and ensuring that the process is aligned with, and capable of, serving them profitably

3. Systematically and routinely minimise and eliminate waste as part of everyday management

4. Find out what poor process quality is costing, and don't rely on financial data alone. Develop a fuller understanding of overall process performance and what the key variables and drivers of performance, quality and cost are

5. Actively manage performance to bring problems to the surface and address them

6. Take a systematic, disciplined and rigorous approach to solving problems and improving process performance

7. Optimise the leadership and management systems and behaviours first. Everything in the business is a reflection of leadership quality, so it needs to be the first part of the continuous improvement conversation

With these potential perils and pitfalls identified, we can more confidently proceed to explore how continuous improvement might serve its singular purpose: to add greater value for all stakeholders.

CHAPTER 16

DEVELOPING A CULTURE OF CONTINUOUS IMPROVEMENT

Introduction

Developing a culture of continuous improvement is a crucial aspect of Business Excellence: a culture where everyone is actively and consistently engaged in systematically improving business processes and cultural capability to create better outcomes for everyone associated with the business. A culture that can also be described as a Thinking People System or Learning Organisation.

Defining continuous improvement

Continuous improvement is the ongoing, rigorous, systematic, consistent and disciplined enhancement of technical and cultural capability to build a high-performing business system that is flexible, agile, responsive and resilient, and that stays aligned with the changing needs of its customers. A system that:

- Meets customers' needs right first time, every time
- Is stable and in control, delivering predictably, reliably and repeatably
- Is cost- and resource-efficient, with work flowing smoothly through the processes with no wasted time, effort or resource
- Has the resilience and flexibility to handle challenges
- Has the agility to adjust to longer-term strategic change and to remain relevant and competitive

- Continuously improves, increasing its capability to add value and reduce waste

Figure 16.1: Core principles of Business Excellence

To achieve excellence, every aspect of the business system should constantly be actively managed and improved. This includes:

- The 'technical system', comprising the operational processes that directly serve the customer, the process-management processes, the operational management system and the strategic management system
- The 'social system', comprising leadership and management development, people management, team-building and culture development, which creates a team of engaged colleagues who collaborate and solve problems well

The system should also be evolved as a complete, coherent and functioning whole, as illustrated in Figure 16.1, with attention paid to the interfaces between the different aspects of the system to maintain alignment between them.

In all of this, continuous improvement should be both:

- Top-down: strategically driven, planned, transformational ('kaikaku') change
- Bottom-up: operationally driven local kaizen improvements and structured A3 projects (more on which later)

And finally, continuous improvement should be an embedded way of thinking and set of practices. Part of normal day-to-day operations.

Why bother

| *'Learning is not compulsory ... neither is survival.' (W. Edwards Deming)*

The performance of your business today is a function of how well-developed and well-managed your people and processes are. And what tomorrow looks like depends on what is done today (and what is not done today) to maintain and improve the systems that deliver that performance.

Plumbing continuous improvement into your business systems builds the capability to consistently develop capability, resilience and agility. And it does this by leveraging existing resources. In contrast, not plumbing continuous improvement into daily management opens the door to the risk of sliding into a non-improving firefighting cycle.

This makes continuous improvement a core organisational capability, and increasing the rate of improvement a task that is of strategic importance.

There are thus four main categories of benefits that come from building a culture of continuous improvement. It:

- Enhances system capability, resilience and agility (and protects against sliding into a non-improving firefighting cycle)
- Optimises the rate of learning and improvement
- Enhances performance and profitability without the need for capital investment
- Enhances colleague engagement, both tapping into, and further developing, people's potential

Let's explore these in turn.

Enhances system capability, resilience and agility

Sustainable high performance requires the:

- Capability to perform to consistently high standards
- Resilience to withstand inevitable turbulence in the operating environment
- Agility to be able to learn and adapt quickly enough and well enough to both a) innovate to create opportunities and gain first-mover advantage, and b) respond to emerging threats and opportunities (both strategic and operational)

Without a systematic approach to continuous improvement, it will be hard to optimise performance and results, particularly in an unpredictable and dynamically changing environment.

Missing this opportunity is bad enough. But it also opens the door for problems to proliferate and for waste and inefficiency to become locked into the system, clogging up the value stream and compromising quality, cost and delivery performance such that the whole system and culture becomes mired in a non-improving firefighting cycle.

This not only limits the business's short-term operational capability, but also further stifles its intrinsic ability to learn, adapt and improve, operationally and strategically.

Optimises the rate of learning and improvement

Perhaps the most profound and wide-reaching benefit is that, when done well, continuous improvement brings (literally) new dimensions to performance capability: second-order capability – the ability to improve the core operational capability – and third-order capability – the ability to turbocharge improvement capability. This furnishes the business with the capability to build capability.

In an era when it has been observed that the only remaining source of competitive advantage is the ability to adapt, these capabilities underpin competitive advantage and make the business a particularly attractive bet for further investment.

Enhances performance and profitability without capital investment, by leveraging existing resources

When done well, continuous improvement drives two key aspects of business performance: adding value and removing waste. And, it is worth emphasising, it does so by leveraging existing technical and social resource – doing better work with what we already have – rather than requiring any additional capital investment. Let's quickly recap what we discussed in Chapter 15.

Adding value: creating loyal customers by discovering, and consistently delivering, what they want and will pay for

The central aim of a business, and golden opportunity number one, is to create loyal customers, and thus secure the consistently profitable revenue streams that are the lifeblood of the enterprise. Satisfied customers may still shop around and look for discounts, but loyal customers willingly return, are low-maintenance and recommend the business to others.

The keys to creating loyal customers are to a) discover and b) consistently deliver what they want and will pay for. That is:

- Understanding with sufficient clarity, depth and accuracy the Voice of the Customer (VoC) – what existing and potential customers want and will pay for, including their unmet needs. And to continually and actively track this to keep it fresh and relevant
- Delivering consistently well by ensuring that the value-adding processes are:
  - Aligned with customer needs
  - Consistently delivering to promise
  - Evolving adaptively to meet emerging needs

All of this serves to consolidate the pool of existing customers and attract new customers through reputation, and in turn to optimise revenue growth and pricing. It also positions the business to gain first-mover advantage in the face of evolving threats and opportunities.

Removing waste: delivering effectively and with optimal efficiency
Waste is anything that consumes time and resource but does not contribute to any monetisable customer value. Waste is public enemy number one. It actively destroys value, damages profitability and hobbles growth potential in two main ways:

- The financial cost of the waste comes right off the bottom line, and
- Waste misappropriates capacity that should be producing chargeable value

The good news is that the reverse is also true. Every cost saving goes right onto the bottom line. And every defect avoided and every bit of waste removed improves flow, delivery performance and productivity and frees up more revenue-generating capacity (including people's time, energy and enthusiasm) to do more productive and profitable things. This results in less variation, greater throughput and greater quality for less cost. All without the need for capital investment and without the risk of undermining performance by playing process Jenga.

Enhances colleague engagement

Continuous improvement is also the ultimate colleague engagement tool, as it:

- Respects colleagues by taking problems that affect their work seriously, and by listening to their ideas
- Develops people, unlocking and bringing into play more of their potential (individually and collectively) as they:
  - Increase their understanding of how their process, and the business overall, works
  - Develop the technical skills required to be an effective problem-solver
  - Develop the emotional, interpersonal and teamworking skills required to problem-solve collaboratively with others
- Increases the pride and satisfaction that people can take from their work
- Equips, empowers and enables people to lead improvement initiatives
- Increases people's confidence in themselves and their willingness to take ownership and responsibility
- Encourages greater and more natural collaborative, cross-functional problem-solving to overcome the horizontal and hierarchical boundaries, barriers and silos imposed by the social structure, which create territorialism and impede vital collaboration

All of this develops and unlocks cultural capability.

A significant opportunity

Continuous improvement - using the field-proven, time-tested tools and techniques that have been around for more than 80 years to empower everyone to solve problems and reduce wasted time, money and materials and serve the customer better - might sound like common sense, particularly in an era of rapid change, but it's still not common practice. Thus, achieving excellence in this key strategic capability remains a significant opportunity for most businesses.

Principles

There nine core principles of effective continuous improvement:

1. Better outcomes for everyone associated with the business

2. Embed continuous improvement and make it an integral part of everyday work at all levels

3. Everything is in scope (all processes, all aspects of the social system, all levels and the collective system)

4. Increase value-add and reduce waste by focusing on right-first-time quality

5. Take a systemic approach (understand system interactions and dynamics)

6. Take a systematic and disciplined approach

7. Involve everyone

8. Develop a continuous improvement mentality

9. Improve continuously

We'll look at each of these principles in detail below.

1. Better outcomes for everyone associated with the business

In an excellence culture, improvement is explicitly aimed at improving the outcomes for, and experience of, everyone the business affects. As Charles Koch put it, creating virtuous cycles of mutual benefit for customers, colleagues, investors, the communities the business interacts with, and the wider environment.

There is both a moral and a practical dimension to this. Continuous improvement works best when everyone is actively involved in driving it, so it is only wise, politic and fair to consider what's in it for the people we wish to engage. If there's nothing in it for them (given that all change and experimentation risks a degree of vulnerability), then they have no incentive (and perhaps a disincentive) to get involved.

2. Embed continuous improvement and make it an integral part of everyday work at all levels

Continuous improvement, it is worth emphasising, should be integral to everyday work and deeply embedded in management routines, disciplines and habits (kata). It is these kata that are the source of stability, resilience and adaptability in the face of change and challenge (and the absence of them correlates strongly with levels of chaos and inconsistency in performance).

These disciplines should therefore be the backbone of the management system, hard-wired in and tightly monitored throughout the management chain from the top, to ensure that they are run as scheduled and to standard.

3. Everything is in scope (all processes, all aspects of the social system, all levels and the collective system)

Businesses sometimes narrowly focus their improvement efforts on the operational processes. But of course, operational process performance will never be better than the wider business system that supports (and often limits, constrains and undermines) it.

Therefore, every part of the business system should constantly be actively managed and improved. This includes all aspects of the systems shown in Figure 16.1; the strategic management system, the operational management system, daily management processes and the operational processes, all aspects of the social system, leadership, operational management, front-line management, and colleague attitudes and behaviours.

And of course, these elements cannot be meaningfully improved in isolation. The technical systems need to work as an integrated, functioning whole, as does the social system, for it to foster the high levels of trust required to facilitate rapid and effective collaborative problem-solving across all parts and all levels of the business. And the technical and social systems need to be integrated and evolved together as a coherent sociotechnical system.

4. Increase value-add and reduce waste by focusing on right-first-time quality

Continuous improvement, as discussed earlier, is the art of finding ways to improve outcomes for all stakeholders by doing two things:

- **Increasing value-add**: Accurately understanding and meeting the ever-evolving needs of the customer, and designing and consistently delivering a product, service or experience that the customer wants, and will pay for, consistently, on time, right first time, every time. This means ensuring that the value-adding processes are:
  - Aligned with customer needs
  - Consistently delivering to promise

- Evolving adaptively to meet emerging needs

- **Removing wasted time, effort, friction and resource** in the process of delivering the promised product, service or experience. This means taking a holistic, systemic and rigorous approach to identifying and removing the superfluous, to allow the process to deliver only, and exactly, what the customer wants, right first time.

There are two important, but often overlooked, points to stress here which sound like common sense, but are far from being common practice. In our zeal for efficiency improvements, it is important to remember that:

- Adding monetisable customer value is goal number one. The primary focus

- The efforts to reduce waste should be intelligently and rigorously researched, designed and tested to ensure that they are actually removing waste rather than inadvertently destroying value

5. Take a systemic approach

The business is a system in which everything affects everything else, so here are five useful insights to guide our interventions. These will increase the odds of success and reduce the danger of unintended negative consequences.

- Address the **'rocks in the river'** and *only* the rocks in the river. Ensure that we are addressing genuine barriers to flow – process constraints which, if reduced, will enhance the quality, delivery or cost performance of the end-to-end process (see Figure 16.2)

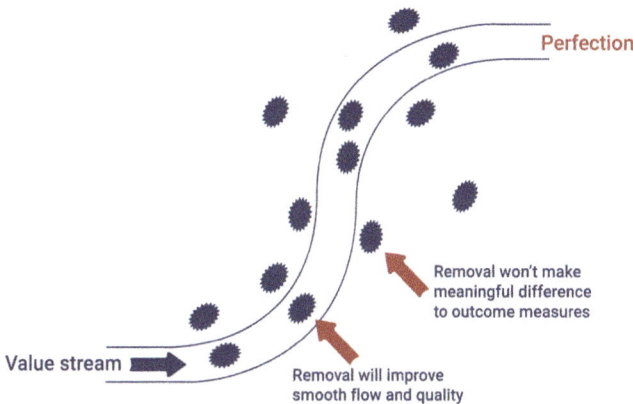

Figure 16.2: Focus on removing problems in the value stream

- Look for, and mitigate against, the risk of **push-down-pop-up problem-solving:** that is, be careful not to make changes in one part in the process that create bigger problems elsewhere

- **Maintain overall systems balance and coherence:** In making changes to component parts as discussed above, and in how we pursue improvement to key aspects of process performance such as quality, cost, delivery performance or colleague engagement, be aware of how 'target fixation' on any one factor, pursued without consideration of the wider system effects, might create imbalance and trigger widespread problems. For example, a focus on cost reduction might affect quality, which might in turn increase rework costs, customer dissatisfaction and colleagues' confidence in management

- Understand the difference between **common causes** and **special causes.** Common causes are factors inherent to the process, related to its fundamental design and management. Special causes are not. They are generally random and hard to predict. They include such things as bad weather and bad luck; for example, delayed delivery due to a flat tyre. Distinguishing between the two avoids the costly error of attempting to address every random factor that affects outcomes, and allows us to focus our short and precious improvement time on factors that will make a sustained difference. (It is also worth noting here that it is important to be aware that arbitrary changes in demand, or changes to process operation made by management, are often themselves the special causes that are destabilising processes and damaging process operation and outcomes)

- **Find and address root causes:** Avoid the practice of simply throwing additional resource at problems or putting in additional checks, steps or processes

6. Take a systematic and disciplined approach

Continuous improvement must follow a disciplined, structured and rigorous approach, based on PDCA thinking, which systematically identifies and removes the root causes of waste and other problems so that they are resolved permanently.

This includes:

- Using daily meetings, informed by reliable facts and data, to understand process performance and identify barriers to optimisation
- Using value-stream mapping (see below) to understand the dynamics of a process and identify waste and other barriers to flow

- Applying Lean principles, including flow, and waste reduction, to identify impediments to process excellence

- Making strategic project selections to target the highest-leverage opportunities

- Using structured problem-solving with root cause analysis to ensure that problems are fully understood and the underlying causes identified

- Planning improvement projects effectively

- Executing projects effectively and seeing them through to successful completion

- Consolidating gains and embedding them into operational standards

- Sharing key learnings across the business to save others time, effort, risk and money

Continuous improvement pursued in this way creates a performance ratchet by consolidating and building on successive gains, as illustrated in Figure 16.3.

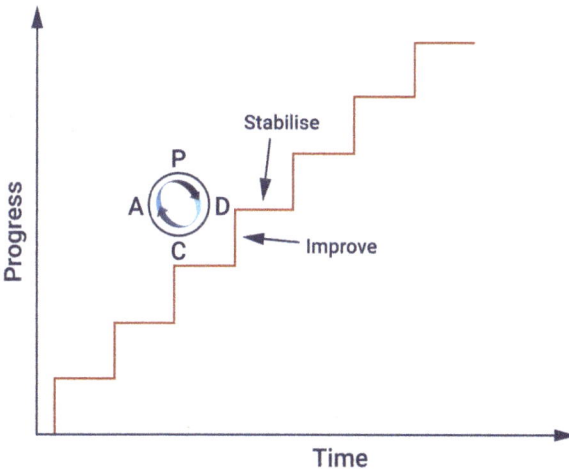

Figure 16.3: The performance ratchet

Figure 16.4 illustrates further how this builds capability progressively over time through both locally led kaizen improvements as part of the daily management process, and top-down strategic breakthrough improvements.

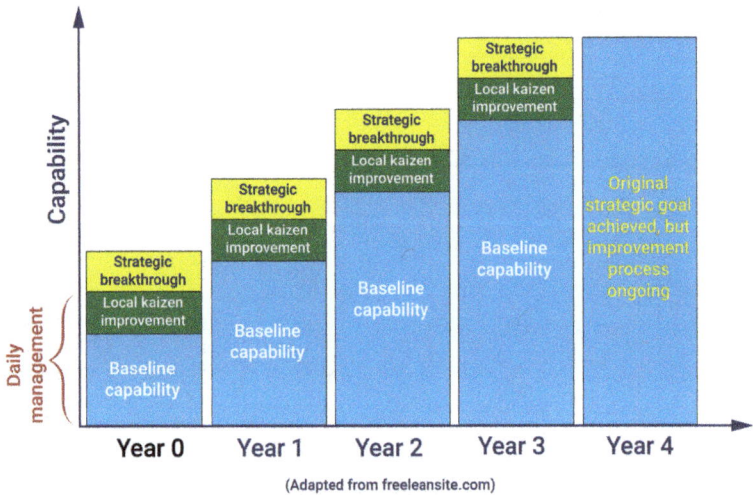

Figure 16.4: Aggregating gains – cumulative capability improvements

7. Involve everyone

'People are rarely the problem but are in fact your most valuable problem-solvers.'(Thomas L. Jackson)

To maximise the potential impact of continuous process improvement, everyone should be actively engaged in it. Everyone on the payroll is, after all, responsible for four things:

- Doing their job well
- Improving how they do their job
- Collaborating with others to enhance their local processes
- Collaborating with others to enhance shared processes and the overall business system

Senior leaders are thus primarily responsible for improving the strategy process, operational managers for improving the operational management processes, front-line managers for improving the daily management process and front-line people for improving the operational processes.

THE SOCIOTECHNICAL NATURE OF CONTINUOUS IMPROVEMENT

Continuous improvement is a sociotechnical process in two respects:

- The improvement of the technical process requires people – usually in teams working collaboratively

- The underpinning social processes of managing and developing people to build capability and foster trust collaboration and teamwork are themselves subject to ongoing development and enhancement

Engaging people in continuous improvement therefore brings the triple benefit of simultaneously a) developing their understanding of the processes and systems and their problem-solving and teamworking skills, while b) improving the process to c) to improve performance. This creates the virtuous cycle (Figure 16.5) which, over time, consolidates into a culture of continuous improvement (aka a Thinking People System or Learning Organisation) which is the foundation of the business's ability to build and maintain capability, resilience and agility.

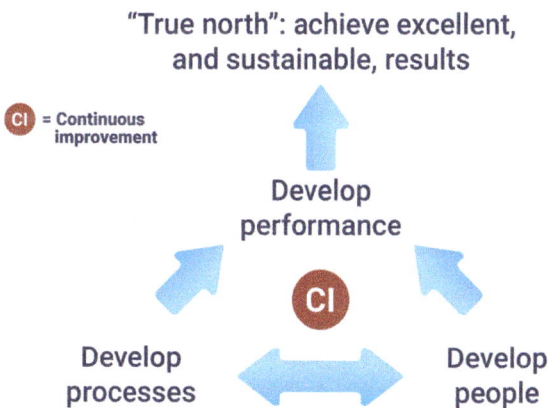

"True north": Achieve excellent, and sustainable, results

CI = Continuous improvement

Develop performance

CI

Develop processes

Develop people

Figure 16.5: Upward spiral of co-development of people, process and performance

8. Develop a continuous improvement mentality

Tools, techniques and systems thinking are of course both valuable and necessary, but what brings them to life is developing the right mindset toward problems, toward experimentation and dealing with setbacks, and toward conflict and debate. We'll look at these in turn.

Attitude toward problems

Opportunities for improvement sometimes present as good ideas, but, more often, come in the shape of problems; quality fails, delays, low productivity, customer complaints, cost overruns etc.

It is therefore important to lead and encourage people to find, expose and eliminate such problems, rather than ignore them, hide them or work around them. As far as possible, to develop a 'stop-and-fix' mentality. To solve the problem there and then, because:

- The longer the delay, the colder the trail and the harder it will be to find the root cause
- If left alone, small problems accumulate in number and grow in size
- It may be forgotten about and recur

Attitude toward experimentation and failures, mistakes and setbacks encountered in the process of learning

Following on from the above, it is useful to differentiate between different types of failure. We are often too tolerant of the wrong kind of failure, and too intolerant of the right kind.

Preventable failures – those caused by inadequate training, poor processes, tools or information, complacency, low standards or arrogance – need to be rooted out.

But it is essential that we recognise that a degree of intelligent failure – temporary setbacks encountered in the disciplined pursuit of improvement through ongoing experimentation and learning – is an inevitable part of the improvement process. Such experimentation yields valuable insights that can inspire subsequent significant breakthroughs. Indeed, many high-performing and rapidly improving businesses advocate the policy of 'fail faster' with respect to the disciplined and systematic pursuit of improvement.

This inevitably involves a level of managed risk, so it is important to value the challenging, complex and risky work involved. Ultimately, that's the leader's job – to encourage and support people to tackle problems and to innovate to make the business better.

Attitude toward conflict and debate

'For good ideas and true innovation, you need human interaction, conflict, argument and debate ... we have to see it as thinking [together], and then we have to get really good at it.' (Margaret Heffernan)

Problems are generally problems because they present a barrier to progress with no straightforward, guaranteed or universally agreed approach to overcoming them. Working through them therefore requires collaborative problem-solving which, at a professional level, works best when supported by appropriate technical tools and social disciplines.

The key technical tool is structured problem-solving – for example, a method such as A3 problem-solving (more on which shortly) that frames discussions and guides them through stages of accurate problem-definition, root cause analysis, proposed countermeasures, and review. This brings a degree of structure, objectivity, rigour and discipline.

A useful guiding concept for the social aspect is John Vervaeke's notion of 'oppositional processing' (in contrast to 'adversarial processing'), where all available, relevant facts, data, insights and perspectives from those involved are sought and drawn out. The journey through root cause analysis to proposed countermeasures is then pursued in an emergent fashion characterised by constructively testing the data, thinking and analysis; by looking for what has been erroneously assumed, missed, rejected or ruled out; and by seeking valuable insights, alternatives, problems or unintended consequences that might have been missed.

9. Improve continuously

'Continuously' means two things; that improvement is:

- **A daily activity,** part of normal operations. Routine work, not a crisis-response: problems should be identified and addressed while small and relatively harmless and not be allowed to escalate into crises. (After all, the best and least expensive time to be wise is before the event rather than during it or after it)

- **Ongoing,** driven by the quest for excellence. The focus on improvement shouldn't end when the issue of the moment has been dealt with. The classic Lean injunction to 'seek perfection' should be pursued; the complete elimination of waste so that the customer can be served exactly what they need, and only what they need, when they need it, with no delay and at minimum cost. It is of course recognised that perfection is not wholly achievable, but that pursuing it maintains humility and high standards, fosters a winning mentality, keeps the business moving forward, and will deliver the best of what is possible – excellence and constant, meaningful progress

Building a culture of continuous process improvement

The above principles lead us to the following steps to build a culture of continuous process improvement. These are to:

1. Develop the right understanding at leadership level
2. Provide leadership to create the right vision and mindset throughout business
3. Equip people with the tools and training that allow them to take a structured approach to problem-solving and to remove root causes
4. Engage people and create the right environment
5. Develop deep understanding of the business processes and systems
6. Embed continuous improvement as a core discipline and habit and constantly build capability maturity

Let's look at these in turn.

1. Develop the right understanding at leadership level

First, leaders will themselves have to genuinely recognise that continuous improvement is strategically vital: that unaddressed waste, errors and inefficiency just increase costs, damage customer service, profitability and morale, and limit the capacity and flexibility of the business and its potential for growth. Then, recognising that, they have to actively lead continuous improvement. First by doing their bit, ensuring that their own leadership processes are fit for purpose and continually improving. Then holding their direct reports accountable for ensuring that their processes are fit for purpose and continuously improving, and directing that they in turn hold the next level similarly accountable, all the way to the front line.

2. Provide leadership to create the right vision and mindset throughout the business

Leaders should establish a mindset throughout the business of actively looking for problems, bringing them to the surface and acting quickly to address them, because problem-solving is a part of daily work and the core responsibility of every front-line manager to lead, not an optional task or something that can be postponed until there is 'enough time'. They should also empower front-line people to be actively involved in continuous improvement.

3. Equip people with the tools and training that allow them to take a structured approach to problem-solving to identify and to remove root causes

Provide continuous improvement tools that everyone can learn the basics of quickly, and then, with the right guidance and coaching, build expertise and experience through solving real problems. (There are additional tools and techniques that will become useful and relevant as more challenging problems are tackled, but these tools, and instruction on how to use them, can be provided as and when required, by a skilled coach.) Also, where problems occur that are beyond the current capabilities of the team to solve, it will be useful to have someone with experience available to provide direct assistance. However, experts such as David Hutchins have observed that in their experience, about 80% of operational problems that arise can be solved with a small number of core tools.

Two powerful tools that everyone can learn to use quite quickly are value-stream mapping and A3 problem-solving.

Value-stream mapping
Value-stream mapping is an excellent visual tool, neatly described by Rother and Shook as 'learning to see', as it graphically reveals information about the process flow and dynamics that is hard to see when we are fully immersed in it. In value-stream mapping, the steps in a process are simply mapped out from beginning to end. Opportunities for improvement (the 'pain points') are then identified by looking for any barriers to flow or for signs of the muda wastes (discussed in Chapter 14).

This is often done in the first instance with sticky notes and a large sheet of brown paper. The main purposes of mapping are to:

* Create a constructive dialogue and develop a shared understanding of the process

- See the whole value stream and understand how it works as a system
- Identify relevant improvement opportunities

In highly sophisticated processes, value-stream mapping can become very technical, precise and detailed, and may require specialised process-mapping software. But most processes, particularly early on in an improvement journey, can be meaningfully and sustainably improved with this foundational approach.

For a fuller explanation of value-stream mapping, see Appendix B.

A3 problem-solving

A3 is a tool that provides the vital structured approach to problem-solving. It takes people along a logical path of problem definition, target-state definition, root cause analysis, solution development, action planning and review. It gets its name from the sheet of paper onto which people are encouraged to fit the entire analysis and solution, to keep their thinking and communication tight and clear.

The nine steps are of A3 problem-solving are:

1. Theme/background
2. Problem definition
3. Goal/target state
4. Root cause analysis
5. Containment measures
6. Proposed countermeasure(s)
7. Action plan
8. Impact check
9. Next actions

Technically, A3 is straightforward enough to be used by all colleagues. It is also very flexible in scope and scale. It can be used to understand and solve operational problems, and also to structure strategic improvement projects.

Developmentally, it sharpens people's critical thinking skills so that they can more confidently propose their own solutions to problems. (And A3 problem-solving is, in itself, an excellent tool for coaching people to develop problem-solving skills.) Socially, it provides a focal point that helps people to problem-solve collaboratively.

For these reasons, value-stream mapping and structured problem-solving are arguably the most practical, powerful and relevant team-building activities available.

For a fuller explanation of A3 problem-solving, see Appendix C.

4. Engage people

Developing a culture of continuous improvement requires that the right environment is created, that adequate time is made, that trust is built, and that the collective and collaborative intelligence across the business is mobilised. Let's explore these in turn.

Creating the right environment

The aim is to develop an environment where problems can be highlighted and discussed openly and honestly without defensiveness, fear, blame or recrimination, and where people are encouraged and supported to take a disciplined approach to problem-solving.

Central to this are regular accountability meetings. People must feel safe enough at these to engage psychologically and socially. When problems are identified, if people anticipate some version of 'Whose fault was that?' being asked, most will be inclined to disengage to protect themselves. If the question asked is, instead, 'How did the process let this happen?' people are more likely to get involved and venture a thought.

Time-blocking

Time for continuous improvement will, of course, never be found. It must be set, prioritised and protected. While there is no rule for how much time should be set aside, Ishikawa suggested that small teams of workers trained in problem-solving spend approximately one hour per week tackling problems and presenting their solutions to their manager. The gold standard for organisations committed to continuous process improvement is typically around two hours per person per week.

Whether or not improvement time is explicitly scheduled is a crucial leadership signal. If it is, people understand through the leaders' commitment the strategic importance of improvement. And if it is not, they can justifiably conclude that it is not something worth committing their time and effort to.

Building trust

Usually, only a small number of colleagues (around 10-15%) will actively engage at first, but this is enough to get things moving. This can be done by encouraging and supporting them to work on a problem that they are keen to tackle and that they know something about. Ideally it will be something they have raised themselves.

There are normally many such opportunities. Early successes will build confidence and show that getting involved is safe, beneficial and enjoyable.

Even if starting from a low baseline of engagement, and beset by an abundance of problems with performance, culture, attitudes and working relationships, this approach establishes constructive dialogue and works through some existing issues while (re)building trust and establishing firm foundations for a more improvement-focused culture.

Developing distributed intelligence
Finally, getting everyone involved develops the invaluable organisational capability of distributed intelligence, mobilising the collective knowledge, experience and insight from across the business and the transformational power of collaborative problem-solving.

5. Develop deep understanding of business processes and systems

The business system is a complex, dynamic set of interacting processes. The more fully we can understand the operation of each process, how they interact and influence each other, and how they operate as a whole to shape the overall outcomes, the better placed we will be to identify the key variables and leverage points and how, where and when we can most usefully intervene to maximise the impact of our continuous improvement efforts.

A deep understanding of the business system and how it operates technically and socially can be developed progressively over time through the process of mapping, measuring and experimentation outlined in this and earlier chapters, informed by an understanding of systems-thinking principles to help identify the connections and dynamics.

6. Embed continuous improvement as a core discipline and habit and constantly build capability maturity

The continuous improvement process can be established by continually cycling through the following steps:

- Establish process ownership
- Identify the process's customers (internal or external)
- Map the existing process

- Establish (or ensure that existing measures provide) relevant, actionable, real-time information
- Monitor process performance (the Voice of the Process) through daily meetings and gemba walks
- Identify status against the 14 process excellence criteria
- Identify improvement opportunities
- Execute the immediately actionable kaizen opportunities
- Prioritise the remaining improvement opportunities
- Address the priorities by taking a structured approach through A3 problem-solving
- Seek perfection: the relentless pursuit of adding value and removing waste
- Rinse and repeat, improving processes and continuously building capability (both technically and socially)

Further building and maturation of continuous improvement capability can be promoted by, first, doing the continuous improvement reps; maintaining focus and discipline by repeatedly running the kata to develop deep process understanding, distributed intelligence and collaborative problem-solving capability. And second, progressively adding to the business's repertoire further – potentially transformational – concepts, tools and techniques from the large range available.

Fully developing and maturing continuous improvement capability requires constancy of purpose and long-term thinking. Leaders can best promote this by supporting a steady and disciplined long-term approach to building capability, balancing this with the need for ongoing delivery of excellent operational performance.

Summary

To achieve excellence, every aspect of the business system should constantly be actively managed and improved. This includes not just the operational processes that directly serve the customer, but also the process-management processes, the operational management system and the strategic management system on which they depend. Social capability must also be consciously and consistently developed, to create a team of engaged colleagues who collaborate and solve problems well. This requires consistent attention to leadership and management development, people management, team-building and culture development.

Engaging people throughout the business in continuous process improvement simultaneously develops their understanding of the process and their problem-solving and teamworking skills, while improving performance. It also creates a virtuous cycle which, over time, consolidates into a Thinking People System (or Learning Organisation), which brings the capability to adapt to changing circumstances rapidly and effectively at all levels.

The key steps in building a culture of continuous improvement are to:

1. Develop the right understanding at leadership level
2. Provide leadership to create the right vision and mindset throughout the business
3. Equip people with the tools and training that allow them to take a structured approach to problem-solving and to remove root causes
4. Engage people and create the right environment
5. Develop deep understanding of the business processes and systems
6. Embed continuous improvement as a core discipline and habit and constantly build capability maturity

All of this requires committed, informed and tenacious leadership to develop it to its full capability and maturity.

PART FOUR: SOCIAL SYSTEM

CHAPTER 17

ENGAGED PEOPLE

Introduction: The people factor

Colleague engagement is, as discussed in earlier chapters, one of the two key interrelated dimensions of Business Excellence, the other being a structured and systematic focus on managing and improving performance (see Figure 17.1).

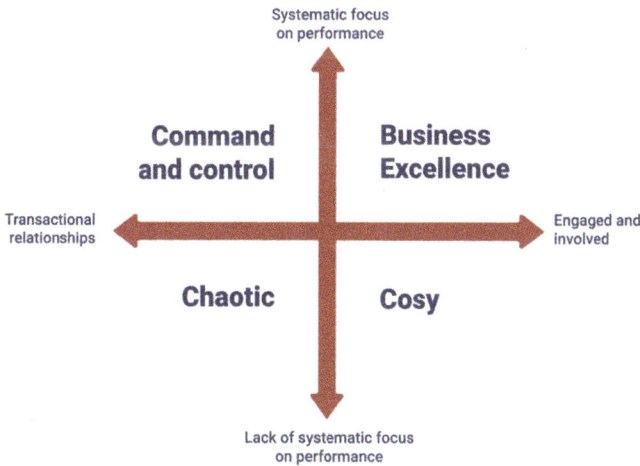

Figure 17.1: Dimensions of Excellence

Engaged people are the driving force of any successful enterprise, supplying the energy, spirit, vitality, creativity and commitment that brings it to life and powers it toward excellence.

When people are engaged, they bring the best of themselves to work. Their 'A-game': positivity, determination, confidence, inventiveness and resilience. They are more likely to take responsibility for their own performance and development, and more likely to get actively involved in managing and improving the processes that serve the customer and move the business forward.

For organisations aspiring to Business Excellence, engaging people is part of the wider vision:

- To create an organisation that respects, and continuously finds ways to add value for, its people, customers and the wider community; a culture of 'omotenashi'
- To create a Thinking People System; a culture built on excellent people management processes that unlock, develop and deploy people's potential and actively involve them in collaborative problem-solving to manage and improve the business

Figure 17.2 positions colleague engagement within the context of the overall Business Excellence model.

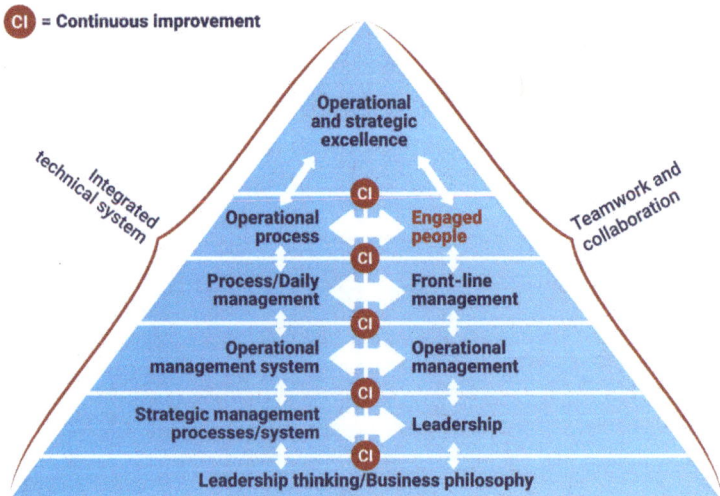

Figure 17.2: Colleague engagement in context

Defining engagement

Before diving into the detail, let's look at how engagement is defined at both the individual and organisational level.

Individual level

At the individual level, engagement can be defined as the application of discretionary physical, cognitive or emotional effort to achieve a goal.

When engaged, people are (a) willing (motivated), (b) able (empowered), and (c) accountable, where:

- Motivation is having the desire and confidence to perform well
- Being empowered means having (a) responsibility, including appropriate decision-making power and authority, (b) information, tools, resources and support, and (c) the requisite skills
- Being accountable means being involved in ongoing, regular, structured reviews of performance (results, attitudes and behaviours), the purpose of which is to:
  - Provide appropriate recognition and encouragement to maintain and enhance top performance
  - Identify relevant improvement opportunities and encourage their pursuit
  - Provide additional direction, motivation or coaching if required
  - Employ proportionate disciplinary measures as a last resort, where attitude, behaviour or performance is unacceptable (and has proved resistant to persistent, positive attempts to support people to move beyond it)

LEVELS OF COMMITMENT

There are different degrees of commitment:

- **Transactional commitment:** Where work is regarded as purely contractual – an exchange of time/effort/expertise for money
- **Rational commitment:** Where people will perform well and solve problems if they believe that it will advance their personal interests by making their life easier and/or enhancing their prospects of improved reward, recognition or progression

---

- **Emotional commitment:** Where people take pride in their job or company, enjoy what they do, and enjoy the challenge of delivering excellent performance. A Corporate Leadership Council report noted that increased rational commitment provides up to a 21% increase in someone's intent to stay, but only a 9% increase in effort. However, emotional commitment to the job can give rise to a 55.9% increase in discretionary effort, peaking at over six times the impact of a rational commitment[2]

- **Spiritual commitment:** Where people's role, or the wider purpose of the organisation, contributes something that is personally inspiring, meaningful and valuable to them: where they feel that what they do is more of a calling or vocation than a job or occupation. This connects with deeper motivations and passions and inspires great commitment, loyalty, effort, engagement and determination

Organisational level

At an organisational level, engagement is defined as the process of communicating with, managing, developing, involving and empowering people, giving them what they need to succeed. It is part of a wider strategy to create a culture of excellence where people can give of their best individually, and collaborate and problem-solve with others.

This requires the right people management strategy and systems, and the right leadership attitudes, skills and behaviours.

Finally, engagement is sometimes narrowly defined as the score on an engagement survey: an indication of how well people feel they are being led, managed and developed. This can be a useful metric within the wider strategy, but there are hidden dangers if an organisation doesn't understand what is driving the score, or is not committed to the underlying aim of empowering and enabling people. Short-term hacks might then be employed to falsely boost the score, which invariably leads only to cynicism about engagement surveys and the leadership's intentions and competence.

---

2   Corporate Leadership Council (2004) 'Driving Performance and Retention Through Employee Engagement: A Quantitative Analysis of Effective Engagement Strategies'

Beyond satisfaction and loyalty

Engagement includes, but goes beyond, people being satisfied with the job. Engagement implies an active commitment to the role, to the aims of the organisation, and to pursuing excellence and continuous improvement at a personal and business level.

Satisfaction may increase people's willingness to stay with the organisation, but this doesn't always mean increased commitment or contribution. Long-serving colleagues may offer only presenteeism, feel entitled, and be disengaged and change-resistant while being unwilling, or unable, to leave. (This is in line with the aforementioned research finding that increasing rational commitment raised intent to stay 21% but resulted in only a 9% increase in effort.)

Also, when organisations introduce initiatives aimed solely at 'keeping people happy', it risks sending the wrong message about engagement; that it is one-way traffic – an effort made only by the business. And it risks raising unrealistic expectations (and possibly a degree of entitlement), which, when not met, is likely to actually increase dissatisfaction.

Not only does satisfaction not guarantee motivation, but motivation does not guarantee performance if people do not have the resources, skills, support etc. that they need to translate motivation into performance.

On the other hand, as the psychologist David Guest pointed out, while happy people are not necessarily productive, productive people tend to be happy. Most people take pride and pleasure in doing their job well; satisfying customers, solving problems, and learning and improving along the way. As a result, they tend to be more fulfilled, confident and resilient, and more ambitious to achieve higher standards.

Respect for people

Effective people management, then, is not about indulging people's less reasonable desires. It is about making 'respect for people' (as Toyota framed it) a guiding principle for the design of the people management strategy, systems, and leadership and management behaviours. This includes (as Kristie Rogers put it) both:

- 'Owed respect' – consistently treating everyone with fairness, civility and dignity

- 'Earned respect' – tribute paid for people's personal attitude, approach, contribution or achievements

Owed respect encompasses respect for people's capabilities, development potential, aspirations, enthusiasms, problem-solving abilities and resilience, and also for their desire to contribute meaningfully, to succeed in their role, and to develop and express their talents as far as they would like to. All of which is aimed at optimising the value they can bring and be rewarded for in return.

Viewed this way, owed respect means providing opportunities for people to take pride in their work, make a meaningful contribution and enhance their impact – giving them the chance to shine and accumulate further earned respect.

Respect of course, as well being due to everyone, is required from them. Respect for colleagues, the company they have chosen to join, its customers and suppliers, and its aims, values, culture and reputation. Central to this is not only encouraging active participation by all colleagues in the management and improvement of the business and the development of a positive and professional culture, but also making it an explicit part of their responsibilities. Specifically, involvement in:

- Daily kaizen: what Masaaki Imai described as ongoing improvements everyday, everywhere, by everybody
- Strategic projects: working toward stretching goals that require them to wrestle with challenging problems

Tackling such challenges necessitates learning and growth and allows people to simultaneously contribute, achieve something of value, and extend their capabilities. All of this fosters pride and builds confidence and self-respect, as well as winning further earned respect from managers, colleagues and customers.

Key aspects of effective people management

Taking into consideration all of the above, the aims of a realistic, comprehensive and balanced people management strategy are therefore to:

- Enable people to be productive and successful in their role by ensuring that they have the information, resources, skills and support they require to succeed
- Develop rounded, balanced and mature professionals with the right attitudes, behaviours and skills to achieve both personal and business excellence

- Create a culture where they can develop and contribute to their full potential, and collaborate effectively with other engaged colleagues

And it should include:

- Setting high standards
- Giving people responsibility
- Providing the opportunity for people to develop and grow through tackling live operational problems, and also through their involvement in challenging strategic projects
- Empowering and supporting people, providing sufficient latitude to take managed risks as they strive to improve things for themselves, for customers and for the company
- Holding people accountable by maintaining a consistent, constructive dialogue about attitude, behaviour and performance
- Providing ongoing coaching and positive developmental challenge
- Where necessary, disciplining the small number of colleagues whose performance, attitudes or behaviours consistently fall below acceptable standards, despite adequate support over an extended period

The good news is that engaging the majority of colleagues is achievable. Most people want to take pride in their work and to do a good job and, if led and managed well, will do so.

Why excellence in people management matters

Effective people management is of strategic importance for organisations aspiring to excellence. High-value-adding people working in a collaborative culture is not a luxury, but a necessity, for delivering the excellent operational performance and the ongoing strategic improvement required to remain relevant and competitive in complex and dynamic mid-21st-century business environments.

The costs of getting people management wrong

The consequences of poor people management are significant, far-reaching and long-lasting, impacting on everything from short-term profitability to long-term viability. Among these are:

- **Immediate direct costs** through:

  - Mistakes and the costs of rework (time, labour, material and the corresponding loss of process availability)
  - Inefficiencies
  - Loss of margin, revenue and customers through poor quality, delivery performance or service
  - Loss of good people, leading to increased recruitment costs, loss of quality if similar calibre replacements cannot be found, and loss of continuity and capability while replacements are recruited and brought up to speed

- **The loss of significant untapped potential,** creating an ever-widening contribution gap – the gap between what people could contribute and achieve, and what they actually contribute and achieve. This is a serious, built-in, recurring opportunity-cost. Poor management can actually stunt the development and expression of available potential, breed attitudinal immaturity and shorten the reach of individuals, teams and the organisation

- **People who are not aligned with the business's aims or values.** If people's needs for belonging, involvement, recognition, esteem and meaning are not met by the organisation, they will seek it in peer groups. Such groups may have their own aims and values. This can create an alternative power base and undermine leaders' influence

- **Reliance on people's personal motivation and discipline.** If people get the message that performance isn't important enough to focus on routinely, they will adjust their standards accordingly . This usually means that a manager will get great attitude and effort, but only from the self-motivated minority. The majority will offer only obligatory potential (more on this shortly). A significant number will be disengaged (evidenced by more absence, unauthorised breaks, low productivity etc.)

- **People who feel disconnected and alienated will focus on their problems and entitlements** and put them ahead of their responsibilities and obligations, such as improving their contribution or playing their part in the team

- **Problematic attitudes and behaviours.** People's attitudes toward the business, customers and colleagues generally reflect the attitude of the business toward them. If this is characterised by mediocrity and a lack of responsibility, care and professionalism, the majority will follow this example in their dealings with customers, and with each other. In extremes, people switch off, give up, withdraw, and won't take responsibility for their attitude and performance

- **Problems and misunderstandings will arise and fester.** This will not only impede the development of the mutual trust and rapport required to access their discretionary potential (see below), but may actually erode it

- **Avoidable frustration and hassle for managers.** Up to 40% of a manager's time can be spent on closely supervising, disciplining and dealing with the grievances of a small number of low-productivity, high-maintenance colleagues. None of which adds value for customers, and much of which is avoidable. This is a significant distraction and means that less time is spent on supporting the colleagues who are striving to move the business forward. Being constantly embroiled in people problems can also skew managers' style, leading them to develop attitudes and behaviours that disengage more people, further exacerbate these problems and create a stuck cycle

- The **lack of accountability** allows poor performers to hide or flourish. Low attitudinal, behavioural and performance standards are accepted and become contagious. Teamwork suffers. The more engaged colleagues become frustrated and ...

- **The best team players get taken for granted, become fed up and leave.** Left without adequate direction, support or encouragement, and with their goodwill exploited by constant requests for more discretionary time or effort to cover for others, they burn out, become disenchanted, switch off, and leave. (And of course, the poor performers who are less attractive to prospective employers stay, and the culture skews increasingly toward entrenched mediocrity)

All of the above impacts on quality, cost, delivery performance and customer service. It creates a business that is slow to spot and grasp opportunities, respond to challenges, improve, and achieve sustained success. It also opens up the significant danger of getting trapped in a culture of self-perpetuating mediocrity.

THE ECONOMICS OF DISENGAGEMENT

Gallup found in 2025 that only 31% of US employees were actively engaged at work, with 52% disengaged and 17% actively disengaged. Globally, only 21%[3] are engaged. This, it was noted:

- Harmed business outcomes. Sorenson and Garman estimated the cost impact for organisations (in 2013) at around US$550 billion (circa 3% of GDP at that time)[4]
- Adversely impacted the lives of millions of employees at work – and beyond

Phil Crosby famously made the point that 'quality is free' (because the cumulative effect of continually fixing defects and the reputational damaged caused is net more expensive than getting things right in the first place).

Bonini, Kalloch and Ton make a parallel point about people management. They observe that: 'You're going to pay one way or the other. Either you invest in a well-paid, well-trained, well-motivated team that will make your company better every day, or you incur endless high penalties for your mediocre workforce in the form of higher turnover, higher inventory costs, lower quality, worse customer service, and less responsiveness and adaptability. Investing in people may seem expensive, but the alternative – a poor-performing operation – is much costlier.'

The potential benefit to colleagues is that excellence in people management is aimed at, and likely to create, more secure and higher-value-adding jobs. And, since a job can only be sustainably paid at a level commensurate with the value it adds (determined by what the customer will pay), increasing monetisable value and customer satisfaction directly influences the organisation's ability to pay.

The benefits of getting people management right

---

3   Gallup (2013), State of the Global Workplace: Understanding Employees, Informing Leaders

4   Sorenson, S. & Garman, K. (2013) 'How to tackle U.S. employees' stagnating management', Business Journal

> *'You don't provide incredible service, tailored problem-solving, superior quality and do it in a rapid time-frame unless you have people who care and people who are committed. ... If we are serious about quality and serious about service, then we must, by definition, be serious about an extraordinary level of attention to people management.' (Tom Peters)*

Unlike machines, buildings and money, people can improve themselves and increase their capability and contribution. They can choose (and thus be led) to learn, grow, develop and improve.

The benefits of effective people management include:

- **Winning the 'war for talent';** successfully meeting the ongoing challenge of:

  - **Retaining talent:** Typically, around 37% of staff in most organisations are actively considering leaving. Around three quarters of this is due to lack of satisfaction, direction and opportunity

  - **Attracting top talent:** The people with the attitudes and skills that you need to move the business forward will be savvy enough to ask the right questions at interview and work out what kind of culture and management style the business has. They are also likely to have options, and tend to prefer to work where they are well managed and have the opportunity to flourish

  - **Getting the best from existing talent:** Developing individual skills that are not readily available for hire, and thus building organisational capability, competitive edge and cultural capital

  - **Deploying talent effectively:** Aligning individual responsibilities with operational and strategic goals

- **Greater control of business performance:** Increasing the ability to produce predictable, repeatable results and continuous improvement

- **Lower-maintenance people:** Fewer distractions for managers and more time to think and act strategically (i.e. add significant long-term value). People who are led and managed with professionalism and respect are more likely to behave professionally and with respect and to be lower-maintenance

- **Better teamwork and collaboration:** People are more able and willing to collaborate and problem-solve within local teams and across the business

- **Greater capacity to learn and adapt quickly and well to new challenges and opportunities,** which requires levels of skill, trust and self-organisation that can only come from engaged people who collaborate effectively

There is, of course, a case to be made that pursuing excellence in how we manage and develop people is also a moral responsibility, as it affects not only people's lives at work, but also their health and well-being beyond, and their longer-term prospects and income potential (and possibly, therefore, their family's longer-term prospects).

> *'What is the net present value of highly developed, engaged people who are continually improving processes over the next 10 years? We have not seen anyone even attempt to calculate this.' (Jeffrey Liker and James Franz)*

VALUING CULTURAL CAPITAL

Cultural capital is the business's combined technical and social capability to add monetisable value. That is, its ability to meet evolving customer needs, to solve problems and to improve operationally and strategically, faster and better than the competition. (With social capability being the ability to recruit, retain, develop, motivate and effectively deploy talent and to internally align the organisation and foster effective collaboration within and between teams across the business.)

Given this:

- What type and level of cultural capital do you need to put you in a position to lead your industry?
- Is your people management strategy explicitly geared to build it?
- Is there an opportunity to measure cultural capital more accurately, to better inform the development and execution of your people management strategy

---

People's potential: from mayhem to excellence

People have the potential to exhibit attitudes and behaviours across a spectrum, from being disruptive to being excellent (see Figure 17.3). What gets developed and expressed depends largely on how people are led, managed and developed. People may be willing, but not able, to do their job well, due to factors beyond their control. These factors are usually down to management, and the constraints and limitations of a less-than-excellent organisational culture.

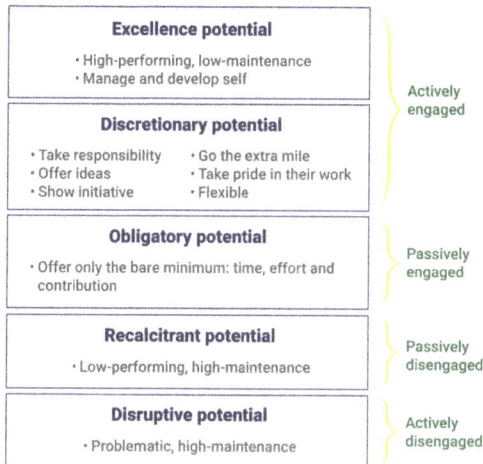

Excellence potential	
• High-performing, low-maintenance • Manage and develop self	Actively engaged
Discretionary potential	
• Take responsibility • Go the extra mile • Offer ideas • Take pride in their work • Show initiative • Flexible	
Obligatory potential	
• Offer only the bare minimum: time, effort and contribution	Passively engaged
Recalcitrant potential	
• Low-performing, high-maintenance	Passively disengaged
Disruptive potential	
• Problematic, high-maintenance	Actively disengaged

Figure 17.3: Levels of potential

Let's start with the bad news...

Disruptive potential: creating mayhem

When actively disengaged, people can be disruptive, difficult, defiant and destructive, looking for reasons to complain, criticise, blame, and hide from responsibility.

This may include refusing to perform tasks, support colleagues or contribute to improvement activities. They may derail meetings with toxic attitudes and behaviours, foment discontent, sour the team atmosphere, and negatively influence others.

In extremes this may include aggression, confrontation, vandalism, theft and sabotage. It happens infrequently, but it happens (in subtle or obvious forms) from time to time in many organisations.

People in this mindset are not only low-performing, but also extremely high-maintenance. They actively impede performance and progress, taking up significant management time and attention for little return. They represent a significant and enduring opportunity cost, as they distract managers from higher-leverage value-adding and strategic improvement activities, which damages everyone's long-term interests.

Recalcitrant potential: reluctance and game playing

People also have the potential to be passively disengaged: awkward, uncooperative, defensive and resistant to change. People in this mindset typically have low standards, an inflated sense of entitlement and an insufficient sense of responsibility. They are reluctant to look at themselves, accept feedback, learn, develop or improve. They are also likely to make excuses and blame circumstances or other people for problems or their own underperformance.

Low-performing and high-maintenance, people in this space are likely to keep pushing boundaries to find out how much they can get away with, and how far they can push or manipulate their manager.

Obligatory potential: the bare minimum

Obligatory potential is the bare minimum that people are obliged to contribute without attracting some form of unwelcome attention. It is pretty much restricted to turning up on time, doing acceptable work, not making too many avoidable mistakes, not having too many questionable absences or unauthorised breaks, and not indulging in too much obviously disruptive behaviour.

There is some degree of engagement, but it is passive rather than active: compliance, but little beyond that. Looking to others to solve problems ('It's not my job'), there is little initiative or contribution of ideas or solutions.

Getting only this from people isn't, of course, enough for excellence.

Discretionary potential: the extra mile

The nature and level of commitment that people offer is, of course, at their discretion. Like getting someone to laugh, genuine commitment can't be forced, but will be naturally forthcoming if the circumstances are right. Dimensions of discretionary potential that can be unlocked include:

- **Physical:** Time and effort
- **Mental:** Thought and creativity

- **Emotional:** Taking pride in the job and enjoying the challenge of delivering excellent performance
- **Spiritual:** When people are committed 'heart and soul' – seeing the job as a vocation, not an occupation or profession

Discretionary potential is the first level of active engagement: 'going the extra mile', being willing, taking initiative, showing goodwill, solving problems, getting involved in improvement activities, contributing ideas, helping others out, and showing commitment and persistence in the face of challenges.

Most organisations have significant reserves of discretionary potential that they could unlock.

Excellence potential: learning, growing, problem-solving and collaborating

Beyond discretionary potential is excellence potential. It draws on people's capacity to learn, change, grow, solve problems and creatively adapt to new circumstances, challenges and opportunities. To achieve personal and professional excellence by both:

- **Enhancing** their existing capacities (learning to work with greater speed and precision), and
- **Extending** their capacities (learning new skills and more adaptive ways of thinking and working)

People who bring excellence potential tend to:

- Be low-maintenance and high-performing
- Be committed to pursuing business and personal excellence, and have a willingness to stretch, to actively develop themselves, and to continuously improve
- Show personal leadership, taking responsibility for their attitudes, behaviours, motivation, development, performance and results
- Be confident self-starters – they see what needs to be done, show initiative and take action
- Be consistently positive and constructive. Problem-solvers (rather than problem-spotters). Thriving on challenges, looking for solutions rather than excuses
- Be reliable: plan and execute in a disciplined way to stay on track and deliver

- Be resilient: have the emotional strength and stability to deliver consistently good performance in a range of conditions, avoiding complacency when things are going well, and not unravelling under pressure

- Have the capacity to learn and adapt quickly and well, as circumstances change

- Be coachable – seeking, listening to, and acting on, feedback

- Collaborate well with others, sharing knowledge, skills, ideas and experience to solve problems, drive improvement and achieve results

- Contribute to an environment where people support, coach, constructively challenge and inspire each other to perform and continuously develop their knowledge, skills, attitudes, confidence and resilience

- Be innovative, always looking to change, create new ways of adding more value, see new possibilities, and continuously reinvent themselves and the business

Since the ability to learn and adapt quickly and well is central to Business Excellence, helping people to develop and use their full range of talents in this way helps the business to excel and to continually adapt to new challenges and opportunities.

Most organisations also have significant underdeveloped reserves of excellence potential.

The engagement spectrum – what we see reflects how well we manage

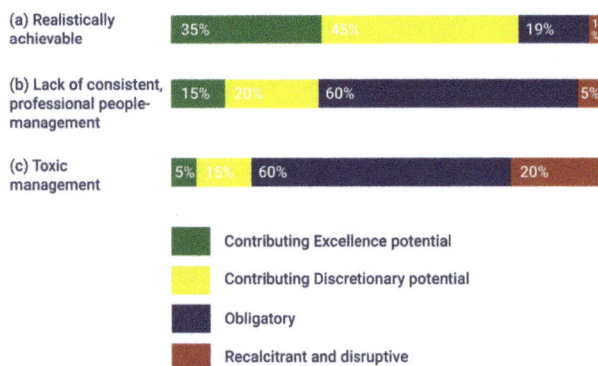

Figure 17.4: The engagement spectrum

The different levels of potential form a spectrum against which every organisation can gauge levels of engagement and thereby gain some insight into the quality of their approach to people management.

The proportions vary from industry to industry, from company to company and from manager to manager. Engagement of above 80% (those contributing discretionary potential or better) is realistically achievable for committed organisations. Best-in-class organisations reach above 90%. (line a in Figure 17.4).

At the opposite extreme, where management is not just ineffective but toxic (line c), only a few hardy souls attempt to give of their best out of sheer personal pride. The majority contribute obligatory potential. A significant minority are actively disengaged.

Where people have not historically been managed and developed in a consistent, systematic and professional way, around 15% of people are actively engaged (line b). It may be claimed, only half-jokingly, that they succeed despite how they are managed, rather than because of it. They are not always used to best effect and their potential is not always fully developed. Instead, they may be asked for lots of favours, taken for granted and largely neglected (while managers spend a significant amount of time dealing with underperformers). This is a huge missed opportunity because it is people in this group who are most likely to be the 'first followers' in the drive toward excellence, and the role models that others will follow. Instead, others see how poorly they are treated relative to their levels of commitment and form a view that it might be better not to risk doing the same.

Here, about 5% of people are actively disengaged, bringing only disruptive or recalcitrant potential. In between are people who are:

- Passively engaged – generally positive about their job and happy to engage more actively, but not getting the opportunities and encouragement to do so
- Passively disengaged – lacking either the opportunity or the motivation to contribute more

Those contributing obligatory potential might be 'watchers' or 'swing voters', because what they do next will depend on whether excellence is supported, encouraged and rewarded, or underperformance is tolerated and unaddressed.

Implications

The upshot is that businesses whose management practices and culture do not actively foster engagement potentially have up to 85% of the workforce bringing less than their full capability to the role – many of whom will, to varying degrees, respond to constructive efforts to engage them more fully.

Unlocking the significant untapped discretionary and excellence potential represents a tremendous opportunity to increase capacity, improve short-term results and build for the future. Significant gains can be achieved by enhancing engagement at every point across the spectrum:

- Those already actively engaged can be further empowered to drive for excellence and to be role models, leaders and coaches who can lead and inspire others
- The passively engaged can be encouraged to develop and contribute more of their potential
- Those who are currently disengaged should be given everything they need to succeed, and both a greater positive opportunity to get more involved, and greater accountability (and clear consequences) for their attitudes, behaviour and performance. This will remove any excuses and will either help them to achieve the standards required, or reveal that they are unable or unwilling to provide what the business needs

Unlocking that extra bit of effort, quality or creativity that people can offer is one of the hallmarks of great managers. The good news is that this can be achieved without the need for capital investment, new technology, or additional time. Indeed, it will save time and hassle in the long run.

FROM ENGAGEMENT TO PERFORMANCE

Figure 17.5: From engagement to performance

Effective management means creating time and opportunities to engage colleagues. Done well:

- This builds the emotional bank account with people (mutual trust, respect, rapport etc.)

- As a result, most people are then inclined to contribute a bit more discretionary and excellence potential (flexibility, goodwill, ideas, desire to learn and improve, to help colleagues etc.)

- This can be deployed to find ways to reduce non-value-adding activity (things that disrupt the smooth flow of work, waste time, money and resources, and frustrate everybody)

- This drives sustainable improvements in processes, KPIs and culture

- This in turn drives the achievement of the strategy to create a culture of excellence which is great to buy from, work for and invest in

Summary

- Increasing engagement is one of the highest-leverage strategies for improving results and is a vital component of achieving Business Excellence

- Engagement goes beyond 'employee satisfaction'. While it includes enabling, supporting and developing people, it also includes setting high standards, giving accountability and providing a positive challenge that helps people to grow and to take confidence from their achievements

- Effective people management unlocks the untapped discretionary and excellence potential that increases the capability to solve problems, improve process and performance, create value, build a positive and confident culture and create an upward spiral of good performance and morale

- Colleague engagement is thus the key to creating a team of high-performing, low-maintenance people. To unlocking the invaluable human capacity to learn and adapt quickly to meet new challenges and opportunities, improve results and maintain competitive advantage. Indeed, given the pace of change in business, this may be the key to survival and sustainable competitive advantage

CHAPTER 18

PERFORMANCE AND ENGAGEMENT FUNDAMENTALS

Introduction

In this chapter we'll first explore the psychology of engagement, and then go on to outline the fundamental factors that underpin engagement.

The psychology of engagement

What disengages

Most people come to work reasonably positive and willing to engage. They want to take pride in their work and to succeed. They want the information, skills and support to allow them to do their job to the best of their ability. But when they don't get what they need to succeed, they may justifiably become frustrated, disengaged, disillusioned and demotivated.

There may be three layers to this frustration:

1. Consistently having to deal with avoidable problems such as:

   • Poor planning, organisation and communication

   • Having to work with inefficient or bureaucratic processes

- Lack of tools, effective equipment or resource
- Not having the training or ongoing coaching to do as well as they would wish to
- Not having the scope to make decisions that would allow them to address some of the problems above

2. Lack of proper management accountability:

- Watching standards not being followed, or underperformance going unaddressed
- Not being listened to when problems are raised and suggestions for improvement offered. People get the message that nobody really cares about quality, performance, customers, profitability or, indeed, them. So they think, why should they? After trying for a while they give up and switch off, and may become cynical

3. When the manager makes matters worse by:

- Pushing for performance regardless of the above issues
- Telling people they are 'empowered' without providing any meaningful empowerment
- Using superficial motivational techniques and pep talks instead of addressing the core problems

The vicious circle of disengagement

If people do not have the right training, tools, processes and leadership, they will struggle to perform and, becoming dismayed and frustrated at the lack of professional leadership, the majority are likely to disengage, withdraw, become defensive, and work (at best) only to their obligatory potential.

When managers (who themselves may lack the right training, tools and processes to manage effectively) misperceive that this is because people are lazy, incompetent, or being deliberately uncooperative – what Douglas McGregor called taking a 'Theory X' view of people – they are likely to respond by adopting a directive, critical and possibly punitive style.

This may alienate even those who are naturally inclined to contribute discretionary and excellence potential and create more, and more deeply entrenched, disengagement all round.

In the managers' eyes, this deepening disengagement confirms their view that people are disinterested, lazy, uncooperative etc. and the vicious circle continues. A lose-lose situation develops where everyone sees everyone else as the cause of the problem.

Over time, this can grind down people's confidence, enthusiasm and optimism and their desire to learn, grow and change, as well as their trust and respect for their managers. Thus, people can go from being 'the company's most important asset' to being problematic and underperforming.

'For many, work becomes stressful; for some downright unbearable. Pathological outcomes multiply to include ... apathy, indifference, and the reluctance to exert any more energy or effort than the bare minimum needed to get by.'(Abraham Zaleznik)

THE SELF-FULFILLING PROPHECY OF TRANSACTIONAL MANAGEMENT

Transactional management, where managers' underlying assumption is that colleagues see work as purely contractual, are self-interested and seeking to minimise personal effort, becomes a self-fulfilling prophecy.

This attitude tends to skew managers' behaviour toward lack of interest in, and engagement with, people, or toward being critical, unapproachable and harsh. All of which contributes to creating a social context that can feel adversarial and leads to:

- **Suppression of people's existing abilities, development and spirit**: As Albert Bandura observed, when people experience attitudes that are 'actively rejectant' they show 'decelerated individual development, relatively poor use of the abilities they do possess, and some lack of originality'

- **Disconnection and withdrawal:** Having no expectation of fair treatment, people tend to give up, become disillusioned, despondent and resentful, and focus on protecting themselves first and foremost. As Richard Pascale noted: 'When we are used, ignored, under-utilised, betrayed, or discarded, it tends to hurt a lot. Over time, employees build up defences against caring too much, investing too much, trying too hard'

- **Push-back:** Behaviour breeds behaviour, so people generally won't give commitment, respect, honesty and support if they don't get it. Instead they tend, as Bandura observed, to become 'emotionally unstable, rebellious, aggressive, and quarrelsome'

The net effect is that when people perceive that their managers are uninterested, aloof, unreliable or even hostile, they tend to do the bare minimum and increasingly, over time:

- Become dependent, and lack initiative and drive: if always told what to do, people will come to always want to be told what to do
- Lack confidence, self-belief and persistence, and drift toward helplessness, hopelessness and apathy
- Become cynical, petty-minded and uncooperative, exerting any negative or disruptive power they have

This breeds a losing mentality that becomes contagious. Managers then see this as confirmation of their initial assumption that people are generally lazy, untrustworthy, uninterested in development and require close supervision. Which starts another turn of the downward spiral of mutual mistrust and tension.

The virtuous circle of positive engagement

The good news is that when people are professionally led and managed, and given the right tools, resources and processes, most tend to be positive and productive, take responsibility for performance and problem-solving, and do a good job.

This can create the virtuous cycle of reciprocal opening. Like the vicious circle, this virtuous circle is driven by managers' attitudes and behaviours: in this case, the belief that people want to do a good job, want to participate, have talent, want to develop, want to take responsibility and can motivate themselves and are capable of solving problems in the right circumstances. (McGregor called this 'Theory Y' thinking.)

This positive mindset generates more positive behaviours: seeing the best in people leads to a more positive, encouraging approach, a desire to engage and be more open and constructive, putting in place proper communication and performance review processes, giving people responsibility, treating them like adults and building their confidence and their desire to succeed.

When managers are thus more 'acceptant–democratic' (as Bandura put it), they are more likely to show greater originality and emotional control.

Most people respond well to this in terms of attitude, performance and results. Most will engage positively, accept more responsibility, be more open and honest, listen, accept feedback and guidance and take advantage of development opportunities. This in turn reinforces the manager's belief in people and encourages them to continue to invest their time, energy and faith in them. (See Appendix D for more on this.)

Realistic positivity

That said, even the most positive and encouraging of managers will, in a career lifetime, encounter a small number of people who respond in a Theory X way to even the most enlightened leadership. In such circumstances, managers can understandably be lured toward losing patience with their progressive approach, and default to more critical and punitive attitudes and behaviours. This has the inevitable result of drawing them into the downward spiral.

Therefore, what I call 'Theory Y+' thinking might be more attuned to the realities of organisational life. That is, for managers to proceed on the assumption that the majority will perform well if led well, while recognising the need to invest additional time and effort in coaching, developing and performance-managing those who do not. This means constructively, skilfully, professionally and systematically managing underperformance by setting clear standards and expectations, identifying gaps (particularly in areas that fall below the 'waterline' of acceptability), creating a performance improvement plan and following it through.

This will either help people to achieve an acceptable level of attitude and performance, or reveal that steps should be taken to discipline or, in extremis and as a last resort, to remove, anyone whose attitude and performance consistently falls below minimum acceptable standards and who has proven unable or unwilling to respond to prolonged and skilled development efforts.

This avoids the pitfall of the Theory X downward spiral. It is also likely to strengthen the virtuous cycle as the more positive contributors (a) see that standards and accountability are taken seriously for everyone, and (b) aren't held back by disruptive colleagues who sour the atmosphere and make it harder for others to succeed.

Psychological factors

A full exploration of motivation is beyond the scope of this chapter, but here are some key psychological factors that underpin effective people management.

1. Provide psychological safety

When in particular work situations, relationships, or in a wider culture that is felt to be either unfriendly, unpredictable or hostile, people tend to feel psychologically unsafe. That is, quite simply, they feel under threat of unjustified criticism, manipulation, exploitation, rejection; of being walked over, ignored, mistreated or made to look or feel stupid. For psychological protection, their fight-or-flight response is triggered. This moves them to be either:

- Closed and cautious – to withdraw (flight)
- Defensive and aggressive – to push back (fight)

Both imply a shift in focus away from customer satisfaction, performance and improvement and toward self-protection. The opposite of what leadership and management are intended to achieve.

To be clear, psychological safety is not pandering, mollycoddling or otherwise tiptoeing around issues that need to be discussed, such as performance, attitude, behaviour and standards. Quite the reverse. It means getting people into the right psychological state to accept the legitimate challenges of professional life and deal with them responsibly and professionally, and over time to do so with increasingly greater speed, comfort, confidence and skill.

David Rock's SCARF model highlights five dimensions that influence a person's degree of felt psychological safety. It forms a waterline model; that is, if any one of the five goes below a threshold for basic trust, then an individual will retreat, shut down or bite back. So a prerequisite for positive engagement is that all five are above the waterline. (Which, again, pretty much just means proceeding with basic levels of courtesy, dignity, respect and interpersonal skill.) Sounds obvious, but it's not a universal constant:

- **Status:** Provide basic 'owed respect' in all exchanges and due 'earned respect' for people's experience, expertise, contribution etc. Avoid saying or doing anything that needlessly threatens someone's social, professional or financial status; for example, diminishing their role, contribution, value, knowledge, expertise etc.

- **Certainty:** With a sense of certainty, people can crack on with their work in a focused and confident manner. But uncertainty creates tension, introduces doubt, causes hesitation, distracts attention and generally impedes the smooth flow of thought and action that characterises top performance. In extremis, Rock argues, it 'can paralyse people's ability to perform'. Due care is then advised to avoid creating unnecessary confusion through being chaotic, disorganised, arbitrary or unpredictable. People should know what is expected of them and have the tools, resources, information and support to succeed. They should also know when they will be held accountable and that this will be done professionally rather than harshly, or in a manner that varies according to their manager's alternating moods

- **Agency:** People need sufficient scope to make and execute their own choices and decisions, especially in stressful situations and circumstances. This includes having sufficient time, resources, reliable information, skill, latitude, empowerment and trust. Without it, we can reliably expect people to react unfavourably to (a) the situation, and (b) the person who is cramping their style. Here again, managers who reduce the scope for positive engagement increase their odds of facing the usual array of self-protection responses, from helplessness and hopelessness, with people withdrawing and switching off, to people pushing back forcefully if they feel cornered

- **Relatability:** The human brain continually makes rapid, subconscious friend-or-foe distinctions on relatability, i.e. how friendly and approachable someone is and how accommodating to our aims and interests they are. We tend not to trust or wish to deal with people whose behaviours are thoughtless, selfish, arrogant, critical, aggressive, uncooperative or hostile. We seek to avoid them and, where that is not possible, to frustrate them, defy them or push back against them

- **Fairness:** People strongly value fairness in regard to:

  - Outcomes, both:

    - Absolute – something that is objectively unfair, and

    - Relative – where one person gets something, but another person in comparable circumstances is denied it

  - Process, i.e. how the decision was reached: by whom, through what process, using what criteria, with what information, considering whose viewpoints and priorities, and with what intention and degree of transparency

Fairness goes straight to the heart of trust, the core of psychological safety. People are especially sensitive to unfairness, quick to perceive it and likely to react strongly, and to hold on to the memory of it for a long time.

2. Foster positive emotions

First, it is important to note that 'positive' and 'negative' are not defined here as indicators of felt happiness, contentment or satisfaction (as important as that might be), but in terms of the impact that a particular emotional state has on someone's performance, contribution, learning, coachability and ability to collaborate. Positive emotions enhance it, negative emotions stifle or damage it.

Given this, one of the defining purposes of leadership and management is to foster positive emotions such as enthusiasm, energy, commitment, determination, creativity, inventiveness, resourcefulness, resilience and tenacity. These are self-evidently the stuff of high performance.

The absence of positive emotions is a problem in itself (and failure to tap into this powerful and freely available resource is a costly oversight). But worse, the vacuum their absence creates is likely to be filled with negative emotions such as apathy, doubt, anxiety, distrust, fear and hostility. All of which increases the probability that people will reduce their focus on, and commitment to, the business and its goals.

Working environments unavoidably throw up problems with processes and performance and in relationships with customers, colleagues and managers. So, while negative emotions will inevitably arise, they cannot be allowed to fester, multiply and become entrenched. Leaders and managers should take care to (a) not be their source, and (b) work to sublimate the frustration, disappointment etc. stirred up by setbacks and challenges into learning, focus and determined, positive action.

3. Develop and tap into intrinsic motivation

Most people take a natural and deep-seated personal (intrinsic) pleasure and pride in doing good work, serving customers well, cooperating with colleagues, learning, improving, solving problems and generally giving of their best. Just for the hell of it.

This intrinsic motivation correlates highly with job satisfaction, performance and improvement, which makes it a powerful motivational tool. And yet, not only is it often underdeveloped (another costly missed opportunity), but it is actively undermined when managers make it unnecessarily hard for people to do a job with pride by failing to provide effective processes, resources and support.

4. Build people's sense of self-efficacy

Self-efficacy (the level of belief in one's ability to succeed in the face of challenge) is another important motivational driver. It is a measure of where people sit on a scale from, at one extreme, having a sense of optimism and belief about themselves and their ability to overcome difficulties and succeed, and at the other, helplessness or despair.

This matters greatly because it affects what someone is willing to take on and how they will react to problems – the levels of effort, persistence, determination and resourcefulness they will bring forth.

People with a strong sense of self-efficacy show greater ambition, entrepreneurial spirit, risk appetite and resilience. They approach things positively, looking for ways to succeed. They bounce back from setbacks more quickly. They innovate, experiment and persist to find a way forward.

With low self-efficacy, people are significantly less resilient, and more likely to duck challenging situations or go into them fearfully and give up easily.

People's sense of self-efficacy is largely psychological. It is also dynamic, changing as a result of learning, experience and feedback. Therefore, how people are led and managed makes a crucial difference.

Self-efficacy can be developed through effective coaching, and given that the four most powerful words in coaching are 'Well done, keep going', the easiest and best place to start is by catching people doing something right: positively reinforcing the attitudes and behaviours that we want to see more of. Then build on this with ongoing encouragement, developmental feedback, constructive challenge, and guidance on how to improve.

In contrast, if they are part of a struggling, poorly led and managed team, routinely failing and subject to ongoing criticism, then without the counterbalance of effective support and coaching, people will lose faith in themselves and their managers, and slide toward helplessness, avoiding responsibility and shifting blame.

5. Manage moments of truth with maturity and skill

Moments of truth are key situations, the management of which makes a disproportionate and lasting difference to all the factors above. There are four main clusters, around how managers deal with:

- Problems, setbacks or mistakes
- Successes, good intentions, strong efforts and people going the extra mile
- Ideas and suggestions for improvement offered in good faith
- Problems and requests raised with them, particularly on issues that would improve their ability to contribute

If the first is dealt with harshly and the latter three are largely ignored, it will have a deep and lasting negative impact on trust, commitment and motivation. Fortunately, the opposite is also true, and this alerts us to a continual stream of opportunities to foster credibility, trust and respect for ourselves as managers, and to build a motivated, confident and committed team.

The performance and engagement fundamentals

It is tempting to think that creating engagement might depend on great charisma. But that's not true. As Peter Block observed, 'Inspiring people is removing obstacles more than lighting fires'. It is, as the Sandhurst Leadership Manual suggests, more prosaic: 'High morale stems from sound training, confidence in equipment, good administration, discipline, self-respect and clear knowledge of what is going on and what is required.'

Looking for the wrong things in the wrong place (Deming's 94/6 rule)

One of W. Edwards Deming's outstanding insights was that 94% of performance problems are created by a failure of the system that people work in and that only 6% are attributable to other 'special' causes, including bad luck and bad weather as well as individual error.

In other words, problems in systems are about 15 times more likely to fail people than people are to fail the system. Nevertheless, a strong instinct remains in many managers to look for someone to blame. Which means that managers, when seeking to improve performance, may often be looking for the wrong thing in the wrong place.

Looking in the right place

The good news, then, is that as managers we are responsible for designing, managing and improving said systems. And if we still want to apportion blame, we don't have far to look!

So, now that we're looking in the right place, we need to know what we're looking for.

Looking for the right things – the performance and engagement fundamentals

So what is the system? It's simply a collection of dynamically interrelated, common-sense elements that shape the context in which people do their work. Elements which, when done well, make it easy for people to do the right thing (and make it harder to do the wrong thing). These include:

1. Positive leadership
2. Hygiene factors met
3. Clear expectations
4. Tools, equipment and resources
5. Capable processes
6. Skills, knowledge and emotional maturity
7. Reliable information to facilitate workflow
8. Appropriate autonomy and responsibility
9. Accountability
10. Effective coaching
11. Structured problem-solving tools and skills
12. Involvement in problem-solving activities

Let's explore each aspect in turn.

1. Positive leadership

Effective people management begins with positive leadership. From the top, leaders and managers are responsible for role-modelling the values, attitudes and behaviours that actively support Business Excellence. They should:

- Provide a clear, positive vision and a credible plan for its execution (after all, who wants to follow a leader who offers no clear path to a valued outcome?)
- Actively build trust and good working relationships, to foster engagement and collaboration
- Ensure that colleagues have everything that follows in points 2-12 below
- Be solution-focused: when problems arise, pursue the question 'How did the process let this happen?' rather than 'Whose fault was that?'

Without alignment to a shared set of values and goals, people are likely to default to their own, which does not always equate to their highest and best contribution.

2. Hygiene factors met

Hygiene factors (as Frederick Herzberg defined them) are basic expectations which, even if met, do not add to people's positive motivation, but if not met will create a black hole of dissatisfaction and distrust that cannot be compensated for by any 'motivator' such as meaningful and positively challenging work, development or sense of achievement.

Putting in effort to engage and motivate people without first ensuring that the hygiene needs are adequately met is like running a bath without putting the plug in.

Hygiene factors include:

- A safe and healthy working environment
- Being treated with dignity and respect
- Adequate welfare provision (clean toilets and places to rest, eat, get a hot drink etc.)
- Competitive/fair reward

(Technical note: Most of the factors below are also on the hygiene-motivator spectrum, i.e. their absence makes it harder to engage people, and the better they are, and the greater their quality, the greater the positive impact.)

3. Clear expectations

Clear, positive expectations around the following are crucial:

*   Performance goals, quality standards, timescales and methods
*   Attitudes and behaviours
*   Organisational values and goals, so that people understand the bigger picture they are contributing to, and the importance and value of it. They know why their jobs are important, how they fit into the overall company structure and the effects of poor performance

Without such clear, positive and meaningful expectations, managers will struggle to engage, inspire and motivate people to achieve any clear purpose or standard. They will also struggle when it comes to feedback, as they will have nothing concrete to measure performance against, and no means of credibly identifying any performance gaps.

4. Tools, equipment and resources

People require tools, equipment and resources of the right quality, available in the right place at the right time. Without this, they will simply be unable to succeed. This will create costly and disruptive delays and quality problems, and people will become frustrated and disillusioned, which may lead to conflict with their managers.

Basic stuff. A perennial problem.

5. Capable processes

Similarly, without well-designed, reliable processes, working within capacity (i.e. not consistently overburdened or under-resourced), we set people up to fail.

People will be left to do things their own way, and may take shortcuts. This creates errors and inconsistency, which affects quality, cost, timescales, teamwork and customer satisfaction ... and creates more conflict.

Handovers between shifts and between different stages of the process become problematic – because, without a consistent approach, people may not know quite what they are getting and what they need to do next.

6. Skills, knowledge and emotional maturity

Through effective recruitment, induction, training and ongoing coaching, people should be equipped with (a) adequate breadth, depth and quality of skills and knowledge – covering technical, self-management, interpersonal, teamworking and problem-solving skills – and (b) the character and emotional maturity to handle the various challenges and vicissitudes of professional life.

7. Reliable information to facilitate workflow

Up-to-date, relevant information should be provided at the right time to facilitate smooth flow of work and its completion on time, to the right quality. This would include, in addition to expectations being agreed at the outset, changes to requirements, circumstances or other issues that might affect progress or requirements.

Colleagues should also be kept informed about what is going on more widely in the company, and about any important strategic developments that affect the context they are working in.

8. Appropriate autonomy and responsibility

People should have the right degree of empowerment, authority, responsibility and freedom to act and be given sufficient latitude to take managed risks to perform and improve their personal and team capability and performance.

9. Accountability

The core principles of effective accountability
People should be answerable for decisions, actions, performance and results, and they should know in advance:

- What they are accountable for
- When they will be held accountable – i.e. when the regular review points are
- What response is expected from them to shortfalls, errors, fails, setbacks etc. and what response they can expect (a) when they respond appropriately and (b) when they don't

Most importantly, people should be able to achieve what they are being held accountable for, i.e. they have been set up to succeed and have the right levels of responsibility, authority, decision-making scope, time, resources, expertise etc., as discussed earlier.

The psychology of effective accountability

People perform best when they feel psychologically safe, confident and valued (but not complacent). So recognition, praise and, above all, encouragement should be offered as appropriate and as a first resort, to identify and reinforce what is there and what is developing. Particularly where people are learning, developing, working on especially challenging issues or battling through difficult times. The four most powerful words in coaching are, let's remind ourselves again, 'Well done, keep going'.

This helps to build and maintain a positive emotional bank account (the reserve of trust and goodwill) with people. This in turn makes it easier to discuss performance and behaviour or attitudinal development opportunities openly and honestly, and thus advance people's development and performance more quickly, painlessly and successfully.

Developmental feedback and guidance are also likely to form part of the accountability mix, but this is unlikely to be the dominant requirement (and it's therefore unwise to make it the dominant flavour). Very direct (and directive) feedback should be reserved for critical areas of underperformance that the person is either not recognising, or not acting on.

Disciplinary procedures may also be necessary, but only as a last resort in a small number of cases where none of the above has worked.

Regular, constructive forums

The 'technology' of accountability comprises the regular, scheduled forums which are part of a wider, coordinated approach to professionally managing the performance of the business. These would typically include daily meetings, gemba walks, performance reviews, coaching, and process-improvement meetings.

Every colleague should be routinely and regularly involved in forums that run at the right frequency, and that have the right focus, to keep them appropriately involved, informed, accountable, heard and supported, and to enable them to achieve excellent and continually improving performance.

All of these forums should be focused on facts and data (rather than dominated by emotion, opinion and the loudest voices). They should also be free from fear, forward-looking, developmental, and focused on performance and improvement.

Beyond these regular forums, managers should also be accessible and approachable so that people can bring improvement ideas, or highlight issues, at any time.

Useable, timely information on performance
Timely, frequent, actionable facts and data on all relevant aspects of process and personal performance should be readily available and easily accessible. This is vital if we are to empower people to manage, and continuously improve, both personal and team performance.

Mutual accountability
Managers should also be accountable to colleagues for the delivery of everything on this list, starting with positive leadership, and open to feedback and constructive challenge if they do not provide it.

Encouraging and fostering adult discussion
People will of course occasionally raise issues that they should be dealing with themselves. And they may make uninformed comments, offer impractical ideas and ... generally behave normally!

None of which are good reasons to discourage discussion around performance and how it might be further improved. Quite the reverse.

Such discussions are excellent opportunities to listen to, and learn from, each other, build a more accurate and more aligned understanding of what shapes performance and outcomes, and invite legitimate concerns and related ideas for useful experiments to see what will work in practice.

Where appropriate, managers can constructively challenge, inform and educate. All of this serves to enhance mutual understanding and strengthen relationships and the ability to engage in dialogue.

This all helps to create a culture characterised not by 'adversarial processing', where people argue against each other to prove a point, but rather, 'oppositional processing', where alternative perspectives, questions, different possibilities and positive challenges are contributed by all those involved, so as to collectively build better solutions. These can then be tested through such ongoing discussion and experimentation.

10. Effective coaching

Using opportunities and issues that arise naturally as part of everyday work, colleagues should be developed to be rounded, confident, responsible contributors with strong job skills, problem-solving skills and interpersonal and teamworking skills, and encouraged to embrace challenges and take on greater responsibility.

11. Structured problem-solving tools and skills

The ultimate aim is to enable and empower people to become active partners in problem-solving and continuous improvement. To facilitate this, the business should have a shared language and toolkit for structured problem-solving, with all colleagues trained to a level that enables them to contribute meaningfully to improvement activities.

12. Involvement in problem-solving activities

Of course, It's no use having the tools and training if there is no opportunity for people to use them and to develop their capabilities and make an impact.

Colleagues, through the formal and informal mechanisms discussed above, should be genuinely empowered to make decisions, solve problems and improve processes, and given time, scope and trust to do so.

Practical steps to enhancing engagement

Oftentimes, companies struggle to identify meaningful actions to enhance engagement because they do not have a model that allows them to identify the key variables that actually drive engagement.

(Quick technical note: the questions asked on engagement surveys tend to measure **outcomes** *rather than* **drivers** *of engagement. The danger of not assessing what actually drives engagement is that you waste time and resource, and that you risk credibility by taking actions that not only might make no substantive difference, but might actually backfire and create cynicism.)*

The model offered here can help to assess the status of the drivers of engagement. And, since most problems with people and performance can be traced back to a shortfall in one or more of these factors, an audit of them will identify practical actions that are likely to lead to meaningful improvement.

It thus informs a three-phase strategy for building strong, positive colleague engagement:

1. Get all the fundamentals above the waterline

The waterline (as in 'sunk below the...') is the minimal level of quality that people require on each factor to be able to succeed. If anything is below the waterline it can sink the whole ship because it will, by definition, render people technically underequipped, and very probably emotionally disengaged if it happens systematically. (People will quickly figure out that they are either working in a system, or with a manager, not committed to excellence. And why, they will ponder, should they be?)

2. Provide further direction, development and support as necessary

With all of the fundamentals above the waterline, most colleagues will be engaged, productive and collaborative. For those who are not yet there, all reasonable excuses for poor attitude, behaviour and performance will, by definition, have been removed. Appropriate additional development and support should be offered. And, as a last resort, appropriate disciplinary action taken.

3. Continuously build and improve toward excellence

With system and individual performance now stabilised, go back to the fundamentals list and identify strategic breakthrough opportunities, i.e. where skilfully chosen improvements can significantly enhance levels of engagement and get a robust, positive, can-do spirit rolling in the overall culture.

Summary

People will generally be engaged, committed and productive when led well, adequately equipped, trained, supported, trusted, respected, involved, and given responsibility and autonomy within a culture of skilled and positive accountability.

The engagement fundamentals and the underpinning psychological concepts discussed here provide tools and insights to get all the key factors above the waterline and moving toward excellence.

CHAPTER 19

DIMENSIONS OF A CULTURE THAT PROMOTES AND SUPPORTS BUSINESS EXCELLENCE

> 'It's not my responsibility to think for 5,000 people. It's my responsibility to create an environment where 5,000 people think.' (Neville Richardson)

Introduction

In the two previous chapters we looked at the key psychological and technical factors that underpin engagement and performance at the individual level. In this chapter we'll look at how culture impacts people's ability and willingness to both perform in the short term and contribute to organisational fitness in the longer term.

Defining culture

Terry Deal and Allan Kennedy noted that culture is simply 'how things are done': the enduring patterns 'invented, discovered or developed by a given group' for making sense of its environment, processing information and responding (as Ed Schein added).

This is best understood as two dynamic – and dynamically interrelated – aspects:

- Internal capability and coherence
- External alignment

Internal capability means maintaining operational performance and cohesion in the face of a range of challenges by establishing robust and time-tested principles, processes, habits and practices and having the discipline and focus to stick to them for as long as they remain relevant. While at the same time continuously improving and evolving them in response both to internally generated insights and to the need to maintain external alignment.

External alignment is the ability to dynamically and responsively track, adjust and adapt to meaningful change in the operating environment so that the business can remain relevant to customers and continue to attract and retain top talent in the face of an unpredictable and ever-changing pattern of threats and opportunities.

The strength of a commercial organisation's culture is, then, a function of these complementary and dynamically related factors which determine its agility and resilience in the face of challenge and change, and thus impact (a) its very ability to survive, and (b) the degree to which it can then go on to thrive.

The relationship between people and culture

It is also important to highlight the relationship between people and the culture of the organisation they work in; a relationship that is reciprocal. The culture of an organisation both reflects and influences how people think about, feel about and behave toward the business, customers and colleagues and toward the various stakeholders' aspirations and problems.

In a culture focused on excellence, people are likely to respond with professional attitudes and behaviours, and thereby maintain and enhance that excellence. Equally, a more transactional and chaotic culture may elicit withholding, reluctance to engage and self-protective attitudes and behaviours which will, correspondingly, negatively impact on the culture's ability to maintain internal capability and coherence internally, and alignment externally.

This is something of a chicken-and-egg situation, but what is clear is that creating the systems that underpin the culture, and setting and maintaining the tone, is primarily down to leaders and managers.

Implications

There are two main implications of this reciprocal relationship between people and culture:

1. 1People need to operate in an environment where they are able to perform, think, learn, experiment, improve, develop and grow: a culture that fosters capable, confident, responsible people who work collaboratively to deliver excellent and ever-improving operational and strategic performance. (This is often described as a Thinking People System or a Learning Organisation)

2. 2There is no great mystique to culture, and it can, to a meaningful degree, be understood, led, shaped, managed and evolved. The three key levers are:

   - Values: the actual values lived out in the organisation (which are not necessarily the ones written on the wall)
   - Management systems and people management processes
   - The attitudes and skills of the leaders and managers

These levers can be used to optimise people's ability to contribute individually and to collaborate with others to solve problems, and, in the process, strengthen both their own capabilities and the cultural and technical capability of wider business.

Done well, this becomes a meta-capability (the capability to improve capability). This has a transcendent impact (or, in more clichéd terms, takes us to the 'next level') in a very real sense as it is, by definition, a higher-level capability with the potential to bring a step change not only in operational performance, but also in rate of improvement. This takes us well beyond one-dimensional people management practices that focus primarily on the performance and contribution of individuals.

Don't ignore culture or leave its development to chance

In some organisations there is a degree of romance or wishful thinking around 'informal cultures'. This is often based on legitimate concerns about the dangers evident in some larger organisations where over-engineered cultures have led to mediocrity (or worse) in customer service, employee experience and financial performance.

As Gary Hamel observed, poorly designed management systems can stifle valuable human qualities that are vital to performance excellence, including the capacities to cooperate, learn, adapt and innovate.

But there is, equally, a danger in surrendering to cultural drift and letting culture emerge without any guiding aims, or attention to the values, systems and leadership capabilities that shape it.

Whatever valued aspects of culture we aspire to, they are unlikely to be achieved and sustained if systems and leadership attitudes don't consistently support them, particularly as things change. Most often, the spirit and focus that we seek to foster can, to a meaningful degree, be captured, promoted and institutionalised. This offers the best hope we have for continuing and enhancing the kind of culture we think is right for the business.

Development of a culture that promotes and supports excellence in people management

Promoting the following factors helps foster a culture of excellence. (Technical note: these factors are both drivers of, and useful measures of, culture.)

Clear and positive organisational purpose and values

It's hard to get people excited about performance and improvement if they feel that they are just there to create short-term shareholder value. Particularly if that aim is pursued through a strategy of squeezing assets, people and processes, and providing sub-standard service to customers.

Having the more intrinsically motivating 'triple bottom line' aspiration of being an employer of first choice, doing something of social value, and being profitable – an aspiration that is pursued by focusing on excellence, quality and customer loyalty – is a prerequisite for developing a culture of excellence.

Pascale and Athos noted the power derived from positive values that are lived out in practice:

> 'Values and trust establish the preconditions that encourage individuals to think, experiment and improve. Learning organisations [demonstrate] an abiding commitment to their people and a faith in the human capacity to find a better way. Once employees know what an organisation stands for, and believe that it is sufficiently trustworthy to warrant their commitment and effort, they begin to truly extend themselves. [Then] If the management provides the basic tools, understanding and latitude to make a difference, great things are possible.'

Clear standards and expectations

Excellence, of course, is synonymous with setting high standards, and with people being developed and supported to consistently achieve them and progressively build on them.

As part of this, it is important that leaders and managers establish the understanding that, while working in an excellent organisation is rewarding and satisfying, it can also be challenging. Individuals need to:

* Commit to achieving high standards
* Be disciplined and consistent in their approach
* Be honest with themselves about their performance and results
* Take responsibility for their attitude, performance and development
* Learn from successes and setbacks
* Create and innovate to identify improvements, and to put them into practice and constantly refine them

They also need to be constantly open to constructive challenge on all of the above.

Likewise, active participation in the management and improvement of business performance is not only to be encouraged, but should be made an explicit part of everyone's responsibilities.

Professional-standard practice around goal-setting and goal-achievement

It is unlikely that people will engage when goals are arbitrary and unachievable, and pursued by any means (i.e. not necessarily ethically) in an environment characterised by chaos, firefighting and blame. People in these circumstances, sensing that they are being set up for failure, are less likely to take responsibility and give of their best, and more likely to shun responsibility, blame-shift and generally look out for themselves.

In contrast, when goals are derived from a credible strategy process, are ambitious, but realistic and attainable, and are pursued through effective, professional management (including regular, constructive reviews where people identify and solve the problems preventing performance), people are more likely to feel that there is a chance of achieving something worthwhile, and are correspondingly more inclined to engage.

Accountability: how performance is reviewed and the response to fails, problems and setbacks

As discussed in earlier chapters, people's feelings about the organisation are often disproportionately influenced by a few key 'moments of truth', particularly around accountability, and especially around what happens when outcomes are not as planned.

Five main factors determine the quality of an organisation's approach to accountability. These are the degree to which:

- Performance is reviewed in a regular, structured and systematic way through a well-designed and well-run management system where the focus is not exclusively on problems. Successes, contribution and effort are also highlighted, recognised and discussed, and all team members are actively encouraged to recognise and praise each other appropriately

- Discussions are informed by relevant, timely and actionable facts and data, rather than driven by managers' emotions and opinions (particularly on the matter of why something went wrong and who is to blame)

- People are assumed to be the solution to the problem, rather than the cause. Recall Deming's observation that the root cause of around 94% of problems lies in the systems and processes that people are constrained by, not in individual error. So it is important that managers ask 'How did the process let this happen?' rather than 'Whose fault was that?' People are more likely to engage with the former and react badly to the latter

- An appropriate balance is struck between (a) maintaining psychological safety and good working relationships, (b) upholding existing standards, and (c) providing sufficient positive challenge to promote continuous improvement

- Managers are accountable to colleagues for providing the performance fundamentals, for maintaining a positive and professional work environment, and for taking legitimate feedback on board and responding appropriately

Remove fear

Business Excellence and continuous improvement requires, of course, that we recognise, tackle and solve problems that affect performance rather than excuse, ignore or avoid them. This means actively exposing problems and bringing them to the surface, which relies on removing any legitimate fear that people will:

- Be ignored, blamed, ridiculed, or labelled as trouble-makers for raising legitimate issues in responsible ways

- Suffer retribution, or

- Have the problems dumped back on them without the authority, resources or support to successfully address them

If it doesn't remove these – often well-founded – concerns, the organisation can end up in the tragicomic position that everyone knows what the real issues are and wants to address them – except the managers.

Create open and honest dialogue to surface and manage conflict constructively

As discussed above, surfacing and working through process and technical-system problems is vital. Constructive dissatisfaction is to be encouraged and approached with the right intentions, attitude, aim and approach. That is, people should be coached, led and managed to acquire the maturity to contribute constructively to enhancing the productive use of time by:

- Identifying and addressing solvable problems. (To offer context on what we are aiming for, Toyota workers make, on average, 33 suggestions a year each, 90% of which are implemented within weeks)

- Dealing professionally with problems that are an unavoidable feature of professional life, including bad weather, bad luck, demanding customers etc.

- Resisting the temptation to indulge in any counterproductive moaning, complaining, bickering or arguing when issues have been professionally discussed and reached a conclusion has been reached, but not the one they wanted

Address social-system opportunities

Social-systems problems – miscommunication, misunderstandings, mistrust, disagreements and conflicts – also need to be recognised and addressed. This is vital to constructive engagement and is a key organisational competence. It relies on the development of the skills and maturity in leaders, managers and colleagues to handle such issues skilfully through proper training, coaching and practice in doing it repeatedly.

Lock in adequate time for continuous improvement and other value-enabling activities

One of the hallmarks of cultural excellence is that the right balance is struck between achieving short-term goals and building the ability to do better in future. Self-evidently, regular, structured time must be prioritised, scheduled and locked in for managing team and individual performance, and for continuous improvement activities.

Until it is, and even if such things are scheduled but routinely postponed, cancelled, rushed or done badly, no one will believe the business is serious about performance and improvement. And they won't take it seriously or commit their time and energy to it.

Managing underperformance

While the whole thrust of excellence is informed by positive psychology – enabling, encouraging, developing, empowering, supporting, collaborating and improving – there may be from time to time (as discussed in earlier chapters) a small number of people who do not respond to an acceptable standard or degree. (And, since falling standards benefit no one, the culture – while first and foremost offering a staircase for everyone to achieve higher performance and better outcomes – also needs to define a baseline that no one can consistently go below.)

Managers need to challenge and address both underperformance, and counterproductive attitudes or behaviour. Otherwise, this will spread and affect others, and ultimately damage the team's results and reputation.

As discussed earlier, however, before we can do this fairly, all the causes that are wrapped up with the system and culture that people operate within must be identified and removed.

CHAPTER 20

PEOPLE MANAGEMENT STRATEGY AND PROCESSES

Introduction

In this chapter we'll look at how to develop and implement a people management strategy designed to successfully support Business Excellence.

We'll explore four key factors:

1. Developing the people management strategy
2. Developing and improving the people management process
3. Developing leadership and management capability
4. Implementing the people management strategy

Developing the people management strategy

The aim of the people management strategy is to build an engaged, stable workforce with the appropriate attitudes, plus the technical and social skills to collaborate effectively, consistently deliver excellent operational performance, problem-solve and continuously improve.

In setting out to create and execute this strategy, we should take care to avoid the trap of what Seth Godin called 'the fruitless search for extraordinary people willing to take ordinary jobs'. That is, we need to recognise at the outset that to develop truly excellent people, teams and culture, the people management strategy must be correspondingly excellent.

The people management strategy typically includes:

- The guiding aims, values and principles. Useful here as an overarching concept for the values is 'omotenashi' ('generous care' for anyone whose lives are touched by the business). For colleagues, this guides us to:
  - Value and respect colleagues to a comparable degree as we do customers and other stakeholders
  - Seek out and listen to the Voice of the Colleague, as we would the Voice of the Customer and the Voice of the Process
  - Include all aspects of people management within the scope of ongoing continuous improvement
- A compelling employee value proposition
- A psychological contract (see sidebar for an example of a Behaviour Partnership, which offers one way to do this)
- The key people management processes
- Standards for leadership and management capability, behaviour and performance
- Standards for colleague capability, behaviour and performance
- People management metrics (see sidebar for some suggested measures)
- Organisational structure
- Culture standards

All of the above should gel as a coherent system and align with the wider organisational strategy.

EXAMPLE OF A BEHAVIOUR PARTNERSHIP

What you can expect	What is expected from you
1. To work in a safe environment and be given adequate training, tools and resources to succeed	1. Work safely, to develop your skills, and to treat company equipment, tools and facilities with respect
2. Positive leadership	
3. Clear direction on company purpose, values, standards and goals	2. To respond appropriately to positive leadership
4. Effective communication	3. To be actively committed to achieving the company's purpose, values, standards and goals
5. A positive work environment where you are treated with courtesy, dignity and respect and where you can openly discuss and address barriers to achieving	4. To communicate effectively
	5. To contribute to a positive work environment, treating everyone with courtesy, dignity and respect and dealing professionally with the routine challenges, setbacks and difficulties that are part of the job
6. To be given a clear understanding of your role, responsibilities, goals and performance standards, and regular, constructive feedback on how you are performing	
	6. To take responsibility for your attitude, performance and results and to accept constructive feedback and respond to it
7. To be coached and developed effectively to deliver excellent results and continuously improve your performance	
	7. To deliver excellent results and continuously improve your performance
8. The support of colleagues in your team and in the wider business	8. To be a team player and support colleagues in your team and the wider business

POTENTIAL MEASURES OF PEOPLE MANAGEMENT EXCELLENCE

- Staff levels (unfilled positions)
- Workforce stability (regretted turnover)
- Technical skills: (a) level, and (b) mix
- Wider workforce capability (self-management, interpersonal, collaboration and problem-solving skills)
- Health and wellbeing: physical and mental (including, but not restricted to, lost days)
- Absence
- Grievances and disciplinaries
- Engagement levels
- Culture: quality, cohesion and effectiveness

Developing and improving the people management processes

There are a number of dedicated people management processes, but it is important to recognise that people's effectiveness and the nature of the culture overall are also strongly influenced by the operational management system. Both are outlined below.

Dedicated people management processes

The dedicated people management processes include:

- **Recruitment and selection:** To bring in the right people with the right attitudes and skills at the right time
- **Induction/onboarding:** To help people settle in and get up to speed quickly and well
- **Ongoing coaching:** To ensure that each colleague is clear about what is expected of them, understands how well they are performing, what their development opportunities are, and gets suitable support and guidance.

This includes regular, structured performance and development reviews and coaching as part of everyday work, to engage people in constructive dialogue about performance and development and to progressively expose them to increasing levels of positive challenge and opportunity

- **Learning and development:** To help people continuously enhance their capabilities, performance and confidence

- **Leadership and management development:** To develop leaders and managers with the attitudes and skills to achieve and maintain excellence

- **Reward:** To offer appropriate intrinsic and extrinsic rewards to retain and motivate people who are contributing positively to the organisation

- **Discipline:** To deal professionally, fairly and legally with situations when people's attitudes, behaviours or performance fall below acceptable standards and all efforts to remedy this have failed

Front-line management processes

The front-line management processes are a vital part of people management. They arguably influence engagement more than any other single factor, as they are the most frequent touchpoint with people and have the most immediate and direct impact on them. They affect colleagues' ability to perform well and shape their experience of, and attitudes toward, the organisation. These processes typically include:

- **Daily accountability meetings:** Short stand-up team meetings at the start of the day to review yesterday's performance, look ahead to the coming day and highlight and prevent any foreseeable problems

- **Gemba walk:** A brief tour of the work area by the manager to see what is happening for themselves, checking in with people individually

- **Coaching:** Responding to real-time opportunities to improve colleague attitudes, skills and performance in the course of daily work

- **Weekly and monthly team review meetings:** To identify, understand and address trends and recurring issues over the period

- **Continuous improvement forums:** To identify and remove the root causes of process problems

The constant positive and professional focus and energy provided by these core routines ('kata') is vital to keep things moving. Without them, there is a communication gap in which confusion, misunderstandings, problems and negativity can take hold.

All of the above processes should:

- Technically

  - Ensure that people have what they need to do their job
  - Hold people accountable for their performance: both what they achieve (results) and how they achieve it (attitudes and behaviours)

- Socially and psychologically

  - Be motivational and developmental: build people's confidence, capabilities and desire to succeed
  - Foster trust, build strong working relationships, and enhance collaboration and joint problem-solving

Developing leadership and management capability

'Job Number 1 is enabling the ongoing engagement and everyday progress of the people in the trenches of your organization who strive to execute the strategy.' (Teresa Amabile and Steven Kramer)

Excellent people management requires leaders and managers with the right attitudes, skills and behaviours. First, leaders and managers need to understand that their role is to:

- Engage people in a consistent, constructive, adult dialogue that enables them to deliver sustained world-class performance and continuously improving results
- Build effective teams that collaborate with other teams throughout the organisation
- Create a positive and productive overall culture

As shown in Figure 20.1 (and discussed in Chapter 2), this implies something of an inversion of the historical command and control hierarchical structure. The primary responsibility of leaders and managers is to serve the people who directly serve the customer; to enable them to deliver excellent service, quality and delivery performance and to improve continuously to create a loyal, stable and profitable customer base.

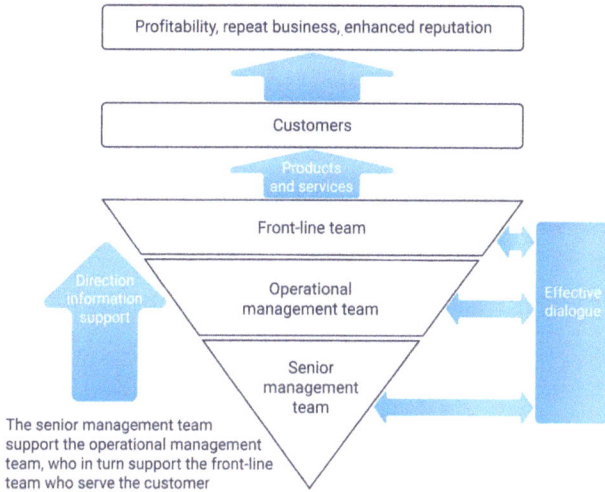

Figure 20.1: Enabling performance by serving the people who serve the customer

There are three broad levels to this:

- First, setting the tone. It is important for leaders to communicate a positive vision of what the business is trying to achieve and what success looks like, and help people see the purpose, value and importance of their contribution. (While some jobs – for example, being a paramedic – might have a more immediate and obvious purpose, most people do something that matters. Picking orders in a food distribution warehouse keeps the nation fed. Testing blood samples in a lab helps keep the nation healthy. Building houses creates homes for people to build a brighter future for their family. It all matters)

- Second, providing people with the engagement fundamentals (outlined in Chapter 18 – see also Figure 20.2, below)

- Third, shaping the culture that people operate in

To deliver on their responsibilities, leaders and managers require a range of skills: they need to be able to manage their own time, emotions, behaviour and performance; to communicate well, to build teams by developing effective relationships, motivating and supporting; to hold people accountable, challenge constructively and coach; and to maintain discipline. So they must, correspondingly, be led, managed, developed, coached, held accountable etc. (Leadership and management capability is covered in detail in later chapters.)

Implementing the people management strategy

Depending on a company's starting position, there may be two distinct phases to implementing the people management strategy. The first sets strong foundations by:

- Putting in place the basic processes
- Establishing core leadership and management skills
- Sorting through any immediate problems
- Beginning the process of knitting this all together to create a Thinking People System (or Learning Organisation)

The second phase builds on this to achieve excellence.

Phase one

Build the foundations – bring the performance and engagement fundamentals above the waterline

The first steps are to bring up to an acceptable standard all the:

- People management processes
- Associated operational management system processes
- Leadership and management capabilities

These three steps should provide a strong enough platform to ensure that the performance and engagement fundamentals are above the waterline (see Figure 20.2):

1. Positive leadership } Example
2. Hygiene factors met } Basics
3. Clear expectations
4. Tools, equipment and resources
5. Capable processes
6. Skills, knowledge and emotional maturity } Enablers
7. Reliable information to facilitate workflow
8. Appropriate autonomy and responsibility
9. Accountability
10. Effective coaching } Involved
11. Structured-problem-solving tools and skills
12. Involvement in problem-solving activities } Empowered

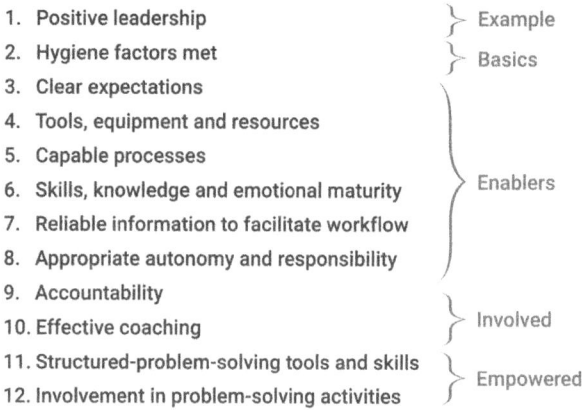

Figure 20.2: Performance and engagement fundamentals

Get people involved and address any immediate issues

Taking the preceding steps should have established constructive forums that will now enable more open discussion around any process, performance, management or culture issues, allow us to act on any relevant issues raised, and assist us in developing greater contextual understanding around anything that either can't be solved immediately, or at all.

This also helps to engage people as active partners in problem-solving and to empower, coach and support them to solve the problems themselves – the ultimate point of engagement. This:

- Respects colleagues by taking problems seriously and listening to their ideas

- Solves real problems, which benefits everyone

- Allows people to bring more of their discretionary potential to the business

- Develops people's technical and social capability, including their understanding of the technical processes and performance, and their collaboration and problem-solving skills

- Gives people pride and satisfaction in their work and confidence in themselves, and enhances mutual psychological safety and trust with their managers

- Encourages people to take increasing responsibility and ownership of their local processes, and their performance and improvement

This should simultaneously address any important gaps, problems and shortfalls and identify and remove all major drivers of colleague disengagement; guide the improvement of the people management processes and the operational management system; and make the culture increasingly professional and well-positioned for the build toward excellence.

Build steadily and consistently

To build trust in the approach and draw in more people over time, it can be useful to start with problems that colleagues raise themselves, achieve some early wins to demonstrate its value, and build momentum from there.

Since there are normally many such opportunities, there is usually no difficulty in finding a place to start. Sometimes, only a small number of colleagues (around 10-15%) are keen to engage at first. But this is enough to get things moving and, if the process works well, the number will naturally build over time as people see for themselves that it is safe, beneficial, enjoyable and productive, and more of them start to engage voluntarily.

Even if we are starting from a low baseline of engagement, and there are problems with performance, culture, attitudes and working relationships, this approach prevents things getting worse and tackles the root causes of these problems. It does so by:

a. Establishing constructive dialogue

b. Working through existing issues and (re)building trust

c. Building the solid foundations of a better culture

Run and monitor

Run and monitor the above (referenced against the strategy and associated measures and process effectiveness). This should surface any significant issues with systems, skills, working relationships etc., and also highlight any areas of resistance so that we can understand and constructively address them.

Ongoing in-flight tactical adjustments should be made as we go and any other, more strategic, learning points should be gathered.

At an appropriate juncture, it would be wise to review Phase one and take learnings from this to inform Phase two, where we will enhance capability maturity and move toward social system excellence in the service of wider organisational excellence. This would likely include:

- Top-level strategic review
- Input from local teams, and possibly focus groups, to get richer detail
- Consolidating the Phase two action plan
- Sharing key points of the action plan with colleagues for comment and refinement
- Actioning the plan

Thereafter, the people management strategic review can be folded into the wider, ongoing organisational strategy cycle

Important note: None of this should be badged or presented as a formal change initiative. This can bring its own problems if people think that it is just another top-down, flavour-of-the month, superficial management move being imposed on them to tick a box. It is, in reality, simply the business showing the vision and commitment to evolve its people management strategy to a level commensurate with its ambitions to achieve operational and strategic excellence.

Phase two

The foundations established in Phase one can then be built upon to move toward being a Thinking People System/Learning Organisation and further enhance people's engagement, commitment and performance. Progress can be achieved by continuously improving the quality and coherence of all aspects of the people management strategy.

The precise content for this stage will of course be highly tailored to the unique circumstances of every organisation, and there is a huge range of possible interventions (too many to cover here). These may, however, include the following broad areas:

- Offering people development beyond the immediate requirements of the job:

  - Professional development: widening or building core technical skills and knowledge to higher levels; developing wider job skills (e.g. priority management, or interpersonal skills), or building new capabilities (e.g. learning a language, doing an Open University degree)

  - Personal development: helping colleagues to take greater responsibility for managing and developing themselves and acquiring the emotional intelligence and resilience to set ambitious goals, overcome setbacks and deal with problems

- Corporate social responsibility activities: e.g. school visits, charity fundraising activities, sponsorship of (and involvement with) local sports teams or other community groups
- Flexible employment policies to help people achieve a work-life balance that works for them
- Social activities: Christmas party, summer barbecue, theatre trips etc.
- A first-rate work environment and amenities, including high-quality rest and food areas
- Making work fun: finding ways to make the job more enjoyable

As part of this phase, it can also be beneficial to establish a more focused approach to measuring engagement. This might include a survey to measure levels of engagement across the business and pinpoint areas for improvement. This would typically involve an annual survey to get the broad picture, supplemented with focus groups to understand in more depth what is driving the scores, and to identify actions that will lead to improvement.

The organisation will, of course, need to decide how far it needs or wants to go with engagement, what level of potential it needs or wants to unlock, and what it is prepared to do to unlock it. While the organisation may not require everybody to be contributing excellence potential (or consider it worth the time and effort it would take to achieve that), it will need everybody to be contributing discretionary potential or better.

Summary

The key to engaging people is getting the people management strategy, processes, management competencies and culture right; setting a clear, positive and challenging vision and helping people to achieve it by providing encouragement, support and development.

This is driven through regular communication, and through forums where people can reflect on personal and team performance using reliable facts and data. They can then be empowered and supported to become active partners in problem-solving, to take the initiative, use their expertise, exercise their creativity, bring more discretionary and excellence potential and optimise their and their team's performance.

CHAPTER 21

TEAMWORKING AND COLLABORATION

Introduction

> *'The best teams stand out because they are teams, because the individual members have been so truly integrated that the team functions with a single spirit. There is a constant flow of support among the players, enabling them to feed off strengths and compensate for weaknesses. They depend on one another, trust one another. A manager should engender that sense of unity. He should create a bond among his players and between him and them that raises the performance to heights unimaginable when they started out as disparate individuals.' (Sir Alex Ferguson)*

A team is the ultimate vehicle for achieving results. Its power derives from the depth of resource, and the bandwidth of capability, provided by the pool of time and energy; from the range and depth of talent, experience, expertise and personal styles; from the rapid, targeted responsiveness created by effective management processes; and from the collective attitudes and behaviours which promote seamless coordination, collaboration, and commitment to success.

High-performing teams tend not to form or sustain themselves naturally, and having talented individuals is no guarantee of having a good team. Building, developing and maintaining them is a process that must be managed.

So, in this chapter we'll look at:

- Definitions of teams, teamworking and team-building

- The benefits of investing time and effort building and maintaining teamworking
- The pitfalls to be aware of and how to avoid them

Figure 21.1 reminds us where teamworking and collaboration fit into the overall Business Excellence meta-model.

Figure 21.1: Teamworking in context

What do we mean by teamworking?

Let's start with three quick definitions.

What is a team?

A team is a group (or groups) of people who perform interdependent tasks and need to collaborate effectively to achieve a shared goal.

High-performing teams comprise a pool of talent with sufficient breadth and depth to handle the variety of situations they are likely to face. They also share responsibility and function as a mutually supportive network.

Teams come in different forms. Variations include:

- Functional or departmental teams (which may include different shift teams)

- Cross-functional teams
- Project teams

These may also be virtual or remote.

There are, of course, other forms of work group that we would not regard (by this definition) as a team needing to be developed into a highly coordinated and collaborative unit to achieve its aims. For example, bus drivers working for the same company rely on mechanics and schedulers etc. to set them up correctly, but each driver has little or no direct collaboration, either with head office or other drivers, in the execution of their primary role.

What is teamworking?

Teamworking is the ongoing, dynamic process of working collaboratively in pursuit of a shared goal.

Teamworking includes the formal management processes that plan, manage and coordinate activities, and the social processes that draw the best out of people with different skills, personal styles and approaches and encourage them to work together – sharing information, knowledge, resources and ideas to solve problems and achieve levels of performance that would not otherwise have been possible.

What is team-building?

'Coming together is a beginning. Keeping together is progress. Working together is success.' (Henry Ford)

Team-building (or team development) is the process of creating, managing and improving the:

- **Operational processes** that allow people to do the technical aspects of their jobs effectively
- **Management processes** that:
  - Recruit the right people
  - Develop them to be effective team players
  - Organise and facilitate coordination and collaboration

- Foster the development of the right attitudes and behaviours toward performance, improvement and collaboration

- **Social processes** that build the mutual understanding, respect and trust that facilitates increasingly natural, spontaneous and seamless coordination and collaboration

To team or not to team?

Building a team can sound like a romantic idea. Easy, natural, fun. It is, of course, anything but. It is a delicate and fraught multi-stage process, requiring great insight, skill, patience and persistence. A high-performing team is the organisational equivalent of a Formula One car. It offers unique performance capabilities but takes considerable time, effort, resource and a degree of risk to build, and is always operating on the edge of a precarious stability, requiring continuous vigilance and effort to maintain. So it is important to understand the purpose and nature of the group you are leading before deciding how to proceed.

There are three variables to consider:

- To what degree is the focus on a **collective goal** (and, correspondingly, on collective responsibility and accountability) versus a set of individual goals (and, correspondingly, on individual responsibility and accountability)?
- Does the group comprise people with **complementary skills** or **similar skills**?
- What **level of coordination and collaboration** is required; do people work in parallel, in sequence, or interdependently? And, where collaboration is required, how fast, seamless and organic does this need to be?

So, where people with complementary skills are required to perform interdependent roles and they need to collaborate in real time to achieve a shared goal (for example, a Formula One pit crew), you would almost certainly benefit from moulding them into a team.

But where a group comprises individuals working more independently (for example, sales people, train drivers or field service engineers, or specialists such as consultants, lawyers or doctors), it might be left to the leader to coordinate activity to whatever degree necessary. People in such groups may collaborate from time to time, help each other by sharing insights, ideas or information, provide absence cover for each other, and need to work closely with a central team for information, material or administrative support – but the degree of collaboration and coordination will differ from that needed by the group working interdependently in real time on a shared goal.

Many and varied possibilities exist between these two poles. The point here is simply to highlight the importance of first assessing where, and to what degree, coordination and collaboration is required, and how natural, spontaneous and seamless it needs to be, before deciding on your goals for, and approach to, team development.

The anatomy of effective teamworking

The main aim is to assemble a group of people with enough breadth and depth of skills, knowledge, experience and personal styles to thrive in the target environment, and then reduce or eliminate friction costs due to poor organisation or coordination, lack of mutual trust etc., to create a quantum leap in productivity, performance and capability.

Four vital mechanisms underpin teamworking:

1. **Framing a meaningful, ambitious, superordinate goal** to bring a sense of being part of something bigger that requires a team effort. This helps to shift people's mindset for 'me' to 'us', from self-interest to collective achievement, and provides a sense of belonging and pride

2. **Compensating** for each other's (temporary or enduring) limitations of:

   - Technical knowledge or expertise, by providing either direct assistance or developing people through coaching

   - Time or effort, by adding their shoulder to the wheel when colleagues are struggling or in need of extra firepower to get something ambitious over the line

   - Morale, by providing emotional support or encouragement when people are having a bad time or stretching to achieve something out of their comfort zones

3. **Complementing** each other's strengths and benefitting from potential synergies in two ways:

   - Significantly enhancing the speed and quality of performance, decision-making and problem-solving by ensuring that people have around them colleagues who bring the information, skills, experience, knowledge or insights that they lack. This allows them to operate confidently in areas where they would otherwise be hesitant, avoidant, slow or error-prone

- Making the most efficient use of specialised talent. For example, the surgeon has other specialists to prepare the operating theatre and so is able to focus exclusively on where he or she adds unique value

4. **Interpersonal dynamics:** Related to the above, the spur to greater levels of insight, inspiration, creativity and commitment typically emerges through the dynamic process of interaction where people elicit ideas from each other, challenge them and build on them while problem-solving in an environment of mutual respect

In well-managed teams, these factors combine to create an upward spiral of increasing trust, success, belonging, pride, confidence, commitment, performance and ambition. All of which adds up to significantly faster and more effective responsiveness in a range of challenging situations.

Not every group is an effective team

When a team is not effectively constituted, built, managed or improved, it can fail to deliver, become riven with internal conflicts and dysfunctionality, and become mired in conflict and dysfunctionality with other teams within or beyond the organisation. It can also become resistant to change and improvement. The reasons for this may include the following:

Ineffective operational process

The technical processes are not properly designed and run, which creates problems with resourcing, quality and flow, spawning operational problems and leading to interpersonal frustrations and conflicts.

Ineffective management process

- Unclear goals
- Poorly designed and run processes for communication, team performance review, continuous improvement etc.

- Poor recruitment, management and development which leave the team with one or more members who display attitudes and behaviours that are antithetical to teamworking, including:

  - Individualism: colleagues who habitually put what they personally want (or don't want) ahead of what others, or the team overall, need from them
  - Competing and creating personal conflict with colleagues: competing for credit, resources, status, power and rewards instead of collaborating to achieve team goals

- Poor recruitment, management and development which leave the team without a wide or deep enough pool of capability (knowledge, skills, experience, styles, emotional maturity etc.) relative to requirements

Ineffective social processes

The group dynamics are characterised by:

- **Lack of commitment:** To the mission, goals, organisation or colleagues
- Absence of trust: People are unwilling to make themselves vulnerable within the group; reluctant to offer insights or ideas, or to go the extra mile, for fear of being taken for granted, exploited, or blamed when things go wrong and when taking responsibility and trying to help others
- **Fear of conflict:** People shying away from constructive professional debate
- **Codependence:** A greater focus on mutual comfort and protection than on results or problem-solving, leading to complacency and low and deteriorating standards as team members are unwilling to challenge each other on poor results, operational problems or counterproductive behaviour
- **People hiding in the crowd:**

  - Social loafing: a decrease in individual effort due to the presence of others
  - Diffused responsibility and accountability: people ducking personal responsibility and accountability for their own performance and results

- **Groupthink:** The team becomes too tight within its own boundaries, too closed to external influences. It becomes cynical about, and dismissive of, outsiders, and unquestioning and uncritical of itself. Unity, conformity and loyalty are valued above discussion of alternative perspectives, dissenting ideas and wider responsibilities (e.g. social and environmental ones). This creates an illusion of superiority and invulnerability which makes the group arrogant, insular and out of touch, leaving it vulnerable to threats that it fails to recognise or take seriously enough

The benefits of team development

If you are leading a group, the best way to succeed is to build a strong and committed team. Benefits include:

- The sheer speed, power and reach created by having a group with a full and coordinated suite of capability, properly coordinated and able to collaborate spontaneously and seamlessly
- The ability to solve problems and grasp opportunities more effectively and more quickly
- Getting the best from people – being a part of a well-run team enhances the individual's sense of belonging and commitment, which unlocks their discretionary and excellence potential and, in turn, fosters greater contribution, responsibility and creativity
- Greater productivity, including higher quality standards, better efficiency and the ability to consistently achieve goals
- Creating a positive cycle of energy, development and success, benefiting everyone associated with it and increasing the chances of sustaining and building on that success

The characteristics of excellent teams

The team competence map in Figure 21.2 captures the essential characteristics of excellent teams. The sections which follow provide an overview of the success criteria for each aspect of the model.

Figure 21.2: Team competence map

Leaders' attitudes, skills and behaviour

Team leaders need to understand the broad architecture of what they are building, and how to build it. They also need to persevere in working through the various stages of team development, known as 'forming, storming and norming' (which each have their unique and varying challenges), to get to 'performing' so that teamworking becomes established habit and practice.

It is important that the team leader:

- Leads by example in their attitudes and behaviour, living the values of the organisation and modelling the attitudes and behaviours expected from the team
- Understands that their role is to drive excellent performance and continuous improvement by actively engaging with people to help them do the best job that they can
- Provides appropriate encouragement, praise and recognition
- Responds constructively to issues and problems raised with them by the team
- Has the right knowledge, skills and attitudes to lead effectively
- Gives people the coaching, support and development to allow them to succeed
- Invites personal feedback from colleagues and acts on it

Colleagues' attitudes, skills and behaviour

Every colleague should bring the right attitude and approach, and the right interpersonal, personal organisation and teamworking skills, to enable them to communicate, collaborate and problem-solve with colleagues.

The aim is that every team member, individually:

- Is committed to the team and its success
- Has a positive, can-do attitude
- Takes responsibility for their attitudes, behaviours, performance and results
- Has the right technical skills and knowledge to succeed in their role
- Has the right interpersonal and teamworking skills to be able to work with, communicate with and successfully resolve differences with colleagues
- Is happy to share their knowledge and experience, and to offer support to colleagues
- Asks for support when they require it
- Is resilient, and stays calm, strong and positive under pressure
- Recognises their own limitations, and is prepared to learn, change and grow
- Is coachable – willing to accept feedback and coaching, and to respond positively

Team performance management

The performance of the team overall requires well-designed and well-run processes for setting, communicating and achieving goals, and for those processes to be run in a way that fosters engagement, accountability, commitment, honest discussion, fast and effective problem-solving and continuous improvement.

Criteria for effective team performance management include that:

- There is a clear team strategy that is aligned with the organisation's overall strategy
- There are measurable performance goals that everyone understands
- Team performance is reviewed collectively against these goals at least weekly
- Accurate, timely and relevant performance data is made available to everyone at these meetings
- Meetings are well-organised, positive and productive. Everyone participates. Performance is analysed and discussed, lessons are learned, and actions agreed, communicated and followed up

- Successes are celebrated, learned from and used to build confidence, pride and team spirit

Effective people management

The management and development of people requires that we devise the right structure in which they can operate and collaborate effectively; get the right people for the right roles; and develop the right personal attitudes and the right technical, personal effectiveness and interpersonal skills.

For effective people management it is important that:

- Each individual understands what the team does and where they personally fit in
- Everyone has a clearly defined role and responsibilities, and clear goals and performance standards to work to
- Every colleague has regular, constructive one-to-one chats with the team leader, to ensure individual accountability, provide feedback, solve problems, and provide support and guidance
- Anyone can discuss, at any time, anything that is stopping them doing a better job
- Underperformance is constructively challenged and managed effectively
- People are actively encouraged and supported to develop. Training and development needs, in technical skills, wider job skills and teamworking skills, are identified and met in a timely fashion
- The team has the right mix of skills, knowledge and experience to make it balanced, flexible and adaptable
- There is a robust recruitment process which selects new team members with the right technical skills and the right personal qualities to fit in with the team
- New people are given a thorough introduction to the company, the team and the job to get them off to a strong, positive start
- There are regular team-building activities to renew focus, review how the team is working collectively, build relationships and identify and address any underlying problems

Effective operational processes

Effective operational processes are part of the bedrock of strong teams, allowing people to operate effectively in the technical parts of their roles. To facilitate effective teamworking, the operational processes should:

- Provide people with the tools, equipment and resources they need to succeed
- Ensure that people get the right information at the right time
- Plan and organise work properly
- Allow high-quality work to be done efficiently

Continuous improvement

The aspiration to excellence implies that the practice of collaborative problem-solving is embedded in the culture and that people have the right tools, time, training and support to drive continuous improvement.

Effectiveness in continuous process improvement requires that:

- There is a culture of continuous improvement where all colleagues are actively involved in addressing problems and enhancing all aspects of customer service and business performance
- The team learn quickly from problems, permanently resolving them by identifying, addressing and eradicating the root causes
- People can speak openly, and without fear, about problems, errors, setbacks or any concerns or barriers to performance
- The team constantly and systematically work to identify and remove waste, inefficiency and unnecessary cost, and to enhance quality and add more value for customers
- A systematic and structured approach is taken to problem-solving, involving proper problem definition, root cause analysis, improvement planning, and follow-through
- People are actively encouraged to challenge existing approaches and offer ideas to improve their effectiveness
- The team accept the necessity of change and are willing to accommodate, shape and drive change to move the business forward

Collective mindset (Culture #1)

Excellent teams focus on intelligent competition: cooperating with each other so that they can compete effectively as a unit. Central to this is an emphasis on sharing: sharing information, knowledge, resources, ideas, and sharing responsibilities, problems, setbacks and success.

The key aspects of this collaborative mindset include:

- Having a strong sense of shared purpose: everyone understands the team's purpose, values and goals and is committed to achieving them
- Being engaged, enthusiastic, results-focused, solution-focused, action-oriented and motivated, creating a can-do culture
- Taking a pride in their work and holding themselves to high standards for quality and service
- Having a winning mentality, belief in themselves and in each other, showing resilience, persistence and determination in pursuing goals, solving problems and overcoming setbacks
- Accepting responsibility for collective decisions, actions and results, and for their impact on customers and the wider business
- Being appropriately self-critical: understanding the team's collective strengths and limitations and what can be usefully improved
- Recognising and celebrating success at individual and team level
- Being positive about, and receptive to, change
- Always looking to push beyond current performance and capabilities

Collective attitudes and behaviours (Culture #2)

The behaviours that people choose, and the underlying attitudes, are crucial if a team is going to gel and create a culture characterised by trust and by enthusiasm for the job, and where people have a sense of belonging and making a contribution that matters.

This includes that, within the team:

- People treat each other with dignity and respect
- Everyone is committed to the team and its success
- Everyone understands the different roles in the team, and respects their importance

- Team members work well as a team: they cooperate, collaborate and problem-solve well, supporting each other to get the job done
- Team members are aware of their own strengths, limitations and personal style, and the impact these have on others, and that they seek to mitigate any potential for creating unnecessary difficulties for colleagues
- People understand each other's strengths and limitations, know how to get the best out of each other and can identify areas where people need support
- Colleagues understand, appreciate and accommodate the range of personal styles in the team
- People make a genuine effort to understand and respond positively to others' opinions, ideas, needs and concerns
- Team members communicate in an open, constructive, adult way, especially when dealing with difficult issues and genuine conflict
- People trust each other, feel they can rely on each other, and have confidence in what each other says and does
- Mistakes, setbacks and performance problems are dealt with constructively. Blame, harsh criticism and recrimination are avoided. People are actively encouraged and supported to improve
- Team members are empowered to make appropriate decisions and changes to allow them to achieve their objectives
- Individuals' focus is the overall team objectives and they accept that they will occasionally have to put wider considerations ahead of their own, and 'take one for the team'
- When someone needs help, colleagues automatically rally round
- Colleagues motivate, encourage and support each other
- There is a positive atmosphere in the team, with good banter and humour

Beyond this, within the wider environment of the organisation and beyond, including relations with other teams, clients, suppliers and wider society, it is important that:

- People understand the team's role, and how it contributes to customer satisfaction and the success of the wider organisation
- Team members know who their external customers are and what they expect
- Colleagues communicate, collaborate and problem-solve well with external customers (where applicable)
- People understand who their internal customers are, their processes, priorities and pressures, and how best to serve them

- Team members help others to understand the team's role in the business and the team's processes, priorities and pressures
- Colleagues communicate, collaborate and problem-solve well with other internal teams to serve the customer and achieve business goals
- Colleagues communicate, collaborate and problem-solve well with external suppliers and agencies (if applicable)
- Where conflict arises between the team and other internal or external teams, it is resolved through mature, constructive discussion

Results and reputation (Excellence)

Ultimately, the success of the team can be gauged by the degree to which it:

- Consistently achieves (or surpasses) performance targets
- Continuously improves performance on all key measures
- Achieves results in a controlled and sustainable way (rather than through regular firefighting)
- Achieves world-class performance, i.e. ranks among the best for the industry globally

CHAPTER 22

BUILDING THE TEAM

Introduction

Building the team involves designing, managing and continuously improving three sets of interrelated processes: operational, management and social.

Effective operational processes allow people to do the technical aspects of their jobs well, both individually and collectively.

The management processes orchestrate the mechanics of coordination and collaboration. They map out who talks to who, when, and about what, and ensure that meetings are run professionally and constructively. This provides a solid platform for the social processes.

Healthy social processes make a team really tick. This requires leaders to foster a spirit of collaboration, encouraging individuals to build mutual trust and strong working relations through how they interact, problem-solve and support each other, not only in formal meetings but in all manner of everyday exchanges.

Building the operational processes

To be effective, people first need to be able to perform their role on time and to the right level of quality. This requires effective operational processes.

While every process is different, there are 14 core factors that are relevant to most:

1. Understand value (VoC)
2. Build in quality and minimise the COPQ
3. Flow
4. Evenness

5. Operate within capability

6. Dynamic resilience

7. Balance

8. Standardise

9. Prime and maintain

10. Resource effectively

11. Error-proof

12. Pull

13. Measure

14. Manage and improve

We have covered this in depth in Chapter 14. The main advice here is to use those materials as your guide, and the associated templates as a starting point; then, iteratively, through trial and adjustment, shape them into what works best for you. To design the optimal approach and gain acceptance, agreement, understanding and commitment, it's important to involve the team. It may be useful to turn parts of this process into projects for individuals or sub-groups to explore.

Building the management processes

The management processes are the bedrock on which great teams are founded. Designing and running them well, and continuously improving them, is a priority. If goals are unclear and communication around them poor, teamwork can unravel quickly and quite badly.

The core team management processes include:

- Daily management/short-interval control meetings
- Weekly performance trend meetings to review, plan and pick up themes, trends and issues only discernible over this period, and implement course corrections and continuous improvements
- Monthly performance trend meetings to review, plan and pick up themes, trends and issues only discernible over this period
- Other relevant forums for planning, control, review and adjustment, and for maintaining dialogue, mutual understanding, motivation, morale and positive working relationships
- Other continuous improvement forums

This should almost 'automate' the management of the business fundamentals and set up a cadence so that the right things are discussed at the right time, at a frequency that matches the speed of the business.

In addition to these overarching team management processes, there are the core people management processes. These include:

- Recruitment
- Induction
- One-to-one reviews and coaching
- Learning and development
- Disciplinary procedures

This too has been covered in depth, in Chapter 20. The advice, as with the operational processes, is to use those materials and the associated templates as your guide, and then iteratively, through trial and adjustment, shape them into what works best for you. Again, you can involve the team in designing the optimal approach and gaining acceptance, agreement, understanding and commitment by turning parts of this process into projects for individuals or sub-groups to explore.

Building effective social processes

Effective social processes build the mutual understanding, respect and trust that facilitate natural, spontaneous and seamless coordination and collaboration. These social processes are, of course, founded on the management processes. How those are run and how things like problem-solving, continuous improvement and conflict are handled, and collaboration is fostered, is arguably the single biggest influence on team culture.

But the social processes go beyond this; they also rely on the informal bonding between team members which builds genuine understanding, rapport, respect, trust and comradeship. A large part of this will happen in the handling of routine day-to-day interactions between team members, where the team leader has no direct influence.

There are, however, steps that a team leader can take to promote and encourage both formal and informal collaboration. These include:

- Ensuring that all formal communication is handled well

- Developing a structured approach to problem-solving to help people deal more effectively with process-related problems
- Creating the interpersonal dynamics that facilitate fast and spontaneous collaboration
- Encouraging informal bonding

Let's explore these in turn.

Ensuring that all formal communication is handled well

Run meetings professionally. Poorly run meetings create dissatisfaction, drain cognitive and emotional bandwidth, and suck up time and energy. Make them happen as scheduled. Ensure that they are run to an agenda that provides an update on activities, status and problems, and that allows colleagues to hold each other accountable. Work also to create an atmosphere of professional respect, recognition, encouragement and problem-solving that simultaneously allows people to work together and to develop increasingly strong working relationships. Ensure that people know what each other are up to and where there are opportunities to give and get support. Help people get to know each other as people.

Developing a structured approach to problem-solving to help people deal more effectively with process-related problems

As described in Chapter 16, collaborative problem-solving both relies on, and also helps build, greater understanding and collaboration. Tools such as value-stream mapping, A3 problem-solving and root cause analysis, when used well, promote the use of facts and data and the application of logical analysis and promote a structured, positive dialogue. This helps bring the best out of people and, when progress is made and success is achieved, creates an appetite for more which can become an upward spiral.

Create the interpersonal dynamics that facilitate fast and spontaneous collaboration

Good working relationships help get the job done better, more quickly and with less hassle and friction costs. But, given that a team is a bunch of imperfect and (potentially) incompatible people trying to overcome this, their individual limitations, and their fears about trusting each other, in order to achieve something worthwhile together, good working relationships tend not to be inevitable or guaranteed. Time, effort and patience are required to build and maintain them.

It is also important to recognise the other side of the same coin; that a level of task focus which neglects or damages relationships will create a constant stream of short-term problems and undermine attempts to create the platform of stable and productive relationships required to maintain performance and solve problems quickly and well enough to achieve excellence.

The main barriers to creating the interpersonal dynamics that facilitate fast and spontaneous collaboration include unresolved conflict, style clashes and lack of trust. To avoid these and to proactively build effective interpersonal dynamics, it is important that everyone in the team understands how relationship dynamics work and what is required of them to contribute positively. This is crucial if the team is going to gel.

Where colleagues have not been developed to this level of maturity, this can be a source of frustration, create tension, limit the quality of the working relationships, and restrict everybody's ability to contribute their best and to grow and develop.

There are four main pillars to creating positive interpersonal dynamics:

- Fostering mutual respect and understanding
- Dealing with conflict
- Fostering mutual recognition
- Actively promoting collaboration

Fostering mutual understanding and respect

It is important for a leader to ensure that everyone recognises that people differ. First, that there are differences in personal style (which can be explored using tools such as DISC, MBTI and Belbin); and beyond this, that differences in all sorts of other human variables mean that each of us has our own unique pattern of strengths, limitations and imperfections.

Sometimes, in the development of a team, it may be possible and desirable to address some of these limitations and develop beyond them. And sometimes it is neither necessary, desirable nor possible, because we benefit from people bringing their full, rich, idiosyncratic selves to the job.

Such patterns of strengths and limitations are both inevitable and desirable in a high-performing team, and what is required of everyone in the team is the maturity and emotional intelligence to understand themselves and others, and to skilfully modulate their attitude and approach to accommodate and work successfully with others. It is part of everyone's responsibilities to contribute to making the interpersonal dynamics work.

Specifically, each member of the team must:

- Recognise their own strengths and how these position them, uniquely, to contribute to the team; and, as far as possible, play to these strengths
- Have accurate insight into their impact on others and on the team dynamics overall
- Understand what others bring to the situation, and allow them to play to their strengths
- Recognise the limitations of their own time, experience, ability etc., avoid taking on assignments that unnecessarily expose their limitations, and recognise when others are better equipped to handle certain tasks
- Modify their contribution to complement other colleagues, and play their part in creating a coherent and balanced team

Dealing with conflict

Conflict can be productive or destructive, depending on what it is about and how it is handled.

Personal conflict is when colleagues fight each other with the primary aim of advancing or defending their personal interests. It decreases the effectiveness of the group by allowing personalities, rivalries, animosities or personal agendas to disrupt team dynamics. It can quickly escalate into hostility and anger, and damage respect, trust, loyalty, satisfaction, commitment and working relationships, reducing members' ability and willingness to engage and contribute anything constructive. This is a triple negative, as the conflict fails to solve current problems, damages the team's ability to solve future problems, and may create more problems.

Issue conflict (the discussion of real issues with the primary objective of developing effective solutions) can be beneficial, engaging people in stimulating and productive discussion, constructively resolving differences through open and honest communication, and drawing on the full range of experience, skills and talents in the team. It has the triple benefit of solving real problems to improve results, making the work better and more satisfying, and enhancing relationships and teamwork.

Team leaders can minimise destructive conflict and keep discussions productive by leading, developing and encouraging colleagues to:

- Remember that we're all on the same team. The goal of the discussion isn't for anyone to 'win' an argument: the goal is to find a productive way forward that the team is committed to
- Assume that everyone's underlying intentions are good
- Be tactful and diplomatic when challenging or expressing differences of opinion. Agree that personal insults, accusations or loaded questions like 'How could you believe that?' are unacceptable
- Look to win people over. Turn any perceived 'foes' into allies through skilled relationship-building, trust-building and persuasion
- Recognise problems and move quickly from spotting them to solving them
- Avoid triggering the downward spiral of the blame game when problems occur, by asking 'How did the process let this happen?' rather than 'Whose fault was this?'
- Be aware of any agendas that are not aligned with the team agenda. Nip this in the bud and refocus on the team agenda
- Challenge constructively. First, colleagues should be encouraged to challenge each other on issues related to performance standards or alignment with team values. This helps to avoid a culture of complacency and mediocrity. Second, when challenging, they should keep it professional, constructive, supportive and solution-focused
- Conduct debate by leading with facts, data, reasoned analysis and a clear, constructive proposal, rather than emotion and opinion. Do not allow discussion to be dominated by loud, opinionated people drowning out humbler – and possibly more useful – voices
- Exercise humility. Respect everyone's viewpoints, and be open to changing their mind when the evidence points in that direction

This all helps to develop a climate where people can discuss issues openly and honestly. It also helps the team avoid, on the one hand, the dangers of too much unproductive and unnecessary conflict, and on the other the dangers of complacency and groupthink. Where issues are debated vigorously in an atmosphere of mutual respect and cooperation, disagreement potentially stimulates deeper thought, decisions tend to be of higher quality, and innovation is more likely. This also fosters the growth of trust and support, so that people feel able to talk freely about their fears, their problems and their own limitations, and to receive help and support from others.

Fostering mutual recognition

Recognition helps build and maintain relationships and is also a powerful motivating force. It makes people feel valued, appreciated and respected by each other. It enhances the relationships and builds trust which, in turn, encourages people into contributing discretionary and excellence potential. In excellent teams, appreciation doesn't just come from the top, it becomes a cultural norm in peer-to-peer interactions. Fostering mutual praise and recognition helps to create the strong spirit that characterises high-performing teams.

Actively promoting collaboration

Collaboration (literally 'labouring together') means pooling time, effort, skills and resources, seamlessly coordinating activities, and dynamically adapting to meet the evolving needs of the situation. It underpins faster and more effective problem-solving, increases creativity, and spurs innovation. But fostering it can be a delicate and fraught process. For it to work, people have to be helped to recognise and accept that, when we collaborate:

- Roles and responsibilities will often become less clear and more fluid. This will unsettle people who like things to be definite and clear-cut
- There will be conflict. As explored above, knowing how to debate trade-offs between options means being able to productively manage such conflict

There are usually many naturally occurring opportunities for collaboration in day-to-day work, especially at interfaces between different processes, both within and between teams, and when problems occur or where innovation is required to achieve strategic breakthroughs. Team leaders can help people to recognise and seize such opportunities for themselves.

Most people are happy and willing to cooperate as long as:

- They know where the opportunities are – where and how their involvement would be beneficial
- There is a reasonable degree of psychological safety; i.e. they know that they won't get endlessly dragged into other people's problems, distracted from

their own roles or taken advantage of, and that they won't be blamed if things go wrong when they are making their best efforts

Encouraging informal bonding

High-performing teams require a level of connection and trust that goes beyond what can be achieved by even the best formal process. So it is important to support and encourage people to invest time connecting in genuine ways. This includes personal conversations in the office and beyond, over coffee or drinks, on non-work topics that lead people to identify shared interests, which fosters deeper liking and authentic connections. This may include social activities and dedicated team-building events.

Building the team mindset

A vital aim within all of the above it is to build a strong team mindset. There are five main facets to this.

1. Commitment to team purpose and goals

Develop a clear understanding of, and genuine commitment to, the purpose, aims and approach of the team. Draw out and underline the importance of what the team does and how its work is meaningful.

2. Sense of belonging

Emphasise the vital importance of the role each colleague plays and the value of their contribution. Begin by providing everyone with a clear understanding of their role and an appreciation of its value and importance to the team. The other side of the same coin is to remember to socialise this so that everyone's role is understood and appreciated by everyone else.

A strong sense of belonging can also be engendered by ongoing recognition of people's personal contributions and achievements, and by giving praise and thanks where due.

The final piece of the jigsaw, to underline that people belong and are integral to the team, is seeking their opinions, ideas and feedback, and acting on it.

3. High levels of trust

Develop throughout the team mutual respect for, and belief in, each other's ability and intentions. Anchor this in the effective, routine communication of the plans, information, status updates and performance data which provide the basic shared understanding of what is expected and how things are unfolding. Trust is also built by facilitating open and honest discussion and debate around performance, process and problem-solving.

At a very practical level, creating a culture where colleagues feel obliged to do what they say they will do, so that people can rely on each other's word, goes a long way to developing a rooted and genuine faith in each other.

Finally, consistency in management and the adherence to agreed standards for everyone and in all situations demonstrates to the team that the leader can be trusted to respect and support their best efforts when they do their bit or go the extra mile.

4. Winning mentality

Build high levels of confidence and motivation in the team and a belief that, no matter what the challenge, they will find a way through. This can be transformational.

Begin building a winning mentality by routinely sharing and recognising successes at the regular meetings. Recognise and celebrate improvements in performance against previous levels, and against industry standards.

At the heart of a winning mentality is developing a habitually strong and effective collective response to tackling and overcoming setbacks and problems; and recognising and celebrating it. Make it part of the story of who you are as an organisation.

Lastly, in all of this, identify and reinforce the valued qualities and attributes that the team show – determination, creativity, skill etc. – and create a narrative around how this defines the team's character and identity.

5. Self-critical, improvement-focused attitude

Another crucial aspect of building an excellence mindset is honing the instinct to continuously improve all aspects of individual and collective performance. Cornerstones of this are encouraging colleagues to challenge any complacency or slip in standards and, indeed, to constructively challenge everything: goals, standards, operational processes, management processes, culture, mindset, behaviours etc., and to plan and take action to address the improvement areas identified.

Managing the stages of team development

Bruce Tuckman devised a classic model to help managers understand and successfully navigate the different phases of team development to achieve excellence. We've represented the model (Figure 22.1) as an S-curve to try and better illustrate the dynamics.

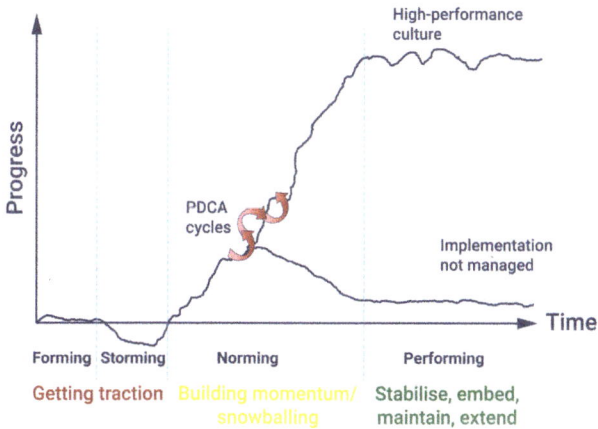

Figure 22.1: Stages of team development

Stage one is **'forming'**. This is where the team is newly formed (or significant changes have been made to an established team). At this stage, people don't know each other well. They may be excited, but also perhaps apprehensive and even suspicious.

Stage two is **'storming'**, represented below as a dip on the S-curve into confusion about roles, jostling for position, and disagreements with the leader and between team members.

Stage three is **'norming'**. Here, team norms are established: that is, understanding and agreement emerges around roles, goals, behavioural standards, processes etc. People begin to understand each other, including their strengths, limitations, personal styles, how they work best and what support they need. As the team works through norming, things begin to settle down and the focus gradually shifts from internal issues to performance, improvement and serving the customer.

Stage four is **'performing'** where, after working through the process of norming, the team clicks. Through many cycles of improvement, the technical process and the social process have been tightened and honed. Trust and mutual understanding have strengthened, and people collaborate and coordinate their activities well. They respond increasingly positively to difficulties and setbacks and support each other well. Performance can still undulate a little (nothing is ever perfect), but the overall standard is significantly higher than at other stages, variations are fewer, and problems are spotted and arrested faster and better.

Finally, Tuckman observed that the model describes a natural sequence that cannot be short-circuited (storming is a vital aspect of sorting through early difficulties and, as such, is healthy and unavoidable), but it is possible to get through the stages more quickly and smoothly when a manager understands the model and its implications and knows how to evolve their approach as the development process proceeds.

Let's look at how best to understand what is going on in the different stages and how to navigate them effectively.

Moving through the four stages of team development

To move successfully through the stages, the team leader needs to maintain a focus on the technical, management and social processes, progressively building them throughout. They will, though, have to adapt the nature of their leadership and interventions as things evolve with each phase of the team's development. Let's look at some of the challenges each phase brings and how to navigate through them.

Moving through forming to storming

Here, the aim is to navigate the challenges of forming so that the team can move through it as quickly and as well as possible, and be suitably positioned to tackle the challenges of storming.

Set boundaries

Setting boundaries at forming is essential to prevent avoidable trouble, and creates an early opportunity to set the right tone for the development of the culture and attitude of the team.

The degree to which this needs to be done will vary according to the situation, but if there are concerns that things might become contentious, it can be advantageous to establish ground rules at the outset. To establish, for example, that everyone will:

- Be treated with courtesy, dignity and respect and be expected to treat others the same
- Be allowed to say whatever they want, as long as the intention is positive and it is delivered professionally and with respect
- Be listened to
- Be open to being questioned, disagreed with and challenged (again, with respect)
- Get an answer on anything they raise – but not necessarily the one they were hoping for

These rules may be enshrined in a document such as a behaviour partnership (see Chapter 20 for an example) and displayed prominently in working and meeting areas if it is felt that a visual reminder or reinforcement might be of value.

The wider aim of this is to build, from the outset, the professional habit and discipline of ongoing adult-adult dialogue. For this to work, we need the safe psychological environment that such guidelines can help to create. Nothing much improves in teams without this environment.

Set the context

Giving people a broad understanding of the context at forming helps colleagues appreciate and accommodate to the broad expectations of the team and the contribution they are expected to make to it. This may include outlining:

- The broad purpose of the team, its objectives and how success is measured
- Who the customers are and what they expect
- The importance of what the team do, and what's at stake for them and the people they serve

Establish processes

It is wise, at forming, to establish the technical, management and social processes, even if only at a basic, 'minimum viable product' level. This brings a broad shape, structure and discipline to team activities and provides a baseline level of good practice that people can constructively critique, build and improve on. Of particular importance at this stage is establishing the foundations of the core management processes of:

- Communication: its content, frequency and style
- The management of team and individual performance, including goal-setting and review
- Continuous improvement

Depending on the situation, it may not be possible at this stage to get the right level of involvement and agreement in the team around these processes, so it may be better for the team leader to simply provide this lead and open things up for discussion and improvement when the team has matured further.

Establish your role as team leader and your style and approach

At the outset, it is also important that, as team leader, you help your co-workers understand:

- How you see your role
- What your goals are
- What your values are and how you work
- What you expect of your team

Bear in mind that, while words are important, winning the team's commitment will depend more on the behaviours that you role-model and how you lead by example.

Get selection right

Perhaps the first and most important consideration at forming is to get selection right. Getting the right people with the right attitude and skills in the right place. While this is impossible to achieve perfectly, particular care should be taken to avoid any potentially risky mis-hires that might hobble the team's development over an extended period.

Bearing in mind the old adage that we often end up 'hiring for skill and firing for attitude', assess suitability on both counts and remember that it may be easier to address skill gaps than deal with the consequences of temperamental or attitudinal misalignments.

Also bear in mind that, while the aim is to build a coherent team, this should not be confused with the need for uniformity among team members. A coherent team that is capable of a fast, accurate, full-spectrum response to all the various circumstances it is required to handle is likely to comprise many personal styles and differentiated skills.

Moving through storming to norming

Here, the aim is to navigate the challenges of storming (the 'storms' of confusion, misunderstanding, frustration and disagreement that inevitably plague the early stages of team development). To move through it as quickly and as well as possible and to position the team to successfully meet the coming challenges of norming.

Storming is where the team leader needs to prepare the ground and lay the foundations for norming (the right principles, vision, tools, processes etc. to aim for). Without laying this foundation at this stage, a team is almost certain to get perpetually stuck in storming.

Particular attention should be paid to:

- Implementing the management processes and managing the fallout from the consequences of their imperfect and incomplete nature (and the fact that some people don't understand them or don't like them, simply because they are used to doing things differently). Make an attempt to use the disquiet to foster constructive debate about how to improve them

- Likewise, implementing the operational processes

- At an individual level, identifying skills, personal styles and other strengths, allocating roles and responsibilities accordingly, and agreeing specific goals and how these will be delivered

Experience suggests that, for most teams at this stage, it will be well-nigh impossible to achieve either universal understanding or agreement. It can be like trying to put up a tent in a hurricane. Just about everything will be disputed, contested or resisted (passively or actively) by someone. So, to put it mildly, this stage is a testing time for team leaders, and how it is handled will have a significant long-term impact on the effectiveness and culture of the team. As a team leader you will require great reserves of calm, patience and resolve, and it is very likely that you will need to:

- Take time to explain and re-explain many policies, processes, decisions etc.
- Ensure understanding
- Discuss, debate, seek agreement where you can, or negotiate for initial acceptance pending further discussion once these ideas have been tested in practice
- Build commitment through influence and persuasion
- Provide reassurance
- Give feedback on progress
- Listen and respond constructively to ideas and concerns
- Handle any personality clashes and issue-based conflicts

Moving through norming to performing

Here, the team leader's task is to navigate the challenges of norming to move through it as quickly and as well as possible, and to position the team strongly for the coming opportunities and challenges of performing.

Consolidate processes, get traction and start building momentum

Norming is, literally, firmly anchoring and consolidating the norms (the team's values, goals, standards, methods, management processes etc.). The primary task is to consolidate the operational and management processes and to begin to foster the social processes that will help individuals to bond and collaborate more naturally and seamlessly.

By this stage, time should have allowed the baseline processes that were introduced at storming to be run and tested in practice, providing real data and allowing informed opinion on what is working and what needs to be improved. Communication and relationships will also, hopefully, have bedded in enough to allow a more reasoned, balanced and fruitful discussion and to begin ratcheting through the PDCA cycles of incremental trial and improvement. All aspects of the operational and management processes are in scope for discussion, including the communication plan, performance measures and individual roles and goals.

Optimise the talent pool

Another vital aspect of norming is optimising the talent pool (sometimes colloquially referred to as 'weed, seed and feed').

In any team, levels of ability and commitment will inevitably vary along a spectrum, and the team's performance will be bounded at the lower end by the lowest standard you accept, and at the top end by the highest level of performance you can elicit from your top talent.

So the first step is to work on engaging people, to get everyone's contribution above the waterline on all aspects of ability and performance and to give them the means and opportunity to move up that spectrum as far as is possible.

This will help you to figure out who is pushing the bus forwards, who is pushing it backwards, and who is just sitting on it and letting others do the work.

Regrettably, it may be necessary to remove any resolutely high-maintenance underperformers, negativists, blockers, vandals, freeloaders or troublemakers. As former All Blacks coach Graham Henry pointed out: 'Don't let any individual damage a positive working atmosphere. If that individual has ability, then it is worth spending time trying to make him or her a better team person. But if it doesn't work, you have to let the person go.'

When dealing with such behaviour, go about it in the right way so as not to violate the principles set out for the culture. This can be achieved by:

- Referring back to the ground rules
- Having an individual chat
- Listening and understanding whether there are substantive issues that might be leading to legitimate discontent that is fuelling the behaviour
- Offering support if appropriate
- Spelling out the consequences if the situation does not improve
- Moving to (and through the stages of) disciplinary procedures where necessary

With any difficulty of this nature settled, the full focus of people development can then be on unlocking the full potential of all colleagues and getting the very best from the most talented and enthusiastic people.

Build confidence, ambition and momentum

Once you have gained solid traction through all of the above, set progressively more difficult goals. Confidence and morale grows as people successfully tackle increasingly challenging tasks. This develops the winning mentality that comes to the fore when the team faces challenges, pulls together and digs in to overcome them. This, in turn, further reinforces team spirit, a winning mentality and belief in their ability to overcome difficulties.

Getting the rate of increase of the level of challenge right is vital, though. Make sure that it is far enough out of the team's comfort zone to represent a meaningful stretch, but not so far as to risk setting people up to fail and inflicting unnecessary damage to confidence and morale.

Begin the focused and disciplined drive toward Business Excellence

Refer back to the team competence map we introduced in Chapter 21 (reproduced for your convenience below) and all the factors outlined in it and cycle through. First, ensure that all aspects are above the waterline, and then pick the areas where improvement will bring the biggest benefits.

Figure 22.2: Team competence map

Foster increasingly strong and spontaneous collaboration and social processes

In all of this, foster increasing collaboration and enhance the social processes. Engage, coach and facilitate. Ask questions to engage people and get them thinking for themselves and contributing more to discussions. Draw people into thinking about:

• What is the highest and best that the team could achieve?
• Where could we usefully improve?

- Their ideas for tackling recurring issues

Remain approachable and open to discussing any concerns, comments or queries that people have.

Maintaining performing

As the old adage goes, getting to the top is one thing - staying there is quite another. Getting the team to the performing stage is an admirable feat. Sustaining and building on it over a long period of time and through many and various challenges represents a different - and arguably more difficult - challenge.

Key factors in meeting this challenge are outlined below.

Maintain consistency of leadership and continue to build capability, confidence and ambition

Continue to use and improve the management processes to maintain regular communication about goals, progress, ideas and action at team, project and one-to-one levels.

Inexperienced team leaders are sometimes prone to making the error of reducing the frequency of communication or performance review meetings when those gatherings start getting shorter, as fewer difficulties are being flagged up. What they have not yet realised is that the perfect meeting is short, boring and (apparently) pointless, but that the real point is to ensure that everything is under control and that all potential issues are spotted early and nipped in the bud. So taking your eye off the ball can be costly.

Team leaders who make this mistake invite all sorts of trouble, including a loss of momentum and a regression to the confusion and frustrations of storming. If the momentum is lost and trust in the ambition, commitment or ability of the leader as a role model for excellence is dented, it is somewhere between difficult and impossible to fully restore it.

Reinforce the winning mentality

Keep the positive feedback and the ideas for improvement flowing. Socialise and celebrate success. Remind people of the importance of their contributions, the value of collaboration, and the principles, culture, systems and habits that were instrumental in achieving these successes. Build tempo, pace and momentum. Get the flywheel incrementally turning faster.

Empower people

Move as far as is possible toward the team self-managing to maximise collaboration, responsibility, mutual accountability and problem-solving. As part of this, encourage co-coaching to reduce dependency on you as team leader, and to allow others to flourish as coaches and get the right support to the right people, from the right people, by the shortest possible route.

Strengthen the social processes

Hold regular team-building sessions to revisit values, goals, processes etc. and do other exercises and activities that renew or deepen relationships and mutual understanding. These might include social activities, awards or quizzes.

Keep actively driving toward Business Excellence

Continue the practice, established during norming, of revisiting the team excellence model and continuously improving all aspects of it toward excellence and world-class performance. Rinse and repeat until perfect.

CHAPTER 23

DEVELOPING LEADERSHIP AND MANAGEMENT CAPABILITY

Introduction

So far ,we have looked at how to design and introduce systems to manage and develop your people and processes. And it is, of course, the leaders and managers who are primarily responsible for making this work. This means that leaders and managers, just like everyone else in the business, must be managed and developed. They must have clear responsibilities, behavioural standards and performance targets. They must be trained and coached to acquire the attitudes and skills they need to carry out their specialised responsibilities effectively. They also need ongoing encouragement, challenge and support to learn and grow, and to be given regular, constructive feedback and coaching on their leadership and management performance.

To remind ourselves of the context, Figure 23.1 shows the anatomy of the culture of excellence: the various component parts and how they all relate. Leadership and management capability forms the foundation of the whole culture and the right-hand pillar of strategic leadership through operational management to front-line management, all supporting the management, development and engagement of front-line colleagues to enable them to power the excellent operational performance that creates loyal customers and underpins the organisation's competitive advantage.

(Note: leadership and management development is a wide-ranging topic, the full depth and breadth of which is beyond the scope of this chapter. Exhaustive coverage is available in other Future Positive resources: find out more at futurepositiveconsulting. com/toward-excellence)

Figure 23.1: Core principles of Business Excellence

The importance of management

Before diving into the detail, it's worth taking a moment to remind ourselves of the fundamental importance of the whole concept and craft of management, and the contribution it makes to the effectiveness of any social entity.

The legendary management writer Peter Drucker observed that management is a social innovation which, he argued, could be seen as being more important, and having greater impact, than any single scientific or technical invention. Quite a claim.

Fully recognising the knowledge base that developed societies have built, he highlighted the fact that it is however management, 'and management alone', that makes all the knowledge and all the knowledgeable people effective and productive: 'The emergence of management has converted knowledge from social ornament into the true capital of any economy [and] the reason that, for the first time in human history, we can employ large numbers of knowledgeable, skilled people in collective, coordinated productive work.'

Management is, he pointed out, itself a body of knowledge and expertise that has evolved the organisation of collective human endeavours beyond 'guesswork, brawn, and toil to the development of systems and the use of information': the meta-capability to organise, deploy and optimise the application of knowledge, expertise and other resources in the service of solving human problems and advancing human progress.

He offered the persuasive example of the role of management as a decisive advantage for the allies in the conclusion of World War Two. 'To the very end, the Germans were the far better [military] strategists. Having much shorter interior lines, they needed fewer support troops and could match their opponent's combat strength. Yet the allies won – their victory achieved by management. The United States, with one-fifth of the population of all of the other belligerents combined, had almost as many men in uniform [and] produced more war materiel than all of the others taken together. It managed to transport the stuff to fighting fronts as far apart as China, Russia, India, Africa and Western Europe.'

THE EVOLUTION OF MANAGEMENT

As Gary Hamel pointed out, management as a professional discipline, and its associated thinking, tools and techniques, continues to evolve. He observed that management was originally concerned with solving two problems:

- Getting semi-skilled employees to perform repetitive activities competently, diligently and efficiently, and

- Coordinating those efforts in ways that enabled complex goods and services to be reliably produced with consistent quality in large quantities

These pioneering industrial age breakthroughs, which Hamel called Management 1.0, occurred in the late 19th and early 20th centuries, led by Henry Ford, Frederick Taylor and Daniel McCallum. They were subsequently augmented by concepts such as annual budgeting, return-on-investment analysis, project management, divisionalisation, brand management, human resource management and business process reengineering, without fundamentally altering the underlying principles of standardisation, specialisation, hierarchy, control, and the primacy of shareholder interests.

Management 2.0, based on the principles of Business Excellence framed by W. Edwards Deming and pioneered by Taiichi Ohno at Toyota and other Japanese businesses, emerged after World War Two. It was subsequently built on by others such as Joseph Juran, Phil Crosby and John Seddon and brought to the attention of the West in 1990 by Womack, Jones and Roos in The Machine That Changed The World. The principles addressed some of the key limitations of Management 1.0, including the inherent inefficiencies, waste, COPQ, lack of adaptability, and inner divisions and disruptions to flow created by departmental silos, and a systematic failure to adequately develop and deploy the talents of the workforce. Excellence principles are aimed at optimising processes, reducing waste, improving workflow and quality, engaging and developing people, and promoting continuous improvement.

These proven, field-tested principles, though common knowledge for decades, remain both under-used and, often, poorly implemented. Many businesses still work with some version of industrial-age Management 1.0 and its attendant poor quality, responsiveness and customer service and underwhelming financial performance.

Organisations today face a new set of challenges and opportunities associated with a volatile, unpredictable, complex and ambiguous global operating environment. They need to figure out how to achieve a degree of ambidexterity, acquiring complementary (and seemingly contradictory) qualities such as:

- Being stable and flexible
- Being resilient and adaptive
- Being focused and efficient, while innovating quickly and boldly enough to stay relevant
- Leading colleagues to remain focused in the midst of constant change
- Recognising the hitherto hidden costs and impacts that the business is responsible for, and acting responsibly with regard to all stakeholders, and to future generations

Management 3.0 continues to emerge in response to this. It is informed by 21st-century breakthroughs in neuroscience, and by social, cognitive and organisational psychology and leadership thinking including systems thinking, Spiral Dynamics, Cynefin, and network leadership.

It is thus important for every organisation to recognise when it has reached the limits of Management 1.0, fully embrace the advances of 2.0 and begin to shape their own version of 3.0.

Defining leadership and management

At its most simple, leadership means influencing people to follow a particular way of thinking or course of action. Management is the disciplined creation and execution of an agreed strategy: the process of systematically planning, organising, executing, monitoring, adjusting and reviewing.

There is inevitably some overlap between the two, and every organisation will develop its own interpretation of and approach to how leadership and management roles and responsibilities are structured.

Leadership activities and mindset

Broadly speaking, in terms of activities, leadership is essentially strategic and includes:

- Monitoring both internal capability, and emerging opportunities and threats in the external environment
- Analysing and making sense of the information gathered
- Strategy formulation: creating the vision for the long-term survival and development of the organisation and setting out a broad approach for how it will be achieved
- Communicating this and enrolling others

Attitudinally and behaviourally, leadership means taking responsibility, taking action and making things happen. It is proactive, pioneering and focused on:

- Tackling novel, emerging or long-standing problems
- Fostering in others more productive and adaptive ways of thinking, acting and relating to difficulties, opportunities, change, stakeholders etc.
- Setting standards

Management activities and mindset

Management activities are essentially operational and include:

- Meeting agreed goals and standards by ensuring smooth and effective business-as-usual performance
- Solving operational and tactical problems to consistently achieve right-first-time quality and on-time, every time delivery to the customer

- Engaging, motivating and developing people and holding them accountable
- Designing, running and improving the operational processes to optimise the use of people's time and talents and other organisational resources
- Strategy deployment: creating and executing structured, achievable and properly resourced strategic plans

Attitudinally and behaviourally, management is process-oriented, disciplined, rigorous and systematic, focused on executing effectively, efficiently and consistently to get predictable, reliable and repeatable results.

In short, strategic management might be thought of as a full-beam headlight: a wide scope look-ahead. Management is a dipped beam, focused on the immediate and intermediate steps to stay on track for the strategic destination.

Leadership vs management

There are two views on the relationship between leadership and management; that they are:

1. **Distinct roles at different levels of a hierarchy,** where leadership is regarded as the preserve of top executives. This thinking is associated with command and control cultures

2. **Both part of every role,** with only the balance varying according to role and situation. This is the Business Excellence perspective, based on the recognition that leadership is something that everyone is capable of. This leads to the view that:

   - Leadership and initiative are to be encouraged at all levels, as appropriate, in the execution of people's roles and responsibilities
   - While still led by senior executives, strategy formulation and deployment, through the use of Hoshin Kanri planning and the catchball process (see Chapter 10), will involve people throughout the business as appropriate

THE USE OF THE TERMS 'LEADERSHIP' AND 'MANAGEMENT': SOME IMPORTANT CAVEATS

- Being called (or calling oneself) a leader does not, of course, a leader make. Some 'leaders', even those in very prominent roles, are leaders only notionally. While the title intends a sense of legitimacy and power, the role, in such circumstances, is essentially to make money for, and preserve the hegemony of, other, more powerful individuals or groups. The leader themself has little scope, power or authority to set or alter the organisation's purpose, aims, values or approach. They are the public face of (and occasional lightning conductor or fall guy for) others

- An elevated position in the hierarchy and the associated authority brings no guarantee that any discernible active leadership is shown

- Where there is leadership, it comes with no guarantees about a) its intentions, or b) its quality. Among the destinations that organisations can be led to is to disaster. Leadership can be focused on preserving personal hegemony, status and power and used to block change, stifle improvement or unnecessarily disadvantage some stakeholders. There's no shortage of examples

- Similarly, the title of manager comes with no guarantee that the bearer:

  - Is committed to personal or business excellence

  - Can manage themselves: their time, emotions or behaviour

  - Can design, manage and improve processes to a standard of excellence

  - Can engage and motivate people and hold them accountable to a professional standard

  - Is commercially aware and understands the impact of their decisions on performance and profitability

- Finally, entrepreneurialism can be an important aspect of leadership and is sometimes regarded as a particular branch of it. But entrepreneurs who lack the management skills to develop processes and lead people may fail to create an organisation that can realise their vision. The same may be true for those who founded organisations as inventors or technical innovators

Underdeveloped leaders and managers: a costly problem

By virtue of their position and role in the business, leaders and managers have a disproportionate influence on people, systems, culture, customer loyalty, business performance, profitability and the organisation's future prospects. Every aspect of business performance is linked to leadership effectiveness: as many businesses have discovered to their cost, a great offering, talented people and plentiful resources are no guarantee of success without it.

Effective management involves a number of high-level self-management, organisation, people management, process management, interpersonal and commercial skills. These take time to understand and some years of focused effort and reflection to properly apply, practice and master.

Despite this, management is one of the few professional roles that people can find themselves in without any experience, aptitude or proven, relevant competence.

This can happen where the importance of management as a strategic capability, and the consequences of underinvesting in it, are not adequately recognised and there is a belief that investment in the ongoing development of the management team to a standard of excellence is either unnecessary (because 'managers are born, not made'), or that, through some unspecified and mysterious process, the development of this highly specialised mentality and skillset will happen automatically (they'll 'pick it up as they go along'). Managers are thus left to develop 'naturally'. Which in practice means slowly, poorly or not at all.

Leaving managers to stumble through a lengthy period of trial and error 'learning', all the while practicing (make that gambling) with the company's people, processes, time, money, assets and reputation, represents a significant, unmanaged cost and risk. This is not something that would be countenanced for other people with significant responsibilities such as train drivers, surgeons or gas fitters.

Thus, without a strategic approach to their recruitment, management and development, leaders and managers may:

- Be appointed to the role without full consideration of their suitability
- Not adequately understand the nature of the role or the seriousness of the responsibilities, or fully appreciate what is required
- Struggle to properly organise themselves and others
- Provide a poor example, attitudinally and behaviourally

- Not communicate effectively
- Lack awareness of how they come across to others, and the impact of this
- Struggle to engage and motivate people with differing personal styles
- Struggle to manage conflict
- Lead teams that fail to gel, cooperate (internally and cross-functionally) or perform consistently well
- Be at odds with fellow managers and fail to appreciate the impact they or their team have on the wider business
- Not take adequate responsibility for team performance, customer satisfaction or results
- Shun responsibility for people management, including holding people accountable and dealing effectively with underperformance
- Fail to follow the management processes
- Oversee operational processes that are not properly designed, maintained or continuously improved, and thus fail to optimise the use of key resources such as time, money and equipment, and fail to systematically improve quality, efficiency and productivity
- Not believe that their position and influence comes with an obligation to continually develop themselves to a high professional standard

The direct impact of ineffective leadership and management

Where managers are thus underequipped, their processes, teams and performance are likely to be suboptimised. They are likely to be routinely embroiled in preventable, and distracting, problems that waste time and money and create barriers, inefficiencies, frustration and conflict, both internally and with customers. The avoidable problems they create leave them little time to focus on improving performance and results. All of this disillusions customers, colleagues and senior managers alike; damages business results, reputation and profitability; and impedes growth.

This represents a built-in cost and an unmanaged long-term risk which directly compromises both short-term business performance and profitability, and the long-term health and viability of the business, in myriad ways. It can lead to:

- **Increased costs,** due to ongoing operational inefficiencies which create unnecessary demands on resources and people's time, including errors, waste, delays, lost production, rework, downtime and low productivity. These costs either come straight off the bottom line or push prices up, reducing demand. Or both

- **Loss of business** through quality problems, poor delivery performance and poor client handling

- **Lower perceived value of the product or service,** which affects customers' willingness to buy, and what they are prepared to pay

- **Poor market reputation** – not being regarded as first-choice supplier due to damaged trust caused by missed deadlines, poor quality etc. This also makes it harder to sell, harder to command a premium price and harder to maintain a strong margin

- **Loss of brand value/equity** (for the reasons above)

- **Time and energy wasted** on blaming, justifying and counter-blaming

- **Further time and energy wasted** on clearing up difficulties that could have been prevented

- **Wasted human potential** as the business fails to leverage its talent to have the impact it should. This is manifested as underperformance relative to potential, and missed opportunities for improvement. Every day

- **Higher levels of absence and the associated cost and disruption.** This includes being short-staffed, having key people in the wrong roles, and possibly overworked, disruption to teamworking, high cost of temporary staff, and all of the related management time diverted from value-adding work

- **Higher employee turnover.** The most talented and committed people get disillusioned at being unable to use and develop their talent, and to get the success and opportunities their talent deserves. They leave. This translates into a loss of value-adding capacity. It impacts on quality, productivity, customer satisfaction and team stability. It also translates into increased costs from the resulting discontinuity, disruption, recruitment and retraining. Sometimes it creates a cascade effect, unsettling others who then start looking for the exits themselves

- **Poor labour-market reputation.** A company's reputation as an employer correlates strongly with the quality of colleagues' relationship with their manager, so a reputation for poor management means that the business is not regarded as an employer of first choice (and is quite possibly seen as an employer of last resort). Top talent is put off. This leaves the business to select from a pool of lower-performance and higher-maintenance people – a recipe for increased hassle and less success

- **Opportunity costs.** Due to the time wasted and the distraction of dealing with avoidable problems, opportunities for improvement are either missed or there is insufficient responsiveness and drive to capitalise on them

- **Major project failures** (due to all of the above)

- **Damaged supplier relationships,** with loss of cooperation, goodwill or valued partnerships

- **Weakening of the collective culture's ability to adapt, evolve and stay relevant.** This is a significant risk if technology, the sales environment and labour markets are competitive and changing quickly

- **Lack of competitive edge.** All of the above accumulates over time and represents a growing gap between potential and actual performance. This opens the door for the competition to build a performance gap (and a reputation gap) that is hard to close

- **Increased risk of business failure.** Carrying the unnecessary recurring costs listed above, commanding poorer margins and having frailties around internal capability, quality and delivery performance increases the organisation's vulnerability to market competition and economic or industry downturns

These are all problems that cause ongoing and accumulating cost, delay and frustration, damage business results and limit reputation, and act as a brake on profitability and future prosperity. It's a recipe for underperformance, frustration, sub-optimisation – much of it avoidable.

But that's not all.

Second-order effects: destructive spirals

Not only are underdeveloped and underperforming leaders and managers likely to invite the above problems, but there is a second-order effect. These people are unlikely to lead any change to a) address the existing, avoidable operational problems, far less to b) lead strategic change that will evolve the business and position it for sustainable long-term success and prosperity. This creates stagnation and a culture of self-perpetuating mediocrity (and potentially a downward spiral) which becomes harder and more costly to change the longer it is left. (See Figure 23.2).

Underdeveloped people and processes

Quality, cost and delivery performance problems

Unhappy customers, colleagues and other stakeholders

• **Managers over-busy and reactive**
• **Value-enabling activities (planning, process improvement and people development) sidelined**

Figure 23.2: The downward spiral of stagnation

The benefits of managing and developing managers

In contrast, managers who are properly managed and developed:

- Are clear about what is expected of them and able to carry it out effectively

- Set an example

- Communicate well

- Build, run and continuously improve both the operational and management processes

- Get the best out of people, managing the performance of individuals and teams to achieve business goals

- Get the best out the financial and other resources they manage

- Build productive working relationships with colleagues, customers, suppliers and other stakeholders

Thus, managers who have been developed to a professional standard consistent with the principles of Business Excellence avoid a raft of common but avoidable issues that plague many companies. This represents significant cost avoidance, improves performance across the board and creates the foundations on which to build strategic change to evolve the business to be fit for the future (see Figure 23.3).

Figure 23.3: The upward spiral of improvement

Conclusion: why develop leadership and management capability

The aim of leadership and management development is to equip leaders and managers with the appropriate attitudes, skills, underpinning knowledge and practical expertise to allow them to effectively lead and manage people, processes and resources and to manage change, so that they can increase the organisation's short-term operational effectiveness and contribute to its long-term strategic growth and development.

But this is not always recognised as being of strategic importance, or done well.

Underdeveloped leaders and managers represent an ongoing avoidable cost and a missed opportunity for operational and strategic excellence; limit the prospects of the business and the people in it; and disadvantage the organisation relative to competitors whose managers are better equipped to succeed.

In short, leaders and managers, depending on their level of development, can be a liability or an asset to long-term performance and future prosperity. It is therefore hard to overstate the fundamental importance of effective leadership and management development.

Managing and developing leadership and management performance

Leadership and management development is an ongoing process that needs to be carried out rigorously and systematically. Starting at the top.

Leaders and managers should, regularly:

- Be (re)acquainted with their responsibilities, capability requirements (skill, knowledge, attitude, behaviour, standards) and performance targets
- Be held accountable for these
- Get constructive feedback to help them understand their impact and to identify and address any blind spots
- Have a chance to discuss and solve problems that are preventing them from doing better
- Identify any development needs and have access to appropriate opportunities to address them

This helps to mitigate against the twin perils of managers a) withdrawing into their comfort zone and not doing the management part of their job, or b) going maverick and pursuing their own ideas and agendas, which are not necessarily aligned with the long-term interests of the business, customers or colleagues.

Creating a system

There are a number of tools that can be combined to create a system and approach to achieve the above. This includes:

- Role descriptions
- Skill profiles
- Leadership standard work and manager standard work
- Competence frameworks
- KPIs
- A performance and development review process
- A reward system that links to organisational values, with managers who meet business targets but score low on values less likely to be favoured for greater influence, status or remuneration

Creating a process

Review of the above can be done formally at six-monthly or quarterly intervals as part of the wider performance review process. Monthly coaching or check-in sessions are highly recommended to maintain focus, build momentum and underline the importance of ongoing development.

The habit of self-review and personal reflection should be strongly encouraged as part of this, as leadership development should become increasingly self-directed.

Getting regular feedback from the team can be built into the systems and culture through:

- Incorporating questions into team members' performance reviews that invite them to offer feedback to their manager
- Managers inviting feedback during team meetings
- 360-degree reviews, where managers can get feedback from a range of relevant people to gain a more comprehensive, rounded and balanced picture
- Employee engagement surveys
- Management team co-coaching, both one-to-one and at management team meetings
- Periodic in-depth team self-review (by the team as a whole)
- Feedback from customers – for example, by visiting, taking to lunch, or otherwise communicating with one customer a month and asking for direct feedback on their experience of the business
- Coaching and mentoring from non-executive directors or outside consultants

These are excellent for raising leaders' and managers' awareness of their performance. It helps provide encouragement and builds appropriate confidence in the right things. It also provides accurate guidance on where development should be targeted for maximum benefit. For any managers displaying toxic attitudes and behaviours – managers whose performance is harming the business and people in it – this leaves no place to hide and no way to dismiss legitimate concerns.

Development methods

Developing managers can involve a number of different approaches, both formal and informal, as suited to the level of the role and the person's experience.

There are some core approaches that are necessary for the development of these complex, high-level professional skills, and other approaches that are useful to supplement these. We'll explore these in turn.

Core strategies and approaches

Formal courses and seminars

Formal courses are an excellent way for new managers to establish the foundational concepts, tools and thinking they need, quickly, well and cost-effectively, and for more established managers to refresh, augment and update their thinking and tools.

They typically cover a great deal of important ground in a short period. They introduce new ideas, concepts, insights and tools and provide inspiration and motivation. With dedicated time put aside for this, managers are able to fully engage with the material, discuss it with other delegates and ask questions of the presenter.

Options can range from short, single-topic courses to comprehensive programmes and lengthy, high-level academic courses.

Sending individual managers to external courses is a great way to bring in new insights and ideas and make new contacts. However, the bedrock of the development of a coherent and high-performing management team must, by definition, be an in-house programme that is tailored to the needs of the business and provides a complete, coherent and consistent system – and, importantly, gets colleagues learning and working together.

It is also easier to implement what is learned from an in-house programme, ensuring that it is applied in practice and translated into progress, results and appropriate return on investment.

In-house mentors who have previously been through internally run development programmes are a powerful, accessible and inexpensive resource to support effective implementation. This can be usefully supplemented by external coaching and mentoring.

Such programmes are the most effective, impactful and cost-efficient approach when one considers a) the costs (outlined earlier) of not addressing the issue at all, and b) how long it takes for managers to develop without structured support, and the direct, hidden and opportunity costs of poor quality encountered endlessly along the way.

Learning on the job: coaching and action learning

Managers can also learn effectively on the job, but only if given sufficient direction and support from their own manager or a skilled coach.

Indeed, if the foundational principles, attitudes and skills have been adequately established, being effectively coached through **'action learning'** to tackle, and learn from, real challenges is the most direct and effective way to develop the relevant technical capabilities and the character, mental strength and resilience to face the challenges that management brings.

Action learning focuses on real requirements and challenges in the workplace. The coach and manager pick an issue; agree on a goal and some initial actions; carry out the actions; and meet again to discuss what they did, what the outcomes were, what they learned, and what they will do next. The process is then simply repeated, progressively bottoming out one opportunity and moving on to the next.

Goals might include changing a process, improving a relationship, delegating more, tightening up how meetings are run, or improving time management; anything relevant. Action learning can be done with individual managers or as a management team, to solve problems collectively, enhance mutual understanding and improve collaboration.

Another on-the-job approach is to use special projects. Giving managers projects to be completed within a set timeframe brings into sharp focus their organisation, planning, decision-making, team-building, execution and performance management skills. This allows these skills to be developed and any problems with them to be identified and addressed. Being relatively self-contained, with bounded timescales and a fairly direct relationship between actions and results, projects can be excellent vehicles for creating a sequence of fast and focused development loops. They can accelerate learning, reduce the risk of expensive mistakes being made on mainstream activities, and bring direct business benefits.

A final on-the-job approach is job rotation. This helps managers develop two invaluable things: a broad and varied range of experience, and an appreciation of, and respect for, the needs and challenges of others in the business. Helping managers develop this perspective and attitude pays great dividends in promoting effective cross-team working (and in reducing misunderstandings and breaking down silos). The business need not be large for this to be an effective approach, nor do managers need to be seconded for months. Even a few days in a different department can be enough to have a powerful and lasting effect. In a similar vein, spending time with customers or suppliers, or even visiting other companies in the same industry, can be a source of excellent insight and development.

For leadership development, periodic **'back to the floor'** visits can be a powerful, immediate and highly relevant learning experience with multiple benefits. Problems with a product or service can be observed and problems with processes recognised. This can build trust and respect, improve dialogue and mutual understanding and provide a morale boost – people feel important and motivated when they see that senior figures care about what is happening at the front line and their experience of it.

Supplementary approaches, sources and mechanisms

There are some other development options for leaders and managers that can potentially be valuable.

Structured open learning materials

There are many excellent open learning programmes. The great advantage they offer is that they provide a complete and structured programme, most often with some kind of test or assignment at the end to check learning. Some are used as part of taught courses with a structure, flow and timescale and with tutor support, while others are more open-ended and self-directed. (The important caveat here, however, is that, while they may offer certificated learning, there is no guarantee of this being translated either into a) workplace practice, or b) capability or enhanced performance.)

Books

Books (eBooks or printed ones) are available at little cost on a wide range of management topics and at every level, from the basic to the academic. (A disconcerting statistic is that less than one in a hundred managers regularly reads management books – so you're already stealing a march on the competition.)

Reading is a simple, inexpensive and powerful way to augment coaching and bring in useful new models, ideas and insights, as well as developing the invaluable lifelong habit of reading management texts. Coaches can use the tactic of directed reading, tasking managers to read a book chapter or article and, at the next coaching session, discussing what they learned and what they can apply in their work.

Podcasts and other audio or video material

Podcasts (and similar video offerings such as MasterClass) can be a very powerful way of learning directly from experts, and can be used to make the most of time spent travelling.

Creating a comprehensive and balanced approach

A combination of the above methods with the focus, structure, direction, expert input and support provided by a senior manager or executive coach offers the most powerful approach to ongoing leadership and management development. It allows a balance to be created, incorporating conceptual learning, practical on-the-job application, and problem-solving that is results-focused and tuned to the evolving needs of individuals and the management team collectively.

WHY FIRST-TIME MANAGERS MAY STRUGGLE, AND HOW TO AVOID THIS

Management recruitment and development can go wrong for many reasons and put the wrong people, with the wrong motivations, attitudes and skills, in the wrong place. Particularly when appointing first-time managers.

For example:

- Many people covet management roles because of the associated money, status and power rather than because of any great desire to assume the burdens associated with management responsibility. As Jack Welch noted, many people want to be a manager but don't want to do management

- People are promoted to management because they are intelligent, hard-working and honest in their technical role, rather than on the evidence of any great ability or aptitude to lead or manage

- No role descriptions, responsibilities or capability framework were used against which to objectively assess capability, attitude or potential

Even if the right people are appointed, becoming a manager requires a shift in mindset and, for some, even a shift in identity. The accomplished technical specialist is a doer who achieves results through her or his own knowledge, skills, expertise, time and effort. In contrast, skilled leaders and managers achieve results by engaging, enabling and empowering others, by managing, developing, motivating and providing direction and support to the team, managing processes, and dealing with customers who exhibit varying degrees of satisfaction and equanimity, and varying levels of expectation and forgiveness!

And the leap is often sudden. As Devi Jankowicz pointed out, if someone has spent years being trained as a specialist to focus intensely on one area of work and is suddenly faced with all the fuzziness and messiness that goes with leadership and management, it's quite a shock for them. They move from being an expert to floundering in unfamiliar and ambiguous terrain. Many choose to run for the comfort and cover of staying hands-on, or resort to copying the style of other managers (good or otherwise), perpetuating a cycle of inconsistency and suboptimal management.

Consequently, when managers are promoted from specialist technical roles, they need to be given a proper induction, training and ongoing coaching to acquire the shift in outlook and the additional skills they require to succeed.

CHAPTER 24

OPERATIONAL MANAGEMENT AND FRONT-LINE MANAGEMENT: ROLES, RESPONSIBILITIES AND REQUIRED CAPABILITIES

Introduction

To develop a culture of excellence, we need managers to understand the nature of the role, the seriousness of their responsibilities and the obligation to perform them well. An obligation that comes with having significant influence over the performance, success and reputation of the business and people's satisfaction, development and career prospects.

In this chapter, we'll look at what is expected from operational managers and front-line managers, and in the next chapter we'll do the same for leadership roles.

Organisations will of course differ in the number of levels of management, the titles used and the specific responsibilities. Offered here is a broad structure that you can adapt to devise an approach that works best for your business. This will hopefully get you to a high standard quickly, saving you significant time, effort, frustration and risk. Figure 24.1 positions this within the overall context of the Business Excellence model.

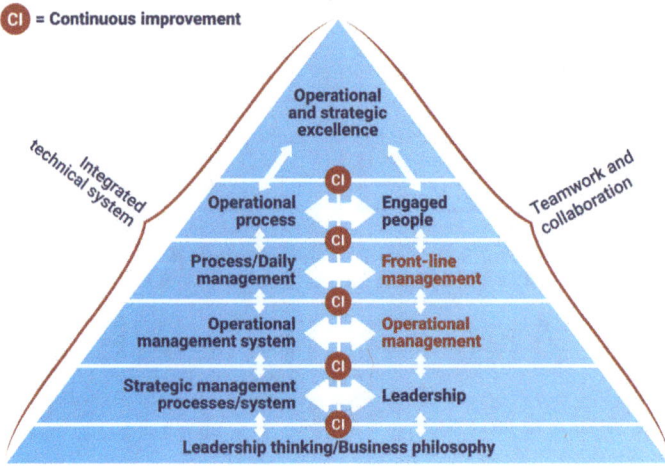

Figure 24.1: Operational and front-line management in context

The role of the manager

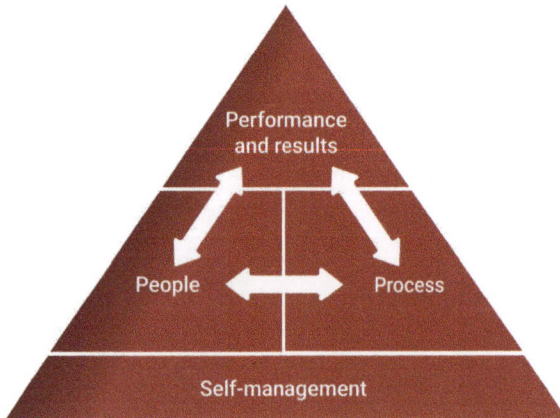

Figure 24.2: The role of the manager

'All management should be directed toward one aim, allowing the individual to perform his or her job to the utmost while [enjoying] his or her work.' (Rafael Aguayo)

In Business Excellence, the role of the manager is to achieve results by enabling and facilitating performance through leading, engaging, developing and empowering people and building, managing and continuously improving processes. This is all founded on effective self-management (as illustrated in Figure 24.2).

The role includes:

- Serving people to enable them to serve to the customer (as illustrated in Figure 24.3), by:

  - Ensuring that front-line colleagues have everything that they need to meet the customers' needs right first time, on time, every time, with zero wasted time or material

  - Empowering the team to improve the system they work in, to help them to do an ever-improving job with greater pride, less effort and more satisfaction

  - Listening to, and addressing, problems that people cannot clear from their own paths

  - Engaging people in a consistent, constructive, adult dialogue to enable them to become high-performing, low-maintenance contributors who deliver sustained world-class performance and continuously improving results

- Recruiting, engaging, motivating, developing and retaining talent
- Building a winning team
- Understanding how the work of the team serves the wider business and how it is expected to collaborate with other teams to optimise the overall system
- Developing a culture that is conducive to excellence

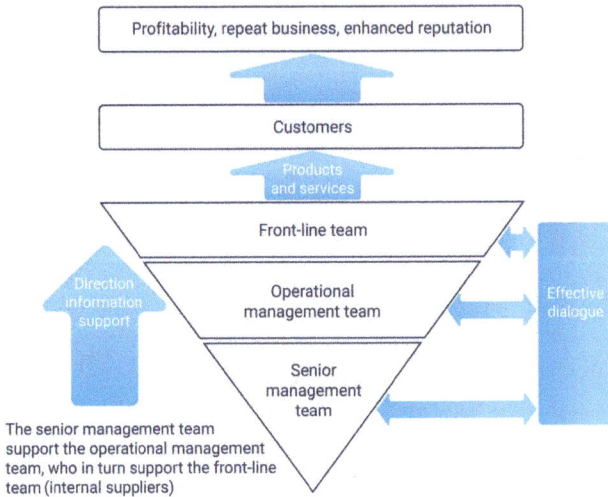

Figure 24.3: How managers enable and facilitate front-line colleagues

Competence model

There are certain core attitudes, skills and other qualities which all good managers in a culture of excellence must possess. These are summarised in Figure 24.4.

Figure 24.4: Management competencies

Let's briefly explore each factor. (NB: you can find the full 65-item framework in both Appendix E, the front-line manager's standards pack, and Appendix F, the operational manager's standards pack.)

- **Attitude and approach:** Being positive, being a problem-solver, and taking responsibility for personal and team performance, and for making things happen
- **Self-management:** Being emotionally balanced, calm, strong, resilient and persistent
- **Personal organisation:** Managing priorities, time and energy effectively
- **Interpersonal effectiveness:** Building strong working relationships with people with different personal styles. Having the ability to handle challenging behaviours and difficult situations
- **Team player:** Collaborating effectively with others within their own departmental team, cross-functionally and at different levels
- **People management:** Having the ability to organise, empower, coach and develop people, and to deal with underperformance and disciplinary issues
- **Leading the team:** Being able to get the mix of characters in the team to work effectively, solve problems and improve processes, as a unit
- **Managing stakeholders:** Ensuring that key stakeholders' expectations and perceptions remain informed and realistic so that processes do not become under-resourced or overburdened
- **Process excellence:** Ensuring that the processes are effectively designed, managed and improved, enabling people to consistently achieve excellent performance
- **Results:** Measures of effective management include:

  - Consistently strong, and continuously improving, performance against key performance indicators
  - Sustained progress toward strategic improvement goals
  - Consistently high employee engagement scores
  - Strong scores on 360-degree reviews

Management responsibilities and standard work

Beyond these broad expectations which all managers share, there are specific responsibilities for front-line managers and operational managers. Below we'll set out:

- The role (literally, the role that a manager in that position is expected to play in the business)
- Responsibilities (what managers in that position are accountable for)
- Standard work – the routine, auditable tasks that a manager at that level should be carrying out, which underpin the delivery of the responsibilities and achievement of the role. (Note: there is, by implication, non-standard work, i.e. dealing with unfolding live events. Nonetheless, successful achievement of the role is underpinned by these core routines/kata)

You can also find these in template format in Appendices F and G.

Front-line management

Front-line management is vital. It arguably influences engagement and performance more than any other single factor, as front-line managers are the most immediate and frequent touchpoint for colleagues, and have the most direct impact on people's ability to perform, their attitudes, their behaviour and their levels of motivation and commitment.

Front-line management focuses on:

- Delivering what the customer needs on time, to quality, within cost, consistently, predictably and reliably
- Making in-flight adjustments
- Making continuous (kaizen) process improvements
- Unlocking individual potential
- Upholding standards: performance, attitudinal and behavioural
- Solving day-to-day tactical front-line operational problems

The front-line manager mindset is:

- Immediate-term

- Customer-oriented
- Pragmatic: focused on people, process, quality, results

Below, we've set out a comprehensive description of the role, responsibilities and standard work for front-line managers.

The role of the front-line manager

To achieve results by enabling and facilitating performance through leading, engaging, developing and empowering people and building, managing and continuously improving processes. This is all founded on effective self-management. The role includes:

- Serving people to enable them to serve to the customer, by:

  - Ensuring that front-line colleagues have everything that they need to meet the customers' needs right first time, on time, every time, with zero wasted time or material
  - Empowering the team to improve the system they work in, to help them to do a better job with greater pride, less effort and more satisfaction
  - Listening to, and addressing, problems that people cannot clear from their own paths
  - Engaging people in a consistent, constructive, adult dialogue to enable them to become high-performing, low-maintenance contributors who deliver sustained world-class performance and continuously improving results

- Recruiting, engaging, motivating, developing and retaining talent
- Building a winning team
- Understanding how the work of the team serves the wider business and collaborating with other teams to optimise the overall system
- Developing a culture that is conducive to excellence

The front-line manager's responsibilities

Achieve results in the areas of:
- Health and safety
- Right-first-time quality
- On-time delivery
- Cost performance

- Colleague engagement
- Ongoing improvement of the capability and performance of both people and process

Self-management. To:
- Set the tone. Be a role model by living the excellence philosophy and demonstrating what effective attitude, behaviour and performance look like
- Provide positive leadership: a clear vision, goals and direction
- Lead with emotional maturity, taking a measured approach to handling setbacks, challenges and change, keeping themself and others calm, focused and professional

Performance management:
- To ensure a safe working environment
- Daily planning and preparation to facilitate optimal team and process performance for each day, week and month
- Daily accountability meeting
- Gemba walk
- In-flight monitoring and course-correction: constantly tracking quality and workflow, and making in-flight adjustments and kaizen improvements
- Problem response
- Live coaching
- Review, learning and improvement

Process management. To ensure that the system that people work in is:
- Fit for purpose (able to deliver requirements on time, to cost, to quality, predictably and reliably)
- Properly resourced
- Operating within capacity
- Continuously improved (by the team) to add increasing value and to eliminate defects, waste and inefficiency
- Aligned with the process stages which precede and follow

People management. To ensure that people:
- Have clear expectations (role, responsibilities, performance standards and goals)
- Have the right knowledge and skills to succeed

- Have the right attitudes and behaviours
- Are supported: that anything stopping them from succeeding or improving is heard and addressed
- Work as a team
- Are held accountable for their performance, attitudes and behaviours
- Are empowered to solve problems
- Are actively encouraged to consistently improve

Resource management:
- To ensure that front-line colleagues have everything that they need to succeed, including equipment, tools, raw materials, consumables and sundries

Coordination, alignment and collaboration. To:
- Collaborate with cross-functional colleagues to ensure the effective management and improvement of the end-to-end processes
- Collaborate with colleagues at different levels (vertically) to ensure strategic alignment
- Recognise and manage the interdependencies within the organisation, resolve conflicts, remove barriers to cooperation, and enhance collaboration within and between teams to improve flow, quality and productivity, and to reduce hassle and frustration and help people to do a better job with greater pride and more enjoyment

Culture. To:
- Actively promote and live the principles of Business Excellence (the pursuit of excellence through continuous improvement, working as a team)
- Develop and maintain the kata (core disciplines) that underpin excellence
- Optimise site performance, not just the performance of their own team (taking one for the team when appropriate)
- Continue improving all aspects of system capability, and attitudes and behaviours, at individual and team level

Strategic management:
- Contribute to the setting of strategic goals for their area of responsibility
- Implement strategic goals for their area of responsibility
- Support implementation of cross-functional strategic goals

Front-line manager standard work (auditable activities)

- Daily management

  - Start of shift handover (if applicable)
  - Daily accountability (Tier 1) meetings: short (5-10 minutes) check-in with the team collectively (where possible, a stand-up meeting in the communications zone where all relevant data are available) to review action and progress from the previous day, and to plan activity and anticipate problems for the day ahead
  - Gemba walk: a brief tour of the work area to see directly what is happening, checking in with people
  - Constantly monitoring process performance, and communicating with front-line colleagues to identify and address emerging problems promptly
  - Live coaching: responding to real-time improvement opportunities in colleague skills, behaviour, attitudes and performance in the course of daily work
  - End of shift handover (if applicable)

- Weekly and monthly team review meetings: to identify, understand and address trends and recurring issues over the period and to look ahead and prepare for the next period
- One-to-one performance reviews to complement the ongoing coaching
- Complete improvement task assignments related to continuous improvement of a) the operational processes, b) the daily management process, and c) projects identified in the strategic plan

MANAGER STANDARD WORK

Business performance comes from the effective management and development of people and process, so standard work emphasises the primacy of the routine and effective execution of the core disciplines/kata, outlined below.

Gemba walk: The gemba is the place where the work is done. A gemba walk is a regular visit by the manager to see for themselves the people and process in action, and to understand what is happening. To talk with and listen to colleagues, ask and answer questions, help people to identify improvement opportunities, and to support people in their improvement efforts. It demonstrates that the manager recognises the importance of the front line, understands what happens there, and cares about the experience of the people who work there. It also signals that they are in touch with, and on top of, things (and therefore not easily misled or manipulated).

Daily accountability (Tier 1) meetings: This is typically a short (5-10 minutes) daily stand-up meeting in the communications zone at the start of the day to review action and progress from the previous day, and plan activity and anticipate problems for the day ahead. The review agenda is typically:

- Part 1 (Review): planned; actual; variance; reason; action
- Part 2 (Look-ahead): planned goals and activities; potential issues and watch-outs

The meeting is likely to be informed by simple, visual process metrics. Tier 1 meetings will feed into Tier 2 meetings (at operational management level), and these will feed into the Tier 3 meeting of the top team so that the site-wide operational status is known early, and issues recognised and dealt with promptly at the appropriate level.

Visual management – maintain up-to-date and accurate visual performance information: Visuals give the performance management process (including daily management and the gemba walk) a sharp and relevant focus. Having access to high-quality data on process performance (with well-chosen and well-structured metrics) allows leaders to track performance, to make in-flight course corrections and to identify improvement opportunities quickly and accurately. (And of course, the faster problems and opportunities are spotted, the cheaper they are to address, and the greater the benefits that accrue.)

Visuals will typically include a performance board featuring:

- Tracking charts showing expected vs actual on key metrics
- Daily maintenance
- Daily 5S actions (see Chapter 14)
- Continuous improvement projects
- A visual map of the process (a value stream map)

Track execution of the plan (expected vs actual) and ensure that variations (defects, misses/fallouts, lates and partials etc.), are identified, and the reasons identified and responded to appropriately.

Operational management

Operational management focuses on coordination and management of process, performance and results. This includes:

- Delivering the operational strategy in line with the organisation's mission, vision and values
- Ensuring the effective running of the whole operation
- Developing the organisation's system and process infrastructure
- Medium- to long-term operational planning
- Reconciling conflicting interests and goals between units
- Recruiting, developing, engaging, motivating and retaining talent

The operational manager mindset is:

- Medium- to long-term
- Inside-outside: boundary spanning, to ensure collaboration and alignment a) within the organisation, and b) between the organisation and external stakeholders
- Facilitating and enabling

The role of the operational manager

To achieve results by enabling and facilitating performance through leading, engaging, developing and empowering people and building, managing and continuously improving processes. This is all founded on effective self-management. The role includes:

- The effective running of the whole operation, overseeing and integrating the management of the core processes end-to-end across the business
- Reconciling conflicting interests and goals between units
- Organising and managing resources to ensure that front-line managers have what they need so that they can provide front-line colleagues with the tools, equipment and resources to deliver what the customer wants, right first time, on time, every time, with zero wasted time or material
- Designing, managing and continuously improving the daily management process and the operational management process
- Developing the organisation's infrastructure appropriately to enable performance

---

- Coaching front-line managers to develop the required skills, attitudes and behaviours
- Overseeing, integrating and monitoring the continuous improvement activities happening at the front line
- Actively contributing to continuous improvement efforts by helping to remove barriers that front-line managers can't
- Implementing the improvement projects associated with the breakthrough goals in the strategic plan
- Developing the management team
- Overseeing the recruitment, engagement, motivation, development and retention of talent
- Developing a culture that is conducive to excellence

The operational manager's main responsibilities

To achieve results, in areas including:
- Health and safety
- Right-first-time quality
- On-time delivery
- Cost performance
- Colleague engagement
- Delivering the agreed strategic improvement breakthrough goals
- Ongoing improvement of the capability and the performance of both people and process

Self management. To:
- Set the tone as a role model by living the excellence philosophy and demonstrating what effective attitude, behaviour and performance looks like
- Provide positive leadership: a clear vision, goals and direction

- Lead with emotional maturity, taking a measured approach to handling setbacks, challenges and change, keeping themself and others calm, focused and professional

Performance management:
- To ensure a safe working environment
- Overseeing front-line managers' daily planning and preparation
- Daily (Tier 2) accountability meeting
- Gemba walk
- In-flight monitoring and course-correction: taking a helicopter view across the whole area of responsibility, tracking quality and workflow across the operational process end-to-end, and making in-flight adjustments and kaizen improvements, ensuring integration both within their area of responsibility and with other teams
- Responding to problems that FLMs cannot solve by themselves
- Live coaching of FLMs
- Review, learning and improvement

Operational management process. To ensure that the operational management system is:
- Fit for purpose: this covers the design, management and improvement of the communications zones, including the visual accountability boards to track operational performance and process-improvement assignments
- Properly resourced
- Continuously improved
- Touchpoints and meetings are fit for purpose and run a) as designed, and b) as scheduled

People management. To ensure that the front-line managers:
- Have clear expectations (role, responsibilities, standards and daily tasks and goals)
- Have the right knowledge and skills to succeed
- Have the right attitudes and behaviours
- Are supported: that anything stopping them from succeeding or improving is heard and addressed
- Work as a team

- Are held accountable for their performance, attitudes and behaviours
- Are empowered to solve problems
- Are actively encouraged to consistently improve
- Are doing the same for front-line colleagues

Infrastructure and resource management:
- To ensure that the operation has everything needed to succeed, including equipment, tools, raw materials, consumables, sundries, wider systems, facilities and amenities. And that it is all in the right place in the right quantities, of the right quality, at the right time

Coordination, alignment and collaboration. To:
- Collaborate with cross-functional colleagues to ensure the effective management and improvement of the whole operational process end-to-end
- Collaborate with colleagues at different levels (vertically) to ensure strategic alignment
- Recognise and manage the interdependencies within the organisation, resolve conflicts, remove barriers to cooperation, and enhance collaboration within and between teams to improve flow, quality and productivity, and to reduce hassle and frustration and help people to do a better job with greater pride and more enjoyment

Culture. To:
- Actively promote and live the principles of Business Excellence (the pursuit of excellence through continuous improvement, working as a team)
- Develop and maintain the kata (core disciplines) that underpin excellence and ensure that front-line managers are doing the same
- Optimise site performance, not just the performance of their own team (taking one for the team when appropriate)
- Continue improving all aspects of system capability, colleagues' attitudes and behaviours, and teamwork

Strategic management:
- Contribute to the setting of strategic goals
- Implement strategic goals for their area of responsibility
- Support implementation of cross-functional strategic goals

Operational manager standard work (auditable activities)

- Daily management:

  - Daily accountability (Tier 2) meetings: a short daily stand-up to review outcomes of the Tier 1 meetings, including action and progress from the previous day, and to plan activity and anticipate problems for the day ahead

  - Gemba walk: a brief tour of the work area to see directly what is happening, checking in with people and being visible and approachable

  - Constantly monitoring process performance, and communicating with front-line managers to identify and address emerging problems early

  - Live coaching: responding to real-time improvement opportunities in front-line managers' skills, behaviour, attitudes and performance in the course of daily work

- Weekly and monthly team review meetings: to identify, understand and address trends and recurring issues over the period and to look ahead and prepare for the next period

- One-to-one performance reviews with front-line managers to complement the ongoing coaching

- Complete improvement task assignments related to continuous improvement of a) the management processes, and b) projects identified in the strategic plan

Vertical development

The assessment criteria set out in this chapter outline the key facets of effective management. Establishing these building blocks to acquire the full set can be usefully seen as horizontal development.

There is also vertical development. This is a measure of capability maturity: that is, how mature the capability in each facet is, and how the person links them together into an integrated whole that brings a versatility and agility to their performance, helping them to respond quickly and well to a range of situations that can change quickly.

The model below (Figure 24.5) sets out four levels of vertical development. The lower on the spectrum we go, the greater the focus on trying to solve problems by throwing more time, energy, effort and force at it. The higher we go, the greater the focus on how well someone reads and analyses a situation, stays calm, thinks clearly, uses skill and expertise (technical and interpersonal), and selects the approach most suited to the situation (situational adaptation). As Deming described it, working smarter, not harder:

- Reactive/chaotic level behaviours include firefighting, blaming and complaining. At this level we may (or may not) solve the problem of the day. But, having failed to address the underlying root causes, we will face the same problem again the next day. And the day after that

- At the tactical level we will anticipate some near-future operational issues and will plan accordingly to avoid or mitigate those we can. We'll also be tuned in enough to read how events are unfolding and make necessary in-flight adjustments. Generally, we'll do our best within the current constraints, but not seek to understand and address the underlying process limitations

- At the improvement-focused level we'll look at the process that is driving the current outcomes (including the problems). We'll (re)design, manage and improve the processes in our purview, address the underlying root causes and improve outcomes on an ongoing basis

- At the strategic level we'll seek to understand how the whole business works as a coherent system, and where future problems and value-adding opportunities are likely to occur. We'll then move to address these proactively, building new, and higher-level, capabilities to create an increasingly more adaptive system over time. Always seeking to increase possibilities and improve outcomes for all stakeholders

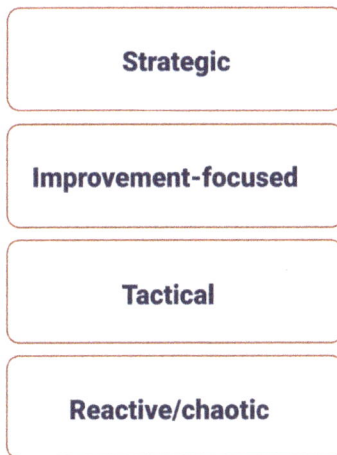

Figure 24.5: Levels of managers' vertical development

You can find managers' standards packs, offering the descriptions of roles and responsibilities set out above in a useable template form, in Appendix E for front-line managers and Appendix F for operational managers.

CHAPTER 25

LEADERSHIP: ROLE, RESPONSIBILITIES AND REQUIRED CAPABILITIES

Introduction

The quality of leadership is the single biggest factor that determines an organisation's ability to achieve and sustain Business Excellence. It is therefore important that leaders understand what the role requires, the seriousness of the responsibilities, and the obligation to perform them well. An obligation that comes with having significant influence over the performance, success and reputation of the business, and the lives and career prospects of the people in it.

In this chapter, we'll look first at what leadership means in the context of Business Excellence, and then we'll share an invaluable practical tool, the leadership standards pack, which captures the leader's role, responsibilities, standard work and core competencies in an auditable form that will aid in their selection, management and development. Figure 25.1 positions this within the overall context of the Business Excellence model.

Figure 25.1: Leadership capability in context

Note 1: Most leadership work is definitively non-standard, i.e. it involves dealing with unfolding events. Nonetheless, successful achievement of the role is underpinned by the core roles, responsibilities and 'standard work' routines/kata, and is correspondingly imperilled by a lack of attention to them.

Furthermore, the work that leaders prioritise should align with their main categories of responsibility and should be carried out to a defined standard. The balance should also be tilted toward shaping the long-term future of the business rather than toward unnecessary involvement in operational matters, far less regular firefighting.

Note 2: If you'd like to read more on leadership, this is covered in other Future Positive resources. Go to futurepositiveconsulting.com/toward-excellence to find out more.

Before we delve into the detail, we'll take two important detours to establish a couple of concepts that are crucial to leadership in Business Excellence:

1. Vertical development in the leadership context
2. The moral dimension of leadership

Vertical development

The capabilities outlined in this chapter set out the lines of 'horizontal development', but it is also important to recognise the importance of leaders' 'vertical development'.

Vertical development is a measure of capability maturity. That is, first, how mature (high-level, practiced, embedded and robust) the skills are for each capability; and second, how well the person links them together into an integrated set of capabilities that equip them to respond in fast, fluid and adaptive ways to the wide range of rapidly evolving situations they are likely to face at the top of their profession.

VERTICAL DEVELOPMENT AND CONSCIOUSNESS

Vertical development relates to the development of consciousness; literally, what we are conscious of and therefore, in highly practical terms, able to see, understand and successfully influence in any given domain, or in life generally.

Greater consciousness allows us to identify more fully, and with increasing subtlety and skill:

- The key variables in play
- How they dynamically interact as a system to shape outcomes
- How to improve outcomes and to tackle increasingly complex challenges

As such, greater consciousness increases our capacity to read the cues in our environment and act effectively on them, and to do so to create better outcomes in increasingly complex, ambiguous, fast-moving, volatile and contested circumstances where there is more at stake and a higher level of risk.

Higher levels of vertical development are characterised by increasing:

- Openness to new information and ideas, and to running experiments to facilitate timely and effective adaptation and evolution
- Degree of systems thinking: the ability to see the bigger picture and be better able to:

- Understand what the different components of the system are
- Understand the current dynamics of the system; how the different aspects interconnect and interact
- Identify root causes of problems
- Anticipate the immediate and longer-term consequences of proposed actions
- Devise lasting solutions rather than reacting to symptoms and applying ineffective quick fixes

- Scope, reach and ability to deliver desired outcomes in increasingly challenging situations

And the lower on the spectrum we go, the more we experience the reverse of this.

The model in Figure 25.2 sets out four levels of leadership vertical development:

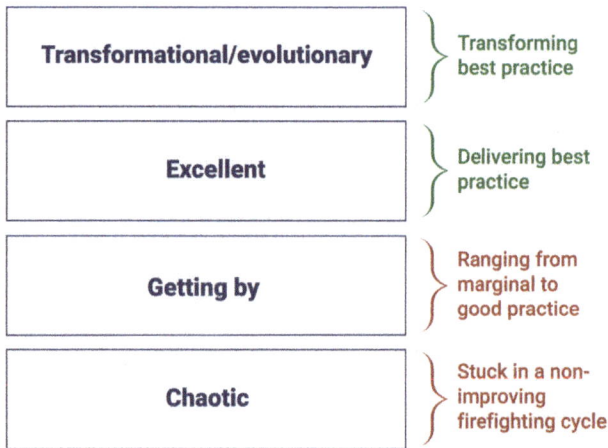

Transformational/evolutionary	Transforming best practice
Excellent	Delivering best practice
Getting by	Ranging from marginal to good practice
Chaotic	Stuck in a non-improving firefighting cycle

Figure 25.2: Levels of leaders' vertical development

- **Chaotic:** Even well-intentioned leaders can be chaotic, should they lack the requisite mindset, discipline, skills and character to deliver results and continuously improve in the face of an inevitable ongoing array of challenges. Where leaders lack such capability maturity, the business may be characterised by conflict, confusion, inefficiency, poor quality and inability to consistently deliver on its commitments – often accompanied by a stream of excuses, rationalisations and blame

- **Getting by:** Leaders here act within the constraints of the existing system, delivering business-as-usual performance with varying degrees of consistency, reliability, quality and efficiency. But because they either don't see the need, or don't feel it is their responsibility, they don't address the factors that are limiting system capability. They are therefore stuck at this level of performance

- **Excellent:** Leaders here are capable of running and improving an operation that has already reached a level of excellence. They deliver best practice, routinely perform well and achieve the SQCDE (safety, quality, cost, delivery performance and colleague engagement) measures. They can also optimise and improve the systems by making kaizen improvements (ongoing small tactical ones), but not the more significant structural and cultural kaikaku changes

- **Transformational/evolutionary leaders** are able to lead a transformation to Business Excellence, evolving the current business model to either:

  a. Respond to (or shape) change in their operating environments to get ahead of the competition and gain first-mover advantage, or

  b. Get to current best practice if the organisation is playing catch-up

Transformational leaders are able to take the initiative and to lead major kaikaku change in some or all of the dimensions described earlier (technical, social, cultural etc.) while simultaneously running the business at an acceptable level. As such, transformational leadership calls for a higher level of ambition, thinking and skill, and a better and more fully integrated set of tools and approaches for both running and improving an organisation

Transformational/evolutionary capability is, in some industries or circumstances, a minimum requirement rather than a hopeful aspiration. Without it, leaders may fail to recognise the existence and value of more adaptive business models and to understand that it is time to change. Instead, they may drift toward an expensive and avoidable crisis which will force change on them (if it's not already too late).

The moral dimension of leadership

Both leadership and management include, but go beyond, competence. We must be confident not only that people in positions of significant responsibility know what they are doing, but also that they are committed to furthering the interests of all stakeholders, and doing so over the long term. That they are not primarily focused on serving their own interests or egos here and now.

'When you were made a leader you weren't given a crown, you were given the responsibility to bring out the best in others.' (Jack Welch)

In organisations aspiring to Business Excellence, it is important that it is made clear to those in senior positions that they have a responsibility to leave the business's performance, reputation and future prosperity better than they found it and on an improving trajectory. So, too, the wellbeing and future prospects of the people in it.

Therefore, in addition to competence, if we are serious about Business Excellence, there is also the separate but related dimension of moral development. Kohlberg offers a useful developmental scale. He identified three broad levels of moral development and maturity:

- At the **pre-conventional level**, attitude and conduct is driven largely by self-interest and the degree of power that one has to do – and get away with doing – what they want. Others' needs and rights are not of intrinsic importance or voluntarily recognised. Constraint is generally external; the threat, or use, of direct sanction or force. At this level of moral development, people are generally opportunistic and self-interested and will test boundaries, possibly with a degree of recklessness, to see what they can get away with

- **Conventional** morality is centred around a recognition of, and respect for, others' needs and rights, within the existing framework of social norms and formal laws. Conformance with conventional morality can be through either a) personal choice, b) social pressure, or c) the threat or imposition of legal authority. Here, leaders are generally transactional and expedient. They remain predominantly focused on their own career prospects, staying as long as it suits them, making decisions that favour their reputation in the short term (and so are not wholly committed to serving the best interests of the business or its people in the long term). They are, though, mindful of others who can impact their prospects, and recognise the need to 'play the game'

- At **post-conventional level,** morality is guided by an intrinsic respect for people; as James Rachels put it, 'giving equal and impartial consideration to the interests of all those affected by what one does'. Here, leaders are motivated by the opportunity (and the felt obligation) to contribute to creating better lives for more people, and to make an evolutionary difference, handing the organisation over to the next generation in better shape and on an improving trajectory on all dimensions. People at this level have an intrinsic respect for honesty and the truth and actively, consciously and voluntarily pursue positive principles, so there is less need for external regulation

This creates four main categories of leadership behaviour, as shown in Figure 25.3.

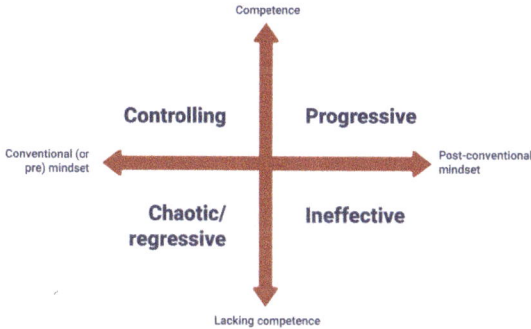

Figure 25.3: Dimensions of leadership

- **Progressive** leaders are skilled both strategically and operationally, and highly resilient. Their aims are guided by the principles of the quintuple bottom line – to create an organisation that is good to buy from, work for and invest in, and which makes a positive social and environmental impact. Their approach is informed by the principles of Business Excellence

- **Ineffective** leaders are generally well-intentioned. They may talk the talk of Business Excellence but, lacking a robust and wide-ranging capability matured through years of mindful practice and experience, are less well equipped to translate their progressive vision into a coherent strategy, far less to successfully implement it. Their approach is likely to lack sufficient focus, rigour and discipline to deliver either consistent operational performance or strategic breakthroughs

- **Controlling** leaders tend to be focused, organised, directive and transactional. In extremes, they can be manipulative and exploitative. Strategy, and operational delivery, may be robust in areas directly linked to driving profitability. The general approach is to push the limits of customer, employee, regulatory and public tolerance as far as they will go without provoking a damaging backlash. To mitigate the risk of this, they usually also excel at image management, to convey an impression of competence, responsibility and trustworthiness and to sell a story that is more palatable than the reality

- **Chaotic/regressive** leaders are typically disorganised, reactive and embroiled in problems. They are operationally inefficient, unable to solve significant systematic problems or make substantive strategic progress. Their organisations are not great to buy from, work for or invest in. They typically operate in markets or niches where they can survive despite this. And, having little ambition beyond this, they tend not to care enough to want to learn, grow or change

Leadership in Business Excellence

> 'My definition of leadership is this: the capacity and the will to rally men and women to a common purpose and the character which inspires confidence.' (Bernard Law Montgomery, 1st Viscount Montgomery of Alamein)

With the scene set, let's now look at the specifics of the role, responsibilities, standard work and competencies required of leaders aspiring to Business Excellence.

A leader's success depends on their ability to make other people successful, individually and as a team. Figure 25.4 reminds us of the key dimensions of this, which leaders bear ultimate responsibility for:

• The quality of the management and development of people, and

• The effectiveness of the systems they work within

Leaders also strongly influence the culture through the example they set personally; the level of commitment to excellence they demonstrate, and their attitudes and behaviour.

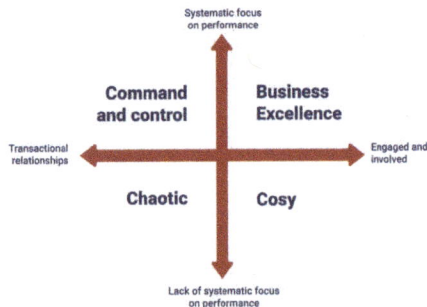

Figure 25.4: Dimensions of culture

Meta-model overview

Figure 25.5 is a reminder of the excellence meta-model and its constituent elements, which leaders are responsible for overseeing the design, management and improvement of.

We'll first recall briefly how the model works as a coherent whole, noting that it represents a fully integrated, dynamic socio-technical system rather than a collection of discrete parts. We'll then explore each aspect in turn, relating each dimension to the leader's role and responsibilities.

Figure 25.5: Business Excellence meta-model

Let's look first at the three-way relationship at the top of the model between people, process and performance.

Organisations' success is tied to their ability to perform. That is, to provide valued, cost-effective service to a target market in a way that is commercially sustainable.

To achieve excellent performance and results requires engaged people working with effective operational processes. When they are led and managed well, this creates an upward spiral of engaged people who both follow and improve the processes; working collaboratively to tackle real issues, solving real problems and grasping real opportunities. This creates increasingly strong results, which further builds people's confidence, motivation and engagement and encourages them to improve further, finding ways to add greater value and remove waste.

The left-hand side shows the 'technical system', the chain of management processes from strategic to operational to daily management, the purpose of which is to equip front-line colleagues with processes that are fit for purpose, lean, efficient, properly resourced, well managed and continuously improved.

On the right-hand side is the 'socio' part; the people factors and their interactions. These necessarily start with effective leadership attitudes, skills and behaviours, running through to operational managers' effectiveness and that of the front-line managers who run the daily management process and directly enable and facilitate front-line colleagues' performance.

The model also, throughout, illustrates the interactivity and interdependence between the various factors. For example, should a leader have great skill, but not an effective strategy process, their effectiveness will be correspondingly diminished. And vice versa: an excellent strategy process in the hands of someone lacking the requisite understanding, skills and discipline to run it well will be similarly compromised. And so on up the chain of people, and the processes they rely on, to the organisation's front line.

The entire venture is founded on the thinking, principles and practices of excellence.

Finally, all aspects of the model are subject to continuous improvement, both in their own right and as a holistic, dynamic business system adaptive to its changing business environment and context.

The key factors and the related leadership roles and responsibilities

With the scene set, let's explore the components in more detail and relate each to the leader's role, responsibilities and standard work, and the capabilities they require.

Excellent performance and results
The leader is the financial and reputational guardian of the business, responsible for both the ethical and effective conduct of it. In organisations committed to Business Excellence, key metrics include the SQCDE measures, framed within the principles of the quintuple bottom line. That is, creating an organisation that is good to buy from, work for and invest in, and that makes a positive social and environmental impact.

Strategic management

Turning now to the technical systems (on the left-hand side of Figure 25.5), the leader's first responsibility is to design, manage and continuously improve the strategic management system – the processes that shape, communicate and implement the strategy for the business – and deploy it to define and implement the organisation's vision, values, ethos, aims, standards and principles and the supporting methodology.

Operational management

The leader is also responsible, in collaboration with operational managers, for the design, management and improvement of the operational management systems, including the daily management processes, which oversee the effective running of the operation at different levels across different timescales. A crucial responsibility within this is ensuring that front-line colleagues have what they need to enable them to serve the customer right first time, on time, every time. Figure 25.6, first discussed in Chapter 18, reminds us of the particulars. A key element of this is (and completing the left-hand side of Figure 25.5) is building, managing and continuously improving operational processes which enable colleagues to achieve excellent performance.

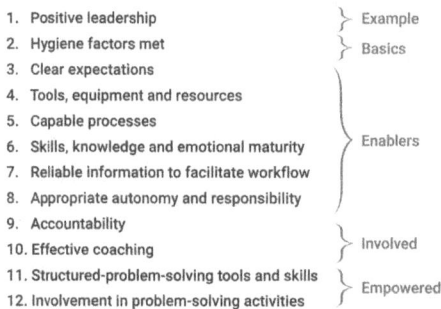

1. Positive leadership	Example
2. Hygiene factors met	Basics
3. Clear expectations	
4. Tools, equipment and resources	
5. Capable processes	
6. Skills, knowledge and emotional maturity	Enablers
7. Reliable information to facilitate workflow	
8. Appropriate autonomy and responsibility	
9. Accountability	
10. Effective coaching	Involved
11. Structured-problem-solving tools and skills	Empowered
12. Involvement in problem-solving activities	

Figure 25.6: Performance and engagement fundamentals

As Teresa Amabile and Steven Kramer suggest, while leaders are not directly responsible for managing operational performance, they remain, ultimately, accountable for it and so should be in touch with what is happening operationally: 'As a senior executive, Job Number 1 is: enabling the ongoing engagement and everyday progress of the people in the trenches of your organisation who strive to execute that strategy.'

This means being aware of operational status and any immediate problems that require a decision or intervention from them. This should be achieved routinely through tiered meetings as part of the daily management process. Leaders should also go to the front line (conduct a gemba walk) as appropriate to see and understand at first hand any significant challenges that people are facing in trying to execute the strategy or use the systems, and to address problems that are beyond the scope of front-line colleagues or operational managers to solve. Of course, the gemba walk also serves another important purpose; that of building up mutual understanding, trust and respect with colleagues and dispelling any sense (all too familiar in some organisations) that senior colleagues might be aloof, out of touch and disinterested in either the colleague, or customer, experience.

Developing people and teams

Let's shift our focus to the right-hand side of the meta-model (Figure 25.5). Here, the leader has ultimate responsibility for recruiting, engaging, motivating, developing and retaining top talent (starting with top management talent) and for gelling people together to create high-performance teams that optimise their collective talent.

Much of this hinges on getting the relationship between managers and colleagues right.

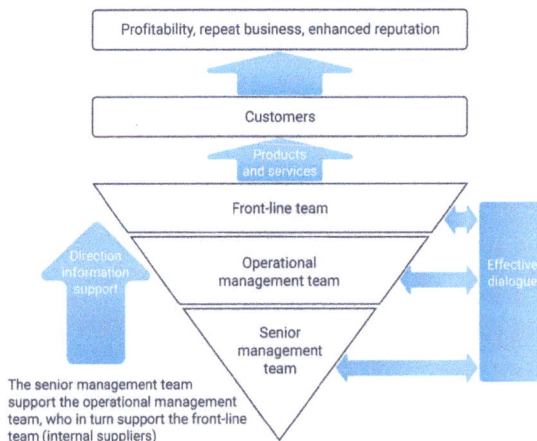

Figure 25.7: Leadership guiding and supporting operational excellence

Figure 25.7 reminds us that senior colleagues are responsible for empowering, enabling and facilitating the performance of front-line colleagues so that they can successfully meet customer needs (and so create loyal customers who return willingly, pay full rate, buy additional items or services and cheerfully recommend the business to others).

Front-line colleagues and managers are, definitively, not there to serve the needs of an inefficient reporting process, nor to be disrupted by senior colleagues' whims or random directives or demands for short-notice reports etc.

As the nature of the relationship is important, so too is the nature of the ensuing dialogue. The leader's role is to engage people in a consistent, constructive, adult dialogue to enable them to become high-performing, low-maintenance contributors who deliver sustained world-class performance and continuously improving results, and thereby:

- Guide everyone to work toward the shared goal of continuously improving quality and customer satisfaction by fostering high standards and a desire for excellence

- Empower the team to improve the system they work in, remove the causes of failure and enable them to do a better job with greater pride, less effort and more satisfaction

- Listen to, and remove, barriers to improvement and systems-level issues that frustrate people's best efforts and waste their time, and that they cannot clear from their own paths

Alignment, integration, teamwork and collaboration
Spanning the right-hand side of the meta-model is the integrative aspect of fostering coordination, collaboration and alignment within the organisation (social cohesion). Correspondingly, spanning the left-hand side is the integrative aspect of creating processes that are aligned vertically and horizontally – end-to-end across the organisation (technical/systems cohesion). This is a crucial responsibility in its own right which is easily, and often, overlooked.

Developing a culture conducive to excellence and continuous improvement
Two things are of particular import here:

- Shaping people's thinking to develop their understanding of, and commitment to, the principles of excellence (briefly summarised below – the full version is in Chapter 3)

- Actively promoting and supporting continuous improvement efforts by:

  - Prioritising time for improvement activities

- Directly executing the high-level improvement projects identified in the strategy
- Monitoring the execution of strategic improvement plans at other levels

---

QUICK RECAP OF EXCELLENCE PRINCIPLES

Business Excellence is based on a clear and coherent philosophy. Key tenets include:

- Sustainable and consistent success depends on **meeting the needs of all key stakeholders**; being first choice to buy from, work for and invest in
- **Recognising that operational excellence is the cornerstone of competitive advantage:** The ability to deliver right first time, on time, every time
- **Process focus:** The quality of the process determines the quality of the result: well-designed, well-run, well-maintained and well-improved processes are the bedrock of sustainable success
- **Quality comes first:** Focusing on right-first-time quality minimises costs, maximises productivity and customer satisfaction and underpins sustainable profitable sales
- **Respect for people:** Recognising people as experts in their roles who wish to work with pride and who, if properly led, will take responsibility for managing and improving performance
- **Colleague engagement drives performance and improvement:** Developing and deploying people's potential and enabling them to be active partners in problem-solving
- **The purpose of performance measurement is to empower and inform:** Clear, understandable, visible performance measures should be available to all colleagues, in real time, and used to understand and improve performance (rather than target criticism)
- **94% of performance problems are due to the system, not people,** so when problems occur, ask 'How did the process let this happen?' rather than 'Who's to blame?'
- **Continuous improvement optimises short-term performance and underpins long-term success:** Sustainable success means building the capability to adapt quickly and smoothly to daily operational challenges, and to wider, longer-term strategic changes

---

- **PDCA thinking drives the management of daily performance and continuous improvement:** At every level, defining a goal, method and measure, executing the plan, reflecting on the outcomes, and applying the lessons learned to the next cycle

- **Systems thinking:** Managing the business as a complete, interconnected system and optimising the performance of the whole, rather than individual elements in isolation

- **Pursue perfection,** the complete elimination of waste, so that the customer is served exactly what they need, when they need it, at minimum cost. While not wholly achievable, pursuing perfection will deliver the best of what is possible – excellence and continuous improvement

- **Constancy of purpose and long-term thinking:** Balancing the need for short-term results with the steady, disciplined building of the capability for sustainable long-term success

In addition to the factors outlined in the meta-model, there are two further aspects of the role of the leader in Business Excellence; managing stakeholders and self-management.

Managing stakeholders
A key part of the leader's role is managing external relations. The leader is the primary spokesperson promoting (and, if necessary, defending) the interests of the organisation. They should also foster active and positive collaboration across organisational boundaries with customers, suppliers, regulatory agencies and (where appropriate) government and academia to enhance cooperation, accelerate learning and create greater ongoing mutual benefit.

Self-management
Effective self-management is foundational. Without it, a leader is unlikely to acquire the emotional stability to think and communicate clearly, problem-solve with others and stay focused on priorities in the midst of the volatile, uncertain, complex and ambiguous context in which they operate.

On such resilience and sustained positive focus the credibility of the leader rests, as do the confidence and trust that colleagues have in them. After all, few will follow a leader who won't face tough realities, lacks conviction and can't see anything through to completion.

The leadership standards pack

Below we outline the leadership standards pack, which will help your organisation to recruit, manage and develop leaders capable of achieving excellence. The pack covers:

- The role (the part that a leader is expected to play in the business)
- The responsibilities (what leaders are accountable for)
- Leader standard work: the routine, regular, auditable tasks/kata that a leader should be carrying out, which underpin the delivery of the responsibilities and achievement of the role
- A capability model outlining a comprehensive and coherent set of competencies that leaders will need

You'll find a version of this in Appendix G that is designed for your immediate practical implementation. Just make any necessary adjustments to create a useable first draft for your business, then:

- Take leaders through a first pass, to start the dialogue and identify strengths and initial development areas and actions
- Review the pack and identify ways to modify it to make it more suited to your business
- Rinse and repeat until the pack is fully customised, functional and embedded in the leadership development processes

This will hopefully get you moving quickly, to a high standard, and save you significant time, effort, frustration and risk.

The framework – as you might hope and expect for such a pivotal role with such a degree of influence and ambition – is reassuringly extensive and detailed. It is purposely slightly over-engineered, with some overlaps and a degree of repetition to reinforce key points and ensure that nothing critical is missed and that it is, generally, robustly fit for purpose.

Job purpose/role (where leaders fit into the big picture and what they do uniquely that no other role covers)

The role of the leader in Business Excellence comprises:

- **Safeguarding the organisation's financial viability, standards and reputation:** Achieving results by following the principles of Business Excellence

- **Self-management:** Setting the tone and example for the culture by living the excellence philosophy and the organisation's values

- **Leading and overseeing the effective strategic management of the business.** To

  - Define and communicate a compelling vision, aims, ethos and standards, and the methodology to achieve it

  - Design, run and continuously improve the strategic management process

- Overseeing the effective operational management of the business. In collaboration with the operational managers, designing, managing and continuously improving both the operational processes and the operational management processes, and thereby achieving excellent and continually improving performance

- People management: Overseeing the recruitment, engagement, motivation, development and retention of top talent

- Alignment, integration, teamwork and collaboration: Creating a unified, empowered and capable team across the organisation, starting at the top. And ensuring that all the technical and management processes are aligned end-to-end (horizontally) and vertically (with the strategy)

- Developing a culture conducive to excellence and thereby achieving long-term outcomes that are attractive enough to maintain the interest, engagement and commitment of all stakeholders

- Managing stakeholders and external interfaces. Successfully managing all stakeholders' expectations and perceptions and being an effective spokesperson to protect and advance the company's reputation in key arenas, fostering collaboration in the organisation's wider network

Main responsibilities (what leaders are accountable for)

Results:
As financial and reputational guardian of the business, to ensure:

- The long-term viability, health and prosperity of the organisation
- The ethical conduct of the company's business; financially, socially and environmentally
- That the business is run in line with the principle and practices of Business Excellence
- That the operational management team achieve the right results, including:
  - Health and safety
  - Right-first-time quality
  - On-time delivery
  - Financial performance
  - Colleague engagement
  - The agreed strategic improvement breakthrough goals
  - Ongoing improvement of the capability and the performance of both people and processes

Self-management
To provide positive leadership that people willingly follow by:

- Exemplifying excellence in personal attitudes, behaviour and performance
- Working well with colleagues in the senior team and wider organisation
- Leading with emotional maturity: actively pursuing a positive vision and taking a measured approach to handling setbacks, challenges and change. Keeping themself and others calm, focused and professional in pursuit of the organisation's vision, aims and standards
- Making and communicating clear decisions that are consistent with the organisation's values, aims and strategy. Doing so in a timely manner, based on the available information, and adapting as events unfold and new information becomes available

Management of strategic performance. To:
- Define and communicate a clear vision, ethos, values, goals, strategy and methodology

- Design a strategic management process that enables the organisation to systematically track both the external environment and internal capability, and thereby optimise the scope and accuracy of its foresight
- Develop and implement a strategy that responds adaptively to (or shapes) unfolding events
- Review and evolve both the strategy and the strategic management process
- Implement the strategic improvement projects assigned to them
- Ensure that the organisational structure is fit for purpose
- Design, manage and improve an infrastructure that is fit for purpose (facilities, amenities, IT etc.)

Management of operational performance. To:
- Ensure a safe working environment
- Ensure (in collaboration with the operational management team) that the operational management system is:

  - Fit for purpose
  - Properly run as a) designed, and b) scheduled
  - Continuously improved

- Oversee the operational managers' planning and preparation for medium- to long-term performance
- Monitor operational performance (through the daily Tier 3 accountability meetings and other appropriate means), liaising with operational managers on appropriate in-flight course corrections and tackling problems that operational managers can't
- Carry out live/situational coaching of operational managers
- Ensure that the operation is adequately resourced to deliver the strategy and goals to the required standards. This includes people, time, equipment, tools, raw materials, consumables, sundries and systems
- Ensure that the operational managers lead and empower colleagues to continuously improve all aspects of organisational capability and performance using appropriate tools and disciplines – and ensure that those activities are strategically aligned
- Address systems and people issues, and other institutional barriers to change

People management
To ensure that the operational managers:

- Have clear expectations (role, responsibilities, standards, daily tasks and goals)
- Have the right knowledge and skills to succeed
- Have the right attitudes and behaviours to lead and manage in ways consistent with the organisational vision, values and standards
- Are empowered to make decisions and solve problems as appropriate
- Are supported: that anything stopping them from succeeding or improving is heard and addressed
- Are held accountable for their attitudes and behaviours, performance and results
- Are actively coached and encouraged to consistently improve
- Work as a team, and lead their teams to collaborate across the business
- Are doing all of the above for the front-line managers

Teamwork, coordination, alignment and collaboration. To:
- Align the organisation:

  - Attitudinally and culturally, making sure that everyone, starting at the top, is following the same broad principles
  - Strategically and functionally so that everyone, starting at the top, is working together and is focused on optimising the performance of the whole organisation vertically and horizontally (end-to-end, not just their silo), and for the long term

- Recognise and manage the interdependencies within the organisation, resolve conflicts, remove barriers to cooperation, and enhance collaboration within and between teams to improve flow, quality and productivity, to reduce hassle and frustration, and to help people to do an ever-better job with greater pride and more enjoyment

Culture. To:
- Promote the aims, ethos, standards and practices of excellence, including systems thinking
- Create a Thinking People System which draws everyone into an ongoing process of collaboration and continuous improvement
- Develop and maintain the kata (core disciplines) that underpin excellence, and to ensure that the operational managers are doing the same

- Ensure a continuing focus on improving all aspects of the business, including system capability, colleague engagement and teamwork

Managing stakeholders. To:
- Effectively manage all stakeholders' expectations and perceptions, including shareholders, investors and headquarters as appropriate
- Be an effective spokesperson and advocate (and, where necessary, defender), to protect and advance the company's reputation in key arenas
- Foster collaboration with key partners in the wider business networks

Standard work (auditable activities that underpin effective leadership)

- Oversee the running of the strategy process of information-gathering, analysis, planning, implementation and review
- Complete task assignments for a) improvement projects identified in the strategic plan, and b) the improvement of the strategic management process itself
- Weekly and monthly review meetings: to identify, understand and address trends and recurring issues over the period, and to look ahead and prepare for the next period
- One-to-one performance reviews with operational managers to complement their ongoing real-time coaching
- Periodic gemba walk: a brief tour of the front line to see directly what is happening, checking in with people, being visible and approachable and building trust, respect and mutual understanding
- Daily management:
  - Daily accountability (Tier 3) meetings: a short daily review of outcomes of the Tier 2 meetings, including progress from the previous day, and to plan activity and anticipate problems for the day ahead
  - Ongoing communication as appropriate with operational managers to be aware of, and address, emerging problems early
  - Coaching: responding to real-time improvement opportunities in operational managers' skills, behaviour, attitudes and performance in the course of daily work

Competence model

There are certain core attitudes, skills and other qualities that all good managers must possess in a culture of excellence. These are summarised in Figure 25.8, which provides a coherent picture that progressive leaders can aspire to, and which allows the assessment of current capability, the identification of development needs and the measurement of development progress.

Figure 25.8: Leadership competencies

Here's a brief summary of each area:

- **Attitude and approach:** Is genuinely committed to Business Excellence, process excellence, continuous improvement and colleague engagement. Maintains high personal standards. Leads by personal example. Inspires confidence and motivates people to give of their best

- **Self-management:** The ability and resilience to deal confidently and professionally with the demands and pressures of the job. Demonstrates commitment to continuously improve their own performance. Develops the ego strength to create and rigorously pursue a positive vision, while growing beyond any tendency toward egomania that may see them become habitually directive, controlling and manipulative, ignoring others' aims, concerns, input or feedback

- **Personal effectiveness:** Works hard and achieves results despite setbacks and obstacles. Is organised, manages their time effectively, focuses on priorities and meets deadlines. Balances operational and strategic priorities on constantly shifting sands. Plans and prioritises to use time effectively

- **Interpersonal effectiveness:** Able to get things done, working with and through others. Influencing rather than relying on orders and authority. Is approachable. Adapts their communication style to suit the situation and audience. Listens well, and makes efforts to understand others' perspectives and needs. Shows respect and acts on what they hear. Is positive, respectful friendly, direct and enthusiastic. Able to assert positively. Brings out the best in people. Persuasive

- **Team player:** Sees beyond their own silo. Collaborates effectively across the business. Gives timely information to all colleagues and to others who rely on their contribution and cooperation. Contributes effectively to the leadership team and their departmental team. Works well with a range of people with different perspectives, experiences, backgrounds and personal styles. Is prepared to take one for the team if necessary

- **Leading people:** Able to coach and develop people, to engage them and draw the best from them as individuals. Sets clear expectations, standards and objectives. Provides clear and constructive feedback on performance. Delegates and empowers effectively. Ensures that people are given the support they need to develop the skills and confidence to succeed and contribute fully

- **Leading the team:** Gets disparate individuals with varying styles, experience, approaches and ideas to work together, creating a whole that is greater than the sum of its parts. Develops the team as a whole and maximises its potential. Creates a sense of shared purpose, establishing clear goals and direction, plans and performance measures. Encourages mutual support and cooperation. Conducts regular, constructive meetings to solve problems, drive continuous improvement and enhance teamworking

- **Managing stakeholders:** Takes the initiative to build and maintain strong, positive relationships with all key stakeholders, including customers, suppliers and external agencies, protecting and advancing the interests of the business. Ensures that they understand the business and how they can add value, provides feedback to help them improve their service, and stands up positively for the company's interests

- **Managing operations:** Highly effective at operational management: leading the design and management of end-to-end process flow, designing effective performance measures, and setting up forums for managing and systematically improving performance, in a way that includes, involves, engages and empowers colleagues

- **Strategic excellence:** Able to design an effective strategy process (based on Hoshin Kanri principles) and to use that to define, implement and review strategy effectively. Is in touch with what is going in the business and in the wider industry and networks. Sets a clear, appealing long-term vision, strategy and goals which has been communicated to everyone responsible for making it happen. Continually evolves both the strategy and the strategy process itself. Translates the strategy into successful action and results

CHAPTER 26

CAPABILITY MATURITY MODEL

Introduction

The capability maturity model, as the name suggests, describes the levels of maturity of the capability reached by an individual, team or organisation in a particular domain. Here we'll focus on organisational capability.

Capability maturity is a must-know concept and assessment tool. It helps us to:

- Recognise the stages on the journey to excellence
- Figure out where we are
- Assess the size and nature of the gap and develop and execute a plan to close it

Overview

Here's a quick overview of the levels of capability maturity. Further detail follows:

- **Level 0: Ad hoc, chaotic, reactive.** Getting through any way you can
- **Level 1: Foundation-building.** This first stage of building toward sustainable progress involves:

  - Establishing Business Excellence thinking at leadership level: the philosophy, the key principles, concepts and attitudes, and the understanding of the practices on which excellence is built

- Establishing (a) effective operational processes, (b) the operational management system, (c) the strategic management system, and (d) the associated measures and kata (basic routines and disciplines) on which excellence is built
  - Bringing QCDE performance under a measure of control to build the platform for...

- **Level 2: Stable, managed and consistent operational performance.** At this level, the operational processes, operational and strategic management systems, ways of thinking, kata etc. are now standardised, consolidated and integrated into a functioning whole. QCDE performance is stable, consistent, predictable and repeatable. But not optimised

- **Level 3: Systematic operational improvement.** The operational processes and operational and strategic management systems are now subject to focused, systematic, disciplined continuous improvement toward the standard of Business Excellence. Proven improvement methods are employed, including value-stream mapping, project prioritisation, structured problem-solving (e.g. A3) and root cause analysis. All of this is guided by relevant and reliable facts and data. Culturally, teamwork, collaboration, responsibility, accountability and a focus on finding solutions are emerging strongly

- **Level 4: Systematic strategic improvement.** The business is fully integrated horizontally (end-to-end along the value stream), and vertically (between levels). It operates increasingly as a network where resource is deployed organically to where it is needed, to quickly and successfully swarm and power through problems and grasp opportunities. The business is increasingly strategically proactive: better tuned to its environment and able to spot and respond to emerging trends, threats and opportunities quickly and well, and to shape and lead its market. The business also develops the capability for meta-improvement: improving its improvement capability

Key dimensions that drive increasing capability maturity

The capability maturity model is a vertical development model. That is, capability rises with each level, and each level is the necessary foundation for the next. The main horizontal dimensions – the capabilities that we focus on maturing and cohering into a system that delivers sustainable excellence and continuous improvement - are of course captured in the now-familiar Business Excellence meta-model shown in Figure 26.1.

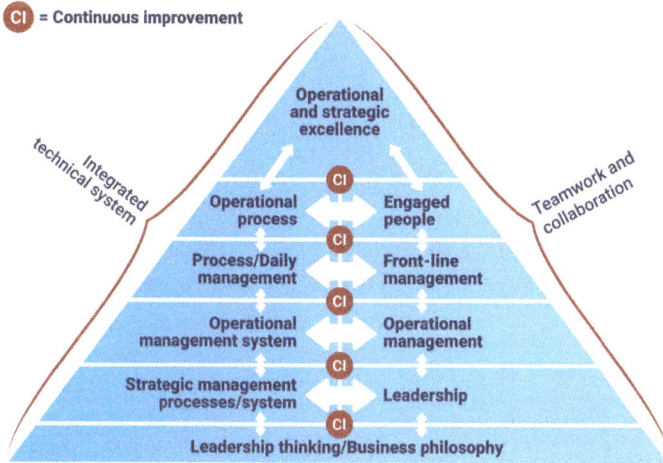

Figure 26.1: Business Excellence meta-model

This includes the:

- Operational processes which collectively comprise the **value stream**

- **Operational management system:** The set of processes that oversee, cohere, coordinate, manage and improve the value stream

- **Strategic management system:** The set of processes that bring structure, focus and discipline to shaping the long-term future of the organisation

- **Leadership and management mindset and skills:** Enhancing these to come into greater alignment with the principles of Business Excellence. Establishing and embedding the core responsibilities enshrined in standard work

- **People:** Developing the right technical, self-management, interpersonal, teamworking, collaboration and problem-solving skills throughout the business so that colleagues have the skills and motivation to engage and contribute fully

- **Teamwork and collaboration:** The collective attitude, commitment, discipline, skill, teamwork, collaboration, responsibility and mutual accountability that underpins excellence

Capability maturity, then, is not just technical, but socio-technical. The degree of capability of the technical system (value stream, operational and strategic management systems) will either constrain or enable the social system (what people can do to perform and improve). And the maturity of the social system – the attitudes and skills of people, individually and collectively – will influence how well the technical system is used and improved. With good leadership, over time, one shapes the other to create a dynamic of reciprocal improvement and opening.

The emergent qualities

The three significant outcomes that emerge as capability matures are:

- The business's ability to create value (i.e. solid QCD performance)
- The ability, in the face of various challenges, to (a) maintain performance, (b) make ongoing kaizen operational improvements, and (c) improve operational performance strategically, via both locally derived projects and those cascaded from the top-level strategic plan
- The degree of attunement with, and responsiveness to, the environment, thus making the business better able to create and exploit strategic improvement opportunities

These are underpinned by the emergence of:

- Greater coherence and integration toward more holistic functioning, technically and socially
- Dynamic resilience (see below)
- Systems thinking – seeing more of the key variables that influence performance, and how they interact to shape the overall system dynamics

---

DYNAMIC RESILIENCE

Dynamic resilience is the capability to maintain and improve performance in (a) the face of operational challenges, and (b) a changing strategic context. This includes:

- Productive capacity: The ability to routinely and consistently meet customers' needs (including the expected variance in them) without hitting the 'wall' of overstretching processes and people
- Recovery capacity: The ability to restore homeostatic balance. To:
  - Routinely get the system reset, primed and ready for each day or cycle

---

- Restore capability and get back on track after disruptive setbacks

- Absorptive capacity: The ability to identify, assimilate and deploy relevant new information, knowledge, concepts and ideas

- Adaptive capacity: Becoming increasingly able to successfully respond to emerging trends and novel threats and opportunities in the ever-evolving operating environment

Moving on up

Since each level is the foundation on which the higher stages must be built, the quality and speed with which each is traversed makes a significant difference to how far, how fast and how well the building of organisational capability proceeds – and the subsequent performance that flows from that:

- Between each pair of levels lies a difficult transitional phase ('storming', as Bruce Tuckman called it) and leaders need not only to successfully navigate this, but, in so doing, build the skill of getting through future transitions more easily, faster and better

- Leadership thinking and skill needs to be at least one level above the level of capability being built, so that it can be both envisioned and executed successfully

- Progress is not always even or linear. Aspects of several stages may run simultaneously

- Progress is not guaranteed. Regression is a constant possibility that must be guarded against. This can come through failing to (a) implement the new practices fully, or (b) anchor and embed them as habit

Attempting to short-cut the required time, effort and investment undermines the improvement process and outcomes. It also undermines people's belief in the achievability of excellence, and in the leaders' capability.

Maturity levels: deep dive

Maturity Level 0: Ad hoc, chaotic, reactive

- Operational processes are poorly designed, under-evolved or ad hoc. Characterised by many 'sticking plasters' and workarounds

- Management systems, tools, skills and practices are inconsistent or entirely lacking

- Planning is non-existent, ineffective or highly reactive (i.e. what plans there are, are constantly changing)

- Much time is wasted dealing with failure-driven demand (demand on the system created by a failure to get things right the first time)

- Performance depends heavily on individuals' personal levels of skill, knowledge and motivation

- There may be much prodigious effort, skill, commitment, ingenuity and general heroics, but it is unpredictable and inconsistent (because even the best people can't consistently outperform a poor process)

- There is no structured or systematic approach to improving the operational processes (what improvement there is, is sporadic, reactionary and less than fully successful or sustained)

- Strategic look-ahead is short (or non-existent), so the business is constantly affected by issues which, with reasonable foresight, could have been avoided or mitigated

- Strategic adaptation (to the extent that there is any at all) tends to consist of top-down-driven 'cure-all' programmes that are not properly selected, thought through, planned, systematically implemented or embedded as habit and practice

- There is no systematic people development to support the development of core technical, self-management, interpersonal, teamworking and continuous improvement skills

- The culture is likely to be siloed, fragmented and fractious, and most colleagues disengaged and frustrated

Maturity Level 1: Foundation-building

- The concepts and thinking that underpin Business Excellence are established in the leadership team and the wider socialisation of them has begun

- The operational processes of the value stream are (re)designed to ensure that it is fit for purpose

- Metrics are developed to measure performance (both outcome measures and in-process measures)

- The operational management system, the strategic management system and the associated kata (disciplines and habits) are established

- QCDE measures are brought under control and a degree of stability, consistency and repeatability is achieved

- The core thinking and tools of process improvement are established, but at a basic, linear, cause-and-effect level

- The processes for managing and developing people effectively are established:

  - Recruitment is guided by clear criteria and underpinned by a structured and consistent selection process

  - All colleagues get a strong basic induction

  - Technical skill levels are raised to acceptable levels

  - Focus is brought to improving relationships within and between teams to enhance teamwork, collaboration and the culture overall

  - Leadership and management attitudes and behaviours are enhanced to be compatible with leading and managing toward a culture of excellence

It is important to stress how crucial, challenging, and vulnerable to failure, this stage is. It is also very protean and it is easy to get stuck in it. The introduction of new ideas can become random and scattergun, and the implementation of them may not be followed through to completion, sustained or integrated to create a coherent, optimised system. This stage takes considerable leadership skill, focus, discipline and persistence to successfully navigate.

Maturity Level 2: Stable, managed and consistent operational performance

- All operational processes in the value stream are now well defined, documented and standardised. They are also integrated into a coherent whole end-to-end, and with the support functions. The different elements, which were, by necessity, standalone at first, are bedded in and increasingly interconnected

- The operational management system is defined, structured and managed, and as a result the operational processes are now managed systematically. Activity is now planned, executed and measured. Appropriate in-flight adjustments and course-corrections are made promptly. The business is now operationally effective (results are reasonably predictable, repeatable and reliable)

- The strategic management system is now defined, structured and managed systematically. As a result, strategic activity is now planned, executed and measured and appropriate course-corrections are made promptly. The business has now achieved a level of strategic effectiveness

- Technical (role-related) skills, and wider job skills (emotional self-management, priority management etc.) and team-oriented skills (including influencing, assertion and negotiation) are systematically developed

- Emergence of systems thinking – understanding how the business works as an overall system within the wider system of its operating environment

Maturity Level 3: Systematic operational improvement

- Process improvement is proactively led, managed and prioritised, and is rigorous and systematic

- Improvement opportunities are actively identified and systematically followed through to completion in various ways:

  - As part of daily management, variations from target are monitored. Meaningful variations are distinguished from random ones (noise). Reasons for variations are understood through rigorous root cause analysis, and corrective and preventative action is taken

  - The value stream is mapped. Waste and issues affecting quality and flow are identified, and the root causes are established and addressed

  - Regular gemba walks identify live issues affecting people and process where the work is done. The root causes are established and addressed

- Measurement systems are improved and developed toward greater relevance and granularity, to provide actionable information to the right people at the right time
- Existing thinking, methods and approaches are constructively, intelligently and responsibly challenged, with better solutions being actively proposed and tested
- Empowered colleagues: everyone is trained to at least a foundational level in continuous improvement tools and thinking. The appropriate tools, time and resources are made available as required to empower people to deploy them
- The culture is increasingly cohesive, adaptable, positive and committed to excellence
- Systems thinking is now more fully established and applied to both the value stream processes and the operational and strategic management processes
- People are increasingly collaborating and problem-solving across boundaries and looking at longer timespans

Maturity Level 4: Systematic strategic improvement

- The organisation is fully integrated horizontally (end-to-end along the value stream) and vertically (between levels) and focused on continuous strategic improvement at all levels and in all areas (value stream, operational and strategic management systems, people and culture)
- Collaboration extends across all internal organisational boundaries and beyond to suppliers, customers and other stakeholders
- Strategic improvement projects are properly cascaded and integrated with daily work
- Systems thinking drives the analysis of both what is going on within the business and its interactions with the environment
- The organisation is increasingly agile and innovative
- The organisation is a learning organisation, optimised, adaptive and resilient, performing at world-class levels, i.e. at comparable levels to the best in the industry worldwide, in terms of both operational performance and strategic improvement and agility
- The business develops the capability for meta-improvement: improving its improvement processes, thinking, skills and tools, to enhance the speed, reach and effectiveness of its adaptability in the face of circumstances that are changing increasingly rapidly and unpredictably

CHAPTER 27

WHAT'S NEXT FOR YOU?

> *'People wait for opportunity to come along, yet it is there every morning.'*
> *(Dennis the Menace)*

A quick summary: businesses thrive to the degree that their people have the right process information, equipment, tools and skills, working relationships and culture they need to succeed in their jobs. This requires effective systems, and above all it requires effective leadership and management. Toward Excellence provides a vision for achieving this and provides the framework, meta-model, insights, tools and methodology to implement and maintain it.

From ideas to action and progress

Here's how we suggest you get started, gain traction and build momentum:

- Assess your business using our top-level culture questionnaire. You can do a first pass yourself to get the feel of it and scope out the terrain, then go through it with your top team to begin raising awareness and to start the dialogue
- Identify the current status. Three things in particular:
  - Existing strengths
  - Waterline issues (factors that are below the critical waterline of minimum acceptable performance)
  - High-leverage breakthrough opportunities
- Prioritise these. Select a place to start, addressing any waterline issues first. (Strategy, the operational management system or leadership skills are typically the highest-leverage places to start)

- Take an achievable action that will build capability, confidence, relationships and a desire to come back and do more
- Review progress, learn quickly, plan the next move
- Rinse and repeat, cycling fast through iterative improvement loops, innovating and building momentum, confidence, insight, understanding and the range of tools in your toolkit, creating an upward spiral
- Progressively draw in more colleagues, both in departmental teams and through creating cross-functional teams, to tackle wider shared challenges and opportunities and to develop and benefit from the range of talents across the business
- Over time, scale this to:
  - Include the whole business
  - Reach further heights by building capability maturity (on all dimensions in all areas) and levels of performance
- Maintain momentum until what once felt impossible becomes routine

It's time

1. You are done with incurring the costs, frustrations and limitations of existing arrangements
2. You have a vision of the success you want
3. You have fully explored every possibility, and are ready to commit
4. You have in your hands a coherent, field-proven, time-tested system and approach that gives you a line of sight to real, sustained progress

Let's get to work.

WHAT IF I'M NOT THE CEO?

The principles apply wherever people are managed. At any and all levels, in any and all businesses: business level, division level, team level, project level. Only two things vary: the size of the team and the autonomy you have to shape things on your own.

In your own business, or if you are leading a self-contained unit of a larger business, you have a significant degree of autonomy. If you are part of a larger corporate, especially if you are in the same building as other teams, you will need more higher-level understanding, support and leadership. Wherever you are, you can start there. You may need the support and cooperation of others higher in the chain, or of people reporting to you.

But there's nothing like understanding the principles, and having done all you can to apply them in practice, for you to be able to lead by example and persuade other people to support your ideas.

GETTING IN TOUCH

If you would like to discuss how we can support you on your journey to Business Excellence, contact us at info@futurepositiveconsulting.com to book a free, no-obligation exploratory chat, or complete the free online assessment at www.futurepositiveconsulting.com and then book a free, no-obligation follow-up consultation.

THE LIMITATIONS OF COMMAND AND CONTROL MANAGEMENT

Introduction

This section looks at the hallmarks of traditional management, and its limitations. It's important to understand these because:

- It's too easy to accept traditional management as 'normal' and inevitable. It's not
- Only when we examine the thinking behind it and the mechanics of how it works can we fully register how deeply dysfunctional it is, and how preventable the problems it causes are
- We need to pinpoint the active ingredients and the root cause of these problems, and recognise that a fundamental shift in the underlying management system is required: that everything else is tinkering, reacting to symptoms. Worthy, but unlikely to achieve significant, sustainable change

There are nine significant, interrelated limitations of command and control management systems:

1. Short-term focus undermines constancy of purpose
2. The measures drive and reward the wrong behaviour
3. The measures hide and embed waste
4. Centralised control adds cost and delay and results in slower, poorer decisions
5. Departmental silos

6. Managerialism

7. They disengage people

8. They are poor at adapting to change and continuously improving

9. They are self-limiting: the business fails to thrive and achieve its potential

Let's look at each in turn.

1. Short-term focus undermines constancy of purpose

Pressure at the end of every period to 'make the numbers' (achieve sales targets, production quotas, financial targets etc.) typically causes a scramble to close deals, get stuff out the door, and cut costs: Often, worryingly, it is accepted that this can be achieved, **by any means**. This inevitably sows the seeds of future problems. For example, rushed, poor-quality work risks complaints, the need for rework, non-payment of invoices, damage to reputation, pressure on price and loss of business.

The pressure to meet short-term goals also prevents underlying problems and inefficiencies being addressed. This locks in waste, delay, errors and unnecessary cost, hindering everyday operational performance and strategic growth. This in turn undermines the ability to steadily build toward sustainable long-term excellence.

There is also a philosophy of providing only a 'good enough' level of service, rather than understanding and meeting customer needs. This stops the organisation building the levels of long-term customer loyalty required to underpin strong repeat business, upselling, and word-of-mouth referral to new customers.

2. The measures drive and reward the wrong behaviour

Though many things may be measured in traditional systems, sometimes to a bewildering degree of complexity, the strongest emphasis tends to be placed on financial and productivity goals. Quality is not usually one of the most strongly emphasised top-level measures, despite the fact that if quality is not right, there's little chance of consistently achieving financial or productivity goals.

Goals tend to be set at the top level. They are also likely to include an ambitious degree of 'stretch', derived with little or no discussion with operational managers around their feasibility.

The goals are also likely to be set departmentally, opening up the possibility of sub-optimisation; one department only being able to meet its targets by doing things that adversely affect other departments and the success of the wider enterprise.

Performance management also tends to be adversarial. When goals are not met, the emphasis tends to be on blame, criticism and threats – loss of budget, bonus, position, etc. – rather than on understanding and eliminating problems. This opens up the possibility of:

- **Gaming:** Managers moving money, people or resources around, or manipulating the numbers (for example, premature revenue recognition) to either meet, or give the impression of having met, the goals
- Plain old-fashioned **cheating;** for example, inventing specious reasons for getting people off waiting lists, or knowingly presenting inaccurate data

Finally, productivity measures that focus on activity, rather than meeting customer needs right first time, create waste. For example, a productivity target of answering phone calls within one minute could be met perfectly while failing to achieve the actual goal of solving the customer's problem in one call. This simply generates what John Seddon called 'failure demand'; additional demand on time and resources to redo the original work and get unhappy customers back onside.

3. The measures hide and embed waste

Traditional financial measures also miss important costs: Costs include:

- Those which directly support **value-adding** activities: what the customer pays for
- **Production-enabling activitie**s such as maintenance, training and continuous improvement, which ensure that the value-adding activities run efficiently
- **Waste:** Any activity that consumes time or resource but adds no value. This includes excessive stock, unnecessary delay, errors, over-elaboration, bureaucracy, and movement of people, materials or information

The first two are usually visible in traditional management accounts, but waste is not. As a result, when there is pressure on costs, value-adding and production-enabling activities get cut, rather than waste being identified and removed. This invariably creates more delays, errors, customer dissatisfaction, rework etc. All of which takes time and money to fix, and results in loss of business. The classic false economy.

Joseph Juran called this the cost of poor quality (COPQ), and the term 'hidden factory' was coined to highlight both the magnitude of the cost of the waste, and its invisibility using traditional measurement. (Waste is of course highly visible with effective in-process measures and value-stream mapping tools.)

W. Edwards Deming pointed out the deep irony that these costs, because they are neither understood nor addressed, can come to be mistakenly regarded as structural, and get built into budgets over time.

4. Centralised control adds cost and delay, and results in slower, poorer decisions

Centralised decision-making and control creates what H. Thomas Johnson and Anders Bröms called the 'information factory': a business within a business producing goals, plans, budgets, schedules, initiatives and directives, and demanding and analysing reports from the operation. Problems resulting from this include:

- **Management reports that add no direct value to the product or service** and often distract managers from their real job of meeting customer needs and engaging people to continuously improve processes. This also creates a culture that serves the hierarchy rather than the customer

- **Centralised decision-making is too slow** to react to problems because, by the time information is gathered, sent, read, analysed and discussed, the actual situation has changed

- **The numbers can't be fully trusted,** because in an adversarial climate, where problems are more likely to be met with criticism and sanctions than support, people are more likely to resort to gaming, cheating and covering up

- Senior managers, whose knowledge is based largely on questionable, historical data, become out of touch with the realities of the operation and **set unrealistic expectations, and impose decisions and initiatives**, including additional tasks, bureaucracy, targets, checks or reports that make it harder for people to do their jobs

- **Undermining and obstructing local efforts** to make positive change

5. Departmental silos

It's logical to structure businesses into departments that perform specialised tasks. The problem is, the value stream – the process that serves the customer –

runs horizontally (end to end) through them. And it needs to run smoothly and efficiently to serve customers promptly and profitably. The dangers of this include:

- A lack of understanding of, and sense of responsibility for, the whole value stream
- Miscommunication, misunderstanding, misalignments and confusion at handovers, resulting in errors, delays and possible missed steps or duplicated effort

While some of this is inevitable in any structure, it is exacerbated by departments being measured separately and judged in an adversarial environment. This mitigates against teamwork, breeds blame and politics, and encourages departments to protect their own interests to the detriment of other departments, the organisation as a whole, and the customer. For example:

- An unwillingness to help a struggling department unless they have a charge number
- The sales team being tempted to achieve targets using tactics that damage long-term customer relationships, or promising features, delivery dates and prices that production can't profitably achieve
- The purchasing team saving money by buying inferior-quality materials that increase end-to-end costs by affecting production efficiency, customer satisfaction and warranty claims
- Production may send faulty product out of the door (or 'over the wall' to the next team) to meet targets, knowing it will result in complaints or create problems for others

6. Managerialism

Operational managers focus on numbers, conformance and discipline rather than on communicating with, leading, coaching and supporting people to solve problems. This is exacerbated by managers not having the tools or training to engage people in process improvement, which leaves them with limited options for achieving performance goals. These are predominantly:

- Pressurising people
- Finding process short cuts
- Cutting visible costs
- Gaming

This culture also tends to attract, promote, encourage and reward managers who can survive and thrive in this adversarial and political environment. Managers:

- With a 'kiss up, kick down' style, reluctant to question or challenge decisions from above, but hard, and sometimes harsh, with front-line colleagues and others with less power
- Who put personal ambition ahead of teamwork, the company or the customer
- Who are comfortable being adversarial, manipulative and political

7. They disengage people

The traditional approach risks both passively disengaging people (not giving them an opportunity to contribute fully) and actively demotivating them. Various things contribute to this, including:

- Lack of effective management. Pushing people, rather than leading by:

  - Ensuring that people have the knowledge, skills, equipment, tools, processes, information and support that they need to succeed
  - Taking the time to coach colleagues to help them improve performance

- The assumption that most performance problems are people problems, and the failure to recognise the impact on individual performance of poor processes, tools, materials, information, training, coaching, support and leadership
- Alienating people through judging, grading, criticising, disciplining, stifling discussion of problems, and preventing people from showing initiative and creativity to solve problems. People's ingenuity is instead applied to self-protection and surviving
- Lack of intrinsic motivation: pride, loyalty and commitment are not valued, so just wither, and the business has to rely more on the extrinsic motivators of financial reward, discipline, intimidation or fear

8. They are poor at adapting to change and continuously improving

Continuous improvement is not seen as an integral part of work. This is because:

- There is a relentless focus on pushing processes and working round problems to achieve short-term goals

- Managers and front-line colleagues don't have process-improvement tools or training
- It is incorrectly assumed that most problems are people problems rather than system problems
- It is believed that improvement means getting everyone to work harder, rather than improving the system (working smarter)
- Manipulated results hide problems
- A fear of speaking up means problems aren't highlighted
- Silo issues mean that cross-functional problems are more likely to result in denial, blame and conflict, rather than acceptance, responsibility and joint problem-solving

Where improvement activities do happen, they can fail because:

- They add more rules, checks and bureaucracy, i.e. more cost and delay
- Significant changes to processes are usually not done by, or don't even involve, the people who do the job, but are done to them by teams of 'improvement specialists'. People can feel criticised and alienated by this approach, and consequently resist it. There is also no transfer of skills or knowledge to allow them to maintain or build on the change, so it often deteriorates quickly
- Improvement activities focus on problems in isolation, not in the context of the whole value chain. So, at best, there may be improvements at points in the value chain (which may or may not flow through to a difference in final quality, cost or delivery performance). At worst, there is a 'push-down pop-up' effect of solving a problem at one part of the value chain, only for there to be bigger, unintended negative consequences elsewhere

All this significantly compromises the organisation's ability to identify problems and their root causes and develop effective long-term solutions. Instead, waste, cost and delay are locked into the system and problems accumulate, creating what Seddon called a 'non-improving firefighting cycle'.

Occasionally the problems explode into a crisis, the reaction to which is often also dysfunctional and counterproductive, with inquests, sackings, restructurings, and more procedures, metrics, reports, checks and bureaucracy. All of which fails to address the ultimate root cause, the management system itself, meaning that it will all happen again sooner or later.

9. They are self-limiting: the business fails to thrive and achieve its potential

This all adds up to a series of in-built limitations that prevent the business from achieving excellence and operating to its full potential.

This is survivable if an organisation has customers with few options or high switching costs; a ready supply of affordable labour with adequate skills; and high enough margins to absorb the costs of the waste and survive the impact of the high employee turnover, absenteeism and other problems associated with disengaged people.

Not every business enjoys these conditions, though, and will be able to survive this level of self-handicapping in the long term.

Conclusion

If you aspire to excellence, but recognise any of this in your business, take heart. These are limitations you don't need to live with.

There is a better way. An approach that evolved from command and control, preserving its benefits and addressing its limitations. And it's practical, well established, and proven to be more successful.

The table on the next few pages takes a deep dive into the difference between traditional management systems and those based on the principles of Business Excellence.

Command and control vs Business Excellence: Key dimensions of difference

Traditional thinking	Excellence model
Purpose	
• To make money for shareholders	• To create sustainable benefits for all stakeholders; customers, colleagues, shareholders and wider society
Philosophy	
• Profits are created by driving the top line, by any means, while cutting the costs that can be identified in financial statements • Focus on driving short-term results (short-term financial results in commercial organisations). All measures and reward systems are geared toward this • Derive numerical measures for everything and manage by analysing these numbers and making decisions based on them • Economies of scale are the key to profitability – keeping utilisation high by doing large numbers of similar transactions/activities • Business is a machine which can be optimised by maximising the output of each individual component • Improvements to the system must be done by specialist experts	• Operational excellence is the foundation of competitive advantage • Aspire to excellence through continuous improvement of processes to deliver better quality, cost and availability • Profits are generated by loyal customers, who bring repeat business and tell others • The primary focus should be on creating value (i.e. products and services the customer will pay for) and driving out waste (most of which can't be identified in financial statements) • Economies of flow are the key to performance. Every activity is performed just-in-time in response to a customer demand, with no batching and queuing • Focus on long-term sustainability; building stable, high-performing systems and strong relationships with customers, colleagues and suppliers • The business is a live, dynamic, interconnected, interdependent system where each part affects the performance of other parts and the performance of the organisation overall • Prioritises end-to-end process performance and ownership over local optimisation • The system can be improved by the people who work in it every day • Do exactly, and only, what matters to the customers

View of the business environment	
• Stable, predictable, controllable	• Fast-changing, unpredictable

Quality	
• Quality is anything above the minimum acceptable standard • Quality is expensive • Inspection is the key to quality: quality control experts and inspectors can assure quality • Acceptance of certain levels of defects • Defects are caused by workers	• Quality is defined by the customer • Quality leads to lower costs • Quality must be built in through effective processes; it cannot be inspected in • Quality is made in the boardroom – the attitude to quality flows from the values and priorities set at the top • Constant pursuit of quality improvement • Most defects are caused by the system

Efficient production	
• Efficiency is achieved through economies of scale (big batches, lower unit cost). This entails the use of 'batch and queue' – doing work in large batches which then waits in a queue for next stage of processing • Keep big inventories 'just in case' • Focus on ends (achieving targets, service-level agreements, quotas etc.) rather than means (developing the most efficient process for getting things done) • Maximise machine utilisation • Standardisation is the 'one best way', to be followed without question • Reactive maintenance	• Economies of flow (minimise time and cost along the whole value chain) • Just in time: activity is triggered by customer demand – lead time as close to actual processing time as possible • Focus on means: developing the long-term capability of the system to deliver excellent cost, quality and delivery performance consistently • Optimise process output • Standardisation as a reference point for existing best practice, but to be continually improved upon • Preventative maintenance

People	
• People are a commodity, to be hired and fired according to demand • People are a cost, to be minimised • The relationship with people is transactional: simply an exchange of time and effort for money • 'Theory X' view of people: that their natural tendency is to want to avoid work and responsibility, and that they can't be trusted, and therefore have to be controlled through close supervision • Reliance on extrinsic motivation: reward and discipline through a management system based on judging, grading, criticising and disciplining • Assumption that most problems are caused by people • Since the system has been designed by experts and is the 'one best way', there is no value (indeed, there are dangers) in empowering or engaging people to identify, discuss and solve problems, or show any kind of initiative or creativity in performing their duties • Fear can be a useful management tool for driving performance and suppressing dissent	• People are a vital resource, and an appreciating asset ('human capital') because they can think, solve problems and actively add value to the business by improving themselves and the systems they work with • 'Theory Y' view of people: that, given the chance, most people will take a pride in their work and, if engaged and empowered, will contribute to improvement activities • Most problems and performance issues are caused by the system. Ensuring that people have effective work systems, training, tools and information is management's responsibility • Emphasis on intrinsic motivation: pride, responsibility, accountability, loyalty, quality work, excellent customer service • Fear leads to disaster, as it drives people to 'play games' and take short-cuts to hit their numbers. It also stops problems from being identified and dealt with in a timely fashion; instead, they build and either create in-built cost, inefficiencies or quality problems, or become crises
Supplier relations	
• The relationship with suppliers is transactional/contractual • Buy on lowest cost • Play one supplier off against another, switching frequently to keep them on their toes	• Buy from vendors committed to quality, since the quality of materials and services purchased significantly affects the business's own costs, quality and delivery performance • Build long-term, cooperative relationships, and work with suppliers to improve quality, cost and delivery performance

Target setting, measurement and performance management	
• Profit is the most important business metric • Management by results: targets are set by senior managers and imposed on the operation. Performance is reviewed through the analysis of numerical performance data • Activity-centred • Financial projections are more likely to be based on assumptions about shareholders' expectations than a sober analysis of market conditions and business capability • The need to serve the demands of the hierarchy, both for performance, and for reports on performance, takes precedence over understanding and serving the needs of customers • Performance data on computer screens available only to managers	• Management by means: performance data is used to help people identify where the system can be improved to provide the high-quality, cost-effective service that satisfies customers and in turn creates financial success • Centred on process flow • Ambitious targets are set through discussion with business units, to ensure that they are credible and deliverable • Visual data, accessible and understandable to all
Attitude to customer	
• Transactional/contractual • Looking for opportunities to maximise short-term revenue • No long-term loyalty	• Partnership, cooperative (looking for mutual benefit) • Understanding their needs and designing products, services and business processes to meet them profitably • Looking to build long-term loyalty to secure repeat business, upsell, and get referrals for new business

Role of management

- Managerialism (impersonal, data-driven). Management is mainly about analysing numbers and making, and enforcing, decisions
- Senior managers' role is to set targets, define methods and create control systems to ensure compliance
- Front-line management is all about supervision, to ensure compliance with process to meet activity/productivity targets. (And to compile statistical reports for senior management)
- Firefighting is valued and regarded as a core skill
- Individual performance is managed by appraisal based on grading, judgement and criticism
- Underperformance is addressed by getting tough with people and demanding more (work harder), and by disciplining and removing persistent underperformers

- Leaders'/senior managers' role is to:

  - Create, and practice, values that put quality and customer satisfaction first
  - Create a management system that actively supports people in delivering quality and customer satisfaction cost-effectively
  - Listen to colleagues to understand and remove barriers to performance that they can't
  - Remove the causes of failure and improve the system. To help people do a better job with less effort and greater satisfaction

- Front-line management is about leadership:

  - Helping people to use performance data to learn and improve their own performance and the system's performance
  - Developing colleagues' level of responsibility and accountability for personal and team performance
  - Developing, engaging and empowering people to bring out the best in them, and allow them to contribute fully by continuously improving their personal and team performance

- To work as a management team to manage, and continuously improve, the whole value chain to improve flow, and the cost, quality and delivery performance of the organisation as a whole

Change

• Resists change: tries to buffer the organisation from it	• Adaptive – responsive to situations as they unfold
• Reactive, often after a string of bad results	• Integral – part of routine work and of everyone's roles and responsibilities
• Mechanistic. Projects are mandated from above and implemented in exactly the same way in different parts of the organisation	• Primarily the responsibility of work groups
• Primarily the responsibility of management and staff specialists	• Embrace change in the business environment and respond flexibly to it

Continuous improvement

• All significant problems can be identified from management reports. No need to see the operation or talk to the people in it	• Continuous improvement of all processes by the people who use them every day, guided by in-process measures
• No mechanisms for colleagues to bring issues to the surface and have them addressed	• Endless search for perfection through continuous improvement. The process is never optimised; it can always be improved
• Fear of the 'shoot the messenger' approach, and generally high levels of disengagement, also dissuades people from highlighting problems	• The continuous improvement processes are themselves continuously improved to give the business a significant competitive advantage through its ability to build and maintain operational excellence
• Sense of acceptance/resignation that certain things cannot be improved	
• React to problems by adding a process – usually an additional step, check or report that adds cost and introduces delay and bureaucracy (rather than identifying and removing the root cause)	• Problems are not something that can be understood from management reports – for this, you need to go and see for yourself
• The processes are changed by specialists with no colleague involvement	• Standardisation of current best practice simply provides the platform for further improvement
• Does not take a systems view of continuous improvement and risks wasting effort or causing unforeseen negative consequences	• Focuses on eliminating waste from the whole value stream (system improvements)

Internal relationships	
• Adversarial - sometimes aggressive • Characterised by mistrust, competition and conflict across the organisation and between different levels of the hierarchy • Cross-functional misunderstandings and blame • Cross-functional competition for resources, budgets, kudos and rewards • Dominated by politics and power struggles	• Partnership, teamwork and cooperation internally allow the business to compete effectively externally • Focused on the bigger picture and bigger, longer-term external success

VALUE-STREAM MAPPING

Introduction

Value-stream mapping (also known as process mapping) is a tool that is used to identify the key components of a process and how they interact to create results. The purpose of value-stream mapping is to help teams discuss, and continually enhance, their understanding of how their process works so that they can ensure it is properly designed, managed well and continually improved.

There are many ways to map a process. In highly evolved and sophisticated processes, maps can become very technical, precise and detailed, but most processes (particularly early on in the improvement phase) can be mapped quite quickly and simply.

The approach we offer here is powerful, simple, visual, versatile and scaleable. An excellent place to start mapping a process (and, indeed, to start learning how to map a process). It may capture enough detail to identify all that needs to be done, and if not, the map can be improved (and people can be developed further in mapping techniques) by adding more advanced techniques as and when necessary.

Why map a process?

The main purpose of value-stream mapping is to get people together to create informed and constructive dialogue aimed at:

*   Helping everyone understand how the process works: what factors influence the results and how they do this

- Identifying improvement opportunities, and building consensus around what can be improved and how it can be improved
- Understanding the impact of proposed improvement suggestions

The process of doing all of this is also an excellent team development tool in itself.

Suggested approach

Here's a suggested approach to getting started with value-stream mapping, and the steps to follow.

The first and most important thing is to get as many of the team who use the process (the process experts) together to contribute. Create a safe, positive space where people can offer their insights, opinions and ideas, identify problems and ask questions, and discuss things openly, honestly and constructively.

Then, using the template below as a rough guide for layout...

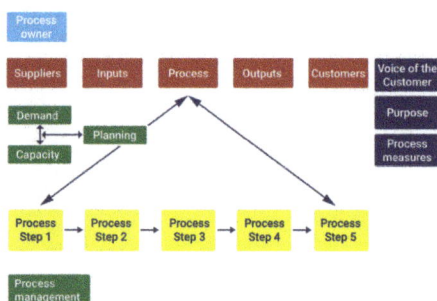

Figure B.1: Value stream map – suggested format

- Get a piece of brown paper about five feet long, some coloured sticky notes (yellow, red/pink, orange and blue work well) and a fine-tipped felt pen
- Along the top of the map, on orange sticky notes, put:
  - **Suppliers:** List who feeds information, tools or material into the process (bearing in mind that the supplier may be internal rather than external)
  - **Input:** List what is required for the process to run effectively. This could include information, tools, equipment, raw material, sundries and trained people

- **Outputs:** List what information and other value-added product, service or experience the process is creating
- **Customers:** Record who the customer(s) are. (This may be an internal customer.) A customer is anyone who uses the outputs of the process

- Then work out what the **Voice of the Customer** (VoC) is – i.e. who uses the outputs of the process, and what they actually want. This is usually defined by some kind of measure of quality, on-time delivery and service (and cost, if it's the end customer). The definition of customer can be widened to include all stakeholders, i.e. anyone affected by the process
- From there, capture the **purpose** of the process in a simple sentence. It will be directly related to the VoC
- Then set out the **process measures:** what measures are used to ascertain the quality, cost, delivery performance and safety of the process (plus any other important factors)
- Then map the **process steps** in yellow sticky notes, running left to right. (If there are decision points, you can capture those on blue notes.) Keep it as high-level and simple as possible for the initial map

The next set of aspects are a bit more advanced, but very important to start thinking about, as these factors have a significant impact on process performance and stability:

- Capture anything you know about the **demand** on the process: timing, frequency, volume. Do you know how much is 'value demand' – activity that adds value for the customer and that they are willing to pay for, and how much is 'failure demand' – demand created on our time and resources by having to correct work that wasn't done right first time?
- Then capture anything you know about the **capacity** of the process: how much work can it do, with what lead times. Identify what factors affect that capacity – for example, staffing levels or equipment availability
- Finally, note how **process management** works. This is often a daily accountability meeting: a short meeting to look at and discuss the measures and what can be learned from them, and to agree actions to both control performance in the immediate term, and improve it in the medium term. This is likely to be complemented by weekly and monthly meetings to discuss longer-term trends, plans and improvement objectives

Identifying improvement opportunities

Once you have a decent first draft of the map, you can begin to identify opportunities for improvement (pain points). Opportunities are anything that is impeding the operation or smooth flow of the process.

The concept of the 'eight wastes' alerts us to key things to look for (though the list is not exhaustive, so feel free to look beyond this – see Chapter 14 for more on waste). 'Waste' here is defined as anything in the process that absorbs resource or adds time, but adds no value to the product or service:

1. **Defects/rework:** Products or services that don't meet the customer's specifications
2. **Waiting:** Idle time awaiting information, materials or decisions
3. **Over-processing:** Unnecessary work, detail or features
4. **Transportation:** Unnecessary movement of material or information
5. **Inventory:** Excessive work in progress
6. **Motion:** Unnecessary movement in accomplishing a task
7. **Overproduction:** Making more than needed
8. **Skill:** Where we could benefit more from people's input (for example, empowering them to make on-the-spot decisions)

These can be captured by sticking onto the map the main pain points, written on red/pink notes. Just stick them near to the part of the process they relate to. Later, they can be captured on an opportunities list to make sure they don't get lost or forgotten.

What next?

From the initial mapping, you'll have a broad idea of how fit for purpose the process is. Most processes have issues that can be addressed through continuous improvement. Some are in such a state that they really need to be substantially redesigned.

Give it a go!

If you think all this sounds a bit daunting, just dive in and see how far you get. Keep it simple. Simple is good. Your first pass may be a bit rough and ready and have a few gaps – no worries, don't sweat it, all we need here is a start point. If more detail or definition is required (either on selected parts of the process, or the whole piece), the relevant parts can either be expanded, or a new, more detailed map drawn. You can learn and improve from there. The only thing you can do wrong is not to give it a go!

A3 PROBLEM-SOLVING: OVERVIEW

Introduction

A3 is a powerful, practical and straightforward problem-solving method that can be used by anyone in any organisation, in any industry. Its nine steps help guide people through the process of problem definition, root cause analysis, action planning and impact verification.

It also provides a structure for recording and reporting the results. (The name comes from the size of the sheet of paper that the report should fit on to, to ensure that it is brief and focused.)

> *'A3 is arguably the best tool for helping front-line people solve problems ... Once you get into it, it is not that complicated. That makes sense, since we want to have everyone in the organisation involved in continuous improvement.'*
> *(Durward K. Sobek II and Art Smalley)*

A3 problem-solving was originally developed by Toyota and is the approach behind their legendary continuous improvement processes. It is based on the simple and powerful discipline of Plan-Do-Check-Act (PDCA) thinking. This promotes a structured approach to problem-solving; a 'scientific' approach of investigating root causes and developing, testing and refining solutions. Often in organisations, problems are not fully understood, superficial solutions are applied and the problems recur. Using A3 helps ensure that problems are understood and permanently resolved.

A3 problem-solving requires no sophisticated mathematical or technical training. The only essential materials are paper and a pencil. People are developed in the use of A3 simply by using the tool to work on real problems with the support and guidance of a coach; this could be their manager, an internal specialist or an external expert. The coach's role is to structure and direct the learner's thinking so that they develop the skill and confidence to solve problems themselves, rather than needing someone else to solve the problem for them. This brings the double benefit of solving problems and simultaneously developing people to become more confident and empowered problem-solvers.

'A3 thinking is as much about developing good problem-solvers as it is solving problems.' (Mike Rother)

When a team have learned this way of thinking about, and approaching, problems, they are more relaxed, engaged and positive about dealing with problems, challenges and uncertainty. Having a team that is skilled and confident in problem-solving also makes everyone's job easier and more rewarding, and allows better results to be achieved. It enables the team to achieve more while doing less (or, as W. Edwards Deming put it, 'work smarter, not harder'), because the previously untapped potential of the team is being used to remove wasted time, energy, materials and cost from their processes.

The approach is useful for more than just dealing with short-term operational problems. It can also be used to achieve stretch goals, through understanding and systematically removing barriers between the current state and the long-term vision.

The nine steps of A3 problem-solving

Taking a structured approach to problem-solving is absolutely vital. Without it, we can fail to properly define the problem and go off at a tangent. We can fail to find the actual root cause and have the problem recur. We can pick the wrong countermeasures. And we can fail to follow up and never really establish if the things we tried actually worked.

Failure at any of these points means that continuous improvements will, at best, be ineffective, and may even be damaging and counterproductive. The A3 structure is designed to help prevent this and maintain structure and focus.

Let's start by looking at the main components of the A3 approach; then we'll look in more detail at each:

1. Theme/background
2. Problem definition
3. Goal/target state
4. Root cause analysis
5. Containment measures
6. Proposed countermeasure(s)
7. Action plan
8. Impact check
9. Next actions

The first thing to note is that the first four stages are about grasping the situation, defining the gap that exists, and understanding what is going on. This strong focus on fully understanding the nature and scope of the problem before moving into planning and action is there to counteract people's natural tendency to dive in.

This is for the simple reason that if we do not understand the problem and its root cause, any action we take is unlikely to be successful. If this is the case, it is likely that most of the time and effort in the A3 process will be spent developing a full and clear understanding of the situation.

Step one – Identifying the theme/background

The purpose of this step is to identify, in a short statement, the main business reasons for focusing on this particular issue. You should also state clearly which key business objectives (for example, quality, cost, delivery or health and safety) are impacted and how. Feel free to show one or two graphs or diagrams if they convey the message better than a bunch of words.

The statement could be, for example: 'Accuracy is a key strategic aim, and process measure, but has fallen below the target of 97.5% in two out of the last three weeks, creating negative customer feedback and a need for rework, which is costing money, creating distraction and frustrating customers.'

Having identified the main theme, the next step is to detail the specifics of the problem. This is a hugely important step that often gets missed or rushed past. If you don't capture this accurately, you are very likely to spend a lot of time and energy going down blind avenues.

Step two – Problem definition

The specifics of the issue may include where the problem is, when it occurs, the size and scope of the problem and the impact on customer satisfaction and other business goals. Where possible, these should be measurable, and illustrated simply and powerfully with graphs or numbers and short bullet-point statements in a way that really makes the problem clear and brings it to life as an important issue to address.

Step three – Defining the goal/target state

After identifying the broad theme and tightly defining the problem, the next crucial step is to define the goal of the improvement activity. This could include three things:

1. A measure; for example, 'achieving 97.5% or better accuracy'

2. How the process itself will work; for example, 'items should be completed in sequence, with no backlog building up at any process stage'

3. A target date for achieving this

As always, simple diagrams or statistical charts often help to illustrate the target state clearly.

Step four – Root cause analysis

Having clearly defined the problem and identified the target state, it is vital to get to the root cause of the existing barriers or problems. Without doing this, all improvement efforts will come to nothing, as they are simply not addressing the right underlying issues. The most popular and effective approach to this is the Five Whys, which we'll look at shortly.

In any attempt to identify root causes, ensure that the discussion sticks to facts and data and does not become dominated by opinion and emotion.

When you feel that you have identified the root cause, before moving on to developing possible countermeasures, check its plausibility. It is too easy to end up with something superficial and general, such as 'lack of training'. Ask yourself:

• Does the root cause look like a plausible explanation for the problem identified in the problem statement?

• If it were removed, would it move performance closer to the target state?

The Five Whys

The Five Whys is an exercise for questioning, thinking and exploring problems. It requires participation and discussion from the people involved to deepen the understanding of what is going on and to sort through the various factors and interactions to get to the most probable root cause.

This is simply asking 'why' a number of times to go down through the layers, from surface-level symptoms to underlying causes – like peeling an onion. The reference to five is just an indication that we need to ask a number of times; it may be less than five and it may be more. Also, we are not constrained to the question 'why'. There are other equally good analysis questions, of course; what, when, where, who and how. This approach is sometimes described as 5W1H.

It seldom works out neatly. At each stage, there may be several different answers that will need to be explored in similar fashion.

Be careful how you ask the questions. Bear in mind Deming's observation that 94% of the problems in organisations are caused by the system of work and not individuals. It is important that the way 'why' is asked does not become a search for someone to blame. Take great care to make sure questioning is constructive. The questions are to engage people in discussion and collectively explore and understand problems, the reasons for those problems and possible solutions. They are not there to allocate blame.

Step five – Containment measures

A containment measure is a step taken to make sure that no quality or delivery problems affect the customer while work is being done to identify and resolve the root cause of a problem. (Or, indeed, to contain any other potentially serious issue.) For example, this may mean increasing final quality checks, or drafting in extra people.

The containment measure is a short-term stop-gap, as such measures are usually expensive and address the symptoms, not the root cause. And it is important to make sure that:

1. The root cause is identified and eradicated
2. The containment measure is removed from the process once the root cause has been eradicated

Occasionally this does not happen and countermeasures are left in place, adding waste – and sometimes just covering up the real underlying problem.

Step six – Countermeasures

The countermeasures are the actions you intend to take to address the root cause and achieve the target state.

If a clear and plausible countermeasure has not yet emerged, then it may be necessary to go back and study the situation in more detail. This is usually a sign that something important has been missed.

There may be more than one countermeasure to address different aspects of the situation. It is, however, important to make sure that proposed countermeasures do not potentially cut across each other and cause confusion.

Before implementing any countermeasure, it is also important to sense check that it will address the root cause and achieve the target state. Look back to the earlier steps in the A3 process and check your thinking. Also, think through any possible unintended negative consequences of the countermeasures. There may be some; just make sure that they are minor and outweighed by the benefits of the countermeasure. If necessary (or possible), think about having a dry run or some other kind of off-line test of the countermeasure before making it live in the real system.

Finally, do not get involved in lengthy discussions about activities or steps beyond the initial countermeasures, because implementing them will change the situation in ways we can't fully predict. This is why the process is built around the PDCA cycle; after implementation, another check is done to assess the situation, and the next phase of countermeasures are developed from there (if indeed any are necessary at all). This processes repeats, ideally in fairly short, rapid cycles to really get to the bottom of problems and solve them by learning through taking practical action.

Step seven – Action plan

Having identified the countermeasures that you think best address the problem and the remove the root cause, the next step is to turn them into a concrete action plan.

Here, the specific actions, the date by which they will be completed, and the person responsible for doing them are all set out in detail – with the knowledge and agreement of the people responsible for each action.

The action plan is then implemented.

Step eight – Impact check

Once the actions that were set out in the action plan have been taken, it is absolutely vital to come back and do an impact check. (Remember, we are following the logic of the PDCA cycle.)

This is to check:

a. That the actions were taken as agreed

b. What impact the actions had on the processes and performance, and if the measures set out in the target state step were achieved

c. What has been learned

It may be that the impact was exactly what was hoped, but it may also be that it was less than hoped for, or even that something backfired. The point here is that you need to check so that you know what to do next to move things forward.

Step nine – Identifying the next actions

Having established the impact of the actions, you'll want to do one of two things (or possibly a bit of both):

- Where the impact check shows that the countermeasures addressed the root causes and achieved the target state, consolidate the gains by establishing the changes you made to the process as the new standard to be followed

- Where further significant room for improvement still exists to achieve the target state (or if it is appropriate now to make the target state more of a stretch goal), go back to step four and go from there through the root cause analysis and the rest of the process again. Keep looping round like this until you are satisfied that the A3 has achieved what it set out to. Then move on to another improvement opportunity, and once again apply the A3 approach from the start

Bringing A3 problem-solving to life

Now that we've outlined the main steps in A3 problem-solving, let's look at how to bring it to life and make it work in practice.

Problem-solving and continuous improvement is of course an iterative, evolving process. In the early stages, it is often unclear what the key variables in the situation are, and how altering them will affect the processes, performance and results. For this reason, A3 problem-solving was designed around PDCA thinking. PDCA is based on the scientific approach of initial analysis, then experimenting by building and testing countermeasures. This makes A3 problem-solving a very practical approach, with the emphasis on learning through action.

So the best approach is to:

- Use short, fast cycles where possible; learning quickly and building and developing the solution incrementally through small, rapid steps. This strategy is sometimes described as 'going to the end of the torch beam', i.e. go as far as you can with the information available, then build and test a solution, see what happens, reflect, learn, and evolve the approach. Then just keep doing this, as it will deepen your understanding of the situation and help you home in on the solution

- Avoid paralysis by analysis. While it is vital to take time to establish the precise nature and root cause of the problem, don't over-analyse. To get the balance between analysis and action right, do a sense-check. Ask:

  - Is more analysis necessary before taking action? If so, will that analysis tell you something of significance that you don't already know, and will it substantially affect any decision on what countermeasure to pursue?

  - Is the planned action credible based on your analysis so far? What do you expect to happen, and what do you hope to learn by taking it?

- Don't plan too many steps ahead, because when you implement the first actions it will change the situation

Coaching A3 problem-solving

If you are coaching people through A3, use the nine steps to bring structure and focus, and to establish the routine in people's minds as a habitual way of thinking so that, in time, they can do it by themselves.

Use your expertise to ask intelligent questions to enhance people's thinking. Do not try and solve the problem for them. An important part of the purpose of A3 is to develop a sense of responsibility, critical thinking skills and improved process understanding.

In line with the advice above, after the initial session to scope the whole piece, aim for short, fast PDCA cycles, with coaching sessions of typically 15 minutes to check action and progress since last time, current state, and next steps.

Where possible, develop your understanding of the situation and go and see for yourself what is happening. Do not rely wholly on what you are told: colleagues may have missed things that your expertise will allow you to pick up on, and you will then be able to devise good questions to help them see what they missed.

MANAGEMENT STYLE

Introduction

Effective processes are one necessary condition for engaging people, unlocking discretionary potential and delivering business results. The other is the right psychological climate, which is largely influenced by management style.

Our attitude to people depends on our assumptions about human nature, our personal values, and how important we believe others' contribution is to the success of the business. Douglas McGregor's classic 1960 'Theory X' and 'Theory Y' model highlighted the influence of our mindset on our behaviour; the impact this has on others' mindset and behaviours; how this, in turn, impacts on results; and how this all creates self-sustaining loops of success, mediocrity or failure. Perhaps the greatest insight we get from this is how powerful our mindset is in creating a self-fulfilling prophecy.

McGregor suggested that managers hold one of two theories about people. If they hold to Theory X, they assume that people are basically lazy, can't be trusted and will only contribute obligatory potential unless pushed. If a manager holds to Theory Y, they believe that people are basically trustworthy and capable; if given the right circumstances they will do a good job, and they have discretionary and excellence potential that they are willing to contribute.

Theory X	Theory Y
Thinking/mindset	
People aren't interested	People will be engaged if managed effectively and given a sense of belonging and purpose, and if they know that their contribution matters
People are basically dishonest and don't want to work. They want to do the bare minimum and go home	People are basically honest and will do a good job if given a chance. People also have discretionary potential and excellence potential which can be unlocked
People can't be trusted to act responsibly	People will take responsibility if we treat them as responsible adults
People have no ideas worth hearing	Everyone potentially has a good idea
People are argumentative, resistant and difficult	When listened to and spoken to with respect, most people are reasonable and open to persuasion
People are the source of errors and problems	People are a source of added value and solutions, with a natural enthusiasm and skill for solving problems and inventing better ways of doing things
Mistakes are mainly due to stupidity and care-lessness	People make mistakes. Many are due to problems with systems or a lack of training. The manager's responsibility is to ensure that the system people work in is fit for purpose, and to coach people to help them to learn from mistakes, put things right and avoid a recurrence
People are basically disloyal	People's first responsibility is to their own career, but they will generally play fair with a fair manager
People are only in it for the money	People are motivated only by money if that is the only measure of success and worth we give them. People also respond positively to other motivators such as praise, recognition, development and meaningful, interesting and challenging work
We need compliance	We need commitment
People need to be supervised and controlled	People can be engaged, enabled and empowered

Philosophy	
The manager's role is like that of a prison guard, there to watch people and keep them in check	The manager's role is to coach: to lead, encourage, support and grow people to get continuously improving contribution and performance
Tough discipline is necessary to keep people in line	Tough discipline gets compliance, not commitment, and generates a backwash of resentment that stops people going the extra mile
It's okay to be harsh with people if they are not performing or complying	People should be treated with dignity and respect at all times (including during disagreements, disciplinary meetings etc.) We need to treat people with the professionalism and respect we want them to show us, each other and customers

Theory X and its problems

Theory X-style management drives low engagement. There is little belief in people's potential and possibilities, and therefore little value is seen in investing time in treating them like responsible adults, or in managing and developing them.

Passive Theory X managers are likely to simply ignore and neglect people, creating apathy, low standards, low energy, sloppiness, and a cynical, defeatist attitude in people. Active Theory X managers regard control and supervision as the key to getting things done, since they do not see people as responsible or trustworthy. They typically favour managing by diktat: giving orders, expecting obedience, being demanding, unapproachable and unwilling to discuss concerns or problems, and being quick to use discipline and punishment.

Sometimes inaccurately described as a 'tough, disciplinarian approach', it is often simply managing by fear. It doesn't win commitment, only compliance (if that). It is also expensive. Due to the belief that people are only likely to comply fully when they are being watched, this requires close supervision, which costs unnecessary and unaffordable time and money. This whole approach also creates a backwash of anger and resentment that will stop people going the extra mile and is more likely to predispose them to be difficult, defensive, fearful and blame-oriented.

Both passive and active Theory X management are likely to:

- Be repressive and stifle creativity, ideas, and other aspects of discretionary potential

- Suppress personal responsibility, stifling initiative and problem-solving
- Stunt people's personal and professional growth, their confidence and the development of technical, personal, emotional, interpersonal and teamworking skills
- Damage trust. In assuming the worst about people and looking for it, Theory X managers draw it out. People live up (or rather down!) to that expectation. The manager's distrust of and lack of respect for people is reflected back on them; they get what they give, and an uncomfortable, damaging and costly low-trust downward spiral is created that becomes hard to escape
- Damage people's commitment. People who feel ignored and undervalued become psychologically disconnected and will work in neutral or actively disengage, becoming alienated, resentful, and possibly even hostile
- Reduce morale, enthusiasm and commitment and create an organisation that is slow to spot and capitalise on opportunities, respond to challenge and grow

Ironically, what keeps Theory X cultures going is the discretionary and excellence potential of some people who draw on their own personal pride and professional integrity and who, because of their own values and standards, wish to serve others well. (However, this still often goes unrecognised by the Theory X manager, who is likely to comment that 'That's what they're paid to do'.)

Taken to the extreme, in this kind of culture, people have no expectations of job security or job satisfaction, and little belief that they could make a valued contribution, or that, if they did make such a contribution, it would be recognised. It breeds a losing mentality, a sense of helplessness and hopelessness, and resentment. Organisations can too easily slip down this path and end up in the position of saying that people are 'our most important asset', while the evidence suggests that people are actually their most dispensable, badly treated and taken-for-granted asset.

Theory X thinking and behaviour is a historical throwback, passed on from one bad role model to the next. It is dangerously out of place in ambitious, progressive businesses in the modern competitive environment. It creates and sustains the conditions for dysfunctional cultures. It wastes time and talent, diminishes everyone and everything and damages results and reputation among potential clients, employees and investors. It's a recipe for underperformance, mutual distrust, frustration, sub-optimal performance and unnecessary trouble. It is difficult to overstate the amount of long-term cumulative damage this can do. It's bad business and it's bad for business.

Theory Y and its benefits

Theory Y takes the more positive (and, research suggests, realistic) view that nobody comes to work aiming to do a bad job, and that the majority of people do have some discretionary potential and would willingly contribute it, and develop it further, given the right circumstances. Managers who take this perspective recognise that their role is to engage, enable and empower people. To:

- Lead, providing clear, positive direction
- Ensure that people have what they need to succeed in their role and do quality work
- Listen to people and remove any obstacle that is stopping them doing a better job
- Empower people to do all they can to improve what they are doing
- Coach and develop people

William Ouchi in 1981 went further with his Theory Z, which incorporated all the best elements of Theory Y and went further, assuming that workers have a very strong desire to learn, improve and work with others and will display strong loyalty. He advocated giving workers almost complete freedom and trust and developing people holistically, equipping them with wider life skills as well as job-related skills. The Theory Y and Theory Z approaches also, to a large extent, become self-fulfilling prophecies. By looking for the best in people, we often draw it out.

The minor flaw in this is that there is usually a small percentage of people (estimates vary from industry to industry, between around 1% and 5%) who do seem to conform to the Theory X view. They will underperform and be difficult and uncooperative, possibly upsetting colleagues and disrupting the team. This means that a pure Theory Y view of the world might be slightly overoptimistic and leave us blindsided by this potentially problematic and disruptive minority and underequipped to deal with them. Fortunately, it is not difficult to modify Theory Y to accommodate this. Since Ouchi has already coined Theory Z, let's call it Theory Y+.

Theory Y+

Theory Y+ recognises that most people can be constructively engaged using the Theory Y approach, but that a small minority invariably seem resistant to it and behave more in line with the assumptions of Theory X.

Theory Y+ style is encouraging, supportive and constructively challenging. It takes the Theory Y approach and adds to it a greater degree of accountability and constructive challenge, and a willingness to discipline firmly and fairly where appropriate. This aims to create a spirit of openness, and promotes honest, positive, adult, supportive working relationships.

For the vast majority, the accountability and constructive challenge will be positive and welcome, taking the form of ongoing coaching to help them continue to evolve, develop and improve their contribution and performance. It will keep them outside their comfort zone just enough to feel a positive and motivating degree of stretch.

For any persistently difficult and disruptive colleagues, the constructive challenge will mean helping them to clearly understand that their contribution, and perhaps their attitude toward their performance, development, colleagues, customers or the business, is below the minimum expectations of what the business believes it is paying for, and that this needs to change; and that if it does not change, it may result in appropriate disciplinary action being taken, possibly leading eventually to dismissal. This will be done professionally, ethically, decently, morally and legally, but it will be done if the person is underperforming or being consistently disruptive, despite being managed in a Theory Y way beforehand and having been given repeated positive opportunities, support and encouragement to perform well and play a positive role in the team.

Theory Y+ strikes the right balance for a culture of Business Excellence. It incorporates the best of the Theory Y approach while recognising the reality that organisations often have a small number of people whose attitudes and behaviours are difficult and disruptive. In promoting constructive accountability and open, honest, adult working relationships, it also avoids the negativity and damage created by the distorted perceptions, and potential over-reactions, of an all-out Theory X approach applied across the board.

FRONT-LINE MANAGER STANDARDS PACK

Introduction

The purpose of this tool is to set clear standards for front-line manager (FLM) capability and performance and to allow FLMs' strengths and development needs to be identified. It is an assessment tool which includes:

- Outline of role, responsibilities and manager standard work
- Capability framework

The suggested approach is to:

- Explain to the colleague the purpose of the tool and what is in it
- Give them some time for self-review and to identify their existing strengths and development areas (in relation to potential future roles, not their current role)
- Prepare your thoughts by identifying what you believe to be their existing strengths and development areas against the criteria
- Then go through the assessment framework with the colleague, recognise their existing strengths, and agree on the key development areas and what action will be taken

IMPORTANT NOTE: HORIZONTAL AND VERTICAL DEVELOPMENT

The assessment criteria below outline the key facets of effective management. Establishing these building blocks to acquire the full set can be usefully seen as 'horizontal development'.

There is also vertical development. This is a measure of 'capability maturity': that is, how mature the capability in each facet is and how the person links them together into an integrated whole that brings a versatility and agility to their performance, helping them respond quickly and well to a range of situations that can change quickly.

The model below sets out four levels of vertical development: Each represents a different stage of emotional and cognitive growth. The lower on the spectrum we go, the greater the focus on trying to solve problems by throwing more time, energy, effort and force at it. The higher we go, the greater the focus on how well someone reads and analyses a situation, stays calm, thinks clearly, uses skill and expertise (technical and interpersonal), and selects the approach most suited to the situation (situational adaptation). As Deming described it, working smarter, not harder:

- **Reactive/chaotic level** behaviours include firefighting, blaming and complaining. At this level we may (or may not) solve the problem of the day. But having failed to address the underlying root causes, we will face the same problem again the next day. And the day after that

- At the **tactical level** we will anticipate some near-future operational issues and will plan accordingly to avoid or mitigate those we can. We'll also be tuned in enough to read how events are unfolding and make necessary in-flight adjustments. Generally, we'll do our best within the current constraints, but not seek to understand and address the underlying process limitations

- At the **improvement-focused level** we'll look at the process that is driving the current outcomes (including the problems). We'll (re)design, manage and improve the processes in our purview, address the underlying root causes and improve outcomes on an ongoing basis

- At the **strategic level** we'll seek to understand how the whole business works as a coherent system, and where future problems and value-adding opportunities are likely to occur. We'll then move to address these proactively, building new, and higher-level, capabilities to create an increasingly more adaptive system over time. Always seeking to increase possibilities and improve outcomes for all stakeholders

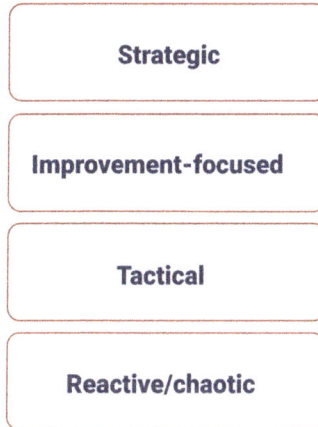

Strategic

Improvement-focused

Tactical

Reactive/chaotic

Figure E.1: Levels of managers' vertical development

By using the criteria in the Management capability framework on pages 500-504, you can assess both horizontal and vertical development and identify development opportunities.

Front-line management overview

Front-line management is vital. It arguably influences engagement and performance more than any other single factor, as front-line managers are the most immediate and frequent touchpoint for colleagues, and have the most direct impact on people's ability to perform, their attitudes, their behaviour and their levels of motivation and commitment.

Front line management focuses on:

*   Delivering what the customer needs on time, to quality, within cost, consistently, predictably and reliably

*   Making in-flight adjustments

*   Making continuous (kaizen) process improvements

- Unlocking individual potential
- Upholding the standards: performance, attitudinal and behavioural
- Solving day-to-day tactical front-line operational problems

The front-line manager mindset is:

- Immediate term
- Customer oriented
- Pragmatic: focused on people, process, quality, results

Below, we've set out a comprehensive description of the role, responsibilities and standard work for front-line managers.

The role of the front-line manager

To achieve results by enabling and facilitating performance through leading, engaging, developing and empowering people and building, managing and continuously improving processes. This is all founded on effective self-management. The role includes:

- Serving people to enable them to serve to the customer, by:

    - Ensuring that front-line colleagues have everything that they need to meet the customers' needs right first time, on time, every time, with zero wasted time or material

    - Empowering the team to improve the system they work in, to help them to do a better job with greater pride, less effort and more satisfaction

    - Listening to, and addressing, problems that people cannot clear from their own paths

    - Engaging people in a consistent, constructive, adult dialogue to enable them to become high-performing, low-maintenance contributors who deliver sustained world-class performance and continuously improving results

- Recruiting, engaging, motivating, developing and retaining talent
- Building a winning team
- Understanding how the work of the team serves the wider business and collaborating with other teams to optimise the overall system
- Developing a culture that is conducive to excellence

The front-line manager's responsibilities

Achieve results in the areas of:
- Health and safety
- Right-first-time quality
- On-time delivery
- Cost performance
- Colleague engagement
- Ongoing improvement of the capability and the performance of both people and process

Self-management. To:
- Set the tone. Be a role model by living the excellence philosophy and demonstrating what effective attitude, behaviour and performance look like
- Provide positive leadership: a clear vision, goals and direction
- Lead with emotional maturity, taking a measured approach to handling setbacks, challenges and change, keeping themself and others calm, focused and professional

Performance management:
- To ensure a safe working environment
- Daily planning and preparation to facilitate optimal team and process performance for each day, week and month
- Daily accountability meeting
- Gemba walk
- In-flight monitoring and course-correction: constantly tracking quality and workflow, and making in-flight adjustments and kaizen improvements
- Problem response
- Live coaching
- Review, learning and improvement

Process management. To ensure that the system that people work in is:
- Fit for purpose (able to deliver requirements on time, to cost, to quality, predictably and reliably)
- Properly resourced
- Operating within capacity

- Continuously improved (by the team) to add increasing value and to eliminate defects, waste and inefficiency
- Aligned with the process stages which precede and follow

People management. To ensure that people:
- Have clear expectations (role, responsibilities, performance standards and goals)
- Have the right knowledge and skills to succeed
- Have the right attitudes and behaviours
- Are supported: that anything stopping them from succeeding or improving is heard and addressed
- Work as a team
- Are held accountable for their performance, attitudes and behaviours
- Are empowered to solve problems
- Are actively encouraged to consistently improve

Resource management:
- To ensure that front-line colleagues have everything that they need to succeed, including equipment, tools, raw materials, consumables and sundries
- Coordination, alignment and collaboration. To:
- Collaborate with cross-functional colleagues to ensure the effective management and improvement of the end-to-end processes
- Collaborate with colleagues at different levels (vertically) to ensure strategic alignment
- Recognise and manage the interdependencies within the organisation, resolve conflicts, remove barriers to cooperation, and enhance collaboration within and between teams to improve flow, quality and productivity, and to reduce hassle and frustration and help people to do a better job with greater pride and more enjoyment

Culture. To:
- Actively promote and live the principles of Business Excellence (the pursuit of excellence through continuous improvement, working as a team)
- Develop and maintain the kata (core disciplines) that underpin excellence
- Optimise site performance, not just the performance of their own team (taking one for the team when appropriate)

- Continue improving all aspects of system capability, and attitudes and behaviours, at individual and team level

---

Strategic management:
- Contribute to the setting of strategic goals for their area of responsibility
- Implement strategic goals for their area of responsibility
- Support implementation of cross-functional strategic goals

Front-line manager standard work (auditable activities)

- Daily management

  - Start of shift handover (if applicable)

  - Daily accountability (Tier 1) meetings: short (5-10 minutes) check-in with the team collectively (where possible, a stand-up meeting in the communications zone where all relevant data are available) to review action and progress from the previous day, and to plan activity and anticipate problems for the day ahead

  - Gemba walk: a brief tour of the work area to see directly what is happening, checking in with people

  - Constantly monitoring process performance, and communicating with front-line colleagues to identify and address emerging problems promptly

  - Live coaching: responding to real-time improvement opportunities in colleague skills, behaviour, attitudes and performance in the course of daily work

  - End of shift handover (if applicable)

- Weekly and monthly team review meetings: to identify, understand and address trends and recurring issues over the period and to look ahead and prepare for the next period

- One-to-one performance reviews to complement the ongoing coaching

- Complete improvement task assignments related to continuous improvement of a) the operational processes, b) the daily management process, and c) projects identified in the strategic plan

Management capability framework

Figure E.2: Competence framework

In the table below, for each statement, tick the option that most closely applies. For a full explanation of what Reactive, Tactical, Improvement-focused and Strategic mean in this context, see the note on Horizontal and Vertical Development on pages 494-495.

Rate the following	Reactive	Tactical	Improvement-focused	Strategic
Attitude and approach				
1. Clearly understands that their role as a manager is to actively engage with all stakeholders to deliver excellent and continuously improving performance				
2. Leads by example. Positive and committed. Inspires and motivates people to give of their best				
3. High work rate and personal drive				
4. Takes the initiative: makes things happen rather than letting things happen or waiting for other people to do something				
5. Problem-solver with a can-do attitude: takes responsibility for addressing problems				

Rate the following	Reactive	Tactical	Improvement-focused	Strategic
6. Persistent and determined: does not give up easily				
7. Reliable: does what s/he says s/he will do				
8. Acts with honesty and integrity. Trustworthy				
Self-management				
9. Accepts responsibility for own attitude, behaviour, performance and results				
10. Resilient: in control of mood and emotions, even under pressure				
11. Recognises own strengths and plays fully to them				
12. Is aware of own weaknesses and shows commitment to addressing them				
13. Acknowledges her/his mistakes, understands them and learns from them				
14. Coachable: welcomes constructive feedback and responds appropriately				
Personal organisation				
15. Is well organised				
16. Stays on top of priorities: focused and disciplined approach to managing own time				
17. Makes adequate time for value-enabling activities (including planning, communication and continuous improvement)				
18. Anticipates potential problems and plans how to deal with them				
19. Decisive: makes decisions in a positive and timely manner				
Interpersonal effectiveness				
20. Treats people with dignity and respect				
21. Looks for the best in people and situations				
22. Is accessible and approachable				
23. Listens effectively to people's perspectives, concerns and ideas				

Rate the following	Reactive	Tactical	Improvement-focused	Strategic
24. Is accurately aware of the impact of their attitudes and behaviours on others				
25. Communicates, and works effectively, with a range of different personal styles				
26. Persuasive: promotes their ideas positively, clearly and convincingly				
27. Deals with conflict and differences of opinion professionally and effectively				
Team player				
28. Delivers on responsibilities and obligations: does not cause avoidable problems or additional work for others				
29. Will muck in to help others as appropriate				
30. Understands and appreciates others' goals, challenges and pressures				
31. Communicates clearly to ensure effective coordination of activities				
32. Collaborative and cooperative: willing to make accommodations for the greater good				
33. Helps and supports colleagues when needed				
34. Asks for and accepts help and advice where appropriate				
People management				
35. Agrees clear standards of performance, behaviour and attitude with each di-rect report				
36. Ensures that direct reports have the knowledge and skills to do the job well. Identifies and meets any learning and development needs				
37. Ensures that direct reports have the resources (including information, materi-als and tools) to do their job effectively				
38. Gives regular, timely and appropriate praise, recognition and encouragement				
39. Holds people accountable: actively reviews individuals' performance and re-sults with them regularly				

Rate the following	Reactive	Tactical	Improvement-focused	Strategic
40. Gives clear, timely, constructive feedback so people know where they can improve performance				
41. Coaches people effectively to help them learn from successes and setbacks and to develop confidence and skill				
42. Empowers and delegates effectively				
43. Deals with underperformance and disruptive behaviour effectively				
Leading the team				
44. Actively communicates a positive vision of the company, its products and services, and how the team contributes to its success				
45. Has clear goals for the team, and communicates these effectively				
46. Prioritises and plans team workload effectively. Allocates work appropriately to make best use of resources and meet deadlines				
47. Recognises and harnesses individual strengths. Gets the most from the abilities in the team				
48. Works to build strong, supportive working relationships between individuals in the team. Actively encourages mutual support and cooperation				
49. Runs regular, constructive meetings to review team performance, solve problems, drive continuous improvement, share knowledge and ideas and enhance teamworking				
50. Actively engages colleagues in continuous improvement activities				
51. Recognises and celebrates team success to build confidence, pride and team spirit				
52. Has developed an environment which is challenging, positive and rewarding				
53. Stands up for the team: promotes the team's successes and interests with all stakeholders				

Rate the following	Reactive	Tactical	Improvement-focused	Strategic
Managing stakeholders				
54. Understands who the external customers are, and what matters to them				
55. Understands how the business delivers value to customers (the end-to-end processes)				
56. Understands the external environment and its challenges and opportunities				
57. Understands the overall business strategy and goals, and the part they play in achieving them				
58. Recognises who their internal customers are and understands and meets their needs				
59. Develops and maintains positive working relationships with suppliers (internal or external)				
60. Actively develops effective working relationships with senior managers				
Builds, manages and continuously improves processes				
61. Ensures that the processes they are responsible for are fit for purpose				
62. Consistently follows processes				
63. Primes and maintains processes (including provision of materials, tools and working equipment) to allow people to work without unnecessary interruption				
64. Ensures effective alignment with, and smooth hand-offs between, adjacent processes				
65. Continuously improves all aspects of process performance				

OPERATIONAL MANAGER STANDARDS PACK

Introduction

The purpose of this tool is to set clear standards for operational manager (OM) capability and performance and to allow OMs' strengths and development needs to be identified. It is an assessment tool which includes:

- Outline of role, responsibilities and operational manager standard work

- Capability framework

The suggested approach is to:

- Explain to the colleague the purpose of the tool and what is in it

- Give them some time for self-review and to identify their existing strengths and development areas (in relation to potential future roles, not their current role)

- Prepare your thoughts by identifying what you believe to be their existing strengths and development areas against the criteria

- Then go through the assessment framework with the colleague, recognise their existing strengths, and agree on the key development areas and what action will be taken

IMPORTANT NOTE: HORIZONTAL AND VERTICAL DEVELOPMENT

The assessment criteria below outline the key facets of effective management. Establishing these building blocks to acquire the full set can be usefully seen as 'horizontal development'.

There is also vertical development. This is a measure of 'capability maturity': that is, how mature the capability in each facet is and how the person links them together into an integrated whole that brings a versatility and agility to their performance, helping them respond quickly and well to a range of situations that can change quickly.

The model below sets out four levels of vertical development: Each represents a different stage of emotional and cognitive growth. The lower on the spectrum we go, the greater the focus on trying to solve problems by throwing more time, energy, effort and force at it. The higher we go, the greater the focus on how well someone reads and analyses a situation, stays calm, thinks clearly, uses skill and expertise (technical and interpersonal), and selects the approach most suited to the situation (situational adaptation). As Deming described it, working smarter, not harder:

- **Reactive/chaotic level** behaviours include firefighting, blaming and complaining. At this level we may (or may not) solve the problem of the day. But having failed to address the underlying root causes, we will face the same problem again the next day. And the day after that

- At the **tactical level** we will anticipate some near-future operational issues and will plan accordingly to avoid or mitigate those we can. We'll also be tuned in enough to read how events are unfolding and make necessary in-flight adjustments. Generally, we'll do our best within the current constraints, but not seek to understand and address the underlying process limitations

- At the **improvement-focused level** we'll look at the process that is driving the current outcomes (including the problems). We'll (re)design, manage and improve the processes in our purview, address the underlying root causes and improve outcomes on an ongoing basis

- At the **strategic level** we'll seek to understand how the whole business works as a coherent system, and where future problems and value-adding opportunities are likely to occur. We'll then move to address these proactively, building new, and higher-level, capabilities to create an increasingly more adaptive system over time. Always seeking to increase possibilities and improve outcomes for all stakeholders

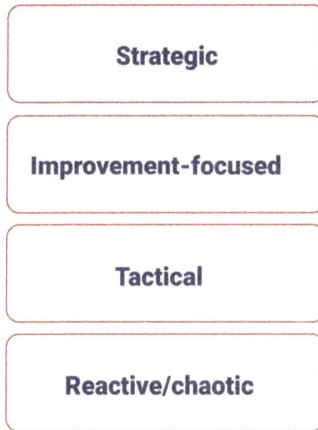

Strategic

Improvement-focused

Tactical

Reactive/chaotic

Figure F.1: Levels of managers' vertical development

By using the criteria in the Management capability framework on pages 512-517, you can assess both horizontal and vertical development and identify development opportunities.

Operational management overview

Operational management focuses on coordination and management of process, performance and results. This includes

- Delivering the operational strategy in line with the organisation's mission, vision and values
- Ensuring the effective running of the whole operation
- Developing the organisation's system and process infrastructure
- Medium- to long-term operational planning
- Reconciling conflicting interests and goals between units
- Recruiting, developing, engaging, motivating and retaining talent

The operational manager mindset is:

- Medium- to long-term
- Inside-outside: boundary-spanning, to ensure collaboration and alignment a) within the organisation, and b) between the organisation and external stakeholders
- Facilitating and enabling

The role of the operational manager

To achieve results by enabling and facilitating performance through leading, engaging, developing and empowering people and building, managing and continuously improving processes. This is all founded on effective self-management. The role includes:

- The effective running of the whole operation, overseeing and integrating the management of the core processes end-to-end across the business
- Reconciling conflicting interests and goals between units
- Organising and managing resources to ensure that front-line managers have what they need so that they can provide front-line colleagues with the tools, equipment and resources to deliver what the customer wants, right first time, on time, every time, with zero wasted time or material
- Designing, managing and continuously improving the daily management process and the operational management process
- Developing the organisation's infrastructure appropriately to enable performance
- Coaching front-line managers to develop the required skills, attitudes and behaviours
- Overseeing, integrating and monitoring the continuous improvement activities happening at the front line
- Actively contributing to continuous improvement efforts by helping to remove barriers that front-line managers can't
- Implementing the improvement projects associated with the breakthrough goals in the strategic plan
- Developing the management team
- Overseeing the recruitment, engagement, motivation, development and retention of talent
- Developing a culture that is conducive to excellence

The operational manager's main responsibilities

To achieve results, in areas including:
- Health and safety
- Right-first-time quality
- On-time delivery
- Cost performance
- Colleague engagement
- Delivering the agreed strategic improvement breakthrough goals
- Ongoing improvement of the capability and the performance of both people and process

Self management. To:
- Set the tone as a role model by living the excellence philosophy and demonstrating what effective attitude, behaviour and performance looks like
- Provide positive leadership: a clear vision, goals and direction
- Lead with emotional maturity, taking a measured approach to handling setbacks, challenges and change, keeping themselves and others calm, focused and professional

Performance management:
- To ensure a safe working environment
- Overseeing front-line managers' daily planning and preparation
- Daily (Tier 2) accountability meeting
- Gemba walk
- In-flight monitoring and course-correction: taking a helicopter view across the whole area of responsibility, tracking quality and workflow across the operational process end-to-end, and making in-flight adjustments and kaizen improvements, ensuring integration both within their area of responsibility and with other teams
- Responding to problems that front-line managers cannot solve by themselves
- Live coaching of front-line managers
- Review, learning and improvement

Operational management process. To ensure that the operational management system is:

- Fit for purpose: this covers the design, management and improvement of the communications zones, including the visual accountability boards to track operational performance and process-improvement assignments

- Properly resourced

- Continuously improved

- Touchpoints and meetings are fit for purpose and run a) as designed, and b) as scheduled

People management. To ensure that the front-line managers:

- Have clear expectations (role, responsibilities, standards and daily tasks and goals)

- Have the right knowledge and skills to succeed

- Have the right attitudes and behaviours

- Are supported: that anything stopping them from succeeding or improving is heard and addressed

- Work as a team

- Are held accountable for their performance, attitudes and behaviours

- Are empowered to solve problems

- Are actively encouraged to consistently improve

- Are doing the same for front-line colleagues

Infrastructure and resource management:

- To ensure that the operation has everything needed to succeed, including equipment, tools, raw materials, consumables, sundries, wider systems, facilities and amenities. And that it is all in the right place in the right quantities, of the right quality, at the right time

Coordination, alignment and collaboration. To:

- Collaborate with cross-functional colleagues to ensure the effective management and improvement of the whole operational process end-to-end

- Collaborate with colleagues at different levels (vertically) to ensure strategic alignment

- Recognise and manage the interdependencies within the organisation, resolve conflicts, remove barriers to cooperation, and enhance collaboration within and between teams to improve flow, quality and productivity, and to reduce hassle and frustration and help people to do a better job with greater pride and more enjoyment

Culture. To:

- Actively promote and live the principles of Business Excellence (the pursuit of excellence through continuous improvement, working as a team)
- Develop and maintain the kata (core disciplines) that underpin excellence and ensure that front-line managers are doing the same
- Optimise site performance, not just the performance of their own team (taking one for the team when appropriate)
- Continue improving all aspects of system capability, colleagues' attitudes and behaviours, and teamwork

Strategic management:

- Contribute to the setting of strategic goals
- Implement strategic goals for their area of responsibility
- Support implementation of cross-functional strategic goals

Operational manager standard work (auditable activities)

- Daily management:

  - Daily accountability (Tier 2) meetings: a short daily stand-up to review outcomes of the Tier 1 meetings, including action and progress from the previous day, and to plan activity and anticipate problems for the day ahead
  - Gemba walk: a brief tour of the work area to see directly what is happening, checking in with people and being visible and approachable
  - Constantly monitoring process performance, and communicating with front-line managers to identify and address emerging problems early
  - Live coaching: responding to real-time improvement opportunities in front-line managers' skills, behaviour, attitudes and performance in the course of daily work

- Weekly and monthly team review meetings: to identify, understand and address trends and recurring issues over the period and to look ahead and prepare for the next period
- One-to-one performance reviews with front-line managers to complement the ongoing coaching
- Complete improvement task assignments related to continuous improvement of a) the management processes, and b) projects identified in the strategic plan

Management capability framework

Figure F.2: Competence framework

In the table below, for each statement, tick the option that most closely applies. For a full explanation of what Reactive, Tactical, Improvement-focused and Strategic mean in this context, see the note on Horizontal and Vertical Development on pages 506-507.

Rate the following	Reactive	Tactical	Improvement-focused	Strategic
Attitude and approach				
1. Clearly understands that their role as a manager is to actively engage with all stakeholders to deliver excellent and continuously improving performance				
2. Leads by example. Positive and committed. Inspires and motivates people to give of their best				
3. High work rate and personal drive				
4. Takes the initiative: makes things happen rather than letting things happen or waiting for other people to do something				
5. Problem-solver with a can-do attitude: takes responsibility for addressing problems				
6. Persistent and determined: does not give up easily				
7. Reliable: does what s/he says s/he will do				
8. Acts with honesty and integrity. Trustworthy				
Self-management				
9. Accepts responsibility for own attitude, behaviour, performance and results				
10. Resilient: in control of mood and emotions, even under pressure				
11. Recognises own strengths and plays fully to them				
12. Is aware of own weaknesses and shows commitment to addressing them				
13. Acknowledges her/his mistakes, understands them and learns from them				
14. Coachable: welcomes constructive feedback and responds appropriately				
Personal organisation				
15. Is well organised				
16. Stays on top of priorities: focused and disciplined approach to managing own time				

Rate the following	Reactive	Tactical	Improvement-focused	Strategic
17. Makes adequate time for value-enabling activities (including planning, communication and continuous improvement)				
18. Anticipates potential problems and plans how to deal with them				
19. Decisive: makes decisions in a positive and timely manner				
Interpersonal effectiveness				
20. Treats people with dignity and respect				
21. Looks for the best in people and situations				
22. Is accessible and approachable				
23. Listens effectively to people's perspectives, concerns and ideas				
24. Is accurately aware of the impact of their attitudes and behaviours on others				
25. Communicates, and works effectively, with a range of different personal styles				
26. Persuasive: promotes their ideas positively, clearly and convincingly				
27. Deals with conflict and differences of opinion professionally and effectively				
Team player				
28. Delivers on responsibilities and obligations: does not cause avoidable problems or additional work for others				
29. Will muck in to help others as appropriate				
30. Understands and appreciates others' goals, challenges and pressures				
31. Communicates clearly to ensure effective coordination of activities				
32. Collaborative and cooperative: willing to make accommodations for the greater good				
33. Helps and supports colleagues when needed				

Rate the following	Reactive	Tactical	Improvement-focused	Strategic
34. Asks for and accepts help and advice where appropriate				
People management				
35. Agrees clear standards of performance, behaviour and attitude with each di-rect report				
36. Ensures that direct reports have the knowledge and skills to do the job well. Identifies and meets any learning and development needs				
37. Ensures that direct reports have the resources (including information, materi-als and tools) to do their job effectively				
38. Gives regular, timely and appropriate praise, recognition and encouragement				
39. Holds people accountable: actively reviews individuals' performance and re-sults with them regularly				
40. Gives clear, timely, constructive feedback so people know where they can improve performance				
41. Coaches people effectively to help them learn from successes and setbacks and to develop confidence and skill				
42. Empowers and delegates effectively				
43. Deals with underperformance and disruptive behaviour effectively				
Leading the team				
44. Actively communicates a positive vision of the company, its products and services, and how the team contributes to its success				
45. Has clear goals for the team, and communicates these effectively				
46. Prioritises and plans team workload effectively. Allocates work appropriately to make best use of resources and meet deadlines				
47. Recognises and harnesses individual strengths. Gets the most from the abilities in the team				

Rate the following	Reactive	Tactical	Improvement-focused	Strategic
48. Works to build strong, supportive working relationships between individuals in the team. Actively encourages mutual support and cooperation				
49. Runs regular, constructive meetings to review team performance, solve problems, drive continuous improvement, share knowledge and ideas and enhance teamworking				
50. Actively engages colleagues in continuous improvement activities				
51. Recognises and celebrates team success to build confidence, pride and team spirit				
52. Has developed an environment which is challenging, positive and rewarding				
53. Stands up for the team: promotes the team's successes and interests with all stakeholders				
Managing stakeholders				
54. Understands who the external customers are, and what matters to them				
55. Understands how the business delivers value to customers (the end-to-end processes)				
56. Understands the external environment and its challenges and opportunities				
57. Understands the overall business strategy and goals, and the part they play in achieving them				
58. Recognises who their internal customers are and understands and meets their needs				
59. Develops and maintains positive working relationships with suppliers (internal or external)				
60. Actively develops effective working relationships with senior managers				
Builds, manages and continuously improves processes				
61. Ensures that the processes they are responsible for are fit for purpose				
62. Consistently follows processes				

Rate the following	Reactive	Tactical	Improvement-focused	Strategic
63. Primes and maintains processes (including provision of materials, tools and working equipment) to allow people to work without unnecessary interruption				
64. Ensures effective alignment with, and smooth hand-offs between, adjacent processes				
65. Continuously improves all aspects of process performance				

LEADERSHIP STANDARDS PACK

The purpose of this tool is to set clear standards for leadership capability and performance and to allow leaders' strengths and development needs to be identified. It is an assessment tool which includes:

- Outline of role, responsibilities and leader standard work

- Capability framework

The suggested approach is to:

- Explain to the colleague the purpose of the tool and what is in it

- Give them some time for self-review and to identify their existing strengths and development areas (in relation to potential future roles, not their current role)

- Prepare your thoughts by identifying what you believe to be their existing strengths and development areas against the criteria

- Then go through the assessment framework with the colleague, recognise their existing strengths, and agree on the key development areas and what action will be taken

IMPORTANT NOTE: HORIZONTAL AND VERTICAL DEVELOPMENT

The assessment criteria below outline the key facets of effective leadership. Establishing these building blocks to acquire the full set can be usefully seen as 'horizontal development'.

There is also vertical development. This is a measure of 'capability maturity': that is, how mature the capability in each facet is and how the person links them together into an integrated whole that brings a versatility and agility to their performance, helping them respond quickly and well to a range of situations that can change quickly.

The model below sets out four levels of vertical development: each represents a different stage of emotional and cognitive growth. The lower on the spectrum we go, the greater the focus on trying to solve problems by throwing more time, energy, effort and force at it. The higher we go, the greater the focus on how well someone reads and analyses a situation, stays calm, thinks clearly, uses skill and expertise (technical and interpersonal), and selects the approach most suited to the situation (situational adaptation). As Deming described it, working smarter, not harder:

1. **Chaotic:** Lacks the requisite mindset, discipline and skills and character to deliver results and continuously improve in the face of an inevitable ongoing array of challenges. Often accompanied by a stream of excuses, rationalisations and blame

2. **Getting by:** Leaders here deliver within the constraints of the existing system, delivering business-as-usual performance with varying degrees of consistency, reliability, quality and efficiency. But through either not seeing the need, or feeling it is not their responsibility, they do not address the factors that are limiting system capability. They are therefore stuck at this level of performance

3. **Excellent:** Leaders here are capable of running and improving an operation that has already reached a level of excellence. They deliver best practice, routinely perform well and achieve the SQCDE (safety, quality, cost, delivery performance and colleague engagement) measures. They can also optimise and improve systems by making kaizen improvements (many small, tactical changes), but not the more significant structural and cultural kaikaku changes

4. **Transformational/evolutionary leaders** are able to lead a transformation to Business Excellence, evolving the current business model to either:

a. Respond to (or shape) change in their operating environments to get ahead of the competition and gain first-mover advantage, or

b. Get to current best practice if the organisation is playing catch-up

Transformational leaders are able to take the initiative and to lead major kaikaku change on some or all of the dimensions described earlier (technical, social, cultural etc.) while simultaneously running the business at an acceptable level. As such, transformational leadership calls for a higher level of ambition, thinking and skill, and a better and more fully integrated set of tools and approaches for both running and improving an organisation.

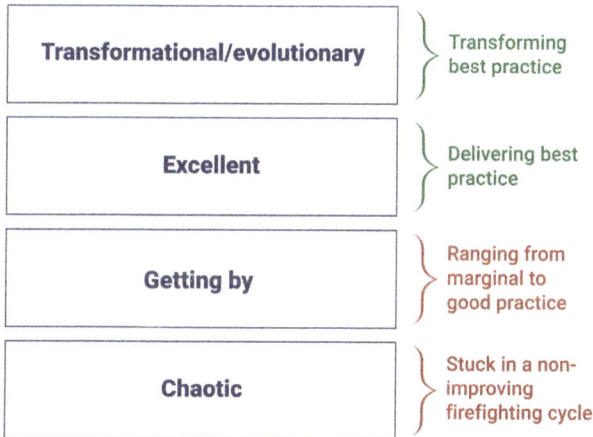

Transformational/evolutionary	Transforming best practice
Excellent	Delivering best practice
Getting by	Ranging from marginal to good practice
Chaotic	Stuck in a non-improving firefighting cycle

Figure G.1: Levels of leaders' vertical development

Job purpose/role

The role of the leader in Business Excellence comprises:

- **Safeguarding the organisation's financial viability, standards and reputation:** Achieving results by following the principles of Business Excellence

- **Self-management:** Setting the tone and example for the culture by living the excellence philosophy and the organisation's values

- **Leading and overseeing the effective strategic management of the business.** To:

  - Define and communicate a compelling vision, aims, ethos and standards, and the methodology to achieve it
  - Design, run and continuously improve the strategic management process

- **Overseeing the effective operational management of the business.** In collaboration with the operational managers, designing, managing and continuously improving both the operational processes and the operational management processes, and thereby achieving excellent and continually improving performance

- **People management:** Overseeing the recruitment, engagement, motivation, development and retention of top talent

- **Alignment, integration, teamwork and collaboration:** Creating a unified, empowered and capable team across the organisation, starting at the top. And ensuring that all the technical and management processes are aligned end-to-end (horizontally) and vertically (with the strategy)

- **Developing a culture conducive to excellence** and thereby achieving long-term outcomes that are attractive enough to maintain the interest, engagement and commitment of all stakeholders

- **Managing stakeholders and external interfaces.** Successfully managing all stakeholders' expectations and perceptions and being an effective spokesperson to protect and advance the company's reputation in key arenas, fostering collaboration in the organisation's wider network

Main responsibilities (what leaders are accountable for)

Results:
As financial and reputational guardian of the business, to ensure:

- The long-term viability, health and prosperity of the organisation

- The ethical conduct of the company's business; financially, socially and environmentally

- That the business is run in line with the principle and practices of Business Excellence

- That the operational management team achieve the right results, including:

  - Health and safety

  - Right-first-time quality

  - On-time delivery

  - Financial performance

  - Colleague engagement

  - The agreed strategic improvement breakthrough goals

- Ongoing improvement of the capability and the performance of both people and processes

Self-management
To provide positive leadership that people willingly follow by:

- Exemplifying excellence in personal attitudes, behaviour and performance

- Working well with colleagues in the senior team and wider organisation

- Leading with emotional maturity: actively pursuing a positive vision and taking a measured approach to handling setbacks, challenges and change. Keeping themselves and others calm, focused and professional in pursuit of the organisation's vision, aims and standards

- Making and communicating clear decisions that are consistent with the organisation's values, aims and strategy. Doing so in a timely manner, based on the available information, and adapting as events unfold and new information becomes available

Management of strategic performance. To:

- Define and communicate a clear vision, ethos, values, goals, strategy and methodology
- Design a strategic management process that enables the organisation to systematically track both the external environment and internal capability, and thereby optimise the scope and accuracy of its foresight
- Develop and implement a strategy that responds adaptively to (or shapes) unfolding events
- Review and evolve both the strategy and the strategic management process
- Implement the strategic improvement projects assigned to them
- Ensure that the organisational structure is fit for purpose
- Design, manage and improve an infrastructure that is fit for purpose (facilities, amenities, IT etc.)

Management of operational performance. To:

- Ensure a safe working environment
- Ensure (in collaboration with the operational management team) that the operational management system is:

  - Fit for purpose
  - Properly run as a) designed, and b) scheduled
  - Continuously improved

- Oversee the operational managers' planning and preparation for medium- to long-term performance
- Monitor operational performance (through the daily Tier 3 accountability meetings and other appropriate means), liaising with operational managers on appropriate in-flight course corrections and tackling problems that operational managers can't
- Carry out live/situational coaching of operational managers
- Ensure that the operation is adequately resourced to deliver the strategy and goals to the required standards. This includes people, time, equipment, tools, raw materials, consumables, sundries and systems
- Ensure that the operational managers lead and empower colleagues to continuously improve all aspects of organisational capability and performance using appropriate tools and disciplines – and ensure that those activities are strategically aligned

- Address systems and people issues, and other institutional barriers to change

People management
To ensure that the operational managers:

- Have clear expectations (role, responsibilities, standards, daily tasks and goals)
- Have the right knowledge and skills to succeed
- Have the right attitudes and behaviours to lead and manage in ways consistent with the organisational vision, values and standards
- Are empowered to make decisions and solve problems as appropriate
- Are supported: that anything stopping them from succeeding or improving is heard and addressed
- Are held accountable for their attitudes and behaviours, performance and results
- Are actively coached and encouraged to consistently improve
- Work as a team, and lead their teams to collaborate across the business
- Are doing all of the above for the front-line managers

Teamwork, coordination, alignment and collaboration. To:
- Align the organisation:

  - Attitudinally and culturally, making sure that everyone, starting at the top, is following the same broad principles
  - Strategically and functionally so that everyone, starting at the top, is working together and is focused on optimising the performance of the whole organisation vertically and horizontally (end-to-end, not just their silo), and for the long term

- Recognise and manage the interdependencies within the organisation, resolve conflicts, remove barriers to cooperation, and enhance collaboration within and between teams to improve flow, quality and productivity, to reduce hassle and frustration, and to help people to do an ever-better job with greater pride and more enjoyment

Culture. To:
- Promote the aims, ethos, standards and practices of excellence, including systems thinking
- Create a 'thinking people system' which draws everyone into an ongoing process of collaboration and continuous improvement

- Develop and maintain the kata (core disciplines) that underpin excellence, and to ensure that the operational managers are doing the same
- Ensure a continuing focus on improving all aspects of the business, including system capability, colleague engagement and teamwork

Managing stakeholders. To:
- Effectively manage all stakeholders' expectations and perceptions, including shareholders, investors and headquarters as appropriate
- Be an effective spokesperson and advocate (and, where necessary, defender), to protect and advance the company's reputation in key arenas
- Foster collaboration with key partners in the wider business networks

Standard work (auditable activities that underpin effective leadership)

- Oversee the running of the strategy process of information-gathering, analysis, planning, implementation and review
- Complete task assignments for a) improvement projects identified in the strategic plan, and b) the improvement of the strategic management process itself
- Weekly and monthly review meetings: to identify, understand and address trends and recurring issues over the period, and to look ahead and prepare for the next period
- One-to-one performance reviews with operational managers to complement their ongoing real-time coaching
- Periodic gemba walk: a brief tour of the front line to see directly what is happening, checking in with people, being visible and approachable and building trust, respect and mutual understanding
- Daily management:

  - Daily accountability (Tier 3) meetings: a short daily review of outcomes of the Tier 2 meetings, including progress from the previous day, and to plan activity and anticipate problems for the day ahead
  - Ongoing communication as appropriate with operational managers to be aware of, and address, emerging problems early

> • Coaching: responding to real-time improvement opportunities in operational managers' skills, behaviour, attitudes and performance in the course of daily work

Leadership capability framework

Figure G.2: Leadership competencies

- **Attitude and approach:** Is committed to Business Excellence. Is a role model. Leads by example. Maintains high personal standards. Inspires confidence and motivates people to give of their best.

- **Self-management:** Deals confidently and professionally with the demands and pressures of the job. A hard worker who demonstrates a commitment to achieving business results. Continuously works to improve own performance. Resilient. Achieves results despite setbacks and obstacles.

- **Personal effectiveness:** Manages their time effectively. Focuses on priorities. Plans and prioritises tasks to use time effectively. Organised. Gets through all key tasks by deadlines.

- **Interpersonal effectiveness:** Is approachable. Influences others by using a range of verbal, written and presentation skills. Adapts communication style to suit the situation and audience. Listens well, shows respect. Makes efforts to understand others' perspectives and needs, and endeavours to create win-win situations. Able to assert constructively. Is positive, respectful, friendly, direct and enthusiastic. Brings out the best in people. Gets things done, working with and through others. Persuasive.

- **Team player:** Gives timely information to all colleagues and others who rely on their contribution and cooperation. Contributes effectively to the leadership team and their departmental team. Works well with a diverse range of people with different perspectives, experiences, backgrounds and personal styles.

- **Leading people:** Sets clear expectations, standards and objectives. Provides clear and constructive feedback on performance. Delegates and empowers effectively. Ensures that people are given the support they need to develop the skills and confidence they need to succeed.

- **Leading the team:** Creates a sense of shared purpose and establishes clear goals and direction for the team. Develops the team and maximizes its potential. Encourages mutual support and cooperation. Communicates goals, plans and performance measures clearly to the team. Conducts regular, constructive meetings to solve problems and enhance teamworking.

- **Managing stakeholders:** Builds strong relationships with internal and external stakeholders. Ensures they understand the business and how they can add value, provides feedback to help them improve their service, and stands up positively for the company's interests. Takes the initiative to build and maintain positive relationships with all key stakeholders.

- **Managing operations:** Allocates responsibilities and matches workloads against priorities and deadlines. Provides the right resources. Plans ahead to avoid potential problems. Regularly reviews progress against performance measures. Has built, and maintains, effective processes. Continuously seeks to improve efficiency, quality, competitiveness and customer satisfaction. Actively involves the whole team in finding more effective ways of doing things.

- **Strategic excellence:** Sets a clear, appealing long-term vision, strategy and goals for their part of the business, aligned to the wider company vision, and articulates it convincingly. Is in touch with what is going on in the business and in the wider industry/networks. Has a credible long-term strategy which has been communicated to everyone responsible for making it happen. Has a credible process for continually evolving the strategy. Translates the strategy into action and results.

Detailed leadership capability

In the table below, for each statement, tick the option that most closely applies. For a full explanation of what Reactive, Tactical, Improvement-focused and Strategic mean in this context, see the note on Horizontal and Vertical Development on pages 520-521.

Rate the following	Reactive	Tactical	Improvement-focused	Strategic
Leadership attitude and approach				
Clearly understands that their role is to engage positively with all stakeholders to deliver excellent and continuously improving performance				
Is genuinely committed to developing operational excellence as a source of competitive advantage				
Understands the overall business strategy and goals, and the part they play in achieving them				
Understands that engaging, empowering and enabling all col-leagues to manage and improve performance every day is a key aspect of business strategy				
Is a systems thinker: sees the business as an interconnected system, with the focus on the performance of the entire value chain, not individual departments				
Is a role model. Lives the values of the organisation and leads by example in their attitudes and behaviour				
Positive attitude: enthuses and inspires others				
Takes the initiative: makes things happen rather than letting things happen				
Actively committed to the continuous improvement of all aspects of business performance				
Takes difficult decisions and accepts responsibility for them				
Is prepared to be challenged				
Responds constructively to issues and problems raised with them				
Reliable: delivers on commitments				

Rate the following	Reactive	Tactical	Improvement-focused	Strategic
Acts with honesty and integrity: trustworthy				
Adapts quickly and flexibly to change				
Takes managed risks in the pursuit of new challenges and achievements				
Provides constancy of purpose: balances the need for short-term results with building the capability for sustainable long-term success				
Self-management				
Has high standards for own attitude, behaviour, performance and results				
Self-motivated. High work rate and personal drive				
Equanimity: calm and composed in difficult situations				
Resilient: determined and persistent in the face of problems				
Recognises own strengths and plays fully to them				
Is aware of own weaknesses and shows commitment to ad-dressing them				
Balanced sense of self-confidence, commensurate with level of ability				
Acknowledges own mistakes: understands them, learns from them and moves on				
Regularly asks for, accepts and acts on feedback from manager, customers, colleagues and team, and responds positively				
Actively drives own development. Continually improves leadership knowledge, skills and performance				
Open to change and to new ideas, approaches and ways of doing things (personally and organisationally)				
Personal effectiveness				
Focus - evaluates priorities, continually concentrating atten-tion and effort on the goals that matter the most				
Organised: plans their time and workload effectively. Stays on top of priorities				

Rate the following	Reactive	Tactical	Improvement-focused	Strategic
Makes adequate time for value-enabling activities (including planning, communication and continuous improvement)				
Anticipates potential problems and plans how to deal with them				
Follows through: completes tasks and gets results				
Meets deadlines				
Decisive: makes decisions in a positive and timely manner				
Interpersonal effectiveness				
Treats people with dignity and respect				
Is accessible and approachable				
Builds and maintains effective working relationships				
Has established and kept trust				
Brings out the best in people				
Listens effectively				
Responds well to people's perspectives, concerns and ideas				
Communicates and works effectively with a range of different people. Modifies their style as appropriate				
Is accurately aware of the impact of their attitudes and behav-iours on others				
Listens to and takes account of diverse views				
Gives constructive feedback skilfully and appropriately				
Persuasive: promotes their ideas positively, clearly and convincingly				
Able to express views, needs and concerns assertively and without being inflexible or aggressive				
Is prepared to say difficult but necessary things				
Invites constructive feedback				
Negotiates constructively and skilfully				

Rate the following	Reactive	Tactical	Improvement-focused	Strategic
Deals with conflict and differences of opinion professionally and effectively				
Team player				
Delivers on responsibilities and obligations: does not cause avoidable problems or additional work for others				
Communicates effectively with other parts of the business to ensure effective coordination and working relationships. Readily shares ideas and information				
Understands and appreciates others' goals, challenges and pressures				
Collaborative and cooperative: is committed to the overall team objectives rather than their own interests				
Contributes effectively to meetings				
Backs collective senior team decisions even when they are at odds with their personal views or preferences				
Asks for and accepts help and advice where appropriate				
Helps and supports others when needed				
People management				
Sets and maintains high standards for people's attitude, performance and behaviours				
Agrees clear responsibilities, standards and objectives with each direct report				
Helps each person understand the importance of their contribution to meeting business objectives, and how they can make a positive difference				
Ensures that direct reports have the knowledge and skills to do the job well. Identifies and meets any learning and development needs				
Ensures that direct reports have the resources (including in-formation, materials and tools) to do their job effectively				
Understands each person's strengths, limitations, preferences and motivations				

Rate the following	Reactive	Tactical	Improvement-focused	Strategic
Gives regular, timely and appropriate praise, recognition and encouragement				
Holds people accountable for attitudes, behaviours and performance				
Gives clear, timely, constructive feedback so people know where they can improve performance				
Challenges constructively				
Actively encourages people to develop, learn new skills and enhance their performance				
Looks for the best in people and shows confidence in them				
Empowers and delegates appropriately to get the most from the abilities in the team				
Helps people develop confidence				
Helps people learn from mistakes. Resists blaming				
Coaches people to help them solve problems, to improve and to develop the required attitudes, skills and behaviours				
Inspires and motivates people to give of their best				
Makes time to listen and respond to the concerns of staff				
Identifies, and responds constructively to, signs of unhappy or stressed people				
Deals with underperformance and disruptive behaviour effectively				
Leading the team				
Creates a positive team identity by setting out a clear vision and strategy for their part of the business, aligned to the wider company vision				
Understands, values and incorporates different perspectives, while remaining focused on getting things done				

Rate the following	Reactive	Tactical	Improvement-focused	Strategic
Runs regular, constructive meetings to review team performance, solve problems, drive continuous improvement, share knowledge and ideas and enhance teamworking				
Recognises and celebrates team success to build confidence, pride and team spirit				
Recognises and harnesses individual strengths. Gets the most from the abilities in the team				
Creates a team culture which is positive and productive				
Works to build strong, supportive working relationships between individuals in the team. Actively encourages mutual support and cooperation				
Actively encourages involvement in decision-making and problem-solving				
Actively engages colleagues in continuous improvement activities to reduce waste and rework and improve customer satisfaction				
Able to rally people to rise to challenges				
Represents and promotes the team's interests positively with-in and outside the company				
Managing stakeholders				
Develops and maintains positive working relationships with suppliers (internal and external)				
Represents the organisation well. Is a good ambassador				
Builds networks of useful contacts inside and outside the business				
Understands who the customers are and what matters to them				
Understands the customer's business objectives, culture, values and challenges				
Meets the customers' needs. Delivers to promised standards				
Keeps the customer informed on key issues, including problems				

Rate the following	Reactive	Tactical	Improvement-focused	Strategic
Responds quickly and flexibly to reasonable customer requests				
Handles complaints quickly, professionally and skilfully				
Manages customers to ensure that no unrealistic expectations and perceptions are allowed to develop				
Develops mutually beneficial partnerships with suppliers				
Ensures suppliers understand the company's business objectives and where they can add value				
Provides clear, constructive feedback to help suppliers meet the business's needs better				
Has earned the confidence of senior managers				
Negotiates effectively with all stakeholders				
Operational leadership				
Maintains a safe working environment				
Sets clear operational goals, plans and performance measures to the team regularly (monthly, weekly or daily, as appropriate)				
Organises the work to deliver to time, budget and agreed quality standards. Creates practical and achievable plans				
Ensures that people have the right resources at the right time to allow them to succeed				
Reviews progress against operational goals (monthly, weekly or daily, as appropriate)				
Rigorous in monitoring and reviewing progress and performance				
Runs relevant, challenging, productive and effective meetings with a clear agenda, constructive discussion and agreed action points				
Understands the totality of a situation and develops accurate, objective assessments of what needs to be done, even in complex and difficult situations				
Makes clear decisions in a positive and timely manner and communicates them effectively				

Rate the following	Reactive	Tactical	Improvement-focused	Strategic
Helps people prioritise effectively. Allocates responsibilities and matches workloads appropriately against priorities, dead-lines and available resources				
Makes the best use of resources, including time, people, money, machinery, vehicles and equipment, deploying them effectively to deliver results				
Thinks ahead to cover staffing and other resource shortfalls				
Anticipates, identifies and deals with potential problems early and effectively				
Shifts resources as priorities change				
Maintains effective processes, procedures and systems and ensures they are followed				
Primes and maintains processes (including provision of mate-rials, tools and working equipment) to allow people to work without unnecessary interruption				
Ensures effective alignment with, and smooth hand-offs between, adjacent processes				
Challenges established practices and processes to improve their effectiveness				
Continuously seeks to improve process quality, cost and delivery performance and customer satisfaction				
Actively leads, engages in, and supports, continuous improvement efforts, helping remove barriers that operational managers can't				
Strategic leadership				
Provides a convincing and clear strategic direction for their area of responsibility that will position the business to thrive in the long term				
Has developed realistic plans for translating that strategy into successful action				

Rate the following	Reactive	Tactical	Improvement-focused	Strategic
Pursues the 'quintuple bottom line' of being excellent to buy from, work for and invest in and having a positive social and environmental impact				
Has an entrepreneurial mindset – always looking out for new business opportunities				
Takes managed risks in the pursuit of new challenges and achievements				
Understands the market the business is in, the key players and the competitive dynamics				
Understands the external threats and identifies those that are of particular danger if left unresolved				
Understands the external opportunities and those that are of particular value or importance				
Keeps abreast of latest developments in technologies, processes and practices				
Understands the unfolding social, economic, environmental and political factors, and how they impact on the business				
Understands how the business works as an entity and the internal dynamics				
Understands the core capabilities required to drive success				
Understands the internal threats and identifies those that are of particular danger if left unresolved				
Understands the internal improvement opportunities and those that are of particular value or importance				
Has designed, and maintains, an effective process for creating and continually evolving the strategy and responding to changes				
Assimilates and makes sense of complex data. Can spot important trends and patterns				
Grasps causes and effects. Can accurately foresee potential consequences				

GLOSSARY

5S – sort, set in order, shine, standardise, sustain: a system for ensuring that everything necessary to do the job right first time, without delay or interruption, is available and accessible

A3 – a problem-solving methodology (named after the size of the piece of paper it should be captured on)

COPQ – cost of poor quality

COQ – cost of quality

FLM – front-line manager

Gemba walk – a regular, focused inspection of the workplace carried out by a manager

Hoshin Kanri – a strategic management model based on the principle that strategic goals are communicated throughout the company and then put into action, ensuring that everybody in the organisation is working toward the same end

JIT – just in time: an inventory control system

Kaikaku – fundamental and transformational changes to an organisation's operations

Kaizen – the continuous implementation of small improvements to an organisation's operations

Kanban – an operational system where demand is pulled through the production process

Kata – deeply embedded habits and routines

KPI – key performance indictor

MCRS – management control and reporting system

Muda – waste

Mura – unevenness

Omotenashi – a mindset of selfless care for others

OMS – operational management system

OTIF – on time in full (performance)

PDCA – Plan-Do-Check-Act: a way of thinking that drives performance management and continuous improvement

QCD – quality, cost and delivery performance

QCDE – quality, cost, delivery performance and colleague engagement

SIC – short interval control

SMS – strategic management system

SPOF – single point of failure

SQCDE – safety, quality, cost, delivery performance and colleague engagement

Takt time – the pace at which production needs to occur to meet customer demand

TPM – total productive maintenance

VoC – Voice of the Customer

VoP – Voice of the Process

VSM – value-stream mapping: a visually led problem-solving methodology

BIBLIOGRAPHY

Books

Aguayo, Rafael, Dr Deming: The Man Who Taught the Japanese About Quality

Anderson, Bjørn and Fagerhaug, Tom, Root Cause Analysis: Simplified Tools and Techniques

Anthony, Jiju, Bañuelas, Ricardo and Kumar, Ashok, World Class Applications of Six Sigma

Arnold, John, Cooper, Cary L. and Robertson, Ivan T., Work Psychology: Understanding Human Behaviour in the Workplace

Ashworth, G., Delivering Shareholder Value Through Integrated Performance Management

Beck, D.E. and Cowan, C.C., Spiral Dynamics: Mastering Values, Leadership and Change

Bicheno, John and Holweg, Matthias, The Lean Toolbox

Bititci, Umit S., Managing Business Performance: The Science and the Art

Bititci, Umit S. and Spanellis, Agnessa, Systems Thinking for Business and Management

Blanchard, Kenneth and Johnson, Spencer, The New One-Minute Manager

Blanchard, Kenneth, Oncken, William and Burrows, Hal, The One Minute Manager Meets the Monkey

Block, Peter, Flawless Consulting: A Guide to Getting your Expertise Used

Boyett, Joseph H. and Boyett, Jimmie T., The Guru Guide: A Concise Guide to the Best Ideas from Today's Top Marketers

Bridges, William, Managing Transitions: Making the Most of Change

Brown, J.A.C., The Social Psychology of Industry

Campbell, Alastair, Winners: And How They Succeed

Capra, Fritjof, The Tao of Physics

Casey, Peter, Tata: The World's Greatest Company

Chomsky, Noam, Who Rules the World?

Christiansen, Clayton M. and Raynor, Michael E., The Innovator's Solution: Creating and Sustaining Successful Growth

Cole, G.A., Management: Theory and Practice

Collins, Jim, Good to Great: Why Some Companies Make the Leap... and Others Don't

Collins, Jim and Porras, Jerry I., Built to Last: Successful Habits of Visionary Companies

Covey, Stephen R., Principle Centered Leadership

Covey, Stephen R., The Seven Habits of Highly Effective People

Covey, Stephen and Whitman, Bob, Predictable Results in Unpredictable Times: How to Win in Any Environment

Cowley, Michael and Domb, Ellen, Beyond Strategic Vision

Crosby, Philip B., Quality is Free – If You Understand It

Crosby, Philip B., Quality without Tears: The Art of Hassle-Free Management

Csikszentmihalyi, Mihaly, Finding Flow: The Psychology of Engagement with Everyday Life

Csikszentmihalyi, Mihaly, Good Business: Leadership, Flow and the Making of Meaning

Csikszentmihalyi, Mihaly and Larson, Reed, Flow and the Foundations of Positive Psychology

Csikszentmihalyi, Mihaly, Gardner, Howard and Damon, William, Good Work: When Excellence and Ethics Meet

Dalio, Ray, Principles

Davidson, Hugh, The Committed Enterprise

Deming, W. Edwards, Out of the Crisis

Deming, W. Edwards, The New Economics for Industry, Government, Education

Dotlich, David L. and Cairo, Peter C., Why CEOs Fail: The 11 Behaviors that Can Derail Your Climb to the Top – and How to Manage Them

Drucker, Peter, The Essential Drucker

Dunphy, Eamon, A Strange Kind of Glory: Sir Matt Busby & Manchester United

Feigenbaum, Armand V., Total Quality Control

Ferguson, Alex, Leading

Ferguson, Alex, Managing My Life

Ford, Henry, My Life and Work

Ford, Henry, Today and Tomorrow

Furnham, Adrian, The Myths of Management

Furnham, Adrian, The Psychology of Managerial Incompetence

George, Michael L., Lean Six Sigma for Service

Gerber, Michael E., The E Myth: Why Most Businesses Don't Work and What to Do About It

Goldratt, Eliyahu M. and Cox, Jeff, The Goal: A Process of Ongoing Improvement

Goldsmith, Marshall, What Got You Here Won't Get You There: How Successful People Become Even More Successful

Goleman, Daniel, Boyatzis, Richard E. and McKee, Annie, The New Leaders: Transforming the Art of Leadership into the Science of Results

Goleman, Daniel, Working with Emotional Intelligence

Goleman, Daniel and Cherniss, Cary, The Emotionally Intelligent Workplace

Greenhalgh, Leonard, Managing Strategic Relationships: The Key to Business Success

Groves, Leslie M., Now It Can Be Told: The Story of the Manhattan Project

Hamel, Gary and Prahalad, Coimbatore K., Competing for the Future

Handy, Charles, The Empty Raincoat

Handy, Charles, Understanding Organizations

Heffernan, Margaret, Beyond Measure: The Big Impact of Small Changes

Hunt-Davis, Ben and Beveridge, Harriet, Will It Make the Boat Go Faster?

Huselid, Mark A., Becker, Brian E. and Beatty, Richard W., The Workforce Scorecard: Managing Human Capital to Execute Strategy

Hutchins, David, Hoshin Kanri: The Strategic Approach to Continuous Improvement

Imai, Masaaki, Kaizen: The Key to Japan's Competitive Success

Jackson, Thomas L., Hoshin Kanri for the Lean Enterprise

Jenson, Bill, Simplicity

Johns, Ted, Perfect Customer Care: All You Need to Get It Right First Time

Johnson, H. Thomas and Broms, Anders, Profit Beyond Measure: Extraordinary Results through Attention to Work and People

Joynson, Sid and Forrester, Andrew, Sid's Heroes: Uplifting Business Performance and the Human Spirit

Juran, Joseph M., Juran on Leadership for Quality

Juran, Joseph M., Managerial Breakthrough

Juran, Joseph M., Juran's Quality Control Handbook

Kahneman, Daniel, Thinking, Fast and Slow

Kanter, Rosabeth Moss, Change Masters: Innovation & Entrepreneurship in the American Corporation

Kaplan, Robert S. and Norton, David P., Strategy Maps: Converting Intangible Assets into Tangible Outcomes

Kegan, Robert and Lahey, Lisa Laskow, An Everyone Culture: Becoming a Deliberately Developmental Organization

Kelly, Walt, Pogo: We Have Met the Enemy and He Is Us

Kohn, Alfie, No Contest: The Case Against Competition

Lampel, Joseph, Mintzberg, Henry, Quinn, James Brian and Ghoshal, Sumantra, The Strategy Process

Landsberg, Max, The Tao of Coaching

Lencioni, Patrick M., The Five Dysfunctions of a Team

Levicki, Cyril, The Interactive Strategy Workout; Analyze and Develop the Fitness of Your Business

Liker, Jeffrey K., The Toyota Way: 14 Management Principles from the World's Greatest Manufacturer

Liker, Jeffrey K. and Convis, Gary L., The Toyota Way to Lean Leadership

Liker, Jeffrey K. and Franz, James K., The Toyota Way to Continuous Improvement

Liker, Jeffrey K. and Hoseus, Michael, Toyota Culture

Liker, Jeffrey K. and Ogden, Timothy, Toyota Under Fire

Liker, Jeffrey K. and Trachilis, George, Developing Lean Leaders at All Levels: A Practical Guide

Mann, David, Creating a Lean Culture

Maslow, Abraham H., Eupsychian Management

Maslow, Abraham H., The Farther Reaches of Human Nature

Maslow, Abraham H., A Theory of Human Motivation

Mehta, Pavithra K. and Shenoy, Suchitra, Infinite Vision: How Aravind Became the World's Greatest Business Case for Compassion

Middleton, Peter (ed.), Delivering Public Services that Work: Volume One

Monden, Yasuhiro, Toyota Production System: An Integrated Approach to Just-in-Time

Montgomery, Bernard Law, The Memoirs of Field-Marshal the Viscount Montgomery of Alamein

Morgan, Gareth, Images of Organization

Nelson, Dave, Mayo, Rick and Moody, Patricia E., Powered by Honda: Developing Excellence in the Global Enterprise

Ohno, Taiichi, Toyota Production System

Ohno, Taiichi, Taiichi Ohno's Workplace management

Pascale, Richard Tanner and Athos, Anthony G., The Art of Japanese Management

Pell, Charlotte (ed.), Delivering Public Services that Work: Volume Two

Peters, Thomas J. and Waterman, Robert H., In Search of Excellence: Lessons from America's Best-Run Companies

Pfeffer, Jeffrey and Sutton, Robert I., The Knowing-Doing Gap

Pugh, D.S. (ed.), Organization Theory: Selected Classic Readings

Pugh, D.S. and Hickson, D.J., Writers on Organizations

Rother, Mike, Toyota Kata

Rother, Mike and Shook, John, Learning to See: Value Stream Mapping to Add Value and Eliminate Muda

Scherkenbach, William W., Deming's Road to Continual Improvement

Seddon, John, Freedom from Command and Control

Seddon, John, Systems Thinking in the Public Sector

Seddon, John, The Whitehall Effect: How Whitehall Became the Enemy of Great Public Services and What We Can Do about It

Senge, Peter M., The Fifth Discipline: Measuring Business Excellence

Shankly, Bill, Shankly: My Story

Shewhart, Walter A., Economic Control of Quality of Manufactured Product

Shook, John, Managing to Learn: Using the A3 Management Process to Solve Problems, Gain Agreement, Mentor and Lead

Sobek II, Durward K. and Smalley, Art, Understanding A3 Thinking

Smith, Hyrum W., What Matters Most: The Power of Living Your Values

Spear, Steven J., The High-Velocity Edge: How Market Leaders Leverage Operational Excellence to Beat the Competition

Spitzer, Dean R., Transforming Performance Measurement

Statt, David A., Psychology and the World of Work

Sutton, Robert, The No Asshole Rule: Building a Civilized Workplace and Surviving One that Isn't

Ten Have, Steven, Ten Have, Wouter, Stevens, Frans and Pol-Coyne, Fiona, Key Management Models: The Management Tools and Practices that Will Improve your Business

Thomas, Angela M., Coaching for Staff Development

Walton, Mary, Deming Management at Work

Warr, Peter (ed.), Psychology at Work

Welch, Jack, Jack: What I've Learned Leading a Great Company and Great People

Wheeler, Donald J., Understanding Variation: The Key to Managing Chaos

Whitmore, John, Coaching for Performance

Wilson, David C., A Strategy of Change: Concepts and Controversies in the Management of Change

Womack, James P. and Jones, Daniel T., Lean Thinking

Womack, James P., Jones, Daniel T. and Roos, Daniel, The Machine That Changed the World: The Story of Lean Production

Wright, Diana and Meadows, Donella H., Thinking in Systems: A Primer

Yokoyama, John and Michelli, Joseph, When Fish Fly: Lessons for Creating a Vital and Energized Workplace from the World Famous Pike Place Fish Market

Audiobook

Peters, Tom, The Leadership 11 Masterclass (Red Audio)

Articles

Amabile, Teresa M. and Kramer, Steven J., 'The Power of Small Wins', Harvard Business Review, 2011

Bonini, Jamie, Kalloch, Sarah and Ton, Zeynap, 'The GJS Can Take Lessons from TPS', Harvard Business Review, 2017

Dawson, Patrick, 'Organisational Change Stories and Management Research: Facts or Fiction', Journal of Management & Organization, 2003

Graham, Julia, 'Developing a Performance-Based Culture', The Journal for Quality and Participation, 2004

Ittner, Christopher D. and Larcker, David F., 'Coming up Short on Nonfinancial Performance Measurement', Harvard Business Review, 2003

Richardson, Neville, 'Hats Off to Great Leaders and Companies Who Care', The Times, 2008

Roberts, Kevin, Pratt, Mike, Gilson, Clive and Weymes, Ed, 'Peak Performing Organisations' in Long Range Planning, 1998

Zaleznik, Abraham, 'Managers and Leaders: Are They Different?', Harvard Business Review, 2004

Online resources

Fit School Blog, https://www.fit-school.co.uk/fit-school-blog

Harvard Business Review, https://www.hbr.org, various articles and blogs

Seth Godin's Blog, https://seths.blog

Shingo Institute Newsletter, sign up at https://shingo.org

Vervaecke, John, After Socrates, https://www.youtube.com/playlist?list=PLND1JCRq8Vuj6q5NP_fXjBzUT1p_qYSCC